Author photo and cover images copyright Pascal
& Maria Maréchaux.

Khadija al-Salami grew up in Yemen in an almost feudal environment. Her
life was devastated by the impact of civil war, which mentally destroyed her
father and made him unable to care for his family. Determined to escape the
poverty, death and destruction around her, Khadija, at the age of 12, asked
the local TV station to let her host a programme for children. She later used
the money that she received for these broadcasts to travel to the United
States to study. She graduated from Mount Vernon College in Washington
DC and, after undertaking postgraduate study in Film production, returned
to Yemen to continue working at the Yemeni TV station. She subsequently
joined the Yemeni Embassy in Paris, where she is currently Press and
Cultural Attaché and Director of the Yemeni Information Centre. She lives
in Paris with her husband, Charles Hoots.

The Tears of Sheba

Tales of Survival and Intrigue in Arabia

KHADIJA AL-SALAMI
with Charles Hoots

WILEY

This edition published in 2004 by   John Wiley & Sons, Ltd, The Atrium, Southern Gate
Chichester, West Sussex, PO19 8SQ, England

Phone   (+44) 1243 779777

Email (for orders and customer service enquiries): cs-books@wiley.co.uk
Visit our Home Page on www.wiley.co.uk or www.wiley.com

First published 2003

Other Wiley Editorial Offices

John Wiley & Sons, Inc. 111 River Street, Hoboken, NJ 07030, USA

Jossey-Bass, 989 Market Street, San Francisco, CA 94103–1741, USA

Wiley-VCH Verlag GmbH, Boschstr. 12, D-69469 Weinheim, Germany

John Wiley & Sons Australia, Ltd, 33 Park Road, Milton, Queensland, 4064, Australia

John Wiley & Sons (Asia) Pte Ltd, 2 Clementi Loop #02–01, Jin Xing Distripark, Singapore
129809

John Wiley & Sons Canada Ltd, 22 Worcester Road, Etobicoke, Ontario, Canada, M9W 1L1

Wiley also publishes its books in a variety of electronic formats. Some content that appears
in print may not be available in electronic books.

British Library Cataloguing in Publication Data

A catalogue record for this book is available from the British Library

ISBN 10: 0-470-86726-4 (PB)   ISBN 13: 978-0470-86726-6 (PB)

Typeset in $10\frac{1}{2}/13\frac{1}{2}$pt by Mathematical Composition Setters Ltd, Salisbury, Wiltshire.
Printed and bound in Great Britain by T.J. International Ltd, Padstow, Cornwall.
This book is printed on acid-free paper responsibly manufactured from sustainable forestry
in which at least two trees are planted for each one used for paper production.

10 9 8 7 6 5 4 3 2

For Judith Hoots and Fatima al-Salami, two kind and generous women who brought such different worlds together through their children

Contents

Acknowledgements

We would like to thank Fatima al-Salami, Amina al-Salami, Afrah Murzah, Muhammad al-Rawdhi, Abdul Kareem al-Salami, and Ghassan Abu Lahum for their generous assistance and patience in helping to research this book; Gene Hoots, Kate Kitchen of Kate Kitchen Public Relations, Susan Hill, Pascal and Maria Maréchaux, and Paul Dresch for reviewing and offering valuable advice on the manuscript and photographs; my agent, Andrew Lownie, and editor, Sally Smith, for having the confidence in us and this book to make it work; and, not least, Muhammad Abu Lahum, Mujahid Abu Shawareb, and Yahya al-Mutawakil for inspiration in the writing of this book.

Paris, France
November 2003

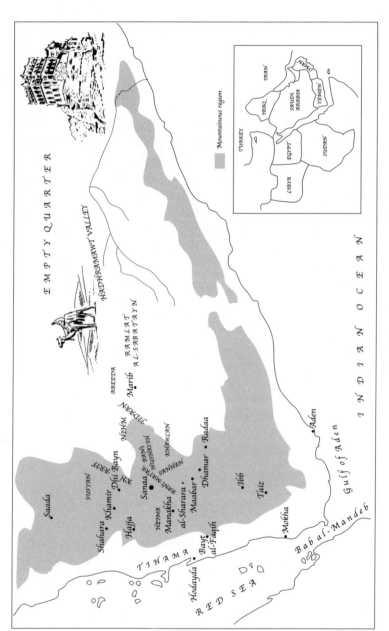

Yemen

Yemen is divided geographically into three distinct regions. To the west lies the sultry Tihama coastal plain, a strip of flat, sterile sand dividing the Red Sea from the central massif. Rain falls rarely here, but bananas, papayas, dates and other tropical crops grow in the rich alluvial soil swept down the valleys by storms in the mountains.

Some 25 miles inland, the central volcanic highlands soar abruptly to over 8,000 feet. The lofty ridges prod the monsoon winds up into cooler air, where they condense to form heavy afternoon showers during the spring and autumn rainy seasons. Rainfall is most abundant in the southern highlands, where the green mountain terraces evoke images of Southeast Asia more than Arabia. But precipitation decreases steadily as one moves north.

Some 90 miles east of where the hills rise steeply from the Tihama, the highlands plunge into the barren eastern desert. This sandstone gravel plain, merging occasionally into rolling sand dunes several hundred feet high, slopes gently across 800 miles to the Persian Gulf in the east.

CAST OF CHARACTERS

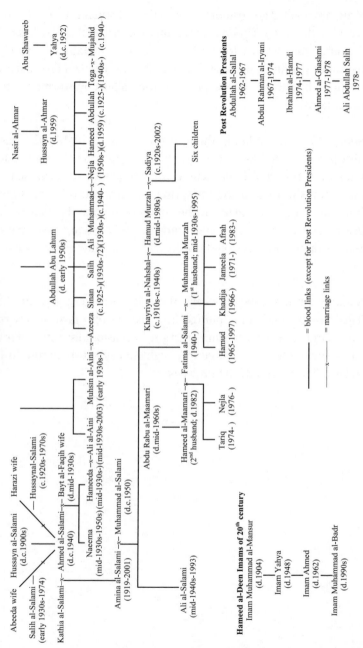

Hameed al-Deen Imams of 20th century
Imam Muhammad al-Mansur
(d.1904)
Imam Yahya
(d.1948)
Imam Ahmed
(d.1962)
Imam Muhammad al-Badr
(d.1990s)

Post Revolution Presidents
Abdullah al-Sallal
1962-1967
Abdul Rahman al-Iryani
1967-1974
Ibrahim al-Hamdi
1974-1977
Ahmed al-Ghashmi
1977-1978
Ali Abdullah Salih
1978-

———— = blood links (except for Post Revolution Presidents)
——x—— = marriage links

Prologue

Billowing clouds stacked up over the western mountains as hordes of late-morning shoppers scurried through the alleyways of the central marketplace. But it was mid-winter and they would bring no rain. Women, enveloped from head to foot in colourful shawls, glided ghost-like between the tiny stalls of the cloth vendors and the spice merchants. Men in white gowns crowded down the passageway where smiths hammered out the curved *jambiya*[1] daggers, displayed at the waist by our proud Yemeni men for the past 3,000 years. Jockeying for position, they shouted orders to storekeepers lounging cross-legged in their workshops, or lingered to take in the tale of a professional storyteller.

At the southern edge of the market, beside the main town gate called Bab al-Yemen, squatted a young sentry in faded military fatigues. Pouring a cup of tea from the kettle on the fire, he slurped loudly and gazed up at the milky sky silhouetting Jebel (Mount) Nuqum buttressing the town on the southeast. The fortress nestled on the summit had wrought havoc upon invaders and pretenders to the throne over the centuries, but that afternoon its cannon would prove impotent against the death and destruction about to rain down on my town of Sanaa.[2]

A mile or so to the southwest, a battered pickup truck lumbered up the far slope of Jebel Atan Mountain. A muleteer swatted his three beasts off the dirt track to let it pass. When the vehicle halted just below the rounded crest, a dozen warriors emerged from a pit carved into the volcanic rock. Their loose robes

---

[1] See Glossary for Arabic words used frequently in this book.

[2] The capital of Yemen, located on the southwest tip of the Arabian Peninsula.

fluttered in the breeze, rifles and ammunition belts slung over their shoulders.

Some of the men headed for the arriving mules, from which they unloaded crates of rifle ammunition and carried them into the stone shelter. The voluminous wool turbans wound round their heads dampened with sweat while they worked, despite the chilly winter air. The others jogged to the truck to remove the tarpaulin from the two rows of 106 mm barrels mounted on the back. When they finished, they lifted three pointed metal cylinders with considerable effort, inserting them into the narrow barrels. Then they hopped down and drove the truck the short distance to the top of the ridge. Sanaa, enclosed behind its mud wall, basked in sunshine below.

The town showed little activity for the holy month of *Ramadhan* was upon us, when, as Muslims, we let neither food nor drink pass our lips between sunrise and sunset. Many of the inhabitants slumbered away the daylight hours of fasting, unaware of the horror in store for them.

The crowd in the marketplace thinned as the sun hovered at its zenith. Grey-bearded men bent with the burden of years emerged from their homes, scurrying along the dark corridors like hamsters in a maze. Each entered his respective mosque and struggled up the spiral staircase to the top of the minaret. Cupping their mouths with the right hand and plugging an ear with the left, booming voices unbefitting their frail bodies urged the faithful to the mosque for prayer.

A faint puff of white smoke suddenly curled up over Jebel Atan. It might have gone unnoticed but for the shiny object that shot forth, zigzagging lazily away from the mountain top. The voices from the minarets crackled with fear as the eerie tube approached, spewing behind it a thin trail of exhaust. A second followed the first, then a third, each lingering a moment before accelerating with alarming speed towards the town. A blood-curdling shriek like fingernails on a chalkboard drowned out the wailing call to prayer as the cylinders hurtled into the heart of Sanaa.

The first missile struck somewhere in the west. I was two years old, and the dull thud of the explosion woke me from a dream with an involuntary twitch. Eyes still closed, I grasped the dummy at my side, tugged the blanket over my head against the frigid air, and drifted back to sleep. My four-year old brother, Hamud, didn't stir. But mother, dozing on the floor beside us, snapped instantly to attention.

Mother knew all too well the terror that accompanied the whirring sound of a Katyusha rocket. She had learned first-hand a couple of days earlier while on her way to buy mutton for breaking the day's fast. We rarely ate meat, but throughout the year mother hid a few coins under the cushion she used as a bed in order to splurge a little during *Ramadhan*.

That day as she neared the Nishwan Primary School next to the *sayla*, the broad watercourse channelling rainwater through the town, one of the whistling projectiles smashed into the street a short distance ahead of her. The blast ripped a gaping hole in a house across from the school, severing the arm of a young mother washing dishes inside. Shrapnel peppered the stone wall beside Mother and red-hot shards of steel danced and hissed on the ground at her feet, but she was miraculously untouched.

The sounds of this new attack aroused in Mother the horror she had felt two days before. She peered apprehensively out of the stained-glass window with innocent eyes that were prematurely sunken from three decades of hardship and uncertainty. One explosion usually heralded the arrival of others, and her ears perked to attention. Sensing the terrifying vibration of the second rocket, she held her breath for the impact.

The house lurched and the window shattered in a display of coloured fireworks. Mother closed her eyes, both to protect them from the slivers of glass pouring down and to beg God to spare her children. Chunks of plaster plummeted from the ceiling and dust from the mud brick walls engulfed the room in a thick haze.

Panicked, Mother snatched Hamud and me from the sheep's wool carpet on the floor where we slept, and scrambled into the dim central corridor. She nearly collided with her father-in-law as he careened down the giant-sized stone steps. His wife, three sons and two daughters trailed close behind, each screaming for the others to follow, cringing when another missile rocked a distant neighbourhood.

Groping blindly along the sacks of grain and firewood on the ground floor, we reached the two hand-turned millstones and squatted between them. No one dared return upstairs to search for a candle. Our solemn clan brooded silently, helpless in the cool obscurity.

Civil war had been raging for over five years when the Katyushas slammed into my neighbourhood in early 1968. Until then the fighting had spared Sanaa, but the destruction I would witness after stepping outside later that morning would forever remain with me as my earliest memory.

The war would also shape my destiny in a way I could not then imagine. By destroying the very fabric of my family, it compelled me to forge my own path in life, rather than follow the route traditionally prescribed for young Yemeni girls.

As I grew older, Yemenis became extremely curious to know more about me and how I had come to choose such an unorthodox path. But I could not talk about my childhood and as a result many people made up their own stories to satisfy themselves.

When I met my future husband, Charles, in the United States two decades later, I had rarely talked to anyone about my past. Charles grew more curious about my life as we came to know each other better. His interest proved to be genuine, and I felt an obligation to tell him more.

He proceeded slowly, realizing how painful it was for me to finally speak of what I had been through. Sometimes I cried, and sometimes the words stuck in my throat, unwilling to emerge. But in the end he helped me at last to say the things I had never been able to say to another soul. I came to see how experiences earlier in life shaped what I am today, and what others are, and that I cannot be ashamed of the suffering inflicted by others.

Yemen's civil war did not affect me alone, of course. The conflict shaped an entire generation of my countrymen, three of whom in particular I would come to know and respect enormously over the years.

These men came to occupy important positions in the government and military, playing instrumental roles in making and unmaking Yemen's rulers. I slowly discovered that the motivations for their actions were numerous and complex, but rarely did they include a simple lust for power. They were all in their early twenties when the cloud of civil war broke over our homeland, when they led their men into battle, and watched their family and friends die at their sides. Instead of buckling under the strain, they transformed tragedy and hardship into opportunity. Yet it is their ability as peacemakers that has most distinguished these men, propelling them into positions of responsibility attained in most other countries by wealth and family connections alone.

Yemen can seem very strange to those who do not know it. It is a land of extremes, both good and bad. Yet the experiences of Yemenis, even those who grew up through the difficult civil war years of the 1960s, show that love, hatred, anxiety, joy, dreams and ambitions differ little between children, teenagers and adults the world over.

Rather than bury the past, I have come to see its redeeming qualities, no matter how harsh the reality. By relating how a handful of men and women have overcome poverty, war and stringent social barriers, I hope that others might be inspired to persevere through overwhelming odds, where despair might otherwise have led them to falter.

CHAPTER ONE

Incense and insurrection

My native Yemen, the ancient Land of Sheba, conjures up images of exotic mystery in both the West and the East. Europeans and Americans know it from the biblical story of the Queen of Sheba, while Arabs from northwest Africa to the Persian Gulf consider Yemen[1] to be the source of much of the world's Arab population today.

Yemen's golden age climaxed some two millennia ago, fuelled by massive exports of frankincense, myrrh and other forms of incense. The resin, collected from aromatic trees and bushes much as sap is collected from pine trees, produces a strong, pleasant odour when burned. In antiquity the plants grew in southern Arabia, the Horn of Africa some 150 miles across the sea, and on a few secluded islands in between.

The original spark to the trade seems to have ignited around 6,000 years ago with pharaonic Egypt's use of the oil from myrrh to embalm its dead. Hauled north to Egypt, the Mediterranean and Mesopotamia (Iraq) by donkey, transportation proved slow and tedious. But a revolution occurred between 1500 and 1000 BC with the domestication of the camel. These beasts could convey heavier loads and travel more direct routes through waterless tracts of desert. This new mode of transport, along with rising demand from the Greek and later Roman empires, whose pagan religions considered the burning of incense

---

[1] The Arabic word 'Yemen' means 'the right-hand side', or 'the South', in relation to the city of Mecca.

indispensable for winning the favour of the gods, led to a surge in the incense trade.

The Bedouin tribes wandering the region developed a vested interest in the trade's success. Many found lucrative employment as guides and guards on the two-month journey from the Yemeni coast to the principal entrepot of Gaza on the Mediterranean. With the predatory Bedouin co-opted into the system, security on the routes improved and trade in other merchandise besides incense thrived. Spices, ebony, silks and textiles poured into Yemen from India for trans-shipment to the north, while rare woods, feathers, skins and metals arrived from Africa.

The caravans returned home to South Arabia laden with gold and silver, setting the scene for the emergence of highly centralized governments. The first state to emerge in southern Arabia was the Kingdom of Sheba, one of whose queens, according to both the Koran and the Bible, paid a celebrated visit to King Solomon in Jerusalem around 1000 BC. But by the fifth century BC, several smaller states to the east began exerting their independence from Sheba.

The trade continued to grow in the centuries before the Christian era. Caravans of 2,000 to 3,000 camels commonly plied the incense route, paved with flat stones in some portions. Any cameleer who left the designated road in order to bypass a staging point, and payment of its inevitable taxes, could be punished by death.

As their appetite for incense became insatiable, the Romans watched with dismay as their wealth drained away to pay for it all. They determined to locate the source of the precious commodity and seize control of it. In 24 BC, Aelius Gallus, the Roman Governor of Egypt, led a force of 10,000 men down the eastern Red Sea coast headed for *Arabia Felix* – Happy Arabia – as they called Yemen. Malaria, lack of water, marauding tribes and deceitful guides all joined forces to thwart the endeavour. Rumours that winged serpents guarded the sacred incense trees did little to lift the spirits of the Roman soldiers, and the emaciated army turned back.

Although the Roman expedition failed, it nevertheless denoted a growing comprehension of the world and its geography that would soon contribute to the decline of the incense route and the kingdoms dependent upon it. Around 50 AD, a storm is said to have blown a Roman ship from the mouth of the Red Sea to India. The captain discovered how to use the monsoon winds for travel in the Indian Ocean and from then on ships from Roman Egypt sailed directly to India and Africa, bypassing the expensive middlemen in southern Arabia.

The unrelenting rise of Christianity in the Mediterranean struck perhaps the decisive blow to the incense trade. Christians, too, burned incense at their religious celebrations, but nowhere near the quantities consumed by pagan worshippers. Demand dropped off sharply.

As the incoming wealth diminished, the South Arabian kingdoms began to neglect their other achievements, notably in agriculture. The Land of Sheba earned lasting fame for its extensive irrigation works, including the enormous sixth-century BC Marib Dam. It watered 25,000 acres and laid the foundation for a sophisticated urban centre. But with the declining revenues, the Shebans allowed the dam to fall into disrepair and eventually collapse.

The various South Arabian states, struggling for a larger piece of the shrinking pie, each attempted to expand its power at the expense of the others. The introduction of the horse into the region in the first or second century AD revolutionized the nature of combat. Recurrent warfare intensified the decay that had already set in and a mass exodus unfolded.

Some families headed north and east, settling much of what is today Oman, the United Arab Emirates and Saudi Arabia, as far north as Iraq. Others immigrated west to the Yemeni highlands, where a new kingdom, Himyar, established itself independent of the incense trade. By the sixth century AD, Yemen's international commerce and the kingdoms built upon it had become extinct.

Christianity began making inroads in South Arabia in the mid-fourth century AD. But half a century later, many Yemenis began converting to Judaism under the auspices of their Himyari king. Yemen's last Jewish ruler did his best to subjugate, and in some cases exterminate, the region's lingering Christian community. But in the process he provoked an invasion by Christian Abyssinia (modern-day Ethiopia) to defend its co-religionists around 525 AD.

Weary of the Abyssinian yoke, Yemen exchanged it for that of Persia (Iran) half a century later. The Persian Shah freed 1,000 prisoners from his jails, sent them to Arabia and drove the Abyssinians into the sea. After 50 years as a Persian province, Yemen submitted peacefully to the new Muslim faith in 628 AD.

Of course Islam was not introduced into Yemen, or any other lands, without resistance. The new religion had to overcome, and in some cases integrate, deeply ingrained local beliefs. For example, the arrival of Islam marked a revolutionary advance in the social status of women in nearly every country in which it took hold. Baby girls in pre-Islamic Arabia were commonly smothered to death by parents who wanted a boy and could not afford to waste scarce resources on a girl. Islam did away with this practice, in addition to institutionalizing female inheritance rights, which rarely existed before.

Abundant rainfall (and the agricultural lifestyle it spawned) bestowed upon Yemen a much greater population density than the sterile deserts of surrounding countries. Yemeni manpower proved crucial to the spread of Islam in the decades following the Prophet Muhammad's death in 628 AD, when 20,000 Yemenis spearheaded the fledgling Muslim expansion out of Arabia. They conquered a swathe of land stretching from the borders of China in the east to the Strait of Gibraltar and northern Spain in the west.[2] Towns across North Africa and up to Barcelona in Spain still bear the names of Yemeni tribes, and many employ the ancient irrigation methods of Yemeni farmers to this day.

---

[2] The name 'Gibraltar' is a corruption of Jebel Tariq – Mount Tariq – named after a Muslim military commander of Yemeni origin.

For most of the past 1,000 years, distinguished members of *Sayid* families – descendents of the Prophet Muhammad – have ruled Yemen. Dynasties rose and fell as *Sayids* jockeyed for support from one another and from the land's numerous tribes. Only a handful of short-lived foreign invasions interrupted this historical chess game. The more recent include occupations by the Ottoman Turks in the sixteenth and seventeenth centuries, and again in the nineteenth and early twentieth centuries.

Yemen's two major tribes, the Hashid and Bakil, furnished the military might behind the *Sayid* rulers, called *Imams*. Popular genealogy has it that Hashid and Bakil were brothers. They descended nine generations from Saba, who lent his name to the legendary Land of Sheba (*Sheba* is the Hebrew word for *Saba*).

An *Imam* could usually, though not always, count on a majority of the Hashid and Bakil to rally behind him in times of trouble. Nothing instilled cohesion in the proud, fractious highland tribes like an invader. The Ottomans were Muslims whose Sultan in Istanbul claimed to be the Khalifa, or leader of the world's Muslims. But such religious credentials in no way made that empire's army any less despised by Yemenis. On several occasions *Imams* gathered the tribes and drove the Turks from the mountain interior back to the malaria-infested coastal plain on the Red Sea. My grandmother told me stories of my great-great-grandfather's role in resisting the Ottomans and the heavy price that he paid for it. The Yemeni warriors inflicted such heavy losses that my country came to be known as the 'Cemetery of the Turks'.

But along with the departing foreigners went the glue that bound the ruler to his people. Relations between the *Imam* and the free-spirited tribes often deteriorated sharply thereafter. Bravery in battle and leadership skills alone were no longer adequate for the *Imam* to sustain popular support during peacetime. He now had to prove himself equally capable in more mundane matters, such as public administration and arbitration of tribal disputes. Perhaps most delicate of all was the generous yet shrewd distribution of the meagre tax revenues the *Imam* managed to prise out of the people. Too much or too little in any one place might easily spell his downfall.

Imams were generally as well prepared as anyone to confront these daunting tasks. Every *Imam* had to be a descendent of the Prophet Muhammad through his daughter, Fatima (none of Muhammad's sons survived beyond infancy). While this condition severely limited the number of potential rulers, additional requirements whittled the choices down still further. For example, the candidate had to be male, generous, courageous, just, of sound mind and body, a skilful administrator, pious and learned in Islamic law.

Some *Imams* bequeathed the title to a son on their death. Such was the case of the four *Imams* of the Hameed al-Deen family that reigned in the twentieth century. But this by no means constituted a strict tradition. The practice was in fact discouraged in that any potential *Imam* had to prove himself capable and worthy of the position before he could secure the crucial support of the tribes and the country's religious scholars.

Numerous candidates often came forth on the death of an *Imam*, at times resulting in bloodshed between their respective supporters. On other occasions no one put forward a claim. Then the Imamate sat vacant until an impending crisis coaxed some brave or ambitious *Sayid* into taking charge.

The first *Imam* had come to Yemen in the late ninth century AD, not as a warrior but as a mediator, invited by the feuding tribes of Saada, 150 miles north of Sanaa. A respected religious scholar and *Sayid* arrived from his native Medina, the burial place of the Prophet Muhammad far to the north. The aging scholar found the simple, ochre-coloured, clay buildings of Saada attractive. Pairs of crescent-shaped horns from the ibex (wild desert goat) embedded in the pinnacled angles of the exterior walls protected the houses from evil. And the cool air of the high plateau revived the body after the searing heat of Medina. The visiting entourage decided to make this pleasant palm oasis its home.

The scholar instructed the Yemenis in Zaydism, one of the numerous sects of Shiite Islam, then declared himself *Imam*, or leader of the Zaydi community. The new *Imam*, like the Prophet Muhammad before him, earned the respect and protection of his followers through his charisma, honesty, justice and mediation skills. His religious authority carried over into more secular activities and, within a few years, the man's sway stretched all the way to Sanaa. Other *Sayid* families from around Mecca and Medina immigrated to Yemen after his death, their number reaching many thousands over the coming centuries.

Yemen experienced a brief revival of its role as a hub for international commerce in the early sixteenth century, when traders began exporting coffee beans from the Red Sea port of Mokha to Constantinople. The Turks soon introduced the drink to Venice, with the rest of Europe catching on a hundred years later.[3]

As coffee's popularity exploded, Europeans dreamed of controlling their own production of the beans. Within a short time they succeeded in smuggling coffee trees out of Yemen, the sole supplier at the time, cultivating them in their respective colonies in the Caribbean, South America and Asia. The Dutch plantations of Yemeni coffee trees on the Indonesian island of Java gave rise to one of the more popular modern coffee beans: Mokha Java. With the consequent rise in world supply, Yemen's monopoly dissolved and export of the bean collapsed.

The medieval era produced its fair share of enlightened rulers in Yemen. But in more recent times, *Imams* and tribesmen alike tended to view with suspicion any innovation that might disrupt the delicate balance between ruler and people. As a result, Yemeni society survived as an anachronistic enclave into the 1960s. Even at that late date, people in my country remained ignorant of and virtually unaffected by the world's technological and scientific advances of recent decades. The country had

---

[3] The word 'coffee' derives from the Arabic word *qahwa*, transformed in Turkish into *kavay*.

few roads, no electricity (apart from a handful of privately owned generators), no paper money and virtually no modern industry.

The ammunition workshop in Sanaa operated on the *Imam*'s behalf and produced a few thousand rounds of rifle ammunition each day. That modest factory comprised the entire modern manufacturing sector of Yemen's northern highlands in the mid-twentieth century.

The country's few imports, mainly textiles from Syria, arrived by boat in the city of Aden on the Indian Ocean. Camel and donkey caravans from Sanaa took 28 days to trek down to the southern port and back with their merchandise. Modest exports of coffee, cotton, animal skins and crude iron and steel paid for the foreign goods. The patriarch of one of the original Sanaani merchant families active in this trade borrowed money from the German Consul in Sanaa at 25 per cent interest in order to finance the caravans in the 1940s. Banks were unknown.

A nearly 90 per cent illiteracy rate reinforced Yemen's seclusion. The country had little educational infrastructure beyond the basic religious curriculum offered in rural mosques. When a group of half a dozen Yemenis took the unprecedented step of seeking the *Imam*'s permission to study engineering in Italy in 1946, he surprised them by granting their request. But rather than issue passports to the students, Imam Yahya Hameed al-Deen, ruler of Yemen from 1904 to 1948, furnished them only with a letter emblazoned with his official scarlet-coloured seal. The handwritten note read, naively but to the point:

> To whom it may concern:
> May these young men be allowed to study in your country and to learn your language, for those who know foreign tongues safeguard themselves against deception.

Imam Yahya brought a handful of Italian and French engineers and medical doctors to work in Yemen after the First World War. All foreigners required express authorization from the *Imam* himself before entering the country.

Ahmed, Imam Yahya's son and successor from 1948 until 1962, viewed foreigners with only slightly less suspicion than his father did. He was well aware of how the European colonial powers had carved up and exploited neighbouring Africa and Asia. Determined to avoid that fate for his country, he rejected all but a few advances made by overseas investors.

In a public speech in 1953, Ahmed justified his isolationist policies:

> I heard someone say, 'Yemen is so backward and Yemen is hungry and naked.' I do not deny these facts ... But I say to them, 'Do you wish progress and to be like those who are suffering from a despotism and an imperialism which have deprived them of their bravery, dignity and freedom?'
>
> God alone knows what I do and that I wish for my people security, prosperity, good fortune and comfort. But I do not wish them to have all of this unless they can preserve their religion, their country and their honour.

Yahya, and Ahmed after him, made nearly all state decisions himself concerning even the most mundane administrative matters. Several days each week, Yahya could be found sitting in the shade of a tree outside the walls of Dar al-Sada palace in Sanaa, a city of only some 50,000 inhabitants at the time. Yellow-bellied doves perched on the branches looked on while plaintiffs and defendants from the humblest of backgrounds argued their cases before the attentive *Imam*.

On other days, Yahya liked to take trips outside Sanaa in his horse-drawn carriage. His bold guard of foot soldiers formed an impressive cortege, singing and frolicking merrily about the coach. Glimmering *jambiyas* twirled high above their heads in tribal dances as they approached the palace on their return.

No one could accuse Yahya or Ahmed of benefiting financially from the state of autocracy in which they maintained the country. Their wealth did not even begin to approach that of the stereotypical Oriental despots of other nations. As *Imams*, they possessed little but the force of their personalities (and to some extent their *Sayid* origins) to distinguish them from the masses. Their handful of 'palaces' hardly surpassed the homes of some of the wealthier merchants (none of whom dared build a more lavish residence than the *Imams*, though many easily could have done so).

Imam Yahya, who died an old man, is said never to have laid eyes on the sea. Indeed few inhabitants of the highlands and desert regions north and east of Sanaa ever set foot outside the country, or in many cases their own communities.

Yemenis from the southern highlands, however, proved more mobile. Several thousand made their way abroad in the mid-twentieth century to study or work in the industrial centres of England and America. Others made it only as far as British-occupied Aden, where they could study in British schools or join the militant labour unions flourishing in the city.

A decree issued by Imam Ahmed in 1952 required that any man desiring to leave the country should present his provincial governor with an attestation that someone would farm his land in his absence. Given that most families had half a dozen sons or more, this condition hindered few. Emigration to Aden became the logical move for any ambitious teenager in the southern highlands with too many older brothers and too little land to farm.

As these migrants returned home with rising expectations and new ideas about the world, the *Imam* came to realize he could not insulate Yemen from the outside world forever. He slowly set about modernizing the country. In 1957, Ahmed initiated purchases of Soviet-made arms from Egypt and brought in Egyptian advisors to assist in building an effective military. In the early 1960s he allowed the Soviet Union to construct a deep-water port in the town of Hodayda, then astutely balanced the political implications of the move, at the height of the cold war, with contracts for American and Chinese companies to build roads linking Yemen's three main towns. The Chinese laid the country's first paved motorway in 1961.

Ahmed proved a less popular and skilled ruler than his father. He could be oppressive in his dealings with the people, and many feared and resented him for it. His father, too, had inspired dread in his subjects, but they knew his decisions would be just. Ahmed, on the other hand, suffering from broad mood swings induced by the morphine he devoured to relieve his arthritis pain, issued edicts with a much more capricious nature.

Yemen's community of religious scholars – *ulama* – had met while Imam Yahya was still alive, and ruled that Ahmed was unqualified to succeed his father as *Imam*. They favoured instead Abdullah al-Wazeer, hailing from another influential *Sayid* family. But Ahmed was nothing if not clever. Months before his father's death, he spread rumours that the *Imam* had died in order to test the reaction of his opponents and the tribes. The results disappointed him.

The astute Ahmed realized that his best chance of becoming *Imam* would come in the aftermath of Yahya's murder. Such an incident just might rally popular support in his favour out of sympathy for his father's assassination. And getting his father killed was hardly a difficult proposition. Numerous plots brewed in the country at any given moment, of most of which Ahmed was aware.

One conspiracy that caught his attention aimed at replacing Yahya with Abdullah al-Wazeer, whose supporters had grown weary of waiting for the aging *Imam* to die a natural death. With his old rival al-Wazeer involved, Ahmed could kill two birds with one stone.

Feigning ignorance of the plot, the ambitious Ahmed let events run their course through early 1948. Then on the day scheduled for the coup's execution, 17 February, Ahmed slipped stealthily out of his palace in the town of Taiz, 150 miles south of Sanaa, for he had learned that his own assassination was supposed to follow upon that of his father. With a supply of gold, he headed for the mountain fortress of Hajja in the mist-drenched highlands northwest of Sanaa, a week's hard march from Taiz.

His gamble paid off. Abhorring the murder of the *Imam*, who reportedly attempted to shield his young grandson from the assassins' bullets, the tribes flocked around Ahmed to crush al-Wazeer and his backers.

Ahmed transferred Yemen's capital from Sanaa to Taiz, enjoying relatively stable rule for his first few years in power. Then in 1955 irate farmers slew three of the *Imam*'s tax collectors near Taiz. The army retaliated by destroying several houses in the farmers' village, but without having sought Ahmed's permission first. When the *Imam* ordered the arrest of the army's inspector general for the attack, the inspector general feared the ruler had discovered his involvement in a coup plot that was brewing at the time. Certain he would be executed, he ordered the army to bombard the *Imam*'s citadel, forcing the ruler to abdicate.

After the *Imam* bribed a large number of the mutineers to join his own camp, however, the coup unravelled within a matter of hours. Safely back on the throne, Ahmed recovered his worthwhile investment by fining the soldiers the exact sum he had paid to bribe them. They considered themselves fortunate to get off so lightly.

The army inspector general and one of the *Imam*'s brothers who supported the coup were not so lucky. Huge numbers of people filed in to Taiz's main square a few days later to watch their public beheading. But Imam Ahmed, short and round as a pumpkin, glaring menacingly at the proceedings from his chair in the middle of the throng, attracted even more attention than the gory executions.

Ahmed excelled at cultivating his mystical image. A pair of binoculars offered to him as a gift, but otherwise unknown in the country, allowed him to discern approaching caravans from the top floor of his palace before anyone else could see them. He then predicted their arrival a couple of hours in advance, astounding those around him.

Ahmed's prestige received a huge boost from his single-handedly putting down the army mutiny, and he basked in the glory as he observed the executions. A distant relative of mine who attended the executions as a young boy, told me much later of the event:

> Imam Ahmed had big bulging eyes that people said he caused intentionally by nearly strangling himself with a cord from time to time. He reinforced the effect for the beheadings that day with a generous amount of *khol* (black antimony) around his eyelids, and the cream he rubbed into his beard made his whiskers stand straight out as if he had his finger in a light socket.
>
> Ahmed described the crime and asked the crowd whether the guilty men deserved to die, and everyone shouted, 'Yes, yes.'
>
> The inspector general sighed. 'A curse on the people,' he said. 'I wanted life for them, but they want death for me.'
>
> When the executions were over, the *Imam* rose to leave the square. The crowd, rather than disperse, pressed round for a better look at the *Imam*, hoping some of his mythical powers might rub off on them. There was a lot of jostling and the *Imam* grew irritated.
>
> 'What's this?' he growled. 'Will you crush me?'
>
> Everybody froze and stared in awe at the *Imam*, whose voice thundered like the roar of a lion. When nobody moved out of his way, Ahmed grasped the huge scimitar suspended from his belt and whipped it from its scabbard. The screech of grating steel echoed across the square and all of us in the crowd recoiled, collapsing onto our backs like dominoes one on top of the other. No one drew so much as a breath until the *Imam* had safely departed.

Such narrow escapes as those in 1948 and 1955 surrounded Ahmed with an aura of invincibility, as though God took a personal interest in his safety. This made each successive attempt to overthrow him that much more difficult to pull off, but new conspiracies surfaced nonetheless.

In April 1959 the *Imam* left for Italy to seek treatment for his morphine addiction. He placed his son, Muhammad al-Badr, in charge during his absence. The inexperienced prince was a different breed from his father. Sympathetic to the progressive ideas of the Egyptian revolutionary Gamal Abdul Nasser, he advocated reforms similar to those in Egypt for his own country.

Imam Ahmed, on the other hand, viewed things from the eyes of an older generation. The revolutionary fervour in the Middle East stirred up by the charismatic Egyptian leader angered and frightened him. In order to stem its tide in Yemen, the clever *Imam* had surprised the world by agreeing to unify his country with Egypt and Syria in 1958 to form the United Arab States. Rebuffing his son's appeals for change, Ahmed instead used the alliance to keep Nasser at bay.

But with Ahmed in Rome, al-Badr could begin to implement some of his beloved reforms. He dismissed military officers deemed too reactionary, took the unprecedented step of creating a seven-member consultative council, and drew up a long list of administrative reforms for the civil service.

Despite his good intentions, Yemenis sensed al-Badr's weakness. He aimed to please everyone, which had taken no ruler very far before him. Though the state treasury was nearly depleted from several years of drought and famine, he caved in to agitation within the military for higher pay. And when they demanded still more, the prince increased government stipends to powerful *shaykhs* (tribal leaders) in the hope of winning their support to counter the increasingly defiant army.

Ahmed got wind of the problems and returned home in August 1959. The unrest that had engulfed the country fired him to uncontrollable rage. When he ordered the *shaykhs'* stipends returned, the emboldened tribes rose in rebellion. The army, still reeling from the dismissals and now threatened with pay cuts rather than further raises, proved unable or unwilling to put down the uprising.

Ahmed summoned two of the revolt's ringleaders: the powerful Hussayn al-Ahmar, *shaykh* of all the Hashid tribes, and Hussayn's son, Hameed. Imam Ahmed imprisoned them, and when the tribes still refused to end their insurrection, he ordered the two men beheaded.

The executions shocked Yemenis, and order returned to the land. But it proved to be only the calm before the storm. The *Imam*'s influence with the tribes never recovered from the deaths of the al-Ahmars. Further unrest ignited and vanished like spring thunderstorms over the next two and a half years as the tribes, in particular Hashid, awaited their chance to take revenge. The rash executions would precipitate not only the end of the Hameed al-Deen family dynasty, but also the extinction of the entire institution of the Imamate in Yemen.

Two years later, in late 1961, Ahmed sealed his family's fate by extracting Yemen from its moribund unity with Egypt. Relations between the two states deteriorated rapidly over the following nine months.

When Ahmed died a natural death in September 1962, his son, Muhammad al-Badr, became the new *Imam*. One week after the transfer of power, a clique of officers bombarded al-Badr's palace and declared the creation of a republic.

Many Yemenis had no idea who or what a republic was when news of the *coup d'état* spread. People announced excitedly to neighbours: '*Jumhuriya* has arrived!' – *Jumhuriya* being a feminine Arabic noun meaning 'republic.'

'Where is this *Jumhuriya* from?' they asked. 'And what has she come to do?'

Imam al-Badr managed to slip undetected from his beleaguered tower in Sanaa. Escaping to the northern mountains, he reverted to the age-old tactic of rallying the tribes to counter the revolution. Many flocked to his cause, but many others refused his plea for help. The Hashid tribes, which had proven so crucial to previous *Imams* in times of trouble, wavered conspicuously in their support. The beheading of their principal leader three years earlier severely curtailed their enthusiasm for the Imamate.

Hashid's snub struck a critical blow to al-Badr. Just as serious, however, was the aid provided to the Republicans by Egypt's

President Nasser. Some 60,000 Egyptian troops soon arrived in Yemen to shore up the wobbly republic.

But al-Badr felt vindicated when Nasser's arch-rivals in the royal family of Saudi Arabia decided to bankroll the *Imam*. The Saudis concluded that the overthrow of a conservative dynastic ruler on its southern border set a dangerous precedent. The tribesmen fighting for al-Badr came to be known as Royalists, and their fickle loyalty ebbed and flowed over the years according to the amount of money at the *Imam*'s disposal.

Egyptian troops finally withdrew in late 1967 from what had turned into a stalemate in Yemen. Some 20,000 Egyptians and 10 times as many Yemenis had lost their lives. With the Egyptians gone, thousands of Royalist tribesmen descended like wolves from the surrounding mountains intent on overrunning the capital and crushing the republic. The subsequent struggle for the town, including frontal assaults and missile barrages like the one my family experienced all too closely, was dubbed 'the 70-day siege'.

CHAPTER TWO

Earliest memories

My mother, Fatima al-Salami, had moved with my brother, Hamud, and me to the capital of Sanaa only a few months before the Katyusha rocket attack rattled the house and sent us scurrying for cover on the ground floor. Mother clutched me against her breast while Hamud anchored himself at her feet between the two millstones. She stroked my hair, so black it almost cast its own shadow in the pitch dark.

I didn't understand enough to be frightened by the explosions, but I sensed the dread in Mother's sinewy body, and trembled along with her at first. Her soothing words slowly reassured me and I felt safe in her arms.

An hour after the barrage, like mice when the lights go out, Sanaa's inhabitants peeked from behind their finely carved wooden doors to inspect the damage. Mother ventured into the entranceway to the house and stepped outside with me still clinging to her. Though she measured not more than five feet tall, the doorframe reached only to her shoulders. Its base dipped a foot below the earthen street level, elevated by the accumulation of dust over the centuries.

Turning left, she headed towards the shouts echoing down the narrow lane. Choking dust saturated the sunlight filtering between the six- and seven-storey houses, the grit seeping under the shawl that covered her from head to toe. Mother tugged the headscarf over her nose and mouth to filter the heavy air.

Suddenly a woman rounded the corner at a trot, her long colourful cloak waving in the breeze.

'Bayt al-Aubeli!' the woman cried, bursting into tears. 'The al-Aubeli house has been hit!'

Mother quickened her pace along the snaking passageway. At the fork, she went right and glimpsed a crowd scurrying to and fro in the grimy smog. When she burst into the bright sunlight, the ghastly scene came into view as her eyes adjusted to the glare. Two perpendicular walls of the five-storey house teetered precariously on their foundations. The elaborate wooden parapet protruding from the fourth-floor window swayed lightly, threatening to crash to the ground. The rest of the structure lay collapsed in a heap of bricks and burning timber supports.

Typical of Sanaa's intimately clustered homes, some built around the time when Columbus arrived in America, the al-Aubeli house rested upon a base of immense basalt cubes called *hajar habash* – Ethiopian stone. The name comes from the volcanic rocks' charcoal colour, resembling the dark skin of the Ethiopians across the Red Sea in Africa. Smaller clay bricks, sun-dried and baked in kilns, form the upper storeys of these dwellings, with delicate abstract reliefs adorning the outer walls. Ground alabaster, mixed with water and plastered around exterior windows and doorframes like icing on a cake, conveys to Sanaa's buildings the distinctive image of giant gingerbread houses.

Soldiers and stunned neighbours sifted with bare hands through the debris of the al-Aubeli house. A teenage soldier, the hint of an incoming moustache above his lip, seized an arm emerging from the pile of bricks like a periscope. Tugging, he slowly extricated the mutilated corpse of a woman. A comrade grasped the victim's feet and they carried her into the house next door.

The two boys returned to where they had left off, tossing aside more bricks. When one of them picked up what looked like a doll, Mother's face contorted painfully. Her thick lips grew pale and the mole under her right eye, at the base of her sharp nose, vanished into the crevice of a wrinkle. She set me on the ground and sprinted across the square, screaming: 'Saeeda!'

Like me, the little girl had been asleep beside her mother when the missile struck. Mother plucked the child from the exhausted soldier's arms and rushed into the makeshift morgue next door. I followed, stopping at the entrance to peer inside. Tearful women, some howling in despair, others silent in bitter reflection, busied themselves tearing white sheets into strips. The dusty, blood-soaked al-Aubeli woman and her two daughters lay prostrate on the floor.

Saeeda drew my inquisitive eyes over to her. We had often played together when Mother went to buy milk and yoghurt, commonly sold by butchers' wives from their homes. A silver necklace and string of beads still hung around Saeeda's neck, chiming along with half a dozen copper bracelets on each arm when someone moved her. I wondered how the al-Aubelis could be sleeping with all the commotion. 'If only Saeeda would get up so we could play,' I thought. I tugged on Mother's arm as she worked.

'What's wrong with Saeeda?' I asked. 'Why doesn't she wake up?'

'Dear Saeeda is dead,' Mother told me. 'She can't wake up. She is going to paradise to be with God.'

All of this was new to me – death, paradise, God. I didn't know what any of the words meant.

Mother ripped a square section from a sheet and slid it under Saeeda, folding the two ends over the top to cover the body. Having died unnatural deaths, the al-Aubelis were counted as martyrs, their souls guaranteed a place in heaven. Martyrs are not washed before burial, and their clothes are left exactly as found. The bodies, wrapped in a white shroud called a *kofn*, must be buried before sundown on the day of their death.

The elder al-Aubeli daughter was in her mid-teens, much older than Saeeda. She had married only a week before and moved in with her husband's family beside the Nishwan School. When the rocket that nearly killed my mother on her way to the market two days earlier blew out the windows in her new home, the terrified girl fled to her parents near Bab al-Yemen, convinced she would be safer there. She, too, had been found buried under the rubble, dead.

The al-Aubelis were butchers, an occupation traditionally passed down from father to son. The father was busying himself at his booth in the market preparing for the late afternoon rush of shoppers when he heard the explosion. Rushing home, he gazed in horror at the smouldering remnants, raised his hands and face to the sky, and wept.

When the women slid the enshrouded corpses onto wooden boards, the waiting men lifted them onto their shoulders and carried them outside. Neighbours, most of whose families had lived beside the al-Aubelis for generations, assembled into a melancholy procession. '*La ilahi ila Allah,*' chanted the crowd as it disappeared down an alleyway. 'There are no other gods but God.'

The mourners, like a snake slithering forth from its den, emerged into the square behind Bab al-Yemen 50 yards away. Exiting under the gate's stone archway, they proceeded along the mud rampart girdling the town; 128 bastions reinforced the 20-foot high wall at intervals throughout its length.

Mother and I shuffled along with the other women, to the rear of the men. But overcome with curiosity, I finally broke free and pranced forward to place myself at the head of the marchers. Every few steps, I swivelled to gawk at the smallest of the three martyrs supported on the pallbearers' shoulders. I was anxious to see this paradise that we were taking the al-Aubelis to, and to see this God that they were going to meet, so I watched everything with great attention.

Qasr al-Silah – the Fort of Arms – lay a quarter of a mile to the east on a foot spur of Jebel Nuqum, soaring 2,000 feet above the town. The imposing castle is popularly believed to occupy the site of the ancient Ghamdan Palace, 20 storeys of marble and granite constructed some 2,000 years ago, but long since disappeared.

Rectangular mounds of dirt framed by small rocks mark the graves in the sprawling Mashhad (Martyrs) Cemetery beyond the fortress. Years later, when I returned to look at the cemetery as an adult, I noticed that over half the tombs belong to infants, shaped more like squares than the rectangles of the adults. They lay so close together as to make the 10-acre graveyard all but indistinguishable from a bare, rocky plain. A stranger might stroll through and never suspect he had trod over a burial ground.

Another cemetery lay closer to Bab al-Yemen. But, too far from the town's defences, it was vulnerable to attack from the enemy on Jebel Atan. Mashhad Cemetery was only slightly less exposed. A sudden assault from tribesmen on the encompassing heights could have caught the funeral assembly out in the open. No one wished to linger.

The women halted at the cemetery's fringe while the men and children entered. The dogs that used the area as refuge from the persecutions of stone-throwing youths scattered before the invaders. A guardian, crouching indifferently under the feathery shade of an acacia gum tree, rose reverently at the sight of the procession and ambled over to the three pits he had dug. The mourners formed an arc around a distinguished-looking elder, who nervously blotted sweat from his forehead while shooting furtive glances at the surrounding mountains for any signs of danger.

'From dust, to dust we return,' he began, in a phrase shared by so many cultures.

Following a brief recitation of religious verse, the men lowered the al-Aubeli mother into the largest tomb. Her head pointed east and her face turned on its side to the north, towards Mecca. With the grave filled, the al-Aubeli father inserted a long, thin stone vertically in the soil over his wife's head. He placed a slightly smaller rock at the waist and a third at chest level, to identify the grave as that of a female. Then he scooped out a circular indentation in the centre of the mound to collect rainwater from which birds might quench their thirst. A few tombs of the wealthier boasted a name and sometimes a date inscribed on the headstone. But these were hard times, and the al-Aubelis' dead lay unmarked.

I manoeuvred through the crowd, craning my neck for a better look as Saeeda's tiny body disappeared into the hollow ground last. I looked all around for God and paradise, but saw nothing I thought might be them. My disappointment turned to horror as the soil from the guardian's shovel splashed onto the little girl's face. The word 'death' now held meaning for me, and I finally understood that my friend wasn't going to wake up, that we would never play together again.

The al-Aubeli father slipped a piece of silver into the guardian's hand for his services, and requested that he recite a few verses from the Koran over the graves from time to time. The old man nodded in assent. The ceremony at an end, the mourners withdrew hastily to the small security of their homes.

With Egyptian troops gone and a new president at the helm of Yemen, the fate of the country hung tenuously in the balance as the al-Aubeli funeral unfolded. The Republicans faced their Royalist foe on their own for the first time as they struggled to withstand the 70-day siege, this last-ditch effort by the Royalists to topple the government.

While one group of Bakil tribesmen attempted to penetrate Sanaa from the north, a second Royalist force dug in atop Jebel Atan and one of the twin peaks of Jebel al-Nahdayn – the two breasts – a mile southwest of Bab al-Yemen. They terrified Sanaa's citizens with their Katyusha rocket attacks.

As Prime Minister and Commander-in-Chief of the Armed Forces, Hassan al-Amri led the heroic defence of the city. He sallied forth personally to fight the besiegers, nearly losing his life on more than one occasion. Yahya al-Mutawakil, a skinny *Sayid* in his mid-20s, served as al-Amri's aide-de-camp. The young man seemed to spend much of his time trying to keep the Prime Minister out of harm's way. Some mornings al-Amri would head out from the town wall in a small convoy of jeeps, determined to combat the Royalist forces. Yahya's job consisted of convincing his fearless commander-in-chief to disengage from battles in which the enemy heavily outnumbered and threatened to overrun them.

After more than two months of probing ground attacks, al-Amri ordered another young military officer, Mujahid Abu Shawareb, to lead a counter-attack against Jebel Atan to dislodge the Royalists once and for all. Mujahid enlisted the support of a tank unit commanded by a close friend, Muhammad Abu Lahum. Both men, though only in their twenties, were intimately acquainted with Imam Ahmed's prisons, and not at all anxious to see the return of the royal family to power.

With 2,000 men, supported by Abu Lahum's tanks, Mujahid moved aggressively out of Sanaa in the first days of February 1968. Intense fire met them from Jebel Atan as they hurtled across the plain in a cloud of dust. After heavy fighting, the Royalists retreated south to make their last stand on a more easily defended ridge. But the Republicans drove them into the territory of the neighbouring Sanhan tribe, from where most of them dispersed to their villages. The siege of Sanaa was finally broken, though at great cost. Muhammad Abu Lahum alone lost three maternal uncles in the battle.

The politics and military manoeuvrings of course escaped me at the time. My only thought had been: 'Why would anyone want to cause so much pain and horror, and why can't Mother make it stop?'

For three decades my thoughts progressed little beyond the philosophical, until my friendship with these three men – Yahya al-Mutawakil, Mujahid Abu Shawareb and Muhammad Abu Lahum – helped me better understand the forces behind the al-Aubeli massacre and, a few weeks later, the terrors wrought upon my own family. Little did I suspect then that those events would ultimately lead me to a life that few Yemeni women could have imagined before.

CHAPTER THREE

The promised land

The original homeland of my al-Salami ancestors lies within an insulated mountain valley in Khawlan territory,[1] 35 miles east of Sanaa. At its western extremity, the valley drains into the Sanaa plain south of the capital, while in the east, the canyons gradually dissolve into the confines of al-Khala – the Emptiness – the great, waterless desert extending across southern Arabia to the Persian Gulf.

The al-Salamis farmed the rock-strewn fields at the highest and widest point in Khawlan's northernmost valley, working their humped oxen or a pair of donkeys year after year. They ploughed the earth and flattened it before the stars of Pleiades appeared low in the west after dusk, the sign that the spring rains would soon arrive and the sorghum must be sown.[2]

The women took time out from their daily chores of cooking and collecting water and firewood to assist the men during the critical late summer harvest. The sorghum had to be cut, threshed,

---

[1] The Khawlan al-Aliya (or Upper Khawlan, to distinguish it from another tribe of the same name further north) is part of the Bakil tribal federation. The al-Salamis descend from the Bani (children of) Ihsam, one of five sections making up the Khawlan. Tribal genealogy, held dear by all of its members (except perhaps by some of the younger generations now living in towns) relates that Ihsam was a son of the original tribal patriarch, Khawlan, himself a descendent of Sheba.

[2] The Muslim calendar is lunar-based, so that each year is approximately 11 days shorter than a solar-based calendar year. As a result, the months fall in different seasons over the decades, forcing farmers to use the stars and the angle of the sun, rather than the date, as a guide to the agricultural seasons.

winnowed and stored before the awaited rains spoiled the yield. If the rains followed soon after the new sowing, then the village would eat its fill that year. But if the monsoon winds failed to convey the moist, tropical winds far enough north to water the valley, disaster could strike.

The al-Salamis dwelled in an area of Khawlan known as Jebel al-Lowz, Mount Almond. They harvested this nut from the lolling 20-foot trees that abound in the high valley. During a few rare years, when God drove away the diseases, locusts and hail that damaged the crop, the trees produced more than the villagers could consume.

In those times of plenty, the al-Salamis would send a handful of their young men with loaded donkeys and camels down to Sanaa to sell the surplus almonds. Entering through Bab al-Yemen, the small caravan would have passed the Great Mosque on its way to the Samsarat al-Mizan, the central weigh station where market officials assessed customs duty on merchandise. The al-Salamis would have stayed the night at the guesthouse at the north end of the coffee *suq*, one of the 40 or so specialized markets making up Sanaa's sprawling Suq al-Milh – the salt market.

Under the stone arches of the guesthouse's narrow gallery, a boy would boil *qishr* for the guests, an infusion of coffee husks without the beans, flavoured with various spices (Yemenis prefer *qishr* to actual coffee). Beasts of burden were couched in a corner of the central courtyard where they waited patiently for dinner, served after the lodging's massive wooden doors swung shut for the night.

In the morning, the al-Salamis would have issued forth from the guesthouse to find the *wakeel*, who acts as wholesaler in the market. Tribesmen today still consider it shameful to sell their produce directly to a retailer, or to tend a shop, no matter how much greater the profits. They will sell only to the *wakeel*, who in turn distributes the produce to shopkeepers.

Having shopped in the *suq* with their profits, the al-Salamis would have returned home to Khawlan with enough supplies hopefully to last them until the next year's almond harvest.

During a trip together to Yemen in 1997, my husband Charles wanted to visit the village of al-Salami in Khawlan. I had never been there, but a friend from the area agreed to take us one afternoon.

As our SUV approached, the entire village of two dozen adults and twice as many children surrounded the car to greet us. The weathered village headman was excited to learn that I was an al-Salami, and adamant that my husband choose a parcel of land for us to build a house on and farm. 'It is a gift from the village to you – for returning,' he said. We thanked him for the generous offer and told him we would consider it.

The al-Salamis' village remains today much as it was over three centuries ago: a dozen square towers of small stones, balanced one on top of the other, without mortar. The *shaykh*'s house, built above a shallow ledge forming a border for the farm-land, looks south over the almond trees and sorghum. Vertical slits around the base of each building, where a stone or two has been omitted, allow a broad field of fire against attackers. For security, the only true windows appear 20 feet up, growing progressively larger as they near the tops of the five- and six-storey fortress-homes.

Behind the village, almost at the foot of the last house, the Khawlan massif plunges abruptly to the plain some 1,500 feet below. A dark patch marking Sanaa glimmers in the distance, 20 miles to the northwest, but the shortest route to the capital winds nearly twice that distance back through the valley.

Someone had been dispatched the moment of our arrival to slaughter a sheep and prepare a feast. After the meal Charles persuaded the headman, an al-Salami like everyone else in the village, to tell us the story of my ancestors' precipitous departure from Jebel al-Lowz – a chronicle that interested Charles far more than me at the time.

'Around 300 years ago,' the headman began over a cup of tea, 'the al-Salamis readied their fields for another planting. But that year the winds refused to back to the southwest and the rains failed. The villagers despaired. Those who sowed their seeds despite the ill breeze produced only stunted plants that soon withered and died. The smaller plots of wheat, millet, and barley fared even worse, their stalks hardly managing to push through the parched soil.'

Three consecutive years of drought made life precarious on Jebel al-Lowz. The people prayed and sacrificed bulls, but nothing could induce the rains to come. They drew on the grain stored in the *mudafin*,[3] but they soon depleted that source. As the livestock lay dead or dying, the only prospect for relief lay in yet another, unpredictable harvest several months ahead.

Many households in the village gathered what possessions their scrawny pack animals could bear and marched south across Khawlan's nearly impenetrable mountain trails. When they reached the town of Radaa, 40 miles as the crow flies, they found that the rains had not faltered completely, so they halted. That branch of the al-Salamis remains around Radaa to this day.

For those families determined to ride out the famine in Khawlan, hunger did not pose the only threat. The drought, like countless others before and since, also sparked unrest in the land. Men turned to brigandage in order to feed themselves, roaming the mountains like packs of hyenas. Those who refused to join the bands of thieves passed the time trying to safeguard what little remained to them.

A climate of grave suspicion swept over the region. Two strangers crossing paths on a mountain track made for a harrowing experience. Each expected the other to set upon him to steal any silver he might be carrying, and each readied himself to pre-empt the assault at the slightest provocation, real or imagined.

---

[3] Plural of *mudfin* – deep shafts dug around villages for storage.

The family of Hussayn al-Salami, one of those who chose to remain in Jebel al-Lowz, became embroiled in such a death during the famine. The origin of the tragedy quickly faded from memory, but the al-Salamis faced the prospect of a bloody feud if nothing were done.[4]

Hussayn's three sons decided to take their families and leave Jebel al-Lowz. Even if the dead man's relatives renounced revenge and accepted the *diya*, the al-Salamis had nothing left to pay with in the aftermath of the famine. Living out their lives forever glancing over their shoulders for fear of being murdered was a price they refused to pay.

The fertile slopes of the western mountains held out the promise of more productive farming than the thirsty

---

[4] Yemen's ancient tribal code calls for either revenge – *thar* – or the payment of blood money – *diya* – in compensation for a death. The aim is to repair the honour of the victim's family and tribe, embodied in the ability to protect its members and territory. Many consider anything less than an eye for an eye as dishonourable, a sign of weakness. The victim's family will often consider accepting the *diya* only if the death is clearly accidental, and not always then.

In some cases, the normal *diya* is increased several fold, such as when the killer and the victim have recently eaten bread together, walked together as travelling companions, or when the victim is from the non-tribal protected strata of society, such as a Jew, an artisan or a woman.

Those opposed to receiving the *diya* will not rest until they have avenged their loss. *Thar* is preferably inflicted on the culprit himself. But if he has fled, a close family member or even an unrelated man from the same tribe is fair game and may be slain in his stead.

Yet revenge and blood money are meant to deter violence, not perpetuate it. A man may think twice before taking a life when he knows that he or his sons will suffer the consequences. The disadvantage is that on occasions when the system fails to contain the bloodshed, retribution can spiral into a nasty vendetta that may endure for generations.

Islam criticized these age-old tribal customs when it took hold in Yemen in the seventh century AD, in particular the concept that the whole tribe is responsible for the actions of any one of its members. While the tribal code ignores considerations of right and wrong, Islamic law introduced moral principles into the equation. Despite their many contradictions, Islamic law, administered by religious judges, and the tribal code, applied by *shaykhs*, have coexisted for centuries in Yemen.

soil of their own valley. One morning before sunrise, the three families loaded their handful of scrawny camels and donkeys with their worldly possessions: blankets, mats, cooking utensils, a wrought copper and brass coffee pot, mortar and pestle, water skins and the women's jewellery. Passing under the precious shade of their beloved almond trees, they departed Jebel al-Lowz forever, bound for a land of which they knew little.

The caravan halted occasionally to allow the women to draw water from a well beside the track to make *qishr*. But they never lingered for fear that villagers would arrive and insist on their staying for lunch. The sheep the villagers would slaughter in their honour might well be the last in those times of want.

It occurred to me how, in Yemen, centuries of poverty and uncertainty have not rendered its people thrifty and prudent, as might be expected. Quite the contrary, any object of value is viewed as a gift from God, which he can withdraw as easily as he provided it. Wealth is not to be saved but spread around, so that when it is gone, those who have received a portion of it might share something of their own in return.

'The frigid air of the upper valley warmed as the caravan filed through the narrow gorges and their maze of huge boulders,' the headman went on. 'But the ravine soon broadened, then opened onto the Sanaa plateau. The Sanhan tribe at the mouth of the valley occasionally blocked Khawlan's access when disputes arose between the two, just like today. But relations were good when the al-Salamis passed through that year and no one challenged them.'

Crossing the plateau, the families then made their way into the Black Mountains west of Sanaa. There they spent the night in one of the small stone shelters erected throughout the countryside for use by sojourners and shepherds, the kind nobody uses anymore. The following day they entered

Bani Matar territory and ascended a ridge onto the al-Sihma plain.

Skirting the heights of Jebel al-Nabi Shuayb,[5] the al-Salamis' hopes began to fade. They had expected to discover a rich, flourishing land as they moved further west. But the al-Sihma plateau, rocky and barren, supported crops only in hollows few and far between. A patch or two of withered sorghum in some of the depressions testified to the passing of a brief shower, but the crops had otherwise failed and the land was void of people – no one even to harvest the few ripened stalks. The families could only plod forward, though for all they knew drought afflicted the whole world.

Mitna village, further on, offered little but the shade of a few thorny acacia trees. Yet for some reason its inhabitants had not fled. In fact, they seemed healthier than anyone the al-Salamis had come across since leaving home. And at the Thursday market town of Suq al-Bowan several hours beyond Mitna, vendors displayed sorghum and even wheat for sale, though the surrounding countryside mysteriously appeared no less parched than in Khawlan.

The route inclined steeply upwards on the far side of the town. It seemed to come to a dead end at the foot of an imposing wall of basalt rock embedded in the earth like a massive meteorite, its ridge worn away into a saw-tooth pattern along its entire length. Rounding the northern edge of the lava block, which marked the border between the Bani Matar and Heima tribes, the al-Salamis couldn't believe their eyes.

A verdant paradise unfurled before them, more spectacular than anything they had dared imagine. The rains had not failed here, and the steep slopes of Heima glittered green with virgin forest and coffee trees crowning golden fields of wheat in the valley

---

[5] The Mountain of the Prophet Shuayb, the highest point on the Arabian Peninsula at 12,368 feet.

depths. Thick clouds rolling in from the far-off sea curled around
the summits, offering moisture and shade. As far as the eye could
see, entire mountains sculpted into parallel terraces resembled
staircases for giants, perhaps those said to have haunted these
parts in pre-Islamic times. The backs of men and beasts had
hauled the soil up over centuries from the rich loam-filled *wadis*
below, and stone walls buttressed the terraces to prevent them
from washing away. The Herculean effort had paid off though,
for no one went hungry here.

The al-Salamis watched eagles plunge into the valley bottoms,
moments later soaring out of the gorges on warm air thermals. In
an instant the thirsty wilderness back home became but a distant
memory as they gazed out from astride what would soon come to
be known as al-Salami Pass (the highest point on the road linking
Sanaa to the Red Sea at 9,400 feet). Months of hunger and
frustration already began to drain away. They knew that this
was where they would settle down.

'A farmer ploughing a field greeted the strangers,' the headman
continued.

'Where are you folks coming from?' he asked.

The al-Salamis looked uneasily at one other. But they had
heard of no one from Khawlan involved in a feud with the
Heima of late, so they risked little in revealing their origin.

'We're from Jebel al-Lowz,' the eldest brother answered.
'In Khawlan.'

The farmer reflected for a moment. He, too, could recall
no outstanding disputes with that tribe. 'Welcome,' he said.
'Where are you headed?'

'The famine just about wiped us out back home,' the
brother explained. 'We're not quite sure where we're
headed yet, so long as it's away from there.' The brother
stared over the mountains before them.

'Looks like you've had all the rain you need in these
parts,' one of the al-Salamis observed.

On hearing of the group's plight, the farmer felt pity, and obligation. 'You must come to my home,' he insisted. 'You'll be my guests for a few days.'

The man led the way down the hill to the tiny one-floor stone house he lived in. The host and his wife and children listened intently that evening over the dim light of an oil lantern as the sons of Hussayn al-Salami took turns recounting the effects of the drought and the lawlessness in their native land.

'*Mash Allah*,' the farmer's wife murmured between tales. She prayed that such misery would never be visited upon Heima.

Early on the morning of the weekly market in Suq al-Aman, below the saw-toothed ridge, the farmer accompanied the al-Salami brothers to purchase a cow from his neighbour. People from throughout the region attended the market. As the throng thickened toward mid-morning, the brothers led their bull into the centre of the commotion. The eldest placed his last silver piece into the outstretched hand of the town herald – *doshan* – and quietly explained their business.

After hearing him out, the *doshan* glanced impassively at the shiny silver in his hand. He adjusted the fringed edges of his long kilt, and cleared his crackly throat as if to seize the crowd's attention. Bursting into a high-pitched litany, he showered praise on the people of Heima and their *shaykhs*, commending the tribe's valour and generosity in the most flattering of rhymed verse; all on behalf of the al-Salamis.

Shoppers, almost exclusively men, strolled hand-in-hand with their friends as they browsed among the stalls. At the *doshan*'s beckoning, they gathered round to view the spectacle. With the undulating chant complete, the eldest al-Salami brother unsheathed his *jambiya*. '*Bismillah al-Rahman al-Raheem* – In the name of God, the Most Gracious, the Most Merciful,' he pronounced, and plunged the dagger deep into the bull's throat.

The blood cascaded from the gaping wound in the bull's neck as it collapsed and died, soaking the earth of Heima's sacred market. With this, the al-Salamis bound themselves in an enduring pact with the land and the tribe. Heima thenceforth considered the three families as much one of its own as if they had lived there for generations. An attack on the al-Salamis constituted an attack on all of Heima; and goodwill shown to them was a favour imparted on all of Heima.[6]

Charles and I left Yemen a couple of days after hearing the story of the al-Salamis' departure from Khawlan three centuries ago. But on another trip to Yemen, in 2000, we visited Heima with my mother and younger sister to learn what befell my family after their arrival there.

We drove for nearly an hour west of Sanaa, parked along the roadside, then trudged up several hundred feet to the Heima village that today bears my family's name. Mother and my sister carried sacks of cookies balanced on their heads as gifts to our relatives, whom they had not visited in several years.

After an excited reunion with the village and meeting its newest additions, born since Mother's last visit, one of the al-Salami elders invited us into the housetop fortress for tea. Seeing our interest, he continued my ancestors' saga from where the village headman in Jebel al-Lowz had left off.

'As new members of the tribe, the Heima offered the al-Salamis land, for any tribesman worthy of the name must own land,' the grey-bearded elder explained. 'They settled on the highest knoll above Suq al-Aman, where we sit now.'

---

[6] The al-Salamis were refugees, just as the Prophet Muhammad had sought refuge in far off Medina from the jealous clans of his native Mecca in the early days of Islam. Anyone requesting succour from another tribe, whether for lack of food or to escape a blood feud, must be welcomed. No shame surpasses that of turning away a man in need, though he may even have murdered your own son.

I glanced out the window at narrow terraces dipping to the valley floor thousands of feet below, into a *wadi* system no less majestic than the Grand Canyon.[7] The al-Salamis had built their fortress-home of stone on the rocky outcrop overlooking their fields, situating it so that no precious farmland went to waste and no attack might catch them by surprise. The roughly hewn boulders of the three-storey tower fitted into place without mortar, while the foundations were made spacious enough to allow room for storing the harvests. Thick timbers supported the roof of dried mud. After decorating the exterior walls with white alabaster to ward off the evil eye, the families settled into their new home.

They farmed as they had on Jebel al-Lowz. Only here the sorghum harvest arrived a few weeks earlier in the warmer air, and the wheat and barley grew stronger and more plentiful under the abundant rains.

The women bore many children, some of whom survived. As the new offspring had children of their own, they built new homes further down the mountain. Within a few generations, the three families had grown to several dozen, and their tiny collection of houses blossomed into three separate villages. The people of Heima called them, collectively, Bayt al-Salami – the House of al-Salami.

The al-Salamis soon realized to their regret that the route winding its way between their villages represented more than just a convenient means of travelling to the region's markets. It was also a strategic thoroughfare, control of which could ensure

[7] Long before the al-Salami's arrival here, undefiled forest blanketed the region. In the early thirteenth century, an uprising sparked by a religious minority in the Haraz region (Heima's neighbour to the southwest) threatened to topple the ruling *Imam*. Tribesmen from across Yemen answered the call to join his army and crush the rebellion. Following their victory, the *Imam* offered his soldiers the forested region west of Jebel al-Nabi Shuayb as theirs for the taking, dubbing it Heimat al-Din – Defender of the Religion – shortened to Heima. When the Sanaa–Hodayda road traversed the area later, the territory north of the road came to be referred to as Upper Heima, while the land to the south became Lower Heima.

success for an army marching on Sanaa from the Red Sea, or for an *Imam* mustering the tribes to block the invaders. Bayt al-Salami's command of this route, at its highest point, prophesied coming hardships beyond the villagers' worst nightmares.

CHAPTER FOUR

The warrior's life

A round the time the al-Salamis settled in Heima, the Ottoman army withdrew from Yemen after nearly 100 years in the country. The Red Sea's importance as a link between Europe and India had declined over the preceding century with the Portuguese discovery of the sea route around Africa in 1497. The Sultan in Istanbul decided that the cost in men and money of holding on to Yemen no longer paid off.

The al-Salamis watched from the roof of their mountain bastion as the retiring Turks marched through the heart of Heima on their way to Hodayda and the ships that would take them home. But the Ottomans would return two centuries later, and Heima's pivotal location would thrust the descendents of Hussayn al-Salami into the forefront of a bloody resistance.

Control over Yemen's Tihama region in the first half of the nineteenth century see-sawed between Yemen's *Imam* and the ruler of Mecca far to the north. Amidst the chaos, the Turks reoccupied the torrid Yemeni coastal plain in 1849. The Ottomans recognized the *Imam*'s sovereignty over the Yemeni highlands and agreed to pay him an annual subsidy. In return, the *Imam* committed himself to stationing an Ottoman garrison in Sanaa.

Istanbul's renewed effort to strengthen its hand in Yemen aimed partly at preventing Britain, whose ships occupied Aden in 1839, from extending its influence further north into the Red Sea. The Turks – ridiculed by the Yemenis on account of their trousers, which only women wear in Yemen – were massacred nearly to a man by the enraged Yemenis on the very day they arrived in Sanaa. The crowd then proceeded to depose the hapless *Imam* who had acquiesced in their unwanted presence there.

But removal of the adversary led to a fresh wave of internecine strife. Nine *Imams* rose and fell from power in the six years following the Ottoman defeat. Anarchy reigned throughout the highlands, culminating in the eruption of a major revolt among the mysterious Mukarama community of Jebel Haraz in 1871.[1]

The Turks, holed up in the Tihama since 1849, used the *Imam*'s bloody repression of the Harazi Mukarama as a pretext for marching once again on Sanaa. Reinforced with troops arriving by sea through the recently opened Suez Canal, they succeeded this time in subduing the capital.

A powerful earthquake shook Heima the following year, as if to warn the invaders. Corruption pervaded the Ottoman administration. Local tax collectors commonly withheld the government's share of the revenue and insisted they had been unable to collect their due. The alleged defiance provoked the government into sending troops to seize land and property from the supposedly delinquent villages. The replacement of Islamic

---

[1] Unlike their Zaydi Shiite neighbours, the Mukarama are Ismaili Shiites. They recognize a largely different chain of successors to the Prophet Muhammad than do the Zaydis, and tend to be very guarded concerning their beliefs and traditions. Everyone from neighbouring Heima knew someone who knew someone who had secretly observed the bizarre practices of the Mukarama in their mountain stronghold of Haraz, such as spouse-swapping and other strange rituals. Of course no one had actually witnessed such abominations for themselves, but like most things odd and unseen, the stories tended to be accepted as truth.

An Ismaili proselytiser had propelled the remote mountains of Haraz into the spotlight of Yemeni politics in the eleventh century AD. Military campaigns expanded the missionary's control to the Tihama and extensive swaths of the northern and southern highlands, to which it soon moved its seat of government, plunging Haraz back into political obscurity. The region reared its head periodically to protest the rule of an overzealous Zaydi *Imam*, such as the thirteenth-century uprising whose quelling gave birth to the settlement of the Heima forest.

law with the Ottoman civil code further angered Yemenis, and sporadic attacks on Ottoman outposts made it clear that the fuse was shortening.

The winter of 1884–1885 hit the highlands with exceptional ferocity. For the first time in living memory, three feet of snow blanketed the slopes of Heima and Haraz for a week. Drought and famine followed on the heels of the blizzard, aggravated when Ottoman troops seized grain from starving villagers in order to feed themselves.

Yemenis needed little prodding to obey the belated call for a general revolt launched by the newly elected Imam Muhammad al-Mansur in 1891. The reluctant *Imam* understood that popular sentiment demanded the expulsion of the Turks, and he had little choice but to take up the cause. When 70,000 angry tribesmen converged on Sanaa soon after, Ottoman units in Hodayda hastened to relieve the beleaguered capital. The troops burned dozens of villages along the way, many of them in Heima.

Hussayn al-Salami, the son of Ihsan, the son of Salih, was a descendent of the Hussayn whose three sons immigrated to Heima from Khawlan two centuries earlier. He had made a name for himself fighting first the Mukarama in 1871, then the Turks marching on Sanaa in the aftermath of that war.

The grey-bearded al-Salami elder in Heima told his story to Charles and me during our visit there:

When Hussayn glanced down from his rooftop in Bayt al-Salami early one morning [in 1891], it was not the first time he had witnessed thousands of Turks on the move. The scene intimidated him not in the least.

He ordered fires to be lit on the mountain tops as a signal for tribesmen to gather with their arms for a fight. Though the carefree days of his youth had passed him by, Hussayn led the fierce peasants into battle, never flinching as comrades fell at his side under the hail of enemy bullets. The daring displayed in his forays so impressed his followers that they made him *shaykh al-mashaykh* – *shaykh* of all the *shaykhs* – for both the Upper and Lower Heima tribes.[2]

When not engaging them in combat, the people of Bayt al-Salami observed the Turks with the curiosity of spectators. One year Ottoman troops advanced triumphantly eastward towards the capital, nothing seemingly able to stand in their way. The next year they shuffled by in the opposite direction, retreating with bloodied tails between their legs to Hodayda on the 150-mile gravel road they had widened in order to move their artillery.

It was an interminable cycle, dictated by the *Imam*'s ability to retain thousands of tribesmen under his sway long enough to defeat the enemy. Each new *Imam* resurrected and focused the unrest that made Yemen so inhospitable to its occupiers. Yahya Hameed al-Deen, who became *Imam* in 1904, abhorred the rampant corruption of the Ottoman soldiers and administrators. He also hated the enforcement of their civil law – the same grievances that had incited the people to revolt under his father.

Imam Yahya wasted no time in taking the offensive once in power. He cut the critical Sanaa–Hodayda road, then rekindled the attack on the Ottoman garrison in Sanaa. The three-month siege reduced the city's inhabitants to consuming cats and dogs to keep from starving. Half the population, estimated at up to 50,000, are said to have perished. The irate Sultan in Istanbul dispatched an additional 10,000 ill-fated troops to Hodayda during the crisis.

The grave al-Salami patriarch continued his story, lowering his voice as if Ottoman spies might still be lurking about.

As the Turk reinforcements moved towards Sanaa to relieve their comrades, Hussayn al-Salami was among the partisans who confronted them. The guerrillas harried relentlessly from behind spurs and boulders as the army lumbered up to the craggy peaks overlooking the Tihama plain.

---

[2] Referred to collectively as al-Heimatayn – the two Heimas.

Once beyond the well-defended Turkish garrison above Manakha town, the route dips sharply into Wadi al-Mawt – the Valley of Death. The tiny scar of a road snaking around rocky outcrops and through deep gorges amounted in places to nothing more than a narrow rock-strewn trail, hemmed in by bluffs on either side. Decimated by the guerrillas, the entire Turkish column surrendered. The garrison in Sanaa did the same when news of the catastrophe reached it.

Far from deterred by the losses, the Sultan raised the stakes, ordering [40,000] reinforcements to Yemen the next year. Despite suffering heavy casualties, this time the army broke through to the capital.

But Hussayn al-Salami continued to flame the fires of revolt in Heima at Imam Yahya's behest. The Ottomans' hold on Sanaa proved tenuous but stubborn. The *Imam* drove them out once, only to watch them capture it again a few months later, and Hussayn and his men passed their time ambushing detachments of Turks patrolling the *wadis* west of the capital.

The proud al-Salami patriarch paused for a moment to allow Charles and me to absorb his story. I would read later that of the 55,000 Ottomans in Yemen, 33,000 are believed to have lost their lives trying to suppress the rebellion.

The new Turkish Governor sent to Yemen in 1911 proved exceptionally harsh. Imam Yahya, secure in his impenetrable mountain refuge of Shahara northwest of Sanaa, this time rallied 150,000 tribesmen to his banner. This biblical plague swarmed onto the Sanaa plateau to teach the Governor and his masters a lesson. The Minister of War in Istanbul responded by rushing 60,000 men to Hodayda, thousands of whom died in the passes on their way up to Sanaa.

The Turkish commander allegedly announced on finally breaking through: 'I could conquer all of Europe with such men as we have just fought.'

The elder from Heima went on as Charles and I listened intently:

'Ahhh, but I took many Turk heads,' Hussayn al-Salami used to boast to his children and grandchildren. And none disputed the claim, for they had seen him in action. But for some unknown reason, perhaps for provoking Turkish reprisals on Heima's villages, Hussayn was betrayed by the inhabitants of al-Ghobar village, a couple of miles down the mountain from Bayt al-Salami.

Al-Ghobar's headman informed the commander of the Ottoman garrison in Manakha one day that it was Shaykh Hussayn who orchestrated the attacks on his troops in the region. The Turkish commander had Hussayn arrested and beheaded, dispatching the trophy to the Sultan himself in Istanbul.

After Hussayn's death, troops from the garrison swooped down upon Bayt al-Salami and demolished the house the three al-Salami brothers had built on the knoll. But the villagers had already left by the time the Turks arrived. On Hussayn's capture, his eldest son, Ahmed, had decided it was best to relocate the family to another village away from the strategic Sanaa-Hodayda route.[3]

Ahmed al-Salami proved equally as wise and courageous as Hussayn. Before long, he stepped into his late father's shoes as *shaykh* of the Heimatayn. It wasn't until I was over 30 years old that I asked my Grandmother Amina about her father, Ahmed. I could hear the pride in her voice as she spoke of him while seated on a cushion in the little room in Sanaa from which she rarely strayed in her old age.

---

[3] The effort required to hold on to the country had by now exhausted the Ottomans. In 1911, the two antagonists signed a treaty in which the Ottomans handed over the bulk of administration in the northern mountains to the *Imam*, in exchange for the latter's nominal recognition of Ottoman sovereignty. Peace had returned, for a brief moment.

'Your Great-Grandfather Ahmed was a handsome and imposing figure, though not a large man,' she said, staring at the wall with her filmy eyes nearly blinded with cataracts. 'He had a long, lean face and a nose as straight as a plough tip. When he was five years old, soldiers came and took him as a hostage to the *Imam* in Sanaa's Qasr al-Silah citadel for a year or two, to guarantee the good behaviour of the Heimatayn tribes. But Ahmed didn't resent it. It was an accepted way for the *Imam* to maintain order.'[4]

Ahmed al-Salami's loyalty to Imam Yahya earned him the rank of captain in the regular army.[5] The *Imam* placed him in command of four *blocks* (the word apparently taken from the English), each *block* made up of approximately 100 men.

In 1915, the ruler of Asir, on the Red Sea coast north of Hodayda, declared himself a British ally in the First World War. To prove his claim, he sent his army to Yemen to attack Germany's Turkish allies (some of whose soldiers remained there even after the 1911 treaty with the *Imam*).

Ahmed al-Salami and his brother, Mubarak, led part of the Yemeni force sent to intercept the new invaders as they swept down the Tihama coast and into the highlands. The two armies engaged in battle in the Haraz Mountains, but the fighting proved inconclusive. The Asiris could advance no further; nor could the Yemenis push them back.

---

[4] The *Imams*, in particular Yahya and his son Ahmed, mastered the art of divide and rule. They brilliantly played the tribes against one another, and the taking of hostages provided an added safety net. The number demanded from any one region depended on the loyalty and behaviour of the tribes living there. The Jawf Bedouins in the eastern desert, and Barat to the north, typically furnished the most hostages. During periods of relative calm, the boys might be taught to read the Koran and even allowed to visit relatives on weekends. But in times of unrest, they could be chained to the wall of their prison cell. A hostage's brother usually replaced him after a year or so, and Imam Ahmed was said to have around 2,000 such detainees just prior to the 1962 revolution.

[5] Military service was voluntary and for life, and a soldier wishing to leave or even retire had to furnish a replacement, often a son.

Grandmother Amina's brother, Abdul Kareem, told Charles and me the story one evening in his home in Sanaa. My great-uncle displayed no less admiration than Grandmother Amina in recounting their father's adventures.

'Clashes continued for several weeks, neither side gaining any ground,' Abdul Kareem recollected from the stories his father had told him as a child. 'Until one day at lunch time a messenger arrived with urgent news for Ahmed. The man's face was grave and Ahmed braced himself for bad news.

'I'm sorry, sir,' the messenger huffed, out of breath from running. 'It's your brother, Mubarak. He's been killed in a skirmish with the Asiris.'

Ahmed's men stiffened, waiting for the lion to vent his wrath on those around him; or worse, to break down in tears. But his stoic expression remained unshakable. Not a hint of sadness or anger crossed his face.

'*Allah yarhama*,' Ahmed murmured. 'God have mercy upon his soul.'

He looked at the compassionate crowd gathered round, detecting a tenderness in his men he had never thought possible. But he needed no sympathy.

'Where's lunch?' he demanded abruptly. A boy hurried in with a tray of meat and cooked millet and set it on the ground. Ahmed sat down and ate as though everything were normal. But a raging anguish fired his insides. After wolfing down the meal, he looked to his deputies.

'Ready your men,' Ahmed ordered. 'We'll attack after sundown.'

When darkness closed in, Ahmed finally unleashed the fury within him. Swiftly and methodically he hurtled through the Asiri pickets, followed closely by his awe-struck troops. His bold determination inspired them, and the unsuspecting Asiris turned on their heels, stampeding through thick undergrowth and over boulders to escape the zealous attackers.

By morning, Ahmed and his men had driven the enemy from the highlands. The old people of Heima and Haraz still speak today with admiration of *Laylat al-Salami* – the Night of al-Salami.

The Ottomans withdrew from Yemen in 1919, following the Empire's defeat in the First World War. Imam Yahya then focused his attention on consolidating his rule, in particular in the Tihama and the eastern desert. These peripheral regions had slipped out of Sanaa's orbit during the decades of struggle in the highlands.

Yahya's forces marched into Hodayda in 1925. The move soon sparked a revolt among the local Zaraniq, used to being left to their own devices. The Zaraniq had long escaped the taxing hand of the *Imams*, and they fully intended to remain that way. The tribe began plundering the trading caravans that plied the route between Sanaa and Hodayda, then further defied the *Imam* by cutting the telegraph lines strung between the two towns by the Ottomans. The final straw came when a party of Zaraniq ambushed the *Imam*'s son, Ahmed, during a visit to the Tihama.

Few of Imam Yahya's predecessors could match his dexterity in carrot-and-stick diplomacy. After the daring attack on his son, Yahya decided the time had come to reign in the Zaraniq once and for all. He dispatched 1,000 men, including my great-grandfather Ahmed al-Salami and the *blocks* under his command, to crush the insurrection in the Tihama in 1927.

News of Ahmed's military and administrative skills in the bloody but successful two-year campaign reached the ears of the *Imam*. In 1931, Yahya sent Ahmed to Marib, the ancient capital of Sheba, to put down a rebellion by the Abeeda and other turbulent Bedouin tribes in the eastern desert. He was largely successful when war broke out three years later between Yemen and the nascent Kingdom of Saudi Arabia, whose army occupied Hodayda. The *Imam* ordered Ahmed back to the Tihama.

My uncle Abdul Kareem, delighted at the questions my husband and I threw at him, told how Ahmed and his men had bivouacked near the town of Bajil, 15 miles inland from Hodayda, when the Saudi army sallied forth from the Red Sea port:

> Gravely outnumbered, Ahmed divided his men into groups of four. He placed them at wide intervals in the form of a deep arc across their foe's likely route. As the Saudis filed unsuspectingly into the crescent ambush, Ahmed's men opened fire from both flanks and the centre. The Saudi commander, believing that the Yemenis outnumbered him, retreated before resuming the drive a few days later. By then, however, a truce was at hand to end the war.

> The four *blocks* under Ahmed's command became known until well after his death as the al-Salami Blocks. Their leader's charisma and valour endeared him to his men, who responded in kind with their own feats of courage. Ahmed had that rare gift of inspiring confidence not only in his subordinates but also in his superiors, including Imam Yahya.

> One day the *Imam* presented him with an invaluable gift of a *hirz*.[6] But it was no ordinary *hirz*. This one preserved its wearer from the clutches of death. So long as Ahmed had that *hirz* pinned to his clothing, no bullet could kill him.

Uncle Abdul Kareem grinned at the thought. I wondered whether it was because he envied his father the *hirz*, or because he mocked his father's belief in its powers.

'Ahmed al-Salami was more than just a warrior,' Grandmother Amina explained to us on another evening over *qishr* coffee at her house. 'He was also a lover of women. He took half a dozen wives, though never more than four at once, as he roamed the country on the *Imam*'s business. He wed his first wife, however, out of convenience rather than any affection for the opposite sex.'

> When Ahmed was 10 or 11 years old, his widowed father, Shaykh Hussayn, and many of the other men in the area

[6] The silver cylinder talisman supposed to ward off bad luck.

were occupied fighting the Turks. He needed not only someone to help look after his son in his absence, but also someone who could help the other women with the farming.

Hussayn arranged for his boy to marry a distant cousin, Kathia al-Salami, from a nearby village in Heima. She was maybe 20 years older than Ahmed, and used to carry her tired husband up the mountain to the village after working in the fields all day.

Grandmother Amina smiled at the recollection of her parents.

Ahmed's third wife came from Bayt al-Faqih on the Tihama coast, a stopping place in the eighteenth and nineteenth centuries for caravans hauling coffee down from the highlands to the port of Mokha, a day-and-a-half's march to the south. The Zaraniq claim Bayt al-Faqih as their capital and profit from the trade in its busy Friday market. Ahmed met the girl's father while stationed in that bustling town during the Zaraniq rebellion, and asked for his daughter's hand in marriage.

Kathia al-Salami became pregnant in the year the Turks withdrew from Yemen (1919). She bore Ahmed a daughter and named her Amina – Fearless; she would become my grandmother.

My belated interest in her youth surprised Grandmother Amina when Charles and I visited her to ask of those days long ago. She loved to speak about it, though she saw nothing very unusual in her upbringing.

She spent the first months of her life in Bayt al-Salami with her mother, Kathia, and her father's second wife, a woman from Haraz. But her father continued to criss-cross Yemen from one posting to another, and Grandmother Amina and her mother followed along.

By the time Grandmother Amina was a couple of years old, her mother wearied of so many strange new homes. Most of all she hated living with her husband's other wives. She forced him to buy her a house in Sanaa, where she and Grandmother Amina stayed several months out of every year.

When Grandmother Amina was 13, her mother scouted out the young bachelors from the surrounding villages. My mother told me later that Grandmother Amina had blossomed into a beautiful young woman as a teenager. Full lips, the trademark al-Salami nose, which is thin and straight, and a seductive black mole under her left eye caught the eye of many a potential suitor. Kathia finally decided on Muhammad al-Salami (a first cousin) for her daughter to marry.

Muhammad served as an officer in one of the four al-Salami Blocks commanded by his uncle Ahmed al-Salami, who now became his father-in-law, too. So when Ahmed headed off to a new town, Muhammad had to go with him. Grandmother Amina took up once again the life of perpetual motion she had experienced as a young child, drifting between Sanaa, the Red Sea, the eastern desert and the southern highlands.

She bore Muhammad a daughter around the time the Second World War broke out in distant Europe. They named her Fatima (after the Prophet Muhammad's daughter). Near the end of her third year, the al-Salami Blocks received orders to proceed to Marib, in the eastern desert 110 miles from Sanaa, where they remained for three years.

Fatima, who would become my mother, loved the dusty open spaces of Marib. And its tall, fierce Bedouin inhabitants fascinated her, greeting one another sometimes by rubbing noses, sometimes by slapping the open palms of their right hands together and emitting an ostentatious kissing sound from their mouths.

The town was relatively new, constructed haphazardly with lots of concrete and corrugated iron. Clustered around a hilltop resembling a giant termites' nest a couple of miles south of the town, three dozen clay towers baked under the harsh sun, remnants of an ancient civilization. Poor families inhabited some of the decrepit buildings, having cleared out the sheltering cobras. Other towers lay crumbling, worn down by centuries of windblown sand and rare showers.

But the ancient part of the town held little interest for Mother. Similar villages, whose ages extended beyond anything she could contemplate, littered all of Yemen. Once in a while Grandmother Amina or the neighbours would take Mother a few miles southwest of the old town to the ruins of the great dam. Its two gigantic stone sluices remain intact more than 2,500 years after their painstaking construction. When the dam burst for the last time shortly before the birth of the Prophet Muhammad, the ingenious structure measured over 3,000 feet long and 50 feet high.

Neither Mother nor anyone else could decipher the extensive inscriptions on many of the stones making up the dam. Researchers later discovered that they are dedications of public works undertaken by ancient kings, but the local Bedouins to this day suspect that the writings indicate the location of hidden treasure, and thus view with suspicion any strangers taking an interest in them. More than one archaeological team has been driven away from the dam and the nearby Temple of the Moon God while attempting to excavate the sites.

The Bedouin tribes around Marib, particularly the Abeeda, enjoy an ambiguous reputation among the settled peoples around them. They are respected for the austerity forced upon them by the harshness of their environment and for a way of life that conjures up memories of a romantic past. They are the guardians of the ancient values with which all Arabs are ingrained to some extent. More than most, they have resisted the seduction of modern, mass-produced conveniences, with the exception of automatic rifles and four-wheel drive vehicles.

Yet the Bedouin also strike fear and resentment into the hearts of settled folk. The Khala wilderness (also called the Empty Quarter), is a land of extremes, a territory larger than France and extending into modern-day Saudi Arabia, Oman and the United Arab Emirates. The face of the desert dweller is more worn, his actions more abrupt, his hospitality grander and his temper quicker to flare than that of the highlander. Images of the Bedouin abound with contradictions. They are considered treacherous, yet honourable; greedy to the point of thievery, yet without rivals to their generosity; ruthless and prepared to kill at the slightest provocation, but willing to defend a guest, no matter what his tribe, colour or creed, more fiercely than they will protect their own lives. Hide something from a Bedouin, and he will steal it from you; entrust him with it for safekeeping, and he will guard it with his life.

My mother recalls with fondness and nostalgia her days as a youth in the eastern desert. 'I learned a great deal from playing with the hardened Bedouin children of Marib,' she says. 'I saw how different they are from the tame Sanaanis, who are quick to insult but rarely come to blows. Bedouin children's stones, on the other hand, prove sharper than their tongues when provoked. They taught me their games and their shepherds' songs and showered me with their boundless hospitality, and I soaked up the freedom of the desert.'

CHAPTER FIVE

Perpetual passage

'I remember being very sad when it came time for us to leave Marib,' my mother told Charles and me one evening. 'I helped my parents tie our belongings into large bundles one hot afternoon before setting out at sunset on the long journey to Sanaa. I was six years old, and Father wedged me between two rolled carpets on the baggage piled atop one of our two camels. I shot 10 feet into the air when the beast stood up.'

The evening air retreated rapidly from the 110° F temperatures of the afternoon as the caravan plodded forward. The family rested under the welcoming shade of a tamarisk tree through the heat of the second day. Sallying forth again at dusk, they plunged deeper into the far-flung desolation of the Jidaan tribe. Black volcanic rocks broke the surface of the sand in patches as if an oil spill had washed over the land. By the end of the following day, they should reach the eastern escarpment leading to the cooler air of the highland plateau 3,500 feet above.

'I didn't sleep well during the daytime stop,' Mother continued. 'And as we started off under the brightening stars, my mother tried to run a rope over my legs to prevent me from falling off the baggage if I dozed off. But I refused. 'I don't want to be tied in,' I complained. 'It hurts. Besides, I'm going to stay awake all night. You'll see.'

I squirmed and fidgeted so much that Mother finally put the rope away. But the gentle swaying of the camel's stride made me very sleepy. My eyelids closed for what seemed like only a moment, when suddenly something struck me on the back of my head and I lost consciousness. When I opened my eyes a few moments later, I was lying on the sand, dazed and the wind knocked from my lungs. I could make no sound while I gasped for breath. My heart raced as the blurry outline of Mother and Father, and behind them the moon, grew smaller in the distance.

Grandmother Amina sat silently with us as Mother told the story over more *qishr*, grinning occasionally as she remembered that night long ago. But now she sat up, forgetting the shawl that fell from her shoulders, and took over the story from Mother.

'Several hours later, around midnight, I poured a cup of water from a goatskin,' Grandmother recalled. 'I had tied one on either side of the two camels so that if one of the animals fell, only one of the skins would be lost. As I reached the cup towards the top of the baggage to hand it to Fatima, I discovered with horror that she wasn't there. I looked frantically into the darkness behind me, then ran to inspect the top of the other camel, hoping I had confused them. But I had not. Fatima was nowhere in sight.'

I shouted her name, but it was like yelling into a pillow. Muhammad immediately realized what had happened. We had both heard a strange thump not long after getting underway that evening.

'What was that?' I had asked at the time.

'One of the water skins must have fallen off,' Muhammad said. 'Let it go. We've got more than enough.'

We had quickly forgotten the incident, but now we realized the thump had been caused by Fatima, and we turned back to find her.

Muhammad felt that his daughter must have broken her neck and died in the fall. Otherwise she would have cried out to them.

But he would never express that sentiment to his wife, at least not before they found the body. Grandmother Amina pushed the same thought out of her mind. She scurried as fast as her legs could carry her back towards Marib, her fatigue silenced by the anguish of losing her daughter.

Most of the striped hyenas in the area had fallen to the bullets of Jidaan hunters. The chances of one of the nocturnal scavengers picking up the little girl's scent were minimal. So if Mother didn't stray from where she had fallen, if the wind didn't strengthen and cover their tracks, then they would find her, dead or alive. Mother was no Bedouin. If she tried to follow after her parents, or return to Marib, she would be likely to lose her way and perish from thirst the next afternoon.

'Muhammad and I hastened across the moonlit waste,' Grandmother Amina went on. 'I studied the horizon, but could make out nothing definite, and steadily lost hope of seeing my daughter alive again.'

Then Muhammad saw something that he might otherwise have taken for a gazelle, but most of the gazelles had been hunted and few remained. He steered toward the distant object without a word, and I soon saw it too. Sprinting forward, I found little Fatima sitting upright in the sand where she had fallen, sobbing quietly and rubbing her swollen shoulder. This time I tied her securely onto the top of the camel, and we retraced our steps westward until well after sunrise.

The family halted at Sirwah, a small town in Khawlan territory at the base of the escarpment. After unpacking their animals, Muhammad strolled into the marketplace. It bustled with morning shoppers under tin awnings extended over the lane from the line of stone shacks. He purchased a lamb and had the butcher slaughter and prepare it. Muhammad distributed the meat to the poor of Sirwah as an offering of thanks to God for sparing his daughter.

Muhammad brought Grandmother Amina a palmful of the pepper-like *mimiya* spice. She ground the tiny black balls into a powder and massaged it into her daughter's badly bruised shoulder to relieve the pain. The rest she tossed into the pot of lamb's broth they had kept for their own lunch.

After a short time in the capital, Muhammad was transferred to Hodayda. Grandmother Amina, who had given birth to a second daughter, decided to remain in Sanaa to raise her two girls in the more hospitable highland climate. But after a year or two, Muhammad wearied of living alone. He came to Sanaa one day to bring his family back to Hodayda with him.

The four of them set out one morning, following the old route from Sanaa through Bani Matar and Heima, with Jebel Haraz looming in the haze off to the south. Not far from the western ridge of the highland plateau, the rugged mountain track steepened its descent. Rain had washed much of it away, so that Mother and her little sister had to dismount from the two donkeys. Muhammad picked up the youngest daughter and carried her in his arms. Mother scurried behind Grandmother Amina, keeping up as best she could. The sight of an occasional waterfall, large-beaked hornbill birds bathing in the pools at their base, steadily lost its mesmerizing effect upon Mother.

'After several hours of marching,' Mother began as Charles and I listened carefully, 'my feet throbbed with a dull pain that worked its way up my legs and into my back.'

'Mother, I'm tired. Will you carry me?' I asked hopefully.

'Come along, Fatima,' my mother said. 'We're almost there. Just a little more.'

But I knew it wasn't true. She and my father had given me the same answer since I had begun asking 'How much further?' several hours earlier.

'But I'm tired. I want somebody to carry me,' I insisted. She said nothing, so I started again.

'Mother, I can't walk any further. Why won't you carry me?'

'Because you're too big for me to carry,' she answered, her patience at an end.

'What about Father? Why can't he carry me?'

'Because he's carrying your sister. Can't you see?'

Half an hour later, we came to a wide flat stone bordering the path beneath a date palm. I plopped down on the rock to sulk, sighing loudly to make sure Mother and Father took notice. Neither of them could convince me to get up.

'All right. Stay here then,' my father finally told me. 'We'll go on without you. But a leopard might come along soon and eat you up.'

My mother and father moved around the bend and out of site. I remained seated for a few moments while my father's words sank in. Then a strange rustling in the nearby bushes scared me. I jumped to my feet and ran down the path as fast as I could. Trailing some way behind, I glanced over my shoulder now and then to make sure nothing was following me.

The next morning, I once again grew tired after several hours of trudging down the steep slopes, overgrown with vegetation. The fatigue deepened as our route flattened out onto the broiling Tihama plain, and I was furious that Father continued to carry my little sister, while I had to walk.

Following a road that wound between parched millet and sesame fields, they approached the market town of Bajil. The strange new world before Mother diverted her anger momentarily.[1]

[1] African influence has penetrated deep into the coastal plain over the centuries. It manifests itself in the inhabitants' physical features and social customs, both of which form composites of Arab and African traits. In the countryside families dwell in round wattle and clay homes. Crowned with a conical thatched roof and hemmed in by a fence of thorny bush to guard the livestock at night, the huts look more East African than Arabian.

Used to the cool air of the Sanaa plateau, mother and her sister suffered miserably on their trek across the Tihama. Temperatures soared to over 110° F, too hot even for mosquitoes. But the locals have grown accustomed to it, even donning sweaters and jackets when the chilly winter days dip into the mid-eighties.

'With just a couple of hours left to Hodayda,' Mother continued, 'Father halted under the shade of an olive tree to perform the afternoon prayer. When he set my sister down on the ground, a viper cooling itself just under the surface reared its head up suddenly from the sand. We watched in horror as the snake sank its fangs into my sister's leg.'

My mother rifled through the bags in a desperate search for a few drops of ambergris.[2] She hoped she might have inadvertently placed some among her spices, but she found none.

Unaware of the gravity of the situation, I found devilish pleasure in the incident. I was certain it was God's way of punishing my sister for being carried all the way from Sanaa, while I had to walk. But remorse overcame my glee when my sister began to boil with fever. Within minutes, sheets of sweat soaked her face and she grew weak. Father carved out a small cavity among the baggage on one of the donkeys' backs for her to lie in and we pushed on towards Hodayda.

Just before sundown we passed a small village and could see the water in the distance, the last of the fishing boats sailing in with the day's catch. Mother and Father debated seeking shelter in one of the huts for the night to allow their daughter to rest. But when they checked to see how she felt, she had already stopped breathing. Father lowered her from

[2] Travellers sometimes carry with them this waxy substance, produced in the intestines of sperm whales. Mixed into a cup of tea to mask the foul taste, the costly remedy supposedly works its way up from the toes to the head, neutralizing any venom in the bloodstream.

the donkey and buried the tiny corpse in the sand beside a thorny caper bush. We continued on to Hodayda in the dark.

When Grandmother Amina's father, Ahmed al-Salami, lived in Bayt al-Faqih during the Zaraniq wars, he married a local woman who bore him two daughters. The girls, Naeema and Hameeda, were both many years younger than Grandmother Amina. Their mother died soon after Hameeda's birth and the two girls lived in Hodayda with their father.

Then the aging Ahmed died too, struck down by a deadly form of malaria that was rampant in the coastal areas. Hussayn, one of Ahmed al-Salami's sons from his Harazi wife, had followed the family tradition and served in the al-Salami Blocks. His father's death left him with responsibility for his two orphaned half-sisters, though he had little time or resources with which to care for the girls.

Children are treated almost like adults from a very young age in Yemen. They are trusted with all kinds of responsibilities that in Europe and America at least seem to come much later. At only a few years old, they may be sent to pick something up in the *suq* for their mothers, deliver a small package across town for their father, or go to school and back on their own, not depending on anyone to drop them off or pick them up. From around a year old, children go outside the home by themselves to play in the alleyways, sometimes with cars and motorcycles passing by regularly. They can take care of themselves for the most part, but siblings and older children always keep an eye on them nonetheless. Every child seems to take care of anyone younger, and in turn is taken care of by those older.

Naeema was 10 years old when her father died, but she had already long since filled her mother's shoes, cooking and taking care of the house and her little sister.

My mother remembers that time with a mixture of nostalgia and pain:

Naeema did a good job handling the house and her little sister. But Hussayn worried about them being left alone for much of the day, so he arranged for Naeema to marry a young man from the al-Shafeeq family, long established in Hodayda. The al-Shafeeqs agreed that Hameeda could come live with her sister in their home too.

After Father brought Mother and me to Hodayda, I went often to play with my aunts Hameeda and Naeema. They were both only a few years older than I was. But I soon discovered that the women in the al-Shafeeq household behaved cruelly towards the two girls, screaming, cursing and ordering them around like servants. I told Mother of the ill-treatment and she stomped over to the al-Shafeeqs and warned them of dire consequences if they didn't conduct themselves with more respect towards Hameeda and Naeema.

But Mother's outburst infuriated the al-Shafeeq women. Naeema's mother-in-law sought the help of one of the family's old servants to get even, sending her the following day to our house for a friendly talk with Mother. The woman seemed very friendly and Mother thought nothing of the visit, even when the woman offered her a new undergarment that she had sewn herself as a present.

When she tried on the gift a few days later, Mother suddenly became nauseous and violent-tempered. She was possessed by a *jini* introduced through the under-garment by the old witch servant sent by the al-Shafeeqs. From that moment on, if anyone spoke harshly to Mother, she would stagger and swoon and a deep, eerie voice came from her mouth – not her own voice, but that of a *jini*.

'Do not trouble Amina,' the voice would command. 'Leave her in peace.'

Her brother Hussayn was furious, and he marched straight over to the al-Shafeeqs. He dragged Hameeda and Naeema out of the house never to return, and demanded that Naeema's husband divorce her.'

Mother did not talk about Grandmother Amina's run-in with the *jini* when Grandmother was around. It would have embarrassed and angered her to hear it, so Mother told Charles and me about it later:

'Naeema and Hameeda had been rescued,' Mother told us after we had left Grandmother's house. 'But Amina's bewitched state showed no signs of improvement. After several months of ill health, vile moods and possession by the *jini*, my father refused to put up with her any longer. He had considered divorcing her even before the spell, but he had feared the wrath of Ahmed, his father-in-law. Now that Ahmed had passed away, nothing stood in his way. He divorced Grandmother Amina, though she had just given birth to a son.'

My father kept me with him, but sent my mother and my newborn brother on a Sanaa-bound trading caravan with instructions to deliver them to Heima. Mother's departure was difficult for me, and the only consolation was the hope that endless meals of fish and rice might finally come to an end.

Mother used to cook the same combination for lunch and dinner seven days a week. It was delicious at first – I'd never even seen a fish before coming to Hodayda – but soon it became monotonous. The taste of fish made me sick and I began eating only rice at meals. But there was little else to eat in the town, and my mother did her best to force me to eat the fish.

The caravan set Amina and my little brother down at the entrance to Wadi Hijran, on Heima's western edge. Men from Bayt al-Salami usually came down the mountain there to meet the convoy and buy wheat, but they were nowhere to be found when the caravan arrived. So the merchants left my mother and brother with the sacks of wheat beside the road to await the men from Bayt al-Salami, and the caravan moved on. They would collect payment when the caravan passed through a week or two later on its return to the Tihama.

Amina did not remain long in Heima. She preferred the easy life of Sanaa, and moved there with my brother a few weeks later. The effects of her spell continued to plague her, so that she couldn't support herself even by sewing. Her only income came from 200 pounds of grain granted her each year by the *Imam* after her father, Ahmed, died. She earned a little more by helping with the harvest in Heima once or twice a year, returning to Sanaa with a donkey-load of grain in compensation.

'A few months after Hussayn rescued his little sisters, Naeema and Hameeda, from the al-Shafeeqs,' Mother continued, 'Imam Ahmed ordered the al-Salami Blocks transferred to Taiz. Both Hussayn and Muhammad, my father, had to go with them, but my father decided that I would stay in Hodayda. One of our neighbours there had looked after me ever since my mother had gone back to Heima. The woman was childless and treated me like a daughter, combing my hair and dressing me nicely every morning. And I loved her in return, though she too served little but fish and rice.'

When Uncle Hussayn told Hameeda and Naeema that they were moving to Taiz, the girls would hear nothing of it. I used to play with them every day, and it was too much for all of us to think about being separated. Hussayn tried everything to persuade them to come along peacefully, but nothing worked.

Then Hameeda and Naeema suggested to their older brother that they might be talked into going to Taiz, on the condition that I come too. Though I loved Hameeda and Naeema, I did not want to leave the woman who took care of me. Nor did I like the thought of another long trek like the one to Hodayda that had taken my little sister's life. But my father reluctantly agreed to bring me with them to Taiz.

Muhammad and Hussayn al-Salami rented a house together in Taiz's al-Jahmiliya neighbourhood. A 20-minute walk east of the old walled town, the house laid along the route to the Salah

Palace three miles away, the only paved road in the country at the time. The palace served as one of two residences for Imam Ahmed, along with three of his four wives. Imam Yahya had chosen each of his sons' spouses with a view towards reinforcing political alliances with other *Sayid* families and the tribes. While few *Sayids* would allow their daughters to wed a tribesman, no such restriction prevented a *Sayid* male, even the *Imam*, from marrying a tribeswoman.

Ahmed's fourth wife resided in Sanaa. The first three cleverly convinced their husband that the fourth would bring him bad luck if she came to Taiz. So the *Imam* had never before laid eyes upon her. He offered her a divorce several years later, but she refused, quite content with the many perks of being a queen but with no husband to have to please in return.

Taiz intrigued Mother, with its three whitewashed mosques from the enlightened Middle Ages,[3] their broad cupolas and thick minarets highlighting the town. She found its energetic, cosmopolitan merchant community very different from anywhere else she had lived. Strong-willed, boisterous women descended Jebel Sabr Mountain in the early mornings to sell their wares in the central *suq*, an occupation reserved in most other highland towns for males. The steep northern face of the 9,800-foot Jebel Sabr formed the southernmost of Taiz's four walls, and numerous streams flowing down its slopes irrigated the banana and papaya trees around the town. The speech of Taiz's inhabitants contrasted humorously with that of Sanaa or Hodayda. The lilting tone and strange pronunciation tickled Mother, and soon rubbed off on her.

'The town's cool mountain air was a shock to my system,' Mother remembers with a shiver, 'after so long in steaming Hodayda.

[3] While Europe foundered in the feudal ages, science flourished in the Muslim world, not least of all in Taiz. One of Yemen's rulers wrote on the magnetic compass and composed a detailed treatise on astrolabes that included several innovations for the time. An astrolabe he made himself is displayed today in New York's Metropolitan Museum of Art.

Within a few days of arriving in our new home, I developed a bad cough. It nearly suffocated me each time an attack came on, and soon I became too weak even to sit up in bed. Already distressed by having to leave Hodayda, I was convinced I was about to die. I told my father I wanted the woman who had taken care of me in Hodayda to come and wash me for my burial, but a few days later the cough went away.'

Mother remembers that her father, Muhammad, and her Uncle Hussayn worked constantly while in Taiz, from early morning until late in the evening. She and her two young aunts were by now old enough by Yemeni standards to take care of themselves. But one day Hussayn received orders to leave the al-Salami Block and move to a new posting in Sanaa. He took his dissenting half-sisters with him, while Mother stayed behind this time with her father.

Muhammad did not relish the thought of his nine-year-old daughter playing by herself around the neighbourhood, and without any womenfolk to keep an eye on her. That was how rumours started of improprieties with the opposite sex that could forever tarnish a family's honour, even at Mother's tender age. A solution soon presented itself, however.

'My father had a close friend in Taiz,' Mother told Charles and me one evening in Sanaa, a bit reluctantly at first. I could feel a rare pulse of emotion rising in her as she spoke. 'He was a *Sayid*, originally from Bani Matar but had lived most of his life in Jebel Haraz. The man knew of my father's situation, and proposed one day that he could marry me. I was young, but my father wouldn't have to worry any more [about the family's honour] with me married. He agreed to the proposal, with one condition: the man would not have sex with me until I had begun menstruating.'

Of course I broke down in tears on learning I was to be wed, but I could do little else to protest. The man took me to Haraz to meet his mother after the wedding, and the three of us returned to Taiz together.

Though he was a *Sayid*, I was petrified of both him and his mother. She had not the slightest sympathy for me. In fact, she found it quite amusing to frighten me into doing what she wanted. She would frequently wave around a hollowed-out vegetable gourd used for storing honey.

'A *jini* lives inside this gourd,' she would threaten. 'And I can free him any time if you misbehave. There's no telling what he might do.'

I'll never forget the vicious smile on her face when she told me that. I cringed every time the woman went near the gourd, fearful she would pull out the wax stopper and free the *jini*.

Several months after the marriage, I found myself one day alone in the house with my husband. I found him acting very strangely, until I finally realized what he wanted.

Mother had not the slightest idea of what sex entailed. Most girls learned of the subject from the cryptic conversations of the older women at parties. The youths easily broke the code words the women used to disguise what they were talking about. The average girl knew everything she needed to know by the time her parents arranged her marriage. But Mother had moved around constantly, spending the last part of her life without her mother, so her knowledge of such things was less than it might have been.

'I managed to get away from the man and out of the house on that occasion,' Mother recalled with a grin that could be taken for humour or pain, or both. 'I spent the next few weeks spying out hiding-places around the house where I could go when he came home. But I eventually ran out of possibilities and he eventually managed to have his way with me. When he did, I dashed out of the house afterwards and ran to my father.'

'You have to let me come back,' I yelled. 'I'll jump off the top of Jebel Sabr and kill myself before I go back to that awful place.'

Father was very angry when I told him what had happened. He went straight over to the man's house and demanded that he divorce me then and there. Father was a tough and intimidating person, and the man he married me to was thankful to get off so lightly. He quickly repeated three times 'Talaqa – I divorce' – and it was done.

Soon afterwards, Imam Ahmed dispatched Muhammad al-Salami to Bab al-Mandeb – the Gate of Tears – at the southwest tip of the Arabian Peninsula. Muhammad left Mother in Taiz with neighbours.

Since his own transfer from Taiz, Mother's Uncle Hussayn had moved from Sanaa to Ibb, a village 40 miles north of Taiz. One day a message arrived for him there: Muhammad al-Salami had died in Bab al-Mandeb from an unknown illness. Hussayn had no choice but to go to Taiz to get Mother and deliver her to Grandmother Amina in Sanaa.

Hussayn's duties in Ibb kept him very busy. He could hardly afford the two weeks required to deliver his niece to Grandmother Amina and return to Ibb, all on foot. So he petitioned Imam Ahmed. Maybe the ruler would allow Hussayn to convey Mother in one of the handful of trucks plying the dirt track between Sanaa and Taiz. All of the vehicles belonged to the *Imam*, and moved on his orders alone.

Though he sympathized with Hussayn's predicament, the *Imam* needed him to stay in Ibb. But the ruler proposed another solution. He had acquired a monstrous metal contraption that astounded the population as it raced down a dirt road and lifted into the air like a large bird, without even flapping its wings. The *Imam* suggested that Mother fly in this machine to Sanaa. That would allow Hussayn to return immediately to Ibb.

A few days later Mother took the ride of her life. The aeroplane reduced an arduous week-long trek to an hour of staring out a window from high above the mountain tops.

'The *Imam* telegraphed Sanaa with the news that I was coming on the aeroplane from Taiz,' Mother remembers with great pleasure. 'And someone was sent to tell my mother. She brought a bunch of friends with her to the landing strip outside Sanaa, and they stared in wonder as this shiny metal box swooped down and rolled towards them on the dirt runway, propellers whirling and kicking up dust. Several of them fled when it came closer.'

We rolled to a stop beside the remainder of the group. The roar of the engines died down, the door popped open and I hopped down the steps and leaped into mother's arms.

'What did you see up there?' everyone asked me. 'What did it look like?'

I explained every last detail and became the focus of attention for the next few days as family and neighbours came to the house to hear about the journey. I loved it.

But once away from the noise of the airplane, my mother was shocked when she heard me speak. I had been so long in Taiz that I had acquired the town's strange accent. My mother, who had only rarely heard such talk, was aghast and slapped my mouth sharply when she heard it. She feared God wouldn't understand my prayers, now that I was old enough to recite them regularly. My mother worked hard to rid me of the Taizi accent, finally sending me to a woman who taught young girls how to pray properly.

My Grandmother Amina's encounters with the *jini* continued to plague her, and the neighbours generously looked after her and the children in Sanaa through the worst of it. She remarried, but the seizures would linger for several more years.

Mother and her younger brother lived with Grandmother Amina in Sanaa until the day Muhammad Murzah's father asked for her hand for his son. Mother had by then reached the more reasonable age of 13 (and wearied of living under the sometimes harsh hand of her mother). Both she and Grandmother Amina accepted.

CHAPTER SIX

The Murzahs

M y older brother, Hamud, took great interest in the Murzah family history. He researched the subject extensively and liked to talk about it, in particular to Charles, who was more interested than I.

The Murzahs came from al-Janat, a tiny village near the large market town of Amran, 15 miles northwest of Sanaa. Hamud discovered that the family may have been Jewish until a few generations ago, but no one knows much beyond that.

Sometime in the late 1800s, one of the Murzah sons left al-Janat for Sanaa, where he married a woman from a prominent family of the Sanhan tribe inhabiting the plateau just south of the capital. He opened a small shop in the central Suq al-Milh marketplace repairing *narghilas*, the common smoking pipes that filter tobacco smoke through water before inhalation. Later expanding his activities into coffee trading, he amassed enough wealth to purchase a few plots of land outside Sanaa's southern gate.

The man and his wife both died soon after their first child, Hamud Murzah, was born. A family in the neighbourhood took in the orphaned boy to raise as their own. By the time Hamud was old enough to claim his inheritance, his parents' land and other possessions had long since been dispersed. Even had he succeeded in identifying the estate, recovering it would have been an uphill battle, for Hamud held no proof of who his parents were. The only such record in most people's possession consisted of a line or two penned on the inside cover of a family

Koran to commemorate the birth, usually by the head of the local mosque (known as an *imam*, but not to be confused with the pre-revolutionary rulers of Yemen). Few others could read or write. Hamud possessed no such Koran, and he had no close relatives to vouch for him.

The al-Nahshal family lived not far from Hamud Murzah's adoptive home, near Bab al-Yemen. Over the years, they had built up their own sizeable holding of farmland outside the town wall. After investing in a handful of retail shops around Sanaa, the al-Nahshals purchased one of the *muhariqs* – the cone-shaped kilns for baking bricks – on the far side of the al-Urdhi military barracks across from Bab al-Yemen.

It was not uncommon for a wealthy family in Yemen to informally adopt a son or daughter from poor relatives or neighbours (provided the latter were not from a much lower stratum of society). The child would move in with the foster family and become like one of their own, working in the house or fields as needed and lifting the financial burden from the real parents' shoulders. When older, the foster parents would sometimes marry one of their own offspring to the adopted child.

The al-Nahshals, cursed with having no sons, desperately needed another man around the house. When Hamud became a teenager, they invited him to come to live with them to help oversee their many business interests. He agreed.

According to Mother,

It was not long before Hamud and the al-Nahshal's only daughter, Khayriya, fell in love. Her parents liked the boy and approved when he requested their daughter's hand in marriage. They released Hamud from the obligation of paying the *shart*,[1] or even the *mahr*.[2] They knew that Hamud could not afford to pay anyway.

[1] Bride-price paid to the family of the bride as compensation for the family's loss of labour in marrying off their daughter.

[2] Dowry paid to the wife as a means of support in case of divorce or widowhood.

The parents were generous and offered the newly-weds a plot of land along the Taiz road to cultivate for their own needs. Hamud and Khayriya continued to live in the al-Nahshal house with Khayriya's parents, and soon God blessed them with the birth of a healthy son, Muhammad Murzah.

Several years later, Khayriya's father fell ill. Sensing his strength fading, he summoned his wife and daughter to his bedside just two days before he died. He made both women swear that on their own deaths they would bequeath the family estate to his young grandson, Muhammad.

The late spring and early autumn rains soaked the earth faithfully in the coming years. Hamud and Khayriya's land thrived – so much that Hamud decided he would take a second wife. As he surveyed the fields one morning, he espied a shepherd girl driving her goats to the slopes of Jebel Nuqum. She subtly lowered her veil as she passed by, and Hamud glimpsed for a brief moment her large moist eyes, parted by a thin nose angled sharply downwards in the middle like a falcon's bill.

Smitten by her beauty, Hamud determined to marry the girl. He returned to the fields that evening and followed her to a small village in Wadi Ajbar, a mile or two south of Jebel Nuqum in Sanhan territory, to discover where she lived.

Taking a second wife proved to be no inexpensive undertaking. Hamud recalled the debate he heard in the mosque after Friday prayer one afternoon. The *imam* of the mosque and a young, educated man conversed politely, but each vigorously attempting to impose his opinion.

'The Koran says clearly that a man may take up to four wives at once. How can you dispute that?' the *imam* asked, exasperated.

'I'm not questioning that,' the haughty youth responded. 'But the Koran also says that each wife must be treated equally by the husband. Does it not?'

'Yes. And so?'

'Doesn't it also state that no man can possibly treat all of his wives equally?'

The *imam* smiled as if to tell the man he was missing the point, but the youth pressed his advantage.

'Then doesn't it follow that it is unlawful for a man to take more than one wife, whom he must, but cannot, treat equally?'

Hamud had no use for such pedantic debate. But he knew he would have to make an effort to treat his wives fairly, which rarely turns out to be as simple as the husband expects. God had blessed him with bountiful harvests, and he saw nothing wrong with taking another wife as a symbol of God's favour. The bride-price and dowry would have to be paid this time, of course. And it would bite deeply into his resources, but he could do it.

Khayriya would be upset. She might even lock him out of the house for a week or two to protest. But she would not leave him because she had nowhere else to go. Everything would turn out all right in the end. He would buy another house in which to install his new wife, while Khayriya continued to live in the old one with her mother and their son, Muhammad.

Hamud's overbearing personality frightened children and intimidated adults. It also tended to prevent him from foreseeing the likely consequences of his actions. And in this case he seriously misjudged the pain he inflicted upon Khayriya.

'She loved her husband immensely,' my mother said of Khayriya. 'And his decision to wed another woman devastated, humiliated her. She sank into deep depression, refusing to eat. After a year of suffering, she died.'

Her son Muhammad was too young to inherit his mother's property right away, as his grandfather had intended on his deathbed. Instead, his father continued to control the estate with the understanding that he would hand it over to the boy in a few years, when he was old enough to manage it wisely.

Before long, Khayriya's mother fell ill. She grew too infirm to care for herself, let alone her grandson. So Hamud took his new wife, Sadiya, and moved in to the al-Nahshal house to watch over them. When the old woman died two years later, Hamud decided his son was finally old enough to do with his inheritance as he saw fit.

But seeing her stepson receive much of what her husband had controlled when they were first married embittered Sadiya. It mattered nothing that the wealth originated from Khayriya's family, and not her own. Sadiya was in the process of building up her own family, having given birth to two daughters and three sons by Hamud and with another son on the way. Her children's inheritance, as she saw it, diminished considerably in the face of their half-brother's gain. Nor did Hamud help matters any by callously pointing out that, over and beyond Muhammad's inheritance from Khayriya, Islamic law required Hamud to leave a portion of his own wealth to Muhammad when he died.

Such talk irritated Sadiya and her children to no end. 'Are you going to leave us empty-handed and out on the street?' they protested.

Hamud brushed aside their concerns and changed the subject. But Sadiya and her children would not sit idly by when the opportunity arose to correct the perceived injustice.

Imam Ahmed began opening Yemen up in a modest way after taking over from his father in 1948. He expanded the community of 30 or so foreigners in the country by bringing in dozens of Russian and other Eastern bloc technicians and advisers. Most of the expatriates kept to themselves, but Muhammad Murzah managed to befriend the small clique of five Italian and four French doctors employed in Sanaa by the *Imam*. In their spare time they instructed him and a handful of other Yemenis in the rudiments of modern medicine.

In the late 1950s, Imam Ahmed resolved to send 10 Yemenis to the United States to study medicine. They would form the nucleus of an indigenous medical corps on their return, and

Muhammad was chosen to be part of the group. The trip to America excited him, though he knew only that it was a far-off land, several weeks' journey by sea. The furthest he had ever expected to travel from home was perhaps to the *Haj* pilgrimage in Mecca one day, if he were lucky. Now he was about to traverse many times that distance. He engrossed himself in studying English while awaiting the *Imam*'s order to send them on their way.

Instructions finally arrived for the students to proceed to Taiz, a week's journey to the south by foot, and eventually on to board their ship in Hodayda. But following their arrival in Taiz, Imam Ahmed experienced a sudden, unexplained change of heart – in keeping with his nature. He cancelled the voyage of the would-be medical students.

Muhammad Murzah returned to Sanaa a disappointed man. The only remnant of his aborted trip was a smattering of English he proudly muttered when my husband met him over 30 years later, to ask for his daughter's hand in marriage.

With his dreams of going abroad crushed, Muhammad's father arranged for him to marry Fatima al-Salami, who lived nearby. The couple stayed with Muhammad's father and stepmother in Sanaa (as, until more recent times, tradition dictated). Fatima gave birth to the couple's first child the following year, but the boy succumbed after a few weeks to 'the cough'. The same illness took the life of their second child when he was four months old. Then Hamud came along, soon after the 1962 revolution, and his frail, spindly body somehow survived that critical first year of life.

Fatima nurtured her children as any mother would. But unconsciously her heart would not permit her to become closely attached to them at first. As late as the 1970s, the chance of an infant in Yemen reaching its first birthday hovered around 50/50, odds too low for the parents to expose themselves fully to the anguish of losing the child. Folk remedies and mystical religious rites represented the only treatments for illness, though by no means all of them were medically useless. Long before any notion of modern medicine arrived in the country, Yemenis habitually pricked their children with thorns scratched on the skin of smallpox sufferers, making an apparently effective vaccination.

But such cures had minimal impact on the staggering mortality rate, so mothers kept emotionally aloof, until their offspring grew strong and developed a degree of immunity to the myriad diseases that cut so many young lives short. As the months passed without serious mishap, a mother would gradually come around to accepting the child as a permanent member of the family.

After the civil war erupted in late 1962, the fledgling Republican government ordered Muhammad Murzah to attach himself to a military unit as a civilian medic. Stationed to various towns on the plateau north of Sanaa, in the thick of the fighting, he dashed around battlefields patching up the wounded. The Egyptian soldiers, who undertook much of the fighting for lack of a well-trained Yemeni army, appeared as giants next to the short, wiry Yemenis. They startled Muhammad when he first encountered them.

'Removing shrapnel from an Egyptian is like operating on a bull,' he explained to his wife during one of his rare leaves from the front.

In the third year of the war, Muhammad was transferred away from the main battle theatre to Maabar, on the Jahran plain 20 miles south of Sanaa. A single dusty street ran through the village in those days. But Maabar commanded the strategic intersection of the road between Sanaa and Taiz, the principal town in the southern highlands, and the recently built motorway from Sanaa to Hodayda, the main port on the Red Sea. A large Republican force garrisoned in Maabar guarded the routes.

Fighting had hardly touched the area during the first years of the conflict, and Muhammad looked forward to more tranquil times than those he had experienced further north. But soon after his arrival, Royalist troops massed ominously on the plain a few miles from the town. Heavy fighting for control of the road ensued. With their advance repulsed, the Royalists withdrew and the region quieted down again for a time.

Fatima moved to Maabar in early 1966 to be with her husband. They rented one of the village's two dozen clay houses. It rose only two storeys high, but when Fatima clambered to the roof to hang the clothes out to dry, she could gaze over the low parapet for a clear view of the extinct volcano protruding like a charcoal iceberg from the plain two miles away.

Fatima had lost yet another son to the ubiquitous cough in the previous year. But in Maabar the couple conceived their fifth child. Towards the end of the pregnancy, Grandmother Amina arrived from Sanaa to assist her daughter with the delivery. A wedding enlivened the town on the day the labour pains started, 5 November 1966. Tribesmen related to the bride and groom flooded in from the surrounding countryside to celebrate. They danced and fired their rifles into the air throughout the afternoon and into the evening, until a careless shot from an enthusiastic participant pierced two of the guests with a bullet.

A doctor had no role to play in childbearing, so Muhammad Murzah limited himself to pacing nervously outside the bedroom while his mother-in-law performed the duties of a midwife inside. A sharp rap at the door startled him from his fond reflections on fatherhood. He opened and a whiff of burning gunpowder from the street eddied into his nostrils. Muhammad knew from the dire countenance of the group standing before him that something was wrong. He snatched his medical kit and followed, relieved to get out of the house and escape his wife's painful screaming.

After removing the bullet and dressing the wounds, Muhammad hurried home for news of his wife's progress. He found an exhausted Fatima nibbling from a bowl of honey, clarified butter, and morsels of bread and chicken, traditionally eaten after giving birth. It was a girl.

The following day, the two injured men sent word to Muhammad encouraging him to name the child Marzuqa –

Blessed – in honour of the father's medical skills. But Grandmother Amina had already picked out a name for me: Khadija.[3]

Mother had proved her worth as a wife by bearing Muhammad three sons (though only one had survived long). But this time she was delighted to finally have a daughter. She allowed herself the perilous luxury of displaying affectionate interest in me from the moment I came into the world.

Grandmother Amina used a whittled twig to apply black *khol* around her granddaughter's eyelids, emphasizing the long lashes and hopefully bestowing strong vision. Like so many Yemeni babies, my large eyes seemed like a pair of hand-me-downs that had to be grown into with time.

Mother wrapped me in a thick white cloth, winding a string around it from feet to shoulders to keep the cloth snug like a cocoon. A hood embroidered with gold thread covered my head, and Mother pinned a *hirz* cylinder to the blanket where I couldn't tear it off. She stuffed a Koranic verse scribbled on a scrap of paper inside the silver talisman to ward off the evil eye, a sort of curse inflicted sometimes unintentionally through the compliments of envious visitors.

Drought aggravated the devastating effects of war, and famine ravaged the land for the next half decade. Farmers butchered their livestock and grain had to be imported from abroad to alleviate the hunger. Yet I grew stronger with each day, and my parents were pleased with the new addition to the household. But my father and I would sadly come to know little of one another.

As the Katyusha rockets rained down on his family in Sanaa in early 1968, my father faced his own hell on the plateau north of the city, to which he transferred soon after my birth. For the past

---

[3] In pre-Islamic Arabia, *khadija* meant 'premature'. Parents used the name to deceive *jinis* and other mischievous spirits that seek to carry away the souls of healthy, hardy creatures into believing an infant was sickly and unworthy of their attention. The Prophet Muhammad's first and favourite wife, a wealthy businesswoman from Mecca, was called Khadija.

three years, the war north of Sanaa had bogged down into a stalemate. The Royalists proved unable to control areas around the main towns and roads, while the Republicans experienced equal difficulty in holding territory away from the principal supply routes in the eastern desert and northwest mountains, along the border with Saudi Arabia. But with the Egyptians gone, Royalist activity picked up and the fighting became heavy again.

A calm, sensitive man who loved music, Father showed little interest in soldiering and counted himself fortunate to have been conscripted as a medic. The death and destruction witnessed on a daily basis affected him profoundly.

Over the years, Mother was able to learn something of what happened on the fateful last day my father spent in the army. I was surprised that she knew anything at all about it, because ever since I could remember my father he had the greatest difficulty in holding a conversation with anyone. But somehow he managed to tell her the story.

During one particularly violent clash with the Royalists, Father went desperately about his work. He cringed from shell bursts and ducked bullets sizzling past his head like grease from a frying pan. In the consuming chaos, he darted towards the horrifying cries of one wounded man after another; they were writhing in pain, sprawled grotesquely on the earth.

Something finally snapped in father that day. The deafening roar of battle intertwined with the screams of his comrades overwhelmed him. Squatting on the ground, he found a rusted oil drum with the top cut off and pulled it over him.

When the hell around him subsided, he emerged from the flimsy barrel miraculously unscathed, physically. Yet Father was a changed man. Oblivious to the dead and dying strewn about, he staggered from the battlefield in a daze. The next anyone knew of him was when he arrived in Sanaa at dawn a couple of days later.

For 2,000 years the sentries' orders remained unchanged: open the gates of Sanaa for no one between sunset and sunrise, for only evil enters then. But the two massive doors of Bab al-Yemen and the other town gates had been sacrificed seven years earlier as a feeble symbol of the arrival of modernity in the wake of the revolution. All had been torn down but Bab al-Yemen, and it remained permanently open now.

The morning sky lightened rapidly, and at the moment the human eye could distinguish a white thread from a black one, the call to prayer rang out from the minarets. Father plodded towards Sanaa across the open ground before Bab al-Shaub gate on the north side of the town wall. Great holes rent his bloodstained uniform and dirt caked his skin like lichen. Long hair and a scruffy beard partially concealed his shell-shocked stare.

Father shuffled through Suq al-Milh, by the deserted stalls of the carpenters, the blacksmiths and leather craftsmen, the cloth merchants, and the corner where the scribes set out their wooden tables. The blended smells of cinnamon, cumin, garlic and incense seeped through the cracks in the shop doors, which the merchants would soon open to spread their wares along the narrow passageways.

He passed the lethargic, blindfolded camel at the mill where Mother took sesame seed for grounding into oil. The yoke on the miserable dromedary creaked and the huge millstone grumbled over the grains in the cavernous workshop, but Father perceived nothing.

He lumbered on mechanically, not even noticing that the al-Aubeli's house lay in ruins; that little Saeeda no longer played in the square while her mother baked bread for breakfast. In front of his own home, the white alabaster smeared over the base of the house and its upper windows had chipped off in the recent explosion, floating to the ground by the door. He walked over it without seeing.

Father plunged his hand through the fist-sized hole in the wall beside the entrance. Sliding the log from the staple inside, the door swung open. The familiar odour of baking bread met him as he closed the door, withdrew the oversized key from its hole, and stomped laboriously up to the third floor.

Mother stood in the kitchen that morning, slapping unbaked bread onto the wall of our rounded clay oven. As she reached down through the hole in the top, smoke belched from the wood fire underneath, dancing out through the ventilation shaft in the ceiling. I reclined on the floor in the corner, where Mother occasionally tossed me scraps of dough, which I pounded diligently with my fists in imitation of her.

Glancing up suddenly, I beheld a strange man, his face devoid of emotion, standing in the kitchen doorway. The room was dark and dreary, brightened only by the tiny window high above and the glow from the fire beneath the oven. But I could make out enough of the wretched figure to be frightened. I stopped patting the dough and watched anxiously.

Father had not been home in over a year. Mother told me years later that he had been very fond of me then, and fretted when she told him that I woke up some mornings with my pillow soaked in blood. Many Sanaani children suffered from nosebleeds. Parents attributed it to the town's dry air and high altitude (7,500 feet). Whatever the culprit, some children never woke up after a particularly serious bout. But mother prayed every day that God would spare her daughter that fate, and the nosebleeds stopped a few years later.

The last time he had been home, during a fortnight's leave from the army, Father had carried me with him in the mornings to the *suq*. He loved it when I clasped my arms affectionately around his neck. While the butcher prepared his order of mutton one day, Father pointed to the fresh liver on the counter. The skinned carcass of the sheep it had belonged to dangled by its hind leg from a nail while a swarm of flies set violently upon it.

'Can you cut off a morsel of that?' he asked. 'For my daughter.'

The butcher smiled at me, snipped off a corner of the still warm organ with a pair of scissors, and handed it to Father. My eyes widened with delight as he swung the raw liver towards my mouth. He and the butcher raised their eyebrows in mock surprise to encourage me, but I needed no prompting, swallowing it whole. The three of us giggled merrily as a drop of blood trickled down my chin, Father neglecting to wipe it away. He collected his sack of mutton and we headed back through the teeming *suq*.

'You should take better care of that girl,' scolded an old woman who seemed to know us. She wore an embroidered shawl over her long silk veil, with large diamond prints over each eye. Father couldn't tell who she was. Like most men, he was unskilled at identifying a veiled female from her gait alone – which suits the women just fine.

'You'll give her the evil eye,' the woman reproached.

Father's heart swelled with pride for his daughter. '*Mash Allah* – God protect her,' he murmured, just to be safe.

But sitting in the kitchen over a year later, I didn't know my father, though I had cried uncontrollably when he had left us last. Mother may not have recognized him either had she noticed him lingering there, for her back was to the door and her attention focused on the oven.

Father froze when he saw his wife. The firelight reflected softly off the side of her face each time she reached for a piece of dough. He gazed intently at the crackling fire, the fumes emerging from under the oven, and his thoughts must have suddenly conveyed him back to the battlefield.

Panic swept over him. He lunged towards mother, seizing one of the long braids of her hair emerging from under her headscarf in his left hand. He tugged violently, and Mother's head snapped back and her mouth and eyes gaped in terror at the ceiling. I screamed as Father slashed at her face with the iron key in his right hand, hacking a deep gash in her mouth.

Mother's atrocious howling brought her in-laws bounding down from the upper floors. They wrenched Father from his wife, who lay on the floor, bruised and weeping, blood streaming from her mouth onto her dress.

Father's two brothers dragged him from the kitchen. His stepmother and sisters helped Mother upstairs to clean her wounds, horrified to find her tongue nearly severed. They would have to take her to the hospital to sew it back on. Forgotten in the commotion, I remained sobbing and trembling on the kitchen floor, eyes riveted on Mother's spilled blood while smoke poured from the burning bread in the oven.

The brothers escorted Father, confused and babbling, down the steps and out the front door. Concerned neighbours had already gathered in front of the house to find out what the screaming was about. The brothers brushed them aside without a word. They led Father to Qasr al-Silah fortress and committed him to the only form of psychological treatment available: jail, where his hands and feet were chained.

CHAPTER SEVEN

Custody battle

After a year of relative peace in Maabar, Father had received orders to return to the northern plateau. Mother could not go with her husband, so she had returned with my brother and me to live with her in-laws in Sanaa. That is where Father found us when he returned in a daze from the battlefield that fateful day.

Father remained in Qasr al-Silah's prison for two weeks after assaulting Mother in the kitchen and nearly cutting out her tongue. Not surprisingly, his stay in jail did little to improve his condition. Heavy doses of sedatives calmed him, but his experience on the battlefield had left deep scars. The family, not least of all my mother, feared he could become violent again.

After returning from his aborted trip to America prior to the revolution, Father had practised medicine from one of two small chambers on the ground floor of his house, originally meant as a storage area. The bleak room opened directly onto the street, while an interior doorway led into the main part of the house.

With Father back home, Mother's father-in-law, my Grandfather Hamud, told her to take her husband and my brother and me to live in the downstairs chamber. But Mother was frightened, for herself and her children. She refused to stay with Father until convinced he was no longer capable of the violence he had displayed two weeks before. Irritated, Grandfather Hamud insisted that Father live downstairs, for he feared his son as much as my mother did. He finally agreed that she and we children could stay in the second storage room around the corner from the one Father would live in.

I despised our new accommodation, a sombre, windowless room a couple of feet below street level, where Mother kept the oil lamp burning throughout the day so we could see. More than the darkness I remember the emptiness of that room; just four bare walls. A prison cell could not have been more cheerful. Father at least had a large window in his room that looked out onto the alleyway.

'Why do we have to live in such a dark, tiny place, when most people live in a big house?' I asked Mother from time to time.

Adding insult to injury, Grandfather Hamud imposed conditions upon the occupation of our grim, oppressive quarters. Possibly on the initiative of his wife, Sadiya, he informed his daughter-in-law that she must pay rent. Mother couldn't believe it. Even were she able to read and write, almost no women worked outside the home in Sanaa. And the only family she might turn to for help was her mother and brother, who both barely had enough income to cover their own needs.

Raised under her own mother's overbearing personality, Mother had matured from a shy, withdrawn young person into a meek, submissive woman, who found it difficult to say no to even her worst enemy. But she had a strong case against her father-in-law. The house they all lived in belonged not to Grandfather Hamud, but to Father. It comprised part of his inheritance from Khayriya. Hamud intended his daughter-in-law to pay rent to inhabit a dreary corner of her husband's *own* home. Yet Mother couldn't muster the courage to resist his tyranny.

'God will work justice in his own time,' she consoled herself.

Resigned to this fate, Mother turned to the only source of income she knew: sewing, which her mother had taught her a few years before. She borrowed an ancient hand-turned sewing machine from Grandmother Amina and laid it in a corner of our lodging. Then she spread the word that she was open for business and soon developed a small clientele, transforming embroidered Indian silk and local cotton material into dresses for weddings and other special occasions.

My brother and I played outside in the street while Mother slaved over the machine day after day. She produced beautiful clothes, but the skill generated little money and she managed to scrape together just enough to feed us and keep her father-in-law off her back.

She paused from her work occasionally to cook and check on her husband around the corner. The fear that Father might turn violent again proved well-founded. A padlock secured the door leading from his chamber into the main part of the house, and late one night he managed to break the lock without anyone hearing. Climbing the stairs, he found a sledgehammer and smashed the clay oven where he had found mother baking bread the day he arrived home from the war.

Languishing hypnotically in his room, Father scrutinized his wife with glazed, uncomprehending eyes whenever she entered. The eerie feeling that she was being watched eased after a few weeks. Mother slowly lulled herself into believing that the fury within her husband had abated, until one afternoon when she brought him a change of clothes. As she approached, Father erupted suddenly from his torpor, seized Mother and thrashed her until she finally managed to break free from his grasp.

Bruised and traumatized, she did not return to see her husband that evening. Early the next morning, she focused intently on her sewing, blocking out all other thoughts. A smack on the open door startled her from her trance and she lifted her eyes to see Father stagger in, glaring through her with drunken eyes. Mother shuddered like stalked prey, but pretended to pay him no attention. As she continued to rotate the hand crank, fear welled up in her and sweat ran down her forehead onto her nose, dripping onto the dress she was making.

Father paused to take in the whirr of the sewing machine. Suddenly his eyes narrowed and his lips tightened in a volatile blend of anger and fright as sounds and images of the battlefield projected through his brain again.

'You devil!' he roared, hurtling towards Mother. He kicked the sewing machine against the wall as Mother threw up her arms in a feeble attempt to protect herself. She was too late. Muhammad hooked the side of her head with his fist, and she sprawled on the floor.

I heard the commotion from the street where I was playing. Darting into the room, I thrust myself between my parents, crying. 'Stop hitting her!' I bellowed to Father.

Father turned to me. I don't believe he knew who I was as he raised his hand to strike me, but Mother instantly collected her wits and grabbed the arm before he could swing. He shoved me aside with the other hand, faced his wife again, and knocked her to the ground with a sharp smack across the face. He left the room with Mother and me sobbing in each other's arms.

When it became clear that Father would not recover rapidly, if at all, from his illness, his stepmother seized the opportunity. Noting Mother's inability to stand up to her father-in-law, Sadiya incited Grandfather Hamud to take definitive control over all Father's property: the land, the shops, and the al-Nahshal house in which we all lived.

In one clean swoop, Sadiya succeeded in securing a healthy inheritance for herself and her children at the expense of her stepson and his family. The beauty of it for her was that the victims could do nothing to counter the move. Years of legal battles would be needed to recover the property, requiring time and money Mother couldn't spare. And a courtroom was hardly the place for a respectable woman to be found anyway.

Sadiya had by no means depended on Hamud financially up to then. Her own parents had bequeathed her a handful of properties around Sanaa. She sold most of them shortly before her marriage, not wanting the burden of having to look after them. But when the civil war wound down in 1970, Grandfather Hamud embarked on a long and tedious crusade to recover Sadiya's property, convinced she had sold it for too little. He would spend years in the courts trying to persuade judges that his wife had been insane at the time of the transactions, even bringing in witnesses he had paid to testify to his allegations. A judge finally conceded in the end, declaring the sales null and void.

Meanwhile Mother continued to struggle to care for her family. She didn't resent father for our predicament. In fact, she pitied him as he shifted from periods of lethargy to spells of violence, which she did her best to anticipate and avoid. Mother became pregnant and bore another daughter, Jameela, in 1971. My brother and I now had another sibling with whom to share the fear and uncertainty that filled our lives.

Several months after Jameela's birth, Mother finally had enough of our precarious and degrading situation. Father continued to abuse her when she let her guard down, and the improvement in his condition for which she ceaselessly prayed never materialized. He had been a caring, warm and sensitive husband before the war, and they loved each other deeply. She believed with all her heart that he didn't know what he put her through now, but remaining by his side was folly. In a burst of uncharacteristic defiance, she gathered her few belongings in a sack, balanced the sewing machine on her head, and took my brother, me and our new sister to live with her mother and brother on the other side of Old Sanaa.

A few days later, Grandfather Hamud showed up at the house. Feigning remorse, he pleaded with her to return, but Mother knew his interest lay in nothing more than finding someone to take care of Father. She could not face her intimidating father-in-law directly, so she informed him through her brother, Ali al-Salami, that she not only refused the request, but also planned to file for a divorce.

Father couldn't speak for himself, so responsibility for the decision fell to his father. But Grandfather Hamud's heart remained as cold and hard as the *hajar habash* stones supporting his house, and he refused to grant a divorce. Mother took her case before the government courts. A judge would impose her request if she could demonstrate just cause; and insanity was considered just cause. Her brother drew up the divorce papers for her and filed them with the court.

When her father-in-law realized Mother intended to follow through with her threat, he instinctively took the offensive. He swore he would take custody of my brother and me, but Mother could not be deterred this time. She returned to her sewing and waited for the long judicial process to run its course.

Mother's divorce application finally came before the court nearly two years later. The judge summoned her and her father-in-law to present their arguments. Mother insisted her husband had lost his mind, while Grandfather Hamud, flanked by a handful of witnesses he managed to browbeat into coming with him, swore that his son was not crazy.

The judge needed little time to reach a verdict. He granted Mother a divorce, much to her father-in-law's consternation, but the bigger question of child custody remained to be settled. Both Mother and Grandfather Hamud determined to keep little Hamud and me: Mother because she loved us; Grandfather Hamud because he wanted to punish Mother for the divorce. Jameela, still an infant, would remain with Mother.

The judge called Mother and we children to the court a few weeks later, on a day I will never forget. Ali, her brother, accompanied us. As we sat on the wooden chairs at the back of the small room, the judge entered and made his way to the desk at the front. The ornate silver scabbard for his *jambiya* curved less abruptly than the more common horseshoe-shaped tribal sheath. Resting at an angle across his stomach, it squeezed the ankle-length *zena* gown around his slim waist in a series of broad folds. He adjusted his neatly bound silk turban and sat behind the desk with a scholarly air, stroking his grey beard now and then as he arranged the papers on his desk.

Grandfather Hamud entered the courtroom next, teeth clenched in a scowl and a determined look on his face. I felt a shiver race through my body when I looked into his eyes. He said nothing to Mother, but forced a grunt and hollow, yellow smile towards Hamud and me. It was the first time I ever remember seeing him smile, and I remained far from convinced of its sincerity. Grasping Hamud and me by the hand, he led us to the corner out of earshot of Mother and Uncle Ali, and placed us each on a chair. He knelt so as to shield us from them.

'In a few minutes the judge is going to ask you a very important question,' Grandfather Hamud explained softly. 'He's going to ask if you want to live with your mother, or with me. Now what are you going to tell him?'

I glared at my grandfather with pursed lips and squinted eyes, and felt my legs tremble under my body.

'You should point to me,' he instructed, pleaded. 'Understood?'

Grandfather Hamud witnessed the anger overcome the fear inside me. Sensing my determined resistance, he placed his hands on my shoulders and shook forcefully.

'Understood?' he repeated, the smile vanishing from his face.

The judge slid the spectacles up the bridge of his nose and looked from his stack of papers at the dozen or so people in the courtroom.

'Mr Hamud Murzah. Mrs Fatima al-Salami,' he called out. 'Please come forward with the children.'

Grandfather Hamud stood up stiffly, forcing a smile back to his face. He patted Hamud and me playfully on our heads and faced the judge, hoping he had spotted the display of affection.

Mother rose with Jameela in her arms and shuffled before the judge's desk. Grandfather Hamud followed, clutching my brother's hand while I trailed behind. Little Hamud and I placed ourselves between the two adults, but Grandfather Hamud stepped in between in order to grasp each of us by the hand.

The judge focused on little Hamud first.

'Now, son. Do you want to live with your mother or your grandfather?'

The boy turned slowly, looked up at Mother, then at Grandfather. His palms began to sweat as Grandfather held his hand more firmly.

'Grandfather says I should stay with him,' Hamud answered innocently.

The judge raised an eyebrow and peered with suspicion at Grandfather Hamud.

'Is that so? But what is it that *you* want, son?' he asked as tenderly as a judge could. Grandfather Hamud increased the pressure on his hand. The boy glanced up, but Grandfather was smiling at the judge.

'I guess ... with my grandfather,' he stammered.

The judge frowned, unconvinced, then turned to me.

'And you, young lady. Who do you wish to live with?'

Grandfather Hamud squeezed like a tightening vice on my hand, though the pleasant expression on his face never wavered. I winced with pain and gazed up with pure hatred into his eyes. Grim, agonizing memories of living in the al-Nahshal house, now called the Murzah house, flooded my mind, numbing the discomfort in my hand. A weight like the lid of a coffin had lifted when Mother finally delivered me from its misery the year before. I could never go back there.

'Khadija?' the judge prodded. 'What do you have to say?'

The blood rushed to my face, ready to explode.

'I won't go back to that house!' I boomed. 'I won't go back!'

I tore my hand away from Grandfather's and burst out of the courtroom. The judge watched stoically as I galloped out the door, past the stunned families waiting their turn outside. He eyed my grandfather disgustedly as Mother started after me.

Grandfather Hamud faced Mother's brother, standing behind him. The veins bulged in his temples and his eyes filled with fury:

'Don't expect me to support that good-for-nothing girl!' Grandfather Hamud snarled at Uncle Ali.

'That is not an option for you, Mr Murzah,' the judge interrupted. 'The law requires that you help support the children no matter who they choose to live with.'

'But I can't afford it,' he pleaded, playing the victim. 'I'm not a rich man, Your Honour. And they're not even my children; only grandchildren.'

'What about the income from the land and the stores you took from your son?' Uncle Ali challenged. 'And his pension, which *you* collect every month?'

'That doesn't even cover the cost of taking care of Muhammad,' Grandfather Hamud countered.

'Enough,' the judge snapped, still glaring at Grandfather. 'You must help pay for the little girl.'

'But I told you. There isn't enough money.'

The tempest within Grandfather Hamud calmed slightly as he channelled its energy into deep thought. An idea came to him.

'What if I disown her, Your Honour?'

The judge hesitated. 'Then you would not have to pay for her. But you would lose any legal rights over her; even the right to see her. Do you want that?'

'I don't care,' Grandfather Hamud growled.

'Well, that's up to you.'

The judge scribbled on a document and looked up again.

'Khadija is to remain with her mother. But Hamud is old enough to stay with his grandfather, which is what he says he wants. I don't believe it, but there's nothing I can do about that. Next case!'

Mother would erupt into tears when she learned of the decision, devastated at losing her son.

A military officer approached Uncle Ali a year or so after the divorce. He was from Jahran, one of the numerous isolated plateaus forming a chain through the central highlands. The visitor inquired as to how long Mother had been divorced, and whether she intended to remarry.

The man's interest pleased both Uncle Ali and Mother. She was nearly 30 years old, and it would not be long before people began calling her *ajuza* – old woman. A divorcee with three small children does not always find it easy to remarry.

Islamic law requires a waiting period of four months before a woman may remarry following a divorce. This allows ample time to make certain she isn't pregnant. Uncle Ali informed the suitor that the prescribed period had indeed passed. Elated by her fortuitous luck, mother instructed Ali to agree on a bride-price and dowry with the officer.

Hameed al-Maamari was *shaykh* of one of the tribes at the northern end of the Jahran plateau. Thirty miles long by 15 miles wide and hemmed in by lofty mountain ridges, Jahran's volcanic soil is extremely fertile. Its vast green fields of ripening sorghum are interrupted only by the occasional patch of dusty, uncultivated earth where land ownership is in dispute.

The 9,000-foot high Yislah Pass separates Jahran from the Sanaa plateau nearly 1,000 feet above it to the north. A mile or two south from the base of the pass, a path leads off from the main Sanaa-Taiz road up a side valley to the west. At the *wadi*'s head, two dozen stone houses make up al-Sharara village, clinging to the lower slopes of the rusty Mushqara Mountains.

The highest dwelling in the village perches on a steep promontory encircled by the other houses. It belonged to Shaykh Abdu Rabu al-Maamari, Hameed's father. Constructed of rough stone and clay mortar, the weight of the four-storey structure is supported by a massive stone arch over the ground floor, where farming implements and grain are stored. The view from the little windows in the upper meeting hall stretches all the way to the tiny speck of Maabar seven miles to the south, where I was born.

Mother told Charles and me about my stepfather and his family after we returned from a trip to Jahran:

'Hameed al-Maamari's grandfather had been a more influential *shaykh* than Hameed was,' she explained. 'His generosity and fairness were renowned throughout the whole of Jahran.[1] The grandfather also possessed exceptional bravery but, like many brave men, his life ended while he was still a young man, murdered by a Bedouin who had come to Jahran to trade salt from the mines in Bayhan to the east.'

Shaykh Hameed's father, Abdu Rabu, also became a respected tribal leader. He involved himself in a constant rivalry with a man named al-Qifri, a *shaykh* of the Bilad

[1] Whose tribes belong to the Bakil tribal federation.

al-Rus (Land of the Mountain Summits), whose territory lay on the far side of the Mushqara Mountains from their village of al-Sharara. Both men cherished their independence above all else.

Like all Yemeni tribesmen, the two *shaykhs* looked unkindly upon intervention in their affairs from outside their territory, not least of all by the government. When civil war consumed the country in late 1962, al-Maamari, al-Qifri and many other tribal leaders throughout the country affirmed their autonomy by accepting money and arms simultaneously from the Republican revolutionaries and the pro-*Imam* Royalists. Despite the generous funding, a great number of the beneficiary tribes declined to back either side definitively, no matter how much largesse they received. Royalists and Republicans alike employed devious methods in an effort to draw neutral tribes into the conflict on their respective sides.

Al-Sharara lies a mile west of the Sanaa-Taiz road. The year before the revolution, an American company had finally transformed the choppy track into a gravel motorway suitable for cars. The Republican war effort depended on control of the strategic route, which entailed the active support of the tribes living in its vicinity. Neutrality was not enough, for the antagonists knew that a little money and rifles distributed by the enemy to the right *shaykhs* could always overcome that, at least for short periods.

Abdu Rabu and al-Qifri accused one another of sometimes pro-Royalist, sometimes pro-Republican sympathies, depending on their own relations with the two sides at that particular moment. The Republican government in Sanaa mistrusted and feared both of the mercurial *shaykhs*, and it made several attempts to capture them – without success.

The government then resorted to the time-honoured tactic of spreading rumours. Yemenis tend to take all they hear at face value, no matter how outrageous, until the tale is proved otherwise. So government officials subtly spread the word that one *shaykh* had criticized the other. The offended man responded with an even sharper insult directed at his rival, and the spiral towards violence became all but impossible to arrest in such tense times.

The slander steadily increased in virulence as the weeks passed. The opposing tribes eyed each other suspiciously in the weekly markets throughout the area, where they came to sell their crops and purchase what they couldn't grow. The slightest false move or misconstrued comment threatened to engulf the whole region in bloodshed and a subsequent cycle of relentless revenge.

Some disputes in Yemen come to involve so many different parties that objective arbitrators from the community cannot be found. That is one of the rare times when the tribes might welcome outside intervention. A neutral figure with no binding links to the region in question may offer the only hope of reconciling the parties.

'The Republican Provincial Governor quietly waited until the situation threatened to ignite,' Mother continued with the story. 'At just the right moment, he sent messengers to Abdu Rabu and al-Qifri, graciously offering his services as mediator. Anxious to bury their differences, both *shaykhs* agreed to meet with the Governor in Maabar. Neither man suspected any sinister intentions behind the proposal.

The two *shaykhs* arrived in the town a few days later. Several dozen of their tribesmen escorted each of them, ammunition belts wrapped around their torsos like jewellery and held in place by their daggers. Each group forfeited its rifles to the Governor's soldiers as an indication that they intended no violence at the gathering.[2]

Abdu Rabu and al-Qifri were dumbfounded when the soldiers seized them and hauled them off to prison. The

---

[2] Both antagonists had little to fear, for arbitration is a sacred ritual. Anyone who inflicts harm at such a meeting gravely offends both his adversary and the arbitrator, and risks losing the support of his own tribesmen.

Governor dispatched them to the mountain castle above Radaa,[3] to keep their men from breaking in to rescue them. The fortress already overflowed with prisoners suspected of pro-Royalist sympathies.

Several days after their arrest, a government official visited the jail. Wearing military fatigues, he addressed the prisoners with arrogance:

'The rule of the *Imams* is finished. The Republic has expelled them and their supporters, and has come to help the people; not to crush them as the *Imams* did.'

The official furrowed his eyebrows and paced slowly by the prison cells, studying the men behind the bars.

'You men are unhealthy,' he explained. 'Many of you are clearly ill. But we're going to make you well. We will give you vitamins, to make you strong again.'

He snapped his fingers and a soldier carried in a box filled with needles and syringes. Once again, Abdu Rabu and al-Qifri suspected nothing as a guard moved from cell to cell injecting each of the prisoners. The alleged vitamins probably contained nothing more than water, and none of the men felt any effect – except Abdu Rabu and al-Qifri, the last in line.

Less than a minute after receiving his dose, al-Qifri dropped to his knees, his face contorted in agony. He lost consciousness and died within seconds on the cold stone floor.

Then the same pain seized Abdu Rabu. He shook with anger as the Governor's role in this treachery became clear to him, from the dispute with al-Qifri to their death in this fortress.

'The Republic has killed us,' he cried out angrily, rattling the iron bars of the cell. 'Though we have done nothing against it.'

He collapsed beside al-Qifri and died.

---

[3] An ancient walled town of ashen clay houses 50 miles to the east.

Abdu Rabu's words deeply moved the other prisoners. News of the *shaykhs'* death spread from behind the prison walls like the call to prayer from a minaret. The people of Radaa rose in revolt, for the Governor had blackened his face by betraying those who had sought his aid.

Abdu Rabu's son, Hameed al-Maamari, commanded a battalion in the elite *Amalaqa* (Giants) Brigade when mother married him. He lived in a rented house within Sanaa's walls. Mother took my infant sister, Jameela, to live with them there, while I remained with my Grandmother Amina and Uncle Ali not far away.

I looked proudly on Mother on her wedding day, dressed in an elegant white gown and matching white crown (called a *taj*) with gold-coloured leaves around it. Though she looked beautiful, I noticed a sad look in her eyes whenever she glanced at me.

When Shaykh Hameed arrived with a procession of celebrators to take Mother back to his home with him, I finally realized that Mother was really leaving. My heart leapt and I nearly panicked. Forgetting my fear of the *jinis* I believed haunted our stairway, I rushed in the darkness to the rooftop to watch Mother's silhouette disappear around a corner with the crowd behind her.

I wept quietly that night after I went to bed, careful that Grandmother Amina would not hear me. But it was winter and the cold finally forced me to seek refuge in her bed to keep warm. I was always afraid to walk around the house in the dark, because Grandfather Hamud told me it was full of *jinis* in order to convince me not to live with Mother and Grandmother after mother's divorce. But that night I mustered the courage to scamper to Grandmother's room in spite of my fear.

Shaykh Hameed was unusual for a tribesman in that he loved to read, a luxury made possible by a rudimentary education at the village mosque during his youth. In the room he used for an office at home, novels and history books littered the desk and clogged the shelves.

Hameed was also unusually tall for a Yemeni, and very handsome. When he sometimes accompanied Mother to visit Grandmother Amina and me, teenage girls hoping to catch a glimpse of him would suddenly turn up to play with me.

'When is your stepfather going to come out of the house?' they would ask me every few minutes.

Hameed could be the gentlest of men. He loved Jameela and me like his own daughters, and sometimes treated me to an Indian or Egyptian film playing at Sanaa's cinema. When we walked together through the streets, friends asked Hameed who the little girl was. He always answered proudly: 'This is my daughter.' I glowed with delight, for nothing could have made happier a child who had been so long without a father.

CHAPTER EIGHT

Growing up

L egend has it that Sanaa was founded by Sam (*Shem* in Hebrew), the son of Noah and ancestor of all Semites, including Arabs and Jews. After the Great Flood, Sam wandered south from Mount Ararat (in modern-day eastern Turkey). Traversing the Arabian Peninsula, he came upon a high plain some 50 miles long from north to south and 10 miles wide. The land seemed productive and the air refreshing, and he began to sink a well. But as he laboured, a bird swooped down, snatched the plumb line in its bill, and dropped it at the foot of Jebel Nuqum Mountain several miles away. Sam dug his well there instead and a town grew up around it, originally named Sam, then Azal, after Sam's brother. It later came to be called Sanaa, indicating an abundance of craft workshops.

The Abyssinians constructed a cathedral in Sanaa during their short stay in Arabia in the sixth century AD. Ancient historians claim the building rose 262 feet high. The reports are surely exaggerated, but nevertheless offer a hint of the church's magnificence. It was said to be the largest Christian structure south of the Mediterranean until its destruction nearly two centuries later. Eastern Sanaa's al-Qalis neighbourhood (from the Greek *ekklesia* – church) marks the cathedral's former location.

Despite the prevalence of Judaism and later Christianity in South Arabia, pre-Islamic Sanaa was a popular pilgrimage destination for pagan worshippers before the arrival of Islam, rivalling Mecca in popularity. But Mecca received a significant boost with the rise of Islam, in particular when the Prophet Muhammad changed the direction of Muslims' prayers from Jerusalem to Mecca, following his betrayal by several Jewish tribes. Though eclipsed by its northern rival, Sanaa evolved into a prominent centre for Islamic learning. The town's Great Mosque stands today largely intact since its construction in the first half of the seventh century AD.

At the dawn of the twentieth century, the town boasted eight public gates carved into its mud ramparts. Bab al-Yemen, a stone arch fitted into the town wall not far from Suq al-Milh, distinguished itself as the newest and most majestic portal, and the point of entry for caravans arriving from the south. In the 1880s Sanaa's merchants insisted on razing Bab al-Yemen's old weaving corridor entranceway, designed for security, and replaced it with the more practical two doors opening onto a broad interior square that remains today.

Sanaa was until the 1970s divided broadly into two sections. The whole resembled a figure eight, stretching some two and a half miles in length from east to west and three-quarters of a mile from north to south. The traditional area of residential homes and markets, called Old Sanaa, lay in the east, towards Jebel Nuqum.

The *sayla* canal bisects the western end of Old Sanaa. It remains dry most of the year, but heavy downpours occasionally send thick walls of water and mud rumbling down the channel, partitioning the town for hours at a time. The more recently built Ottoman administrative district was situated in the west. It boasted numerous gardens, the *Imams'* principal palace, and a Jewish quarter.[1]

---

[1] Yemen's Jews have traditionally specialized in crafts, particularly metalworking, smithing, and jewellery and glass manufacture. A hint of their former importance is indicated by the ubiquitous Stars of David carved into lintel stones above doorways and fired into the coloured glass of both Jewish and Muslim houses in numerous Yemeni towns.

Physically, Yemeni Jews are all but indistinguishable from Muslim Yemenis, except for the Jews' long hair ringlets dangling in front of each ear. Like the

The house I lived in with my Grandmother Amina occupied a narrow street corner in the modest Hurqan neighbourhood, at the far northwest corner of Old Sanaa. Made from roughly hewn white stones of widely contrasting sizes, bound together with clay mortar, the tiny two-storey dwelling is dwarfed by the elegant mansions across the *sayla* on the east side of Old Sanaa.

Grandmother Amina's house also lacked the elaborate exterior friezes and abstract reliefs decorating even the neighbours' homes. Three flimsy wooden planks formed the gate leading into the narrow courtyard. The timber lintel above the doorsill sagged menacingly, and the alabaster coating over the house's stone base peeled away with every rain shower. The ground floor sat dark and vacant, devoid of even a well.

In typical Sanaani houses, the first floor is equipped with a hand-cranked flour mill, shallow compartments for storing grain and a well. Bedrooms are situated on the second floor, while a meeting room with large windows and a view of the town make up the third floor, both facing south to take advantage of the sun's

---

Muslim women, Jewish women dress in either the long *sitara* or *sharshaf*, and many veil themselves when leaving the home.

The Jews of Yemen, whose sons are commonly named Yahya (John) or Yusuf (Joseph), are not members of the tribes among which they live. They form a protected class alongside artisans, merchants, *Sayids* and other non-tribal sectors of society. As such they take no part in tribal disputes and are exempted from contributing a portion of the *diya* to pay off the blood debts of the tribe in whose territory they reside. An offence or insult perpetrated against a Jew, who traditionally carries no weapon, may be fined up to 11 times what the same action would have cost had the victim been a tribesman.

Most estimates put the number of Jews in Yemen at some 70,000 in 1948. Then Israeli Jews began coming to Yemen and promised Yemeni Jews houses and jobs if they immigrated to Israel. Yemeni Jews tended to be slightly better off materially than their Muslim countrymen. But the twentieth century had brought with it a rising flood of cheap imported goods into the country, hurting demand for the Jews' own craftwork. In contrast to the bleak economic future in Yemen, the Israeli recruiters portrayed Israel as a paradise waiting for them. All but a few thousand Jews decided to migrate, and even many Muslims wanted to go if what they had heard was true. Some asked their Jewish friends to send word back once they were settled, to let them know if it was worth them going too.

warmth. The upper storey contains the kitchen and bathroom, facing north so that the predominant winds disperse odours. The value of a home drops considerably if this orientation is not respected, but Grandmother Amina's house was too small to be designed in the style of most homes.

Grandmother Amina, like Mother, had sewed to earn extra money since the departure of her last husband. The hand-cranked sewing machine and piles of clothes and material filled most of the room next to the kitchen where Grandmother and I slept. Grandmother Amina's son, Ali, a student at the military officers' training school, lived in the small compartment on the other side of the kitchen with his wife.

I was too young to go to school when I first moved in with Grandmother. I passed the days helping around the house, sneaking away to play in the street or on the rooftop terrace when some other task occupied Grandmother Amina.

I rose every morning at dawn, awakened by the call to prayer from the nearby mosque. After setting the chickens loose from their pen in the courtyard and looking for eggs (Grandmother Amina always made me drink a hen's first egg – 'It will make you intelligent,' she said), I grabbed a pail and skipped to the well behind the Azeri house next door. A furrow leading out from the well's base emptied into the vast walled garden beside it, irrigating the soil twice a week through a network of canals. A rich Sanaani had bequeathed the garden to the mosque. In turn, the mosque rented the land out for growing herbs and vegetables around two sprawling tamarisk trees.

I returned home with a bucket of water balanced on my head, climbed the steps to the parapet roof, and watered the basil, mint and thyme that grew there. Sometimes a startled snake emerged from the vegetation, and I would play with the tiny reptile before placing it back in its home.

I loved to sit in the kitchen and watch Grandmother cook. She ground the wheat on the millstone outside the kitchen, tossing scraps of dough to me like Mother used to do. I took them outside in the street, where the neighbourhood girls would build a small fire with papers and twigs and pretend to bake bread.

I also adored scaling the outside of the Azeri house. After my chores (and sometimes before), I would wait until the women had gone out to visit friends for the day before scurrying up the jagged stone wall to the third-floor terrace. But each time I raised myself triumphantly onto the landing, it dawned on me that I couldn't climb down. I had to wait hours for the family to return and let me out through the inside of the house. If they were in a bad mood, one or two of the women would follow me home and inform Grandmother Amina of the mischief I had got into that day. They were all the more inclined to do so if they found some of the eggs missing from their hen house. I frequently coaxed a friend into swiping them.

Grandmother would apologize humbly and invite them to stay for tea. When they left, she would chase me round the house for a beating that made my blood boil.

'*Ajuzat al-kahna!*' I would snarl at grandmother as I squirmed to avoid the blows. 'You old witch! Leave me alone!'

I scowled like a frightened monkey in an effort to appear intimidating, but it was all Grandmother could do to keep a straight face when she heard my crude tongue-lashing. Later in the evening, after I herded the chickens back into their pen and wearied of pouting, I would silently enter the bathroom and scrub Grandmother's back, as she bathed, in a gesture of reconciliation. She returned the favour, and after dinner, when the dull flame in the alabaster lamp consumed the last of its oil, we would fall asleep side by side on the floor among the piles of clothes.

On nights when I had trouble falling asleep, I would imagine the posters on the walls of some of the neighbours' houses that I so adored. They portrayed giant waterfalls beneath snow-capped mountains in the Alps; green meadows teeming with flocks of geese and sheep fatter and woollier than I imagined possible. It was science fiction to me, and I didn't believe it when Uncle Ali told me such places really did exist.

When Ali explained that the white blanket on the mountain tops was only solid water, it reminded me of how one frigid winter morning the water in the bottom of the pail I left out overnight had hardened. I had squeaked in astonishment when I tried to pour it out and it refused to budge.

Grandmother Amina married seven times, though she refused to speak on the subject. 'She ran one of her husbands out of the house brandishing a shoe,' according to Mother, 'and he never came back.'

While Grandmother Amina was autocratic and demanding with her family, she could show infinite generosity to others. The pension from her deceased father and the income from her sewing hardly met the expenses of feeding herself and me, yet she would not hesitate to offer whatever might be left over to anyone in need. Visitors from al-Salami village in Heima came all the time to Sanaa, some to find work, others for medical treatment at the hospital, and some just to visit. Grandmother Amina would feed them all and insist that they stay with us, which many did.

Grandmother's overbearing demeanour affected me differently than it had my mother. Rather than resign myself in diffidence, I took after Grandmother. I developed my own commanding personality, a trait that would both reward and punish me over the years.

Few children in Yemen had anything but home-made gadgets to play with when I was growing up. Boys fashioned miniature chassis from wire and carved wheels from discarded wooden blocks to make cars. Girls fastened together sticks or wire into human shapes, then persuaded their mothers to sew scraps of cloth into clothes for their new dolls. Manufactured toys from abroad only appeared from time to time in the *suq*. They cost too much for most families to afford, but Mother occasionally splurged when she came to visit me.

I was thrilled when she turned up one day with a doll whose eyes closed when laid on its back. I took the doll outside and,

with the concentration of a surgeon, smashed its head open with
a rock to find out what made it blink. Running back into the
house, I demanded that Mother buy me another one. She grew
angry and refused, but I cried so hard that she finally gave in.

The stray dogs patrolling the town for scraps of food fascinated
me as much as the weeping toy. I could watch them for hours at a
time. Most Yemenis consider canines quite unclean, but I was
particularly fond of the puppies. I learned to recognize pregnant
dogs when they skirted into the tiny opening at the sides of
houses, used as a drain for the toilet on the upper floor. Propping
the swinging door up with a stick, I would sweep my long
hair over my shoulders and watch the birth of a new litter,
undeterred by the horrendous stench.

Once each week, a man from the *hamam* – bathhouse – passed
through the neighbourhood with his donkey and cart, collecting
fuel for the fires that kept the baths hot and steamy. He halted
before each house, scooped up a spadeful of ashes from his cart,
and spread them inside the latrine. He then shovelled up the
contents, the odour stifled by the ashes, and dumped them into a
tin tub on the cart. Once burned under the baths, the ashes served
as fertilizer for the town's gardens, like the one by the well behind
our house.

The amiable fellow that passed through Hurqan with his
pet baboon provided a much rarer attraction. Cries from the
neighbourhood children of 'The monkey man! The monkey man
is here!' preceded his arrival, and I would dash into the street
in a burst of excitement to watch the leashed baboon turn
somersaults to the audience's applause.

In between the infrequent visits of the monkey man, I found
other entertainment. Grandmother Amina's sister, Hameeda,
and Hameeda's husband, Ali al-Aini, liked to go for a drive on
Friday mornings, the Muslim Sabbath. They took me with them
as they visited some of the villages near the capital. I loved to
view the surrounding mountains up close, watching over the
town like tireless sentries. The best time was after the summer
rains, when the barren, khaki slopes burst into infinite shades of

green. I tried to imagine myself as courageous and steadfast as the peaks, and their example helped me through many a crisis as a little girl.

When the arrival of the rains tarried, I lost myself in the giant crowds that assembled outside Bab al-Yemen. Sombre as a funeral gathering and led by an old camel, the procession plodded along under the shadow of the town wall to the foot of Jebel Nuqum, reciting Koranic verses and beseeching God to send water to their scorched land. '*Bismillah al-Rahman al-Rahim*,' one of the men cried out before sawing open the camel's rubbery throat. Some people struggled to place a hand on the dying camel (in the ancient belief, I learned much later, that their sins might flow from their bodies and into the camel's blood as it poured onto the ground). They hoped God would find the sacrifice pleasing and grant them their request for rain.

I didn't understand the importance of rain to the farmers then, but I was as happy as anyone else when it finally came. I would roll up my trouser legs and stomp through the muddy streets, playing with the other kids. The goal seemed to be to go home as dirty as possible, and it was well worth the fury we provoked in our parents after soiling the furniture.

I rarely fell ill as a child. The only real scare came when a high fever left me delirious for several days, haunted by grotesque, human-like spectres all around me. Mother, who had come from Shaykh Hameed's house to care for me, rushed into the room when I cried out after one of my hallucinations. I pointed a trembling finger at the hideous creatures groping towards me.

'There's nothing there, dear,' Mother tried to comfort me, stroking my burning forehead.

'Look! There they are. Can't you see them?' I insisted, then collapsed back onto the cushion, drenched and spent from the effort.

Mother and Grandmother were relieved when the fever lifted a few days later. Mother told me I could have anything I wanted as a reward, and I mulled over the proposition carefully.

'I know what I want,' I announced a few minutes later.

'What?' Mother asked.

'Shoes. Those high heel ones I saw in the *suq*.'

'But you're too little to wear high heel shoes, dear,' mother protested, laughing.

'But you said ...'

'All right. All right,' Mother interrupted. She knew me too well to try to go back on her word. 'We'll go and pick them out.'

I smiled contentedly with the thought of high heels adorning my feet. The following morning we visited the modern shops in al-Tahreer Street. I donned the new *sharshaf* mother made for me, like the one fashionable young women wear: a black ensemble of long skirt, cloak, veil and head covering, introduced into Yemen by the Ottomans in the nineteenth century.

When I found nothing I wanted in my size there, we headed for the *suq*. I trotted ahead of Mother into the market like a newborn gazelle. The pungent odour of burning incense perfumed the air. Rummaging carefully through the shops, I finally realized that they didn't make high heel shoes for little girls, so I settled on a pair for adults. I lifted the glittery shoes aloft triumphantly, a prizefighter with his belt, while Mother went to bargain with the shopkeeper. But he had already sold one pair of shoes that morning, so he waived her on to the next merchant, who had not. Fortunately the second shop had an identical pair. They were far too big for my little feet, but that hardly mattered.

Before the shopkeeper could hand Mother her change, I was already clanking proudly down the dusty market corridor towards home. As I cut a path through the crowd of shoppers with my head held high, two Chinese men, probably expatriate workers, stopped to snap a photograph of me. I craned my chin up even further, raised my eyebrows, and placed my hands on my hips in a pose. The Chinese were still laughing when Mother ran by to catch up with me.

I had never been more than a few miles from Sanaa when word arrived of a wedding in Grandmother Amina's native village of

Bayt al-Salami in Heima. Grandmother and her sister, Hameeda, decided they would take me with some of our distant male relatives to attend the ceremony.

We crammed into someone's car in Sanaa and squeezed out an hour later at the foot of the crag from which Bayt al-Salami gazes down at the world below. The panoramic view of Heima's emerald mountains unfolded before us with breathtaking beauty, razor-sharp crests enshrouded in mist, rolling like waves to the west.

Our group set off on foot up a narrow path that disappeared among the boulders above. The track was so steep that in places I crawled on my hands and knees for what seemed like an eternity, but I loved the freedom of the countryside.

Bayt al-Salami did not impress me. Even the fact that it was Grandmother's native village captivated my interest for no more than a few seconds. And it would be years before I heard the stories of my great-great-grandfather fighting the Turks from there. On arriving at the summit to the welcoming songs of the village women, I cringed with fear when the men fired off a dozen volleys from their rifles in honour of their guests from Sanaa.

Though sore and fatigued from the climb, I could find no repose. The village idiot took great pleasure in jumping out from behind walls and doors to frighten me. Grandmother Amina told me the retarded man was only playing and quite harmless, but I remained unconvinced. His distant, unfocused look reminded me too much of my father.[2]

The wind picked up after sunset in Bayt al-Salami. It howled ferociously through the ancient stone village, shaking the houses

[2] The psychologically ill are much more accepted in Yemeni society than in the West, provided they are not violent. This man, for example, lived freely in his village where everyone watched over him. It was the same for my father, once the medications calmed him enough not to pose a threat to anyone. Someone in the neighbourhood was always giving him a cigarette, or grinding food up for him when his teeth grew too weak for him to chew. They are treated essentially as children.

and pounding the cactus-like euphorbia bushes grown up around them. I wept through the night and swore I could not endure another day in the village my al-Salami ancestors had founded 300 years earlier. Grandmother sent me back to Sanaa the next afternoon.

I began my first year of school soon after returning from the brief visit to Bayt al-Salami. I settled quickly into my studies, which provided a much-needed diversion from home life.

Little but grief and pain had filled my world up to then, and hardly a day passed when I did not shed tears from the memories. The occasional Friday drives outside Sanaa with Aunt Hameeda and her husband provide some of the rare fond recollections from that period of my life. But now I could mercifully concentrate my energy on schoolwork, holding at bay the gloomy thoughts of separation from Mother, and Father's illness.

I felt strongly even at that age that with an education I could become anybody and do anything I wanted. People would one day look up to me because of my diploma, and not because of what family I belonged to. As a result of the hope I placed in education, I became a different person at school, where I felt that people valued me more, and I valued myself more.

I faced a dilemma on the very first day of class when the teacher asked each pupil their name. No one had ever wanted to know more than my first name, so when my turn came I answered simply: 'Khadija.'

'*Bint min?*' the teacher probed. 'The daughter of whom?'

I hesitated at what for the other students was a simple question, but my life was anything but simple. Normally I would have taken my father's first name as my own middle name, and his last name as my last name: Khadija Muhammad Murzah.

But I had never known Muhammad Murzah as a father. Furthermore, my Grandfather Hamud carried the Murzah name too, and I hated no one in the world more than him. Walking to school one day a few years after the episode in the courtroom over custody of my brother Hamud and me, I had rounded a corner and seen Grandfather shopping in the *suq* a short distance ahead. My muscles had tightened and my heart filled with a loathing deeper than any child should ever know. Try as I might, I hadn't been able to command my legs to carry me away from the place. I stood gawking in terror until the man moved on through the *suq* and out of sight.

I would be damned if I took Grandfather Hamud's name. Besides, he had disowned me after the judge ruled I could stay with Mother following the divorce.

'Al-Salami,' I finally stuttered to the teacher. I had replaced Murzah with my mother's name, since Yemeni women keep their maiden name throughout their lives. 'Khadija al-Salami is my name.'

CHAPTER NINE

An unexpected visitor

Grandmother and I received occasional visits from friends and relatives in Sanaa. One afternoon a strange man called out Grandmother Amina's name from the street in front of the house. She and I peered out of the tiny upper window at a middle-aged, sunburned figure clad in a long *zena* and sleeveless sheepskin cloak. He wore the thick fur against his lanky frame and the tanned leather turned out. Neither of us recognized the man.

'Who is it?' Grandmother shouted. She positioned herself behind the open window so as not to reveal her face to the stranger, which would have been shameful.

'Is that you, Amina?' replied the stranger gruffly. Grandmother had heard his peculiar accent somewhere before, yet too long ago to remember where.

'And who are you?' she challenged.

'I guess you wouldn't remember me. I am your brother.'

During his days in Marib, Grandmother Amina's father, Ahmed al-Salami, had taken two wives from among the Bedouin. One hailed from the Bayt Yusuf clan of the Abeeda tribe, the other from the *Ashraf*, descendents of the Prophet Muhammad through his grandson Hassan.[1]

The Abeeda trace their ancestry back to Qahtan, the patriarchal ancestor of the southern Arabs and the great-great-grandson

---

[1] As opposed to the *Sayids*, who descend through Hassan's brother, Hussayn – a distinction that has become clouded in recent decades.

of Noah, according to the biblical book of Genesis. The tribe is prevalent around Marib today, and although their neighbours refer to them as Bedouin, most of the Abeeda are settled in small, fortified villages on the arid plain between the Ramlat al-Sabatayn (the Sands of the Two Shebas) to the east and the great Khala desert to the north. Only those populating the extreme northern reaches of Abeeda territory are true Bedouin, dwelling in wool tents and driving their camels and sheep across the sandy wastes in a perpetual quest for green pasture.

The predatory Abeeda strike dread into the hearts of peoples far afield. Groups of several dozen Abeeda until recently prowled the barren rim of the Khala for hundreds of miles around, mounted atop their swiftest riding camels. The warriors' bare torsos shimmered in the starlight from the sesame oil and indigo they smeared on against the extremes of heat and cold. Avoiding contact with the inhabitants, unless it was to lift their livestock, the marauders survived on balls of sun-dried buttermilk prepared by their women for the journey. Though Imam Ahmed succeeded in extending his influence over the desert regions during the 1950s, such raids continued into the following decade. The blood debts incurred on some of the forays remain in effect today.

From her father's marriage to the Abeeda woman, Grandmother Amina had a younger half-brother in Marib. But she had not seen him since she was last in Marib 30 years before, and didn't even know if he was still alive. When the stranger revealed his identity, Grandmother rushed down the steps and flung open the door as the man entered the courtyard through the outer gate. Back straight and head held high, he approached as quickly as dignity permitted and embraced his overjoyed sister.

I had never met anybody quite like Uncle Salih al-Salami. As far as I was concerned, he might as well have come from the moon (whose terrain is not all that different from his Abeeda country). He exuded the hardened physique and proud, suspicious character of dwellers of the eastern desert. Once or twice I had glimpsed men like him in the Suq al-Milh. A handful of their women sometimes trailed behind in bright flowing robes, with strings of colourful beads suspended from their head coverings to partly conceal their faces. They wandered among the stalls, rifles strapped over their shoulders,[2] picking up objects and handling them, curious at all of the strange wonders to be found in what to them was a grandiose city.

Shoppers in the *suq* maintained a healthy distance from the Bedouin visitors, as if from a poisonous snake. They knew them to be quick-tempered, owing allegiance to no authority but their hearts. Grandmother Amina, however, had lived in Marib and saw beyond the townsmen's dread of the desert dwellers. She was delighted to see her long-lost brother.

Uncle Salih's goat-hide sandals, designed to scare off serpents and scorpions in the sand, clacked sharply against his heels with each stride. He climbed the steps and entered the long, narrow sitting room as Grandmother Amina scurried off to the kitchen. I didn't follow Grandmother as usual, but instead crouched by the door and stared with wonder into my great-uncle's penetrating eyes, darker than the well pit I drew water from every morning. I looked quickly aside when his gristly but not unfriendly gaze fell upon me, returning when he diverted his attention elsewhere.

Grandmother entered and poured Salih a cup of *qishr* from a brass kettle. He sipped slowly, pausing to wipe a strand of long swarthy hair from his mouth and tuck it into the strip of

[2] Firearms are officially banned inside Sanaa. Traditionally the town, like many market towns throughout the northern plains, enjoys the status of *hijra* – a refuge from tribal conflicts. The *diya* for any offence committed in a *hijra* is multiplied several fold, and violating the sanctity of a *hijra* is considered a grave insult to the *shaykhs* of the tribes in whose territory the town is situated.

But despite its status, Sanaa's sentinels dared not challenge a Bedouin toting an automatic rifle as he passed through Bab al-Yemen with his women to shop. Attempting to deprive him of his weapon, even for a few minutes, represented too risky a manoeuvre for any but a well-armed platoon. And even if they succeeded, the Bedouin's tribesmen might resort to the age-old response of cutting the roads leading into their territory to all government vehicles, including military, until amends had been made for the affront to the man's, and thus the tribe's, honour.

chequered cloth wrapped loosely around his head for a turban. Salih inquired about the family, most of whom he had never met, and many he had never even heard of.

Grandmother Amina and I liked Salih immediately and as the conversation took a more familiar turn, with prompting from me, Grandmother persuaded the reserved man to tell us about his life in Marib.

Like many Bedouin, Salih had gone into the transport business, which had converted from camel caravans to trucks by the early 1970s. He had made a few runs north to Saudi Arabia with friends, where they bought Western goods from the markets over-flowing with the fruits of that country's oil wealth, returning to sell the merchandise in Yemen's *suqs* for a handsome profit. Salih eventually borrowed money from his family, combined it with the profits from his trips to Saudi Arabia, and purchased a brand new Mercedes truck to go into business on his own account.

He loved the work, steering by the stars around border posts, avoiding their prohibitive customs duties, using routes known only to the Bedouin. Many inexperienced drivers followed the wrong tracks far into the desert, usually to a Bedouin camp long since deserted. Many ran out of petrol while trying to find their way out and perished of thirst.

The work proved lucrative, but the danger extended beyond just getting lost. Brigands tarried around the markets in Saudi Arabia, spying out smugglers purchasing a load of goods. They watched carefully for when a truck was fully loaded and the driver likely to head back to Yemen, which usually occurred at night to avoid border patrols. The bandits would set up an ambush, seize the truck, then dump their victim's body into a nearby hollow, where it might be discovered weeks later by another smuggler. Otherwise drifting sand buried the corpse forever. Yet Salih didn't dwell on the hazards of his occupation. When death is written, no amount of precaution can prevent it.

It was nearly dark, and the call to sunset prayer rang out as Salih rose to take his leave from Grandmother Amina and me.

Promising to return, he pushed a shiny silver piece into my hand, then poured a pile of the coins into Grandmother Amina's hand. She protested vigorously, but Salih would have none of it and swore he would divorce his wife if she refused. Grandmother knew her brother would carry out the threat – such oaths are not made light-heartedly – and she reluctantly accepted the money.

Salih declined our invitation to remain with us for a few days. He had more business trips to make. But our joy over finding a long-lost relative more than offset the sorrow of seeing him go. I glued my nose to the window as my great-uncle climbed into his big Mercedes truck. The flowers and waterfall scenes and *Mash Allah*s painted on the vehicle's doors to ward off the evil eye caught my attention. Beaded strings and Koranic verses hung from the ceiling and rear-view mirror inside the cab.

The neighbourhood children gathered round to admire the truck. Few Sanaanis could have afforded it, and they wondered what its driver was doing at my house. I waved good-bye from the window, and Salih's perfect white teeth glittered in a smile as he drove away in a cloud of dust.

Uncle Salih did not come often to Sanaa, but he had opened the way for renewed ties between our branches of the family. His mother and sisters visited Grandmother Amina and me every few months, sipping *qishr* and gossiping the afternoon away.

The women of Marib fascinated me as much as Uncle Salih did. At home, they spent most of their days either shepherding their goats and sheep, or collecting water and firewood to prepare the meals.

'Aren't you afraid to be out in the desert all by yourselves?' I asked.

'We have our rifles,' the women explained. 'And we know how to use them just as well as the men do.'

They kept me spellbound, and I watched the Bedouin women intently as they unwound their headscarves without the slightest reservation, revealing the thick braids of black hair flowing down their backs and over their shoulders. But nothing could induce them to remove their veils, composed of a thin strip of gauze-like cloth tied behind the head and draping loosely over the nose and mouth to the chest. I chuckled at their modesty.

'Why don't you take your veils off?' I finally mustered up the courage to ask. 'There are no men here.'

Grandmother Amina shot a scolding glance, but I ignored it, anxiously awaiting the answer.

'We Abeeda consider it vulgar for a woman to display her mouth.'

I laughed.

When Grandmother served lunch, the women sopped up the bitter green fenugreek sauce with morsels of bread. Reaching under their veils, they shovelled the gooey balls into their mouths, followed by handfuls of honey-soaked pastry, lettuce, onions and rice. The visitors ate with all five fingers of their right hand, rather than just the thumb, index and middle fingers as is the etiquette in Sanaa, and I giggled again at their strange custom.

My cousin, Aisha, came over to the house during one of the Bedouin women's visits. The two of us squatted side by side, studying the guests' every move. One of the older women noticed us during a break in the conversation.

'You're very beautiful,' she complimented Aisha matter-of-factly. We both blushed.

'And you, too, are a cute girl,' she continued, turning now to me. 'There's a certain light in your eye. I can see you're going to make something of yourself.'

We snickered with embarrassment, but I would always remember the woman's prophesy.

One day Salih's mother and some other women from Marib, dressed in black from head to toe, presented a solemn sight before the courtyard door. Grandmother Amina and I sensed that they had come with terrible news. I would learn the details of what happened only 20 years later, while sitting in the

Café Deauville on Paris's Champs-Elysées with Muhammad Abu Lahum, members of whose own tribe were intimately involved in the story:

> Salih al-Salami prodded his Mercedes over steep sand dunes somewhere on the Yemeni-Saudi border early one morning, careful not to jostle the cargo on the truck's open bed. Crossing the border without a hitch, he accelerated across the pebble-strewn plains of the Jawf, less than two hours from Marib.
>
> Salih dipped into a shallow *wadi* bed and emerged on the opposite bank to find the unsettling sight of a dozen armed men crouching in the shade of a boulder. They sprung up at the sound of the approaching vehicle and waved for Salih to stop. Bandits abounded in this sparsely populated region, but that was no excuse to abandon someone who might be in genuine need of assistance. Who knew? The following week he might be the one stranded and in need of help.
>
> Salih grew suspicious when the men declined to meet his greeting of 'Peace be upon you' with the customary reply of 'And also upon you', a religious formality after which violence is strictly forbidden. Neglecting the formula leaves open the possibility that foul play is intended, and Salih's doubt increased when the group offered no explanation for being alone out in the Jawf wilderness, far from any villages. They said only that they had run out of water and were thirsty.
>
> Salih had no choice but to offer to convey the men to a nearby well where he sometimes filled his radiator. The grim-looking party climbed onto the bed of the truck, grasping the low side railing for support and searching for a place to put their feet among the bulky load.
>
> It happened that Salih wasn't hauling the usual freight of cigarettes and boxed consumer goods that day. He carried more profitable merchandise: rifles for delivery to supporters of al-Habeeli in Marib.

The al-Habeelis are a family of *Ashraf* and the former rulers of Bayhan, 30 miles southeast of Marib. In the aftermath of the British withdrawal from Aden in 1967, a radical pro-Soviet regime filled the political vacuum there. These Marxists rapidly expanded their control to the dozens of independent sultanates extending across southern Arabia, from near the Bab al-Mandeb strait in the west to Mahra,[3] 600 miles to the east. The country came to be known as South Yemen. What came to be referred to as North Yemen, on the other hand, occupied an area stretching from the Saudi Arabian border in the north to about 50 miles south of Taiz. The Red Sea hemmed in the country on the west, while the desert served the same role in the east.

Relations between North and South Yemen deteriorated rapidly following the British departure from Aden, and the two governments closed their mutual border in 1967. North Yemen, whose civil war showed signs of finally winding down, was just then beginning to open up to international markets and seek integration into the community of nations. South Yemen, however, set off in the opposite direction. It retreated from its role as home to one of the busiest seaports in the world in Aden, and isolated itself from all but its Soviet backers in Moscow. Its leaders professed their goal of establishing a Marxist state in South Yemen, the only one in the world with an official religion: Islam.

Despite numerous calls for unity by both countries in the 1970s and 1980s, North and South Yemen remained bitter rivals. Serving as proxies during the cold war for the United States and the Soviet Union respectively, each government supported insurgent groups, attempting to overthrow the other through low-intensity warfare and sabotage campaigns.

---

[3] Where the inhabitants speak a language believed to be a remnant of the ancient tongue spoken by the Shebans.

The Marxists in South Yemen drove the conservative al-Habeelis out of Bayhan and into exile in Saudi Arabia after taking power. The Saudis then used the al-Habeelis to foment unrest back home, to keep leaders in Aden focused on domestic problems rather than on ways of overthrowing the Gulf monarchies.

Salih al-Salami's trip through the Jawf that day was somehow mixed up in these Byzantine politics. As Salih released the clutch and pulled slowly away, one of the men riding on the back leaned over and shouted into the cabin.

'We've changed our minds,' he said. 'Take us to the well between here and Mahjil. Do you know it? You can leave us there.'

Salih knew the watering hole. It was situated many miles off to the northwest, considerably out of his way, and he had heard recently that the well was nearly dry. As he reflected, the ominous reality of the situation struck him like a kick from an angry camel: his passengers intended to kill him.

Salih nodded his head in feigned agreement to the man, then rapidly mulled over a depressingly limited number of options. Instinct took over, and he coolly floored the accelerator. The truck jerked forward in a sudden burst of power. Five or six of his would-be assassins lost their grip and fell off the truck. Next Salih swerved violently, whipping the steering wheel as quickly as he could from side to side, continuing to accelerate. More toppled off.

But three of the men managed to dive onto the truck bed and cling to the side with one hand. Salih meandered too violently for them to stand up, but one of them pulled himself laboriously up to the front where he could grasp the bar running horizontally behind the truck cabin. He raised himself to a crouch, swinging wildly to and fro. Salih watched in the rear-view mirror as the man raised a rifle to his hip with one hand. He swerved hard in a desperate effort to throw him off, but it was too late. The bullet pierced the rear window and struck Salih in the head, killing him instantly.

Someone found Uncle Salih lying face down in the sand a few days later, well preserved in the dry desert air. The identity of the killers could not be immediately determined, but the slaying had occurred within Jidaan territory, which placed responsibility in that tribe's hands no matter who actually committed the crime.

Such treachery demanded revenge by the Abeeda, unless the Jidaan found the killers and brought them to justice themselves. The irascible Abeeda would not likely accept the payment of *diya* in compensation for such a heinous offence. Only vengeance would preserve their honour.

But the Jidaan *shaykhs* tarried in uncovering the perpetrators, until the Abeeda suspected that the Jidaan themselves must be the culprits. While the Abeeda threatened to take matters into their own hands, the al-Salamis from far-off Heima got wind of the killing. They arrived on the scene demanding revenge for their fallen cousin, raising the stakes considerably.

As the eastern desert teetered on the brink of war, the *shaykhs* of Bani Hushaysh, the tribe wedged between Sanaa and the Jidaan to the northeast, intervened. The three antagonists accepted their mediation, handing over rifles to the Bani Hushaysh as guarantees of their goodwill. Following several months of investigation, the arbitrators finally pieced together the details of Salih's murder. Someone had informed the leaders in Aden of Salih's supply effort on behalf of their enemies, the al-Habeelis. The Marxists requested one of their contacts among the Jidaan to kill Salih and prevent the weapons from reaching their destination.

The Bani Hushaysh *shaykhs* identified the man who fired the shot that killed Salih, but he had died in an unrelated incident a few days afterwards. The Abeeda and Heima decided not to pursue the vendetta against the man's relatives (at least as of this writing, some three decades later).

The Jidaan are not to be tangled with lightly. All the desert trembled during the winter raiding season in dreaded expectation of these infamous marauders, particularly in years when the rains failed or when the black clouds of locusts devoured crops and left families destitute. A few extra livestock lifted from another tribe could spell the difference between life and death for the weak and vulnerable.

But of course the Jidaan's victims did not sit idly by and watch their livelihood driven off. They assembled pursuit parties and chased the raiders to one of the two or three watering holes at which they were forced to stop. The object was for the raiders to reach the wells far enough in advance of their pursuers to water their looted camels and be off again before their agitated owners caught up.

Mabkhut Naji Kaalan (whose last name means 'the two testicles') was one of the two Jidaan *shaykhs* who tried and failed to identify Great-Uncle Salih al-Salami's killer. In the first half of the twentieth century, this larger-than-life character led countless raids into the dunes of the Ramlat al-Sabatayn. Once he feigned death for half a day while the victorious tribesmen pursuing his band watered their recovered camels before setting off for home.

Muhammad Abu Lahum, related to Mabkhut (and me) through marriage, tells of one expedition in 1948:

Mabkhut and his 16 raiders hid their camels and moved forward on foot to attack a camp of Karab and Sayar tribes that roam the southern fringe of the Khala. But the enemy caught wind of them and cut them off from their camels. Unable to escape, Mabkhut came up with a plan, calling out to the enemy to send their best man forward for a one-on-one duel with him.

At sundown, Mabkhut and his opponent rose and came slowly forward, rifles in hand. Mabkhut fired first, and the bullet struck and killed the Karabi. The wily Mabkhut then slipped away under cover of darkness, managed to find one of his mounts and sped away for help.

When Mabkhut returned the following day with more Jidaanis, all but one of his comrades were dead. The lone survivor had been overrun in the end, but had managed to wrestle his assailant to the ground. Before plunging his *jambiya* into the man's heart, the Jidaani heard the man cry out: 'Spare me, and I will protect you.'

The Jidaani stopped. 'It is done,' he promised, and returned his *jambiya* to its sheath. And none of the Karab and Sayar could thereafter lay a hand on the Jidaani, as he was under the sworn protection of one of their own tribesmen.

Hardly had he arrived back home before Mabkhut came to see my father.[4] Father disapproved of Mabkhut's stirring up so much trouble in the desert, but revenge would have to be taken nonetheless. He agreed to accompany Mabkhut back to Karab and Sayar territory. 'But on one condition,' my father insisted. 'You must inflict no more losses upon them than you yourself suffered on the last raid.'

Two hundred Nihm tribesmen assembled a few days later in Mabkhut's village – a few clay houses on a rise above the Jawf plain. The villagers welcomed the warriors, led by my father, with song and dance and improvised poems in praise of the tribe's valour. Mabkhut and a handful of the surviving male villagers fired rifle shots over their visitors' heads and came forward to rub noses with the Nihmis in greeting.

Equipped with daggers and rifles, and with ammunition belts wrapped around shoulders and waists, the men listened to the Jidaan women's shouts of encouragement from atop their sleek riding camels. A young boy, still several years short of growing a beard and carrying a large drum, followed up the rear as the party set off to the east.

---

[4] Abdullah Abu Lahum, the *shaykh* of the Nihm tribe and great uncle to Mabkhut's wife.

On finding their foe several days later, my father and Mabkhut ascended the crest of a dune to survey the enemy. The Karab and Sayar, lined up before their camp, recited a rather uncomplimentary poem to which the Nihm and Jidaan responded with their own derisive verse.

On the other side of the dune, the impatient drummer boy suddenly began thrashing his drum as hard as he could. The staccato roll thundered through the air to the Karab and Sayar camp, whose men froze in terror, for no such instrument existed in their land.

Someone cried out that the Nihm and Jidaan had brought with them a powerful new gun with which to slaughter their enemies. At this, the Karab and Sayar broke ranks and fled before their attackers could even launch an assault.

Memories are long in the desert. When North and South Yemen unified in May 1990, the border that separated the Jidaan from the Karab and Sayar reopened for the first time in 23 years.

Fascinated by the desert, my husband visited the Ramlat al-Sabatayn in 1992. 'A flurry of Karab men and boys rushed from their tents to meet my three Yemeni companions and me,' Charles told me on his return. 'They levelled their Kalashnikov rifles at our Toyota Land Cruiser as we approached.

On seeing that we meant them no harm, the Bedouin invited us into one of their three tents and the 60-year-old *shaykh* ordered the slaughtering of four sheep in our honour. While we sipped tea and the women prepared the meal, one of the older men slid a cushion over for me to lean on.

'What are the names of your tribes in Europe?' he asked me.

With the ice broken, they all chimed in with their own questions: 'How long does it take to travel to America by car? How much salary do you earn? Why don't you have any children? Is it true that Westerners confine the elderly to special homes, away from their families?'

Later a Karab man presented me with an antique Czech-made rifle and asked if I knew how to fix it. Like many Yemenis, he believed Westerners have the answer to just about everything, and he seemed more confused than disappointed when I said I couldn't help him. I nearly ended up having to accept the rifle as a gift when I made the mistake of admiring it aloud.

Just before going to sleep, I asked the *shaykh* why the Karab had seemed so tense on our arrival earlier that evening.

'We thought you might have been the Jidaan,' he answered gravely. Everyone in the tent grew silent at the mention of their traditional enemy.

'We had some problems with them a few years ago,' he said. When he described the 'problems', I realized he was referring to Mabkhut's raid nearly 45 years earlier.

Scars

I applied myself diligently to my first year of studies and was rewarded with excellent reports, particularly in mathematics. Midway through the first year at the Liqiya School in Sanaa, I had the highest results in my class.

I set out eagerly for school every morning except the Friday Sabbath from Grandmother's house. The school sat in the big square in front of Qasr al-Silah fortress a little over a mile away, and the route took me across the *sayla* creek and skirted round the Fulayhi Mosque. Houses on three sides of the mosque made the tip of its whitewashed minaret only just visible from the street. A few women begged outside the mosque entrance, and sometimes I handed them the coins Grandmother gave me to buy sweets with.

I loved school. It was challenging, and it took my mind off my family problems. But a traumatic experience one day left an indelible mark on me.

The classroom windows looked north onto the broad square used as a makeshift market two or three mornings each week. Qasr al-Silah loomed off to the right, with the seven whitewashed cupolas from the magnificent Bakiliya Mosque just beyond it.

As my two dozen classmates and I struggled to concentrate on our lessons one morning, a crowd began pouring into the square. It wasn't even a market day, but the throng hummed with excited anticipation of some unknown spectacle. People soon filled the square completely, except for a wide circle left vacant beside the white domes of the *hamam*. Bodies pushed against the stone walls of the three-storey houses ringing the square, pressing like water threatening to burst a dam. Unable to talk above the din, the teacher finally laid down his piece of chalk and walked over to the window to see what was going on.

A series of explosions set off by South Yemeni-supported Marxist guerrillas had rocked Sanaa over the preceding weeks, causing numerous deaths and significant damage. The random blasts frightened and outraged Sanaanis, who demanded that something be done. The day before the crowd convened in the square beside my school, the authorities had arrested two men, charging them with sabotage. The Prime Minister decided that heads would roll this time, and he ordered the execution of the culprits in the hope that it would dissuade further attacks. Nobody realized, however, that the Liqiya School, with its six-year old pupils, offered a front-row seat on the square where the two men were to be put to death that morning.

With the crowd assembled and the hour upon them, the prisoners staggered into the square. A soldier on either side of each grasped the men's elbows. The prisoners had their arms bound behind their backs, and were clothed only in baggy trousers. The crowd made way as the guards tugged the miserable convicts toward the vacant spot.

Behind them trailed a government official wearing a flowing white *zena* gown who was holding a megaphone. The onlookers grew silent as the official addressed them. He called attention to the government's efforts to end the insecurity, and encouraged citizens to remain patient and vigilant in the face of the bombings. Then he read out the prisoners' crimes.

By now my classmates and I had joined our teacher at the window to watch. When the official ended his winded monologue, he lowered the megaphone and waved his hand to proceed. Two soldiers pushed the first prisoner to his knees and instructed him to lean forward. A hulk of a black man[1] then made his way

---

[1] Men of African descent, the sons of former slaves brought from Africa, were commonly employed as public executioners since they belong to no tribe and so remain excluded from blood debts.

through the excited throng, his powerful hands clinging to a massive steel sabre. He seemed taller to me than the giant minaret of the Salih al-Din Mosque just off the square, the crescent moon at its summit so high I could hardly see it.

The two soldiers stepped back from a prisoner as the executioner hovered over his victim. The crowd held its breath and the pupils in the classroom gasped in astonishment when he raised his sabre high into the air. I cupped my face with both hands, but spread my fingers just enough to make sure I could see.

The sword came down swift and hard. A sharp thud preceded a melancholic groan, and the prisoner convulsed and rolled onto the ground, the sweat on his back glittering in the morning sun. The other students and I groaned in unison with the man, and I felt the steel on my neck as clearly as if I were the victim. The soldiers rushed clumsily to return him to his kneeling position, his neck covered in blood but still intact. The embarrassed and shaken executioner raised the sabre again, hurriedly this time. Another thud and another moan, softer this time, long and whining.

The executioner nervously adjusted his sweat-soaked tunic, swivelled his head to loosen his neck muscles, and brought his sword down a third time. The prisoner's head finally dropped to the ground, rolling a short distance from its body.

The soldiers dragged the corpse to the edge of the crowd, placing the head alongside it, upright and gazing at the onlookers. The second set of soldiers then thrust the other prisoner forward, trembling.

The executioner wiped his blade clean with a cloth, slowly regaining his composure. Under the watchful eye of the crowd, the sword rose, more confidently this time, and split the air with a deadly whirr. The head hurtled through the air, a fountain of blood surging from the open neck on the ground.

The scene horrified me. I did not understand the official's words used to justify the execution to the crowd, and I could not comprehend that anyone would deserve such a fate. The victims seemed random to me, and I felt their pain. The memory haunted me each night when I slept for years to come.

I spoke to no one the rest of that day. That in itself was not unusual, but nor did I pay attention in class, which was unlike me. The scene in the square that morning would not leave my mind.

Instead of going home after school, I headed for Bab al-Yemen gate, towards which the soldiers had hauled off the headless bodies. The executions remained the exclusive topic of conversation in Suq al-Milh market as I pushed my way through the swarm of afternoon shoppers.

Emerging into the open square in front of Bab al-Yemen, book bag over my shoulder, I cautiously approached the gate. I slipped unnoticed amid the vendors selling knick-knacks from wheeled carts, and exited through the stone archway. The top of one of its enormous doors contained a gaping two-foot hole from a tank shell fired on the opening day of the 1962 revolution.

I scanned the surroundings for any sign of the bodies. Grandmother had said once that the heads of violent criminals, and Royalists during the civil war, were displayed on the wall outside Bab al-Yemen. But the civil war had ended a couple of years earlier, and violent criminals were few and far between. So I had never actually seen any heads for myself; only the occasional severed hand of a professional thief exhibited on a stone block beside the gate.

The row of iron spikes hammered like meat hooks into the bricks around Bab al-Yemen remained empty that day. Not even a trace of blood stained the surrounding wall. Relieved, I started for home when a reflection caught my eye from the refuse heap a little further along the wall. A shiny buckle betrayed a shoe, then a pair of shoes, lying behind the mound of old clothes, fruit peelings and other rubbish. Noticing that the shoes seemed to be attached to someone's feet, I crept closer until the headless cadaver of one of the prisoners came into view. Close by him lay the second, their heads nowhere in sight.

I froze, then finally mustered the courage to tiptoe over to the first body, as if trying not to awaken it. Squatting for a closer inspection, I couldn't look away despite my disgust, convinced the man would wake up any second. When he didn't, I stood up and kicked his leg lightly. The lifeless body quivered, then returned to its motionless calm.

Panic overtook me. Without a sound, I turned and sprinted under the portal of Bab al-Yemen, but after only a few steps my legs buckled, casting me to the ground and skinning my hands and knees on the hard dirt. A vendor tried to help me, but I pushed him away, picked myself up, and staggered on towards the *sayla*. Unable to control my legs, I stumbled several more times before finally reaching Grandmother's house.

Mother had come to visit Grandmother Amina that day, and the two of them had begun to wonder where I was. Then they heard the door slam shut downstairs, followed by a thud as something hit the earthen floor. Grandmother Amina lit a candle and followed Mother down the steps, where they found me sprawled unconscious on the ground. Mother carried me upstairs and laid me on a cushion in my room. She stroked my hair and recited verses from the Koran, while Grandmother brought water to splash on my face.

I awakened, breathless and sweating, eyes wide open with fear.

'What happened to you?' Grandmother Amina asked.

I remained silent, gazing blankly at the ceiling, and Grandmother fetched a glass of water and a bowl of soup. I sipped the water, but wouldn't touch any food. When Mother picked me up to wash me in the bathroom, my legs folded and I collapsed to the floor.

My condition remained unchanged for several days: uttering not a word, unable to walk or eat. The execution scene in the square ran non-stop before my eyes, and I could think of nothing else. Even if I could have spoken, I probably would not have told what had happened. Mother would have been angry that I had wandered over to Bab al-Yemen after school.

Nearing despair over my condition, Mother and Grandmother turned to a last resort. Grandmother occasionally consulted a *hajama* when she had a particularly nasty fever. The elderly woman cut a half-dozen small incisions in her patient's back, placing hollowed-out cow horns over them as suction cups to draw out the bad blood. But even the *hajama* admitted that what I had was too strong for her remedies. She told Grandmother Amina about another woman, a kind of sorceress skilled at countering spells, spirits, the evil eye and many physical ailments, one or more of which I obviously suffered from.

Mother wrapped me in a warm blanket and carried me into the street with Grandmother Amina. We wound down several alleyways until finally arriving before an ancient, nail-studded, wooden door. Grandmother knocked the shovel-shaped clapper sharply against a protruding iron slab. A rope tugged from one of the upper storeys unlatched the inner crossbar and we entered. Feeling our way across the dark antechamber, we trudged up the knee-high steps to the third floor, guided by the greeting, '*Haya, haya* – Welcome, welcome', from above.

Inside a dimly lit room, a hunchbacked woman stoked the glowing embers of a fire on the hearth. Her loose-fitting robe failed to conceal the plump body underneath as she turned to greet us with a wrinkled, toothless smile. Coming nearer, she pulled the blanket back to see my face better.

I jumped with fright at the sight of the old woman, then calmed enough to take in the shelf-lined walls crowded with glass vials of various liquids and powders. I stared suspiciously at the doctor, who peered back with a hideous grin that did little to reassure me.

'How do you feel?' the doctor inquired. I didn't reply, watching, studying.

Mother laid me on a thin mattress spread on the floor and explained what she knew about my condition. Kneeling beside me, the woman looked again into my eyes through the flickering firelight, then examined my hands and feet.

'How long has she been like this?' the woman asked.

'A week,' Mother replied.

The doctor nodded knowingly, rose and walked over to the fire. Taking a long iron rod from beside the hearth, she thrust an end into the flame.

'There is only one cure for what the girl has,' she asserted, twirling the iron in the coals. 'This is not a normal illness. Something has frightened her, and she must be frightened again in order to be rid of its hold over her.'

The doctor withdrew the rod from the fire a few minutes later and considered the glowing red tip contentedly. I watched carefully, until suddenly it dawned on me what was happening. Before I could resist, Mother and Grandmother Amina each gripped an arm to restrain me, and I looked on in horror as the woman came nearer.

The doctor pulled the blanket away and raised my flowery dress above my stomach. Helpless, my eyes closed as the broiling flat tip of the rod seared into the skin just above my belly button. After what seemed an eternity, the woman released the pressure to reveal a circular blister an inch and a half across.

I squirmed and shrieked with pain, the first sound from my mouth in many days. When finally calm enough for Mother and Grandmother to release me, I rose sluggishly from the mattress, shot a vicious scowl at the three women, and staggered out of the room and down the stairs. Mother pushed a handful of bills into the doctor's hand, invoked God's blessing on the woman, and hurried after me.

I pouted for several days afterwards, but was walking, talking and eating again normally.

Though not timid, I talked little as a girl. One of Grandmother's friends used to chide me when she visited. I liked to sit silently and listen to their gossip, bringing tea or biscuits when Grandmother Amina instructed me to. Occasionally the guest would remark somewhat maliciously to me: 'Can't you speak, young lady? It seems like you have no tongue.'

Remembering similar comments from teachers and classmates, I began to wonder if something was wrong with me, that maybe I didn't know how to speak properly.

I made few friends among my classmates, and rather than linger to play after school, I usually came straight home. I had very good reports, and occasionally someone would ask me to help them with schoolwork, which I didn't mind. But overall my classmates knew little about me, and tended to assign me to a separate category than themselves: neither inferior nor superior, just different. For one thing, I picked out all of my clothes myself. They had to fit perfectly and I was adamant that they be clean and ironed before wearing them to school. Few other children, or even their parents, worried about such matters.

On one occasion, parents were invited to school to watch a play put on by the children. When I came on stage, my hair brushed perfectly and my clothes spotless and pressed, mother noticed one of the parents in the audience point to me.

'That must be [Yemeni] President al-Hamdi's daughter,' they said.

Mother chuckled to herself.

But my reluctance to speak didn't fully explain my lack of friends. The house I lived in with Grandmother Amina was tiny and old, situated in a secluded corner of the walled town where the homes are not so majestic as in the eastern section. Even within our own Hurqan neighbourhood, the surrounding buildings dwarfed our home in both size and décor. The modest dwelling embarrassed me, and I made certain that none of my schoolmates discovered where I lived.

The house also frightened me. On the day Mother took us away from the Murzah house, Grandfather Hamud had pulled me aside.

'You're going to live in that old, decrepit house with your grandmother?' he taunted. 'But it's not safe there. You'll see. It'll all come down on your head one day.'

I didn't repeat the words to anyone, for it was still a thousand times more agreeable staying with Grandmother Amina than with the Murzahs. But I lived in fear every day, expecting Grandfather's prophecy to come true.

Even more discomfiting to me than the house, however, were the skeletons in the family closet. I felt ashamed of Father's illness (which I could not grasp at my age), that my grandfather had disowned me, and that Mother was married to someone who wasn't my father. The other children would make fun if they knew, or even worse, some might pity me, which was the last thing I wanted. I made certain that no one at school found out about any of it.

For some reason, the few friends I did manage to make tended to be from influential families active in politics, such as the al-Mutawakils and al-Arshis. The girls occasionally invited me to their homes to study after school. Their luxurious, spacious houses impressed me, with their chairs and tables to eat on, sit-down toilets, and servants who catered to their every wish.

I never invited these friends to my house, though. I would have died if they saw where I lived. And, worse, were they to come over they would inevitably ask questions about the family that I dreaded answering, such as where my father and mother were.

But my friends and their parents seemed just as happy with the arrangement. Being from prominent families, they were even more protective of their daughters than most, and didn't fancy them traipsing all over Sanaa with their friends. All the way through my primary school years, not one of my schoolmates learned of Father's illness or my family situation.

Mother soon bore a son to Shaykh Hameed al-Maamari, her second attempt at a husband. As the labour pains intensified, she walked to her mother's home, where Grandmother Amina once again performed the duties of midwife. Waiting outside on the roof, I listened anxiously to mother's agonizing groans. When it was over, Grandmother Amina called me into the room to watch her sever the umbilical cord of my new brother, Tariq.

The army transferred Shaykh Hameed from Sanaa not long afterwards, and I did not see him or Mother for many months.

They stayed for a while in Ibb, before moving to Dhamar, a collection of mud-brick buildings wedged between two volcanic craters 60 miles south of Sanaa.

It was in Dhamar, a pre-Islamic town and former refuge for *Imams* during tumultuous times, that Mother could no longer ignore her husband's drinking problem. Alcohol was officially banned in the country for Muslims (Jews could make wine, but neither sell nor consume it outside their own homes). Whisky and various other spirits nevertheless trickled into Yemen, smuggled on dhows across the Red Sea from Africa.

Mother discovered Hameed's fancy for alcohol soon after their marriage. Though quite gentle when sober, he sometimes beat Mother during drinking bouts, but she believed he would change with time. By then pregnant with another child, Mother infuriated Hameed by confronting him when he came home drunk one evening in Dhamar. Mother told me the story many years later, though the emotion had hardly faded even then:

> When I yelled at him, he stormed out of the house in such a fury that I wondered if he would ever come back. But half an hour later he returned, holding in front of him a stray dog that he had skinned. He nailed it to the living room wall by its hind leg like a goat in a butcher's shop.
>
> 'I'll do the same to you if you don't stop nagging me,' he warned.
>
> I was terrified. It was the first time Hameed had lost his temper with me, but I decided right then that I wouldn't wait around for a second time. I managed to get a message to my brother, Ali, in Sanaa. He came to Dhamar the next afternoon and took Jameela, Tariq and me home with him.
>
> Hameed came home from work that evening to an empty house. I guess he felt bad about what he had done, because a few days later he came to Sanaa and pleaded with Ali to convince me to return to him. I refused, and asked for a divorce instead.

Mother rented a tiny one-storey house beside the children's cemetery around the corner from Grandmother Amina's house, where she moved with Jameela and Tariq. I joined them, and my little brother Hamud came from his grandfather's from time to time to spend the night. Another addition to the family arrived a few weeks later when mother gave birth to a baby girl: Nejla.

I was delighted to have Mother back and a new sister, but the happiness would not last for long. I was around 10 years old when disaster struck one of our neighbours. The incident moved me intensely and foreshadowed a similar tragedy in my own life.

The Minfakhs' house looked onto the garden behind my Great-Aunt Hameeda's house, beside the children's cemetery. They were related by marriage to Hameeda's husband, Ali al-Aini, and one of the younger sisters of the Minfakh wife came frequently to the house to babysit. I would see her when I visited Hameeda and played in the courtyard.

I admired the 14-year-old Minfakh girl's beauty, her feminine mannerisms and the care she took in combing her long black hair to make it look just right. As she approached a marriageable age, she obsessed over finding a young man from an influential, preferably rich, family to marry and live happily ever after with.

The al-Ainis were also related by marriage to the Abu Lahum family of Nihm, forging another of those seemingly bizarre alliances not uncommon in Yemeni politics.[2] Some of the Abu Lahums occasionally telephoned the Minfakhs' house to ask how the family was getting along and the Minfakh wife's younger sister answered the phone one day while she was babysitting. Her soft, pleasant voice intrigued one of the Abu Lahum women, ever on the lookout for suitable wives for her sons. She asked later

---

[2] This one linked a family of conservative tribal *shaykhs* on the one hand, with the reform-minded al-Ainis, prominent Socialist Baath Party activists, on the other. Yet Yemeni politics are nothing if not complicated and alliances are forged according to relations and whose side your friends and enemies are on, more than on ideology.

who the young lady was and whether she was married. The Minfakh girl was so excited by the prospect that she talked non-stop about it for days, though her older sister and I teased her. An Abu Lahum would make an excellent catch for a husband.

The girl came over to babysit for her sister with growing frequency over the coming weeks, in the hope that the Abu Lahums might call while she was there. Then one afternoon she failed to turn up at the right time. The family grew worried and the men fanned out across Sanaa in search of her, but they came up with nothing by late that night, nor throughout the following day.

A week later the girl's parents received a phone call from Bayt al-Zogabi, the women's prison in Sanaa. Their daughter was being held there. The family was shocked that she was in Bayt al-Zogabi, where only women of disrepute were supposedly held. There had to be some kind of misunderstanding, they thought.

'Some soldiers brought her in,' the prison warden stated coldly when the family arrived to see the girl. 'Said they found her loitering around with some men.'

The news devastated the family. It was difficult, impossible, to imagine anything worse for a family, even death. The sons escorted their stunned mother back to the car while their father convinced the warden to release their daughter. When the guards finally brought her out, he saw her beautiful long hair had been shaved. The girl was a wreck and she said nothing until getting in the car. Then the words poured off her tongue in a torrent.

'I was walking along the street,' she stammered, 'when a car pulled up beside me and stopped. Two soldiers got out. They grabbed me and shoved me into the car.'

The girl paused, tears welling up in her eyes when she saw the dumbstruck expression on her mother's face.

'They raped me,' she screamed, sobbing uncontrollably.

At home the inevitable debate surfaced as to whether to believe the story or not. Had the girl provoked the soldiers? Or had she been minding her own business? At the end of the day it didn't really matter. She was no longer a virgin, no matter whose fault it was. No one would ever have her as a wife, and the accusation of loose morals levelled at their daughter would blacken the family name for generations to come.

The parents in the end took the view that their daughter had provoked the encounter with the soldiers. The family locked her in her bedroom, and for weeks she couldn't come out. Meals were shoved through when the door had been opened a crack.

Then, after several months of captivity, the girl began vomiting blood. A few days later she collapsed on the floor of her bedroom and died. Rumours spread but nobody ever knew for sure what had befallen her.

Deep down, I believed the girl had told the truth, however unlikely the story seemed. She had thought of little but landing a good husband from a respectable family. With promising interest shown by the Abu Lahums, it would have been unthinkable for her to jeopardize all her hopes by behaving in the way of which she had been accused.

The girl swayed her hips ever so slightly when she walked, and beautiful eyes highlighted by thick lashes beamed out from behind her veil. Some young soldiers anxious to prove themselves, or perhaps an influential officer, probably saw her strolling by, kidnapped her, raped her and then threw her in jail to cover their own guilt. Otherwise, if the girl had gone of her own volition, why would the soldiers have thrown her in jail and accused her?

The girl's death did not in itself shock me. I knew it was probably the most compassionate end for her. A woman whose honour has been so blatantly and completely stripped away wishes only to die. But the injustice of the incident distressed me. The fact that she had been found with strange men made the girl guilty in the eyes of much of society. She had no chance to defend herself, for no one would listen to her side of the story, and the men implicated with her received not even a reprimand. It was acceptable for them, while the girl had to go to prison for the same offence.[3]

The tragedy was an extreme case, but it frightened everyone who heard the story, sowing exaggerated visions of equally horrible events befalling their own families. Yet there is one remedy that goes a long way towards alleviating such worries: marriage.

[3] Nor could religion justify such a double standard. The Koran states that four eyewitnesses must back an accusation of adultery, and that both the man and the woman are to be punished if found guilty (Koran, 24:2–10). That was far from the case here.

CHAPTER ELEVEN

Revolt

Mother and Uncle Ali had a cousin named Muhammad al-Salami. Grandmother Amina breast-fed Muhammad when he was a child, and Mother and Uncle Ali therefore considered him their brother. He lived in Sanaa, working as a low-level public servant swallowed up within the vast bureaucracy of the Ministry of Health.

Muhammad had developed a taste for left-wing politics over the years. He considered himself a Socialist, which Yemenis associated with Communism and atheism. Muhammad didn't escape the epithet, even within his own family, and Grandmother Amina referred to him derisively as *al-kafir* – the pagan.

Muhammad had a close friend in the Socialist movement named Ahmed, who was in his late twenties and studied in Damascus, Syria. He wanted to marry a girl from home, and Muhammad approached Uncle Ali with the idea.

A graduate of officers' training school, Uncle Ali worked at the time in the Army's Criminal Division and, like Muhammad, had manoeuvred himself into a safe bureaucratic post. His ears provided fertile ground for Muhammad's proposition, all the more so after he found a love letter smothered in cheap cologne left for me by a boy I hardly knew outside our door one day.

'Khadija is growing up,' Muhammad told his cousin. 'It's best to find her a husband before something unfortunate happens.'

Muhammad didn't mention the Minfakh affair from several months before. He didn't have to, for the event lingered in everyone's mind. Uncle Ali wanted no such catastrophe to taint his own honour and jeopardize his career. He requested a couple of days to think it over, but he required little pestering before he went along with the advice. With my father ill and Grandfather Hamud's refusal to have anything to do with me, Uncle Ali was responsible for me. His decision would stand.

Mother couldn't believe her ears when Ali broke the news to her. She had already squashed one proposal for my hand. Soon after her divorce from Hameed al-Maamari, one of the *shaykh*'s close relatives suddenly began turning up at our house, ostensibly to visit Hameed's children, Tariq and Nejla. The man lived in Saudi Arabia, and he brought gifts for all the children when he came. But Mother noticed that he never failed to reserve the best present for me, though we were not even related. My favourite was a Polaroid Instamatic camera, which I had never seen before. The man confirmed Mother's suspicions when he asked her if she would consider marrying me to him. She promptly banished him from the house, never to return.

But Uncle Ali's plan constituted a much more formidable threat. Mother recalled her own terror when her father arranged her wedding at nearly the same age. She didn't wish the same experience on her 11-year old daughter.

Mother protested vigorously, but Uncle Ali always dangled the Minfakh example before her, which he considered sufficient justification for his action. It was the middle of the school year, and the best Mother could do was make Uncle Ali agree that the wedding would not take place before I completed my fifth-year exams that spring.

I was speechless when I returned home that afternoon to learn my fate. My success in school, where I continued to have the highest marks in class, had made me determined to continue studying all the way through high school, maybe even to university some day. The classroom was one of the few places where I felt comfortable. I didn't have a family to brag about, or material wealth, but other students came to me for help in school and that made me feel valued for something. The attention was satisfying, and offered the glimmer of hope that I could perhaps make something of myself through education. Marriage, however, would almost certainly put an end to any academic aspirations. And after witnessing the suffering two marriages had brought upon Mother, the idea of a husband hardly appealed to me.

Several years earlier, I had gone with Grandmother Amina and Aunt Hameeda to attend a collective wedding ceremony outside Sanaa one weekend. We arrived in the village just before nightfall and I covered my ears as intermittent rifle fire stoked the sky with tracer bullets for the festivities.

Inhabitants from the surrounding countryside crowded into a square amid the clutch of stone buildings. Powerful oil lamps illuminated the 25 grooms, who reclined stoically on wooden chairs along the exterior wall of the largest house, with necklaces of sweet-smelling basil and jasmine flowers draped over their necks and tucked into their colourful turbans. Each sported a ceremonial dagger in a silver-plated scabbard at his waist, held fast by a thick belt embroidered with gold and silver thread.

The women assembled in another square away from the furtive glances of the men. Colourfully decorated brides dripping with gold and silver ornaments moved like a conveyor belt in and out of a house requisitioned for the weddings, checking their dresses and make-up incessantly to ensure that all was perfect. A veiled woman belted out a melancholic tune while tapping a broad tin plate with a spoon for an instrument. A younger apprentice accompanied her with a small drum, and the two broke into a whiny but captivating duet on the refrains. The guests took turns dancing, resting every so often to pick morsels from the heaped pile of rice and goat meat on a tray nearby.

Towards midnight each husband conveyed his respective bride to his parents' house, where the couple would live out their lives, or until they collected sufficient funds to build their own home. The rest of the village continued with the gala for several more hours.

The following morning, I tagged along with the women to visit the homes of each of the 25 grooms. On entering the first house, I noticed before anything else a large white sheet spanning the wall beside the bedroom door, suspended from a nail at each corner. A dark red stain attesting to the virginity of the bride adorned the centre of the spread, with the groom's and the bride's mothers standing proudly beneath it. Every house we visited boasted the same trophy; some displaying tiny stains and others larger ones, but no sheet was without its proof of chastity.

When I asked what the vermilion streaks on the sheets were, Grandmother Amina said it was *sharaf* – honour – and I understood that the stains came from the blood of the brides. I curled my nose indignantly, dreading my own wedding day. Little did I suspect it would come so soon.

I burst into tears and tore from the house when Mother told me the news of my engagement. I ran until I reached a public garden on the far side of Old Sanaa where, exhausted, I plopped down under a fig tree, the tears etching deep canals down my dusty cheeks.

The scene left Uncle Ali unmoved. 'A woman's role in life is to marry and be a good wife,' he lectured Mother. 'She is meant for nothing else but the grave.'

He threatened to send me to live with my Grandfather Hamud if I didn't marry. 'And the first thing he'll do is marry her off,' he warned. Mother had no doubt about that.

There seemed no way out. Mother loved me immensely and, though she had never been to school herself, she had encouraged me to keep studying as long as I could. But she had hardly a confrontational drop of blood in her body. She could never muster the force needed to stand up to Uncle Ali, so she reluctantly conceded defeat.

Yemenis typically marry at an early age though, at 11 years old, I was still considerably younger than the norm. Parents usually search out a handful of potential mates for their son or daughter with a view towards enhancing family alliances and, in the countryside, avoiding the break-up of family lands through later inheritance. The parents always have their preferences, but should their child bitterly oppose their choice, two or three other suitors are usually available to fall back on. Happy marriages are not uncommon in Yemen, and couples frequently evolve from nervous beginnings to sharing a deep love and respect for one another.

Overbearing parents, however, sometimes line up only one husband or wife for their child and try to force through the union should any opposition arise. Uncle Ali chose this strategy. Even if he had presented me with other options for a husband, I was hardly old enough to be expected to choose.

It was an unfortunate situation. Uncle Ali felt little of the paternal love for me that would have prevented Father from marrying me at such an age. He could think of nothing but relinquishing his responsibility for me, and marriage was the easiest and safest route.

I spent hours begging Grandmother Amina to have the wedding called off, but she, too, had resigned herself to my fate. I next turned in desperation to Mother, but she only tried to console me with assurances that I was about to discover a new life by travelling and seeing the world. And she reminded me that my fiancé had agreed to allow me to continue my studies.

In an effort to appease Mother, Uncle Ali had told her that he had obliged my future husband not to have intercourse with me for three years, until I reached the age of 14. 'So you have nothing to worry about,' Mother told me, though she still felt obligated to try to introduce the subject of sex, albeit in a very indirect manner. The prospect terrified me when I remembered the bloodstained sheets hanging on the walls the morning after the 25 weddings a few years before.

Mother's soothing talk did little to reassure me. I had reached the conclusion that I could depend on no one but myself to find a solution to my predicament, but I could come up with no way out of it. The next six months were a nightmare for me. Studying proved next to impossible, and whenever I opened my books my mind would drift back to my wedding. The tears would flow down my face and onto my papers, smearing whatever I had written.

My marks steadily deteriorated as the end of the school year approached. Following the exams that spring, Uncle Ali and I boarded a plane for Jedda, the gateway to Mecca on Saudi Arabia's Red Sea coast. Several members of my fiancé's family lived in Jedda, part of the extensive Yemeni expatriate community in Saudi Arabia.[1]

Uncle Ali had signed the marriage contract with Ahmed in Sanaa before we had even left for Saudi Arabia. The two had agreed on payment of the *shart* (bride-price) to Uncle Ali and the *mahr* (dowry) to me, which Mother used to buy me gold jewellery. Ali presented me to Ahmed at the airport in Jedda, where Ahmed had come to visit his family during the summer break from university.

I hated Ahmed before even meeting him, for helping force me into a marriage I wanted no part of, for not realizing that I was a child and not meant to be with a man yet. When I finally met him, I despised him even more.

Ahmed drove Uncle Ali and me to his family's home in Jedda. He showed me to my bedroom and returned to the living room to chat with my uncle alone. Uncle Ali's earlier promises to Mother began to ring hollow when he came to my bedroom an hour or so after our arrival.

'Your husband will come back here in a few minutes,' Uncle Ali told me, 'and you are to do exactly as he tells you.'

I understood immediately what he meant.

---

[1] During the mid-1970s and 1980s, up to 40 per cent of North and South Yemen's male population worked abroad, mainly in Saudi Arabia and the other Arab oil kingdoms of the Persian Gulf. They found employment in various jobs from construction, which attracted the mountain tribesmen, to currency changers, which generated fortunes for the business-minded families of the Hadhramawt Valley in South Yemen.

'But you said he has to wait until I'm 14,' I protested.

'I don't care,' Uncle Ali replied.

I paused, mortified. The lump in my throat swelled so that I could barely breathe. I thought desperately for a way out.

'I won't do it,' I finally growled. 'You can't make me.'

Uncle Ali anticipated opposition, but the anger grew inside him anyway. He had already prepared it, rehearsed it.

'Don't you embarrass me,' he warned. 'You're talking about my honour. I won't go back home with my face blackened just because you're too stubborn to do what your husband tells you.'

'I won't do it,' I repeated, on the verge of tears.

'Maybe you're not a virgin after all,' Uncle Ali taunted. 'Why else wouldn't you do it?'

I broke into tears.

'All you want is the blood-stained sheet,' I accused. 'So you can show all your friends. Well, you won't get it from me.'

'You'd better not embarrass me in front of Ahmed,' Uncle Ali repeated.

I frowned and folded my arms in defiance. But Uncle Ali believed his message had got through, and he left the bedroom.

A few minutes later, I heard footsteps in the hallway again. The door opened and in came Ahmed. I glared at him with a hatred I had formerly reserved only for my Grandfather Hamud.

He came slowly towards the bed and sat down beside me. Placing his hand on my knee, he caressed it over my fluffy dress. My eyes widened in horror and a steely shiver ran through my body. With the other hand, Ahmed brushed the knee-length hair over my shoulder to uncover my face, still fixated on the floor. As he settled closer, his breathing became rapid.

I would not go down without a fight. Springing to my feet, I landed a kick to Ahmed's shin. Approaching again, he reached for my skirt and I backed away in haste, kicking and clawing. But I was tiny and he strong, and in my desperate struggle I lost my balance and fell on the bed. Ahmed pounced like a cat. Slipping his hand between my legs, he poked my vagina with his finger, then withdrew. The blood on his fingertip seemed to satisfy him, and he wiped it onto a white handkerchief he had in his pocket. He left the room with me screaming on the bed.

The next morning, Uncle Ali returned to the bedroom and yelled at me for resisting Ahmed. But it did not last long, for he was in fact very proud to return to Sanaa with the bloodstained handkerchief Ahmed had given him. He cared nothing for how it had been obtained, and was ignorant of the trauma it caused me.

'Now do as he tells you. Don't bring disgrace to our family,' were Uncle Ali's last words. He left a few minutes later for the airport to return to Sanaa. I found myself alone with a stranger in a foreign land, and nowhere to turn for solace.

Three or four days later, Ahmed and some friends drove with me to Taif, 80 miles east of Jedda. The mountain city's cool, refreshing air attracts many of Saudi Arabia's lowland inhabitants in the sultry summer months. On our way back to Jedda, we stopped in Mecca to pray before the Kaaba stone in the mosque there, towards which Muslims the world over face when performing their five daily prayers.

Despite Ahmed and his friends' efforts to cheer me up, I continued to sulk. The thought of being in Holy Mecca, which only a few months earlier would have thrilled me, now meant nothing.

I had been fairly religious up to then. I prayed at Grandmother Amina's side and attempted to keep the fast during the month of *Ramadhan*, despite Grandmother's insistence that I was too young to fast. She would give me a biscuit and send me behind the door to eat it, saying the angels wouldn't see me if I ate it there. Then she would pretend to sew my mouth shut when I had finished, so that no one would know I had broken the fast.

Since arriving in Jedda, however, my views on religion had suffered a serious blow. God must have abandoned me, I believed. In the months before leaving Yemen, I had always held a glimmer of hope that my wedding would be cancelled, or indefinitely delayed. But now the deed was done. God had allowed it to happen, and I was angry with him. So when Ahmed parked the car near the mosque in Mecca, I refused to get out, waiting inside while the others prayed.

Ahmed and I flew to Damascus a few days later, where he lived alone in a small house. I sat on the bed in my room one evening a few days after our arrival, thinking of Mother and school back home. The door creaked open and Ahmed entered, cautious, testing the water more carefully this time.

'I hope you're happy here,' he said soothingly from the doorway. I glued my eyes to the carpet, silent. Ahmed closed the door and approached the bed, sitting down beside me.

'You're very beautiful,' his voice crackled nervously. 'Though you don't have any breasts yet.'

Ahmed reached for my knee, but I foresaw the move and countered it. Landing a powerful blow to his knee with my foot, I darted into the bathroom before he could recover and locked myself in. Hysterical, I beat my head over and over against the tile wall around the bathtub. I wanted only to die.

A container of cleaning fluid in the corner caught my eye. I tore the cap off, lifted the jug to my mouth and felt the cool blue liquid flood into my stomach. The container slipped from my hands as my insides churned violently, paralysing me. Pain welled up inside like an oil strike ready to burst. My knees swayed and the liquid suddenly exploded from my mouth as I fell hard to the tile floor.

I had no idea how much time had elapsed when I regained consciousness. The sun had already risen and my body ached on the cold floor where I had collapsed. My head spun and my stomach groaned wrathfully, while the odour of vomit and chemicals filled the bathroom like thick steam. Picking myself up slowly, I was suddenly embarrassed at what I had tried to do, how weak it seemed to try to end my life.

I cleaned up the mess on the floor and did my best to leave no trace of what had happened. Then I pressed my ear to the bathroom door to listen for any sounds outside. Unlocking the door, I peaked outside to see if anyone was there before going to rest on the bed.

One of Ahmed's friends, a Yemeni student, moved in with his wife and infant daughter not long afterwards, to share the rent. A friendly couple, they tried to put me at ease in my new surroundings, but with little success. I remained terrified and bitter, and every day my heart hardened against Ahmed. He liked to show me off to his friends, but even they made fun of him for marrying someone as young as I. They hid their remarks from him, but I overheard them and felt humiliated.

As had happened to Mother as a young girl in Taiz, my hide-and-seek with Ahmed became a daily, life-or-death routine. But in Mother's case she had had her father to turn to, and in the end he helped her. I felt as though I had no one. The people I loved and believed loved me – Mother, Grandmother Amina, Uncle Ali – I felt they had all put me in this situation. I had begged them to help me, but no one would listen.

Ahmed's friends occasionally convinced me to come out of my room when Ahmed left the house. They took me to the enormous al-Hamadiya covered market and to other sites around Damascus. Ahmed occasionally accompanied us, but I always walked as far away from him as I could get.

No matter how hard they tried, they couldn't cheer me up. I kept my pain to myself, not mentioning a word to any of Ahmed's friends. 'If my closest family could not understand me and help me, what could I possibly expect from strangers?' I thought. So I spoke to no one unless spoken to, and answered as briefly as possible.

Ahmed finally had to admit defeat. After three weeks in Syria, he arranged for me to return to Yemen, where an outraged Uncle Ali met me at the airport. At home, I ran to Mother's outstretched arms, though I resented her at that moment for not being strong enough to stand up for me. I gave her the biggest hug of my life, tears streaming down both our faces. She hardly recognized me, so pale and skinny was I from not eating.

'She has disgraced us,' Uncle Ali started in immediately to Mother. 'What are people going to say?'

'I don't care what anybody says,' Mother answered.

'You'd better straighten her out,' he warned. 'So that she doesn't play any more games when she goes back to her husband.'

I unlaced my arms from around Mother and turned to Uncle Ali with a vicious stare as he started to leave.

'I'm not going back!' I screamed. 'You don't care about anything but the *shart*,' I said, referring to the fact that Uncle Ali would have to reimburse the bride-price paid by Ahmed if I didn't go back.

Uncle Ali slammed the door behind him. He would threaten Mother to disown me over the coming weeks, just as Grandfather Hamud had done. And he would finally do it when he saw I would never return to Ahmed.

My uncle's abandonment was painful because up to the time his cousin had put the marriage idea in his head, Ali had been one of the few male relatives to treat Mother and me with respect. He had helped Mother in her divorce from Father, and sheltered me from the wrath of Grandfather Hamud. I had even begun to convince myself that he could be the father I did not have, and had taken his name, Ali, as my middle name.

When he forced me to marry and, in my mind, oversaw my rape, the world crumbled before my eyes. It seemed he didn't love me after all, and my resistance only made me the bad one, the guilty one. I had learned early in my childhood that life is not fair, but this injustice terrified me, convinced me that life is a battle to be fought and won. There were no allies but my own will.

For several years afterwards, Mother prayed every day that God would burn her cousin Muhammad's heart as he had burned mine by giving Ali the idea to marry me off.

School had already started by the time I returned to Yemen, but I was in no state to go to classes straight away. The distressing ordeal consigned me to bed for a week. Mother stayed by my side offering valuable moral support, until she finally encouraged me to get out of bed and start living my life again. The load on both our shoulders was bigger than ever now, but we would find a way to get by.

Iman al-Arshi, from a family of *qadhis*,[2] was one of the few friends I had made at school the previous year. She worried when I failed to attend the first week of school. Someone told her they thought I lived in the Hurqan neighbourhood and she went there after school one day to ask around for the al-Salami house.

She found it, and when Mother showed the girl into my room, I felt shock and embarrassment that my friend had managed to track me down. I prayed that none of the mice that sometimes emerged in the night would choose to make an appearance just then. I had awoken once to find one of the rodents crawling up my trouser leg.

But Iman seemed to take no notice of our tiny house. Instead she was terrified at my skinny, pale appearance. She sat down on the floor beside where I lay and asked what had happened to me; why I hadn't returned to school. I calmly told her about the marriage, and by the end of the story Iman was weeping. I realized then that I hated to be pitied.

I returned to school the following week, as ready as I would ever be to face the world again. It horrified me that Iman had seen where I lived, that I had opened up to her about what had happened to me. What if she told others at school?

I concentrated more than ever on my studies, becoming increasingly distant from my classmates. I was different now, sharing little in common with them. I had no father, my grandfather had disowned me, and my uncle had attempted to tear me away from what little I had. I could rely on no one, trust nothing. At the same time, I noticed the other students surrounded by the love and attention of close-knit families.

---

[2] An educated, bureaucratic elite of judges whose members filled many important administrative posts both before and after the 1962 revolution. Imam Ahmed in particular often favoured *qadhis* over *Sayid* families in government positions in order to prevent the latter from challenging his authority. The title has come to be inherited by whole families in Yemen, whether they maintain the strict educational standards of *qadhis* or not.

I joined the fledgling Guides organization that autumn. For some reason I admired their military-style uniforms, and thought that through the Guides I might reach closer to the stature enjoyed by boys. I sometimes heard parents remind their daughters, 'But you're only a girl,' when they aspired to something not normally suitable for girls, a comment that I came to resent. I also hoped the afternoon Guide meetings would take my mind off my personal problems after school.

A few weeks after joining, my Guide section and a troop of Scouts attended a youth festival in Libya where Muammar al-Qadhafi came to meet us. One of the scouts showed great interest in me on the plane ride to Libya, and when we visited the Roman ruins in Leptus Magna outside Tripoli, I noticed him staring at me constantly. He was two or three years older than I, and quite handsome, like the photos of European movie stars in popular Arabic magazines. I learned through the other Guides that he lived in Hodayda. His mother was a Yemeni from Hajja, and his father was Syrian, which explained the boy's light hair and green eyes.

We were both too embarrassed to exchange even a single word directly. But on the flight back to Yemen he walked by my seat and dropped a small package discreetly into my lap. My heart beat quickly as I unwrapped the box to find a necklace and a bottle of perfume, along with a letter from the boy, whose name was Nabeel. We stared at each other from our seats the rest of the way home, still not daring to speak.

A few days later, back at school, the principal interrupted my class one day to say that one of my relatives wanted to see me. Surprised, I stepped out of the classroom to find a middle-aged woman standing in the hallway.

'Who are you?' I asked.

'I'm Nabeel's aunt,' the woman explained pleasantly. 'He's outside. If you could just come and say hello, it would mean so much to him.'

I was angry with Nabeel for having the nerve to send his aunt in to get me, despite the courtesy he had intended by it.

'I can't see him,' I snapped. 'I don't have time.'

'But he really wants to see you,' the woman pleaded on behalf of her nephew.

'I can't see him. Tell him I'm engaged to be married.'

I returned to the classroom, and after school I sneaked out of the back exit in case Nabeel was waiting for me at the front.

His attempt to see me was annoying, though the harshness of my reaction surprised even me. His efforts in no way aimed at offending, and should have flattered me, but I could not help remembering what had happened to me in Jedda. I felt anger towards all men, and could never imagine marrying again. When Nabeel showed that he was serious about forging a relationship with me, I cut him off abruptly.

On returning to Sanaa from Libya, Yemen's President Ibrahim al-Hamdi held a reception for the Guides and Scouts at the military Officers' Club. Decked out in my fatigue-like uniform, patiently waiting in line to receive my gift, I studied the President's clean-shaven baby face, tanned and innocent. He was 30 pounds overweight, with a thick crop of wavy black hair.

When my turn arrived, I furrowed my eyebrows, stared straight into the President's eyes, and marched down the red carpet with feet stomping and arms swinging high like a soldier on parade. I brought my heel down with a sharp clack in front of al-Hamdi, raising a stiff right hand to my temple in salute. Pride radiated from my face, and I looked as if I had just single-handedly liberated the country from an invader. Al-Hamdi smiled, almost laughed, in his khaki polyester trousers and matching button shirt. He handed me a small radio set, and I proffered another salute before marching away.

CHAPTER TWELVE

Career woman

During the trip to Libya, I met another Guide with whom I would maintain a much longer relationship than I did with Nabeel. Amat al-Aleem al-Suswa, a few years older than I, worked at the Yemeni radio station in Sanaa. We got along well, and Amat, who would later become Yemen's first female ambassador[1] and Minister of Human Rights in 2003, first planted the idea in my head of getting a job.

Amat grew up in Taiz, the bustling merchant town in the southern highlands. Taiz's inhabitants place a premium on education, and local customs impose looser restrictions on what roles women play in society compared to the northern highlands. Few Sanaani women would ever consider working outside the home, believing it reflects poorly on the family by implying that their husband or father lacks the resources to care for them. Taiz and the southern highlands in general take a different view on the subject and women are frequently seen occupied in work outside the home.

Despite being from Sanaa, I found myself freed from the domestic barriers that might have opposed my taking a job. My father and grandfather had disappeared from the picture, Uncle Ali had disowned me after my divorce, and Mother knew that now I would do what I wanted despite what anyone told me.

It was no secret to me that Mother struggled financially to care for my siblings and me. She occupied herself much of the day by

[1] To the Netherlands in 2000.

sewing to help make ends meet, and I resented being a burden on her. Realizing through Amat's example that a woman could work and support herself if she set her mind to it, that's exactly what I did.

Adolescence is an extremely brief period in Yemen. Children are handed enormous responsibility at an early age, in particular girls, as we saw with my Great-Aunt Hameeda running her household before she was 10. I had what turned out to be the added advantage of appearing older than my age. By my eleventh birthday, I could pass for 14 or 15, so when I requested a job on the afternoon shift at the telephone exchange, no questions were asked. But I tired of the low-paying desk job after a month or two and left to search for something else.

My friend Amat introduced me to Fatin, a young woman who worked at both the radio and television stations in Sanaa. She was a pioneer and a star for me – pretty, intelligent, outgoing – and I admired her greatly. Fatin told me the radio needed someone my age to read a part in the weekly drama programme broadcast by the station, and I gladly accepted.

Radio had fascinated me since a young age. I listened to both Yemeni and foreign short-wave stations at home when I got bored, marvelling at how it worked and appreciating it as a small opening to an unknown world beyond Yemen.

Grandmother Amina noted with concern my attachment to the radio as a youngster, fearing I would neglect my prayers to listen to it. She told me repeatedly the words she had heard someone say once: 'You will know the end of the world is near when men dress like women and metal talks.' The radio, as far as Grandmother Amina was concerned, was metal talking and so signalled the approach of Judgement Day. 'Yes, the end is near,' she would sigh, then urge me to be diligent in my prayers.

Yet her warnings failed to overcome the radio's allure. One day when I was seven years old, Baba (Papa) Abdul Rahman, a famous radio host for a children's programme, visited my school. He interviewed students to appear on his weekly show and I was among the seven chosen. It was the happiest day of my life up to then, and I ran home as fast as I could after school to tell Mother and Grandmother that I would be talking on the radio in a few days' time.

The show was pre-recorded and I woke before dawn on Friday, the morning the show would air, afraid of missing it. I nestled between Mother and Grandmother Amina in the sitting room to listen. The show so delighted me that I dreamed of one day working at the radio station.

As I went to work one day at my new job, a man sitting in the reception area called to me as I passed. 'Young lady, come here for moment. What is your name?'

Not used to having strange men hail me in public, I put him off. 'I'm late,' I said, and continued on my way to the meeting.

As I sat down with the other station employees, the man who had called to me entered. When the station director introduced him as the Minister of Information, I turned bright red.

'So' he smiled, turning to me. 'Now will you tell me your name?'

Fatin and I became friends and she took me with her one day to watch the recording of a show at the television station, lying atop the summit of a heavily guarded hill overlooking Sanaa from the north. The previous year, my school class toured the Sanaa television station, established in 1976 soon after public electricity was introduced to the capital. The lights and cameras of the studio were mesmerizing, and after watching Fatin's programme being filmed, I decided I wanted to be on television, too.

Fatin arranged a meeting with the television station director. On entering his office, the exceedingly polite man made several male visitors clear a seat for me, curious to discover my business. I sipped from the cup of tea placed on the wooden table in front of me, focusing my attention on the director.

'I want to work at the television station,' I asserted.

The director leaned back in his chair, running his fingers through his hair pensively. The television station was still in its infancy and it so happened that he had been trying to develop a children's programme for some time, he explained. But he had no children who could host the show, so the project had not progressed beyond the planning stages.

'But you're still in school, young lady?' the director asked.

I slid forward anxiously, sensing his interest. 'Of course. But I can work in the afternoons, after class.'

'And your parents won't mind?' he probed.

'Oh, no,' I reassured him. 'They won't mind at all.'

The director mulled over the possibilities while I looked on with the other men in the office, eagerly awaiting his response.

'Why don't you come back tomorrow afternoon?' he announced. 'We'll see what you can do.'

I glowed with joy.

I passed my first test at the television station, and continued working every afternoon. The director designed a sort of variety show in which I interviewed guests and oversaw various forms of entertainment for a live audience. I loved it.

Returning home from work one evening, I found Grandmother Amina and Mother watching a recorded version of my programme on television. Grandmother glanced up from the TV set when I entered the room and her mouth dropped open in amazement.

'But ... you're on the television,' she stuttered. 'How can you be here, too? May God forgive them for this magic.'

I laughed, recalling the stories of Sanaani women drawing their veils across their faces while watching television so as not to be seen by the male announcers, whom they believed were always staring at them rudely from the TV set. And later I had to convince Mother that the gratuitous violence in the action-packed B-films frequently shown on television was acted out and not real; that no one actually died, or even got hurt.

My burgeoning professional career inevitably sparked the ire of certain relatives from Mother's side of the family. Various aunts, uncles and cousins suddenly turned up on our doorstep to complain about me.

'Look at your daughter on television, showing her face for everybody in the world to see. She doesn't even wear the veil,' they lectured. 'And why does she use the name al-Salami? She's not an al-Salami. She's a Murzah. She brings shame on our name.'

Most girls in large towns begin veiling at around puberty, either at their mother and father's behest or on their own – it makes them feel grown-up, some say. But I neglected even to cover my hair with a scarf now. I had done so for a few weeks when one of my female colleagues at the radio station pressured me.

'You have long, beautiful hair,' the woman told me. 'The wives of many of the men working here don't have hair like yours. You'll attract them if you don't cover it.'

I felt guilty and wore a headscarf for a while. But by the time I moved to the television station, I no longer put it on.

None of the plaintiffs who came to our house ever asked Mother how she was getting on, or whether she or her children needed anything. They cared only for the perceived slight to the al-Salami honour. The ceaseless barrages upset her, and she would tearfully confide in me when I returned home, but I showed little sympathy. Mother's emotion even angered me.

'Why do you listen to them?' I demanded. 'You're letting them make our lives miserable.'

I locked myself in my bedroom and cried, wondering why the rest of the family insisted on giving Mother and me a hard time when we had never interfered in any of their lives. I slowly realized that their wrath stemmed from the fact that I, a young girl, proved capable of taking care not only of myself, but of my mother and sisters as well. I posed a challenge to the rest of the family, who ironically feared people might question their ability to provide for Mother and her children (which they neglected to do anyway).

Uncle Ali and his cousin, Muhammad al-Salami, could envision the evening conversations in households across the town: 'Why, isn't that the al-Salami girl? Ali's niece? What's she doing on television? Poor Ali and Muhammad. What grave misfortune has befallen them that they must send their women out to work?'

The highly visible job I had added to the family's rancour, but in the end they could do nothing to change the situation. The harder they tried to break Mother's and my spirits, the stronger and more confident I became that they would not succeed. My determination frightened them, but they could no longer crush it.

My salary didn't make us rich, yet it generated more income than Mother or Grandmother Amina could dream of making from sewing. I came home at the end of every pay day and distributed one stack of Yemeni riyal notes to Mother, and another to Grandmother. But the most satisfying aspect, not least of all to me, was that neither Uncle Ali nor anyone else could play the puppet master to us any longer.

In the summer of 1978, Algerian President Houari Boumedienne paid an official visit to Sanaa. The Yemenis held a singing and dancing exhibition for this prominent member of the Non-Aligned Movement, who had ruled the former French colony since 1965. I was one of two young girls chosen to welcome Boumedienne and Yemen's President Ahmed al-Ghashmi to the spectacle. We handed the two men a bouquet of roses and a *jambiya*, then introduced and commented on the dancers over a microphone.

Boumedienne left later that day, and the following afternoon the station director hurried into the television studio to see me. He had just received a phone call.

'The President wants to see you,' he announced dramatically. 'Immediately.'

I broke out in a cold sweat, oblivious to the murmurings of my colleagues, who wondered what was going on. 'What could the President want with *me?*' I pondered as I left the station.

Debilitating fear engulfed me as I remembered how former President al-Hamdi had died on 11 October 1977, just a few days after I had received the radio from him on returning from

Libya with the Guides. It was widely believed that his successor, al-Ghashmi, was behind the plot that had flown two French girls to Yemen a few days before and killed them. Next al-Hamdi was murdered and the girls' bodies placed alongside his at his house in order to disgrace the former ruler in death.

My thoughts ricocheted from one horrid scenario to another. 'Is he going to try the same trick again? Or maybe someone else wants to give him a taste of his own medicine,' I considered. 'But why me?'

The station director ordered a car to chauffeur me to the President's office, located a couple of miles outside the walled town. I contemplated my options as the vehicle sped through the deserted streets of Sanaa at an hour when most Yemenis were at home eating lunch.

We pulled into the short driveway of al-Ghashmi's modest, two-storey stone house, from where he sometimes worked, and my heart shifted into overdrive. A handful of lethargic guards picked themselves up from the shaded ground beside the house to see who had arrived, their cheeks swollen with *qat* leaves.[2]

Their nonchalance surprised me, as did the tiny size of the President's house. I studied the scene and an idea suddenly came to me. If something, anything, strange happened in the house,

---

[2] Afternoon *qat* chewing sessions are an institution in Yemen. The tender young leaves of the *qat* tree, a mild stimulant, are chewed to produce a caffeine-like effect after several hours of chewing. People meet every day after lunch to chew *qat* together, the men in their quarters and the women in theirs. By the sunset call to prayer, the floor is littered with the branches of *qat* trees, meticulously plucked of their edible leaves.

The habit's most serious consequence is the strain it places on the meager salaries of Yemeni households, some of which devote over half their income to acquiring good quality leaves. But whatever the effects on health and pocket, *qat* cultivation is an effective redistributor of wealth from Yemen's cities to its rural areas. Farmers today cannot hope to make money from grain production, with the massive influx of heavily subsidized wheat and flour dumped on Yemen as aid by American and European governments. Yet, thanks to *qat*, Yemen has to a large extent managed to avoid the deserted countryside and mass migration to sprawling, poverty-stricken urban areas common in so many poor countries.

I would excuse myself to the bathroom and hopefully find a window through which to slip out and escape.

I felt slightly reassured now that I had a plan, and a short man with a twinkle in his innocent eyes and a ready laugh met me outside the front door. Ali al-Shater, a presidential adviser, sometimes organized youth theatres in Sanaa. I recognized him from one I had acted in, which eased my mind further.

Noticing my apprehension, Ali asked me about school and work at the television. Leading the way inside, he left me alone in a reception area that would have been the living room in a normal house. It smelled pleasantly of expensive incense burning on charcoal. He returned a few minutes later trailed by the other young girl who had greeted al-Ghashmi and the Algerian President with me the previous day. She smiled and sat down beside me.

'At least she's still alive,' I thought. 'That's a good sign. But then again, maybe he wants to kill us at the same time.'

After sitting quietly for a few nerve-racking minutes, the sudden opening of a door startled the two of us. Al-Ghashmi entered the room. Every time I had seen the President on television (and in person a couple of days before), he had worn military fatigues and an intense, preoccupied expression on his face, with dark brows creased over distant eyes. But today he was dressed in a long white *zena* and glided about coolly, portraying a more benevolent image.

The moment of truth had come. However, rather than a dagger, as I half expected, al-Ghashmi thrust forward his open hand. I shook it awkwardly, trying to hide my relief.

'Congratulations,' the President boomed as his mouth wedged open into a broad smile. 'You represented your country well yesterday.'

I had never seen al-Ghashmi smile before. The warmth astounded me, revealing a human side to his character that many people had said did not exist. The President handed me a tiny leather-bound box. I opened it in front of him and the brilliant reflection from a Rolex watch blinded me momentarily, ignited by the cheap chandelier overhead. The brand name meant nothing to me at the time, though I could see it must have cost a lot. Then al-Ghashmi handed me a stack of bills wrapped with a thin strip of white paper. '5,000 riyals' was printed on the paper – about US$1,200 – a significant amount of money at the time, and unheard of for a 12-year-old.[3]

Relieved that I had not found it expedient to excuse myself to the bathroom and flee the house, I thanked the President and followed Ali al-Shater out to my waiting car. Back at the television station, my colleagues waited impatiently for a report on what transpired. I told them about the watch, and though I neglected to mention the wad of bills, my colleagues knew that no one met the President without asking for a house or at least a large sum of money to help with some concocted family tragedy.

The next day at work, rumour had it that I asked for and received 20,000, maybe 25,000 riyals from al-Ghashmi. I just smiled, because I knew they would listen to their own gossip before they believed me.

The money I received thrilled me, though the amount came to considerably less than what my colleagues made it out to be. I pondered long and hard over what to do with it. No one in Yemen deposited money in the bank, of which only a handful existed anyway. Banking, like television, was still a new phenomenon, and the idea of giving a stranger your money to safeguard takes time to catch on, even if the bank is willing to pay for the privilege.

Most women take any large sum of cash they receive, such as a wedding dowry or inheritance, and buy silver and gold jewellery, coral or pearls. These are all simple to conceal at home, gratifying to show off on special occasions, and convenient to carry away

---

[3] Even al-Ghashmi's enemies recognized his prodigal generosity, reflective of his background from a family of *shaykhs* of the Hamdan tribe nearby Sanaa. The al-Ghashmis had managed to supplant the earlier *shaykhs* of Hamdan when the latter lost favour by supporting the Royalists after the 1962 revolution.

in the event of misfortune, such as divorce. The rest they hide under a mattress or use to purchase a goat or a few chickens to supplement their income with milk or eggs.

Abdullah Zayn headed the television and radio stations in Yemen when I worked there. His wife, Nadia, was born to an Algerian mother and a Yemeni father. I had come to know the couple well since beginning to work at the television, and Nadia and I adored each other. Abdullah travelled frequently, and in his absence Nadia sometimes asked Mother to let me stay with her for a few days. Nadia prepared me before going to the television station, applying my make-up, showing me new styles for my hair, braiding it and roping it like a serpent around my head, all of which pleased me no end.

Nadia grew up in Algeria, a country heavily influenced by French culture during its 114 years of colonial rule. She was very different from other women in Yemen, and I found her enormously intriguing. She could speak French, didn't wear a veil and loved to travel.

Abdullah met Nadia when he went to Algeria on an academic scholarship. They married and Nadia accompanied Abdullah to France to continue their studies. I loved to hear stories of when the couple lived in Paris. Descriptions of the Sorbonne, the Eiffel Tower, *Notre Dame* Cathedral and how the Europeans dressed and acted captivated my attention. Some of the stories were simply inconceivable, such as how Nadia used to sit in a street café on the Boulevard St Michel, *alone*, waiting for her husband to finish class. I found that extremely provocative. No woman would ever sit by herself in a café in Sanaa, but Nadia explained that things were different outside Yemen.

Abdullah and Nadia had saved their money and wanted to build a new house in Sanaa. They nearly had enough to begin construction and, to help, Nadia decided to sell an intricately worked gold belt her mother had given her on her wedding day. I used 4,000 riyals of the money al-Ghashmi gave me to buy the belt from Nadia, who was sad to see it go but pleased it would remain with someone close to her.

Ever since a brief border war between North and South Yemen in 1972, talks concerning the unification of the two countries had plodded slowly forward. Much remained to be done, as the conservative, Western-leaning government in Sanaa remained diametrically opposed to the radical Marxist regime in Aden, and vice-versa.

An emissary from South Yemeni President Salim Rubaya Ali arrived at the Presidential Office in Sanaa on 24 June 1978, less than a week after I met al-Ghashmi. The talks between the two leaders aimed at pushing ahead the unification. Ali al-Shater, who had welcomed me a few days earlier, met the envoy at the airport and drove him to al-Ghashmi's office. As editor-in-chief of the weekly newspaper *26 September*, Ali had been a close friend and confidant to both President al-Ghashmi and his predecessor, Ibrahim al-Hamdi.

'I showed the envoy into the reception room,' Ali remembers, 'and couldn't help but notice that he seemed extremely nervous. I asked him, 'How's the weather in Aden? Must be hot this time of year,' trying to strike up a conversation. For some reason he seemed really confused by my question.

'It's exactly 90 degrees,' he answered matter-of-factly.[4]

'I assumed he was joking,' Ali continued. 'But when I turned to look at him and saw the blank expression on his face, without the slightest hint of humour, I couldn't believe it. I was wondering if he hadn't had a nervous breakdown. 'It's just like them in Aden to send a guy like this,' I thought.'

> I bent down to take the briefcase from him – just to be nice – and he jerked it away from me. But I was polite and insisted. I guess he felt confident I wasn't going to open it, and he finally handed it to me. It was a beautiful briefcase, brand new, and when he wasn't looking, I tossed it up in the air,

---

[4] Aden in the summertime is one of the hottest places on earth, nestled in and around a volcanic crater on the humid Indian Ocean. But Yemen uses the Celsius temperature scale, and 90° Celsius is nearly 200° Fahrenheit, impossible even for Aden.

studied it in the light, spun it around to get a good look at the quality of the leather. It was like playing Russian roulette, only I didn't know it at the time. I looked at the guy and smiled and told him, 'I'd like to have a case like this one.' I had hoped he might promise to send me one when he got back to Aden. But he didn't say anything; just stood there wiping the sweat from his forehead. I left him in the reception room and went to inform the President of his arrival.

'He has a briefcase with him,' I told al-Ghashmi. 'Should I open it before he comes in?'

'That won't be necessary,' the President said. 'Just show him in.'

I went back to the reception room and led the envoy down the hallway to the President's office. Two soldiers stopped us before we entered and studied the man carefully.

'This isn't the one who usually comes,' one of the soldiers said. 'We should search him.'

I was embarrassed in front of the envoy and said angrily, 'What do you mean, search him? Do you want to insult our guest?'

We walked past the soldiers and I showed the man into the President's office, closing the door to leave them alone.

I was heading back down the hallway to talk to the guards when suddenly I remembered that the President had mentioned something about having an official photograph taken of the meeting. I stopped, debating whether to go back and ask al-Ghashmi if he still wanted a photographer before they became too engrossed in their conversation, but before I could decide, there was an explosion.

Everyone thought it was an attack from outside, and the guards grabbed their rifles and prepared to defend the President. Then we realized the explosion had come from inside the President's office. The soldiers were horrified and they all ran out of the building and disappeared.

A few days later, as investigators pieced together what had happened, the guards at the Presidential Office that day turned up and accused me of being involved in the assassination plot.

'We wanted to search the envoy,' one of them told the investigators. 'But Ali wouldn't let us.'

'I had no idea what was going to happen,' I pleaded. But the guards didn't believe me and the investigators weren't sure.

I was certain they would interrogate me further. But then Ali Abdullah Salih[5] turned up. Fortunately he defended me, pointing out to the investigators that no one had been closer to al-Ghashmi than me.

'He wouldn't have killed the President,' Ali Abdullah said. 'Al-Ghashmi trusted no one more than Ali. The only house the President would eat in besides his own was Ali al-Shater's house. He feared being poisoned by anyone else.'

I was relieved.

'Besides,' Ali Abdullah continued. 'If he were going to assassinate the President, why would he do it in such an elaborate way? He could have just shot him.'

I of course found it in my best interest to vehemently back up these arguments, and the guards finally dropped their accusations.

It turned out that after Ali al-Shater had showed him into the President's office, the envoy laid his briefcase on the desk, flipped the two latches and opened it. A bomb inside the briefcase sent the room up in a cloud of fire and smoke, killing al-Ghashmi and the emissary.

Salim Rubaya Ali in Aden followed the North Yemeni President to his death a few hours later, executed in an internal power struggle brought to the fore by al-Ghashmi's assassination.

[5] The military commander of Taiz Province who would soon become president.

Abdul Fatah Ismail, a hard-line Marxist exile from North Yemen, became South Yemen's new strongman.

It seemed that the South Yemeni emissary was almost certainly unaware of the contents of his briefcase. But had the guards searched him, they would have discovered a pistol strapped to his thigh, which probably explained the man's uneasiness with Ali al-Shater.

South Yemeni President Salim Rubaya Ali had personally handed a briefcase to the envoy before sending him off that morning. But at the airport, Salim Rubaya's political rival, Abdul Fatah Ismail, relieved the man of that case and exchanged it for another one. One of Salim Rubaya's men noticed the manoeuvre and later informed the South Yemeni leader of the switch. He immediately attempted to reach al-Ghashmi on the telephone to warn him, but it was too late.

A Soviet warship docked at Hodayda's port weighed anchor and steamed away within minutes of the deadly explosion in Sanaa – a thin shred of evidence, but one that led many Yemenis to speculate that Moscow had masterminded the scheme.

Immediately following al-Ghashmi's death, a four-man interim Presidential Council took over executive authority in the country. My school friend, Iman al-Arshi, came to school the following day in a state of shock. Her father, former Finance Minister Abdul Karim al-Arshi, had been named to head the Council, becoming North Yemen's de facto ruler. With two presidents assassinated in eight months, the whole al-Arshi family feared for Abdul Karim's safety. I remember Iman's relief when the Presidential Council named Ali Abdullah Salih as Yemen's new President three weeks later.

CHAPTER THIRTEEN

Blossoming

I awoke one morning when I was about 13 years old to find my trousers soaked in blood. The sight terrified me, and I was certain that some fatal illness afflicted me.

I recalled the time I was just a little girl playing in the lane outside Grandmother Amina's house. Rolling around in my baggy white trousers, mud had splashed onto my crotch. When grandmother came outside and noticed the dark stain, she thought it was blood and that I had prematurely ruptured my hymen. She ran back inside to get the iron rod she used for measuring her sewing fabric and began beating me with it.

'Now you've done it!' she shouted hysterically. 'You're never going to find a husband!'

The rod was painful and I ran screaming into the house, ignorant of the reason for my punishment or its connection with a future husband. She used to warn me not to jump around too much or be too rough when I played, so as to preserve 'the thing that belongs to someone else'. That was her way of referring to the vagina, since it would one day represent the honour of whomever I married. But I had no clue what she was talking about. I came to consider my vagina as the source for all my misery and pain, and wished more than anything not to have it any longer. Only years later, on witnessing the stained sheets with Grandmother Amina and Aunt Hameeda at the 25 weddings, did I understand why Grandmother had acted the way she did.

But by now my *sharaf* had already been proved in Jedda. There wasn't supposed to be any more blood, and the fact that there was terrified me. Desperately thinking of some way to make it stop before Mother found out and worried to death, I tiptoed into the living room and felt along the shelf for the bottle of pills Mother took for bleeding. I prised off the cap and swallowed several tablets. The blood ceased after three or four days, but returned the following month. The pills obviously didn't help, so I stopped taking them.

It was around this time that Grandmother Amina began placing two small Chinese teacups over my chest when she visited us. Then she prayed that God would not let my breasts grow to be bigger than the cups, for Grandmother thought big breasts were a curse for a woman.

That suited me just fine. I was so embarrassed when my breasts began to grow that I let out the seams along the sides of my shirts so they wouldn't be so tight and show my chest.

I started secondary school that autumn. The Queen Arwa Girls High School was nearly a mile from my house, just beyond the construction site of Sanaa's first luxury hotel. A new student joined my class that year, and one afternoon she handed me a folded note, slipping away before I could read it. There was a charming poem inside, its pleasant verse expressing the girl's belief that I had a kind heart, and her wish that the two of us could be friends. The prose concluded: 'I see a profound sadness in your eyes.'

The girl's intuition startled me and I struck up a conversation with her the next day. Her wish came true and we became friends. Her name was Siham Makawi, and I soon perceived that the pain Siham recognized in me reflected her own scars.

The Makawis came from South Yemen. Siham's father, Abdul Qawi Makawi, had played an influential role in the Front for the Liberation of Occupied South Yemen (FLOSY), a political party sympathetic to the charismatic Egyptian President Gamal Abdul Nasser. FLOSY opposed the British occupation of Aden, and jockeyed for power, often violently, with the more radical activists of the National Liberation Front (NLF) in the countdown to the British withdrawal in 1967. The NLF quickly overran FLOSY, declaring South Yemen a Marxist state and driving its foes into exile, mostly to Sanaa.

The NLF leadership could be a vindictive lot. They hated Abdul Qawi Makawi with a vengeance, considering anyone more moderate than they to be British agents and imperialists. Makawi's involvement in opposition activities against the Aden regime further provoked their wrath. Following threats to his life, Makawi moved from Sanaa to Cairo, Egypt, where he believed his family would be safer.

But Makawi didn't like the thought of his children being completely severed from their roots, so he sent some of them to Sanaa when they were older to attend school there. That was how Siham came to be in my class at Queen Arwa Girls High School. Siham's older sister, who had remained in Sanaa when the rest of the family moved to Cairo, was the school principal.

I liked Siham, but once again found myself reluctant to allow the friendship to develop far for fear she would learn too much about my family. I never invited her to my house, but I did go a few times to Siham's, who lived with her older sister.

My new friend frequently probed me about why I looked so sad. I resisted at first, but as we grew closer, Siham chipped away the armour ever so slightly. I eventually described my nearly fatal marriage, but could delve no further into the past without breaking into tears.

Then one day Siham opened up about her own past, and I learned the inspiration behind the girl's poems. Siham's father had continued to be a thorn in the side of the Aden regime. The NLF leaders considered ways of sending him a clear message, and finally decided to dispatch a team of assassins to Cairo. As Siham's three brothers left their flat together one evening, they were gunned down in the hallway in front of their door. All three of the boys died. The killers escaped, but the Makawis had no doubt as to who had ordered the operation.

Sanaa in the 1970s was not the most cosmopolitan of towns. Foreigners were few and far between, comprised for the most part of military advisers from the United States and the Soviet Union, living side by side. North Yemen's leaders attempted to steer a balanced political course between the two superpower rivals.

While I played in the street one day as a little girl, I noticed an extraordinarily long shadow pass over me. Startled, I glanced up to see a blue-eyed, blond-haired man with skin white as flour, his face hairless and smooth as a frying pan. 'It must have been a Russian,' Grandmother Amina informed me later. I decided then and there that I would like to marry one of these handsome, exotic Russians one day. Tall and fair-skinned, with subdued mannerisms, they seemed the very antithesis of the boisterous, ebullient Sanaanis.

I had also glimpsed foreigners on another occasion. Grandmother Amina and Aunt Hameeda took me once when I was a little girl to pay a visit to a relative who worked in the port of Hodayda. While promenading along the beachfront (my first trip to the sea), we crossed paths with a handful of European women, probably the wives of contractors working on the port expansion project there.

The foreigners intrigued us, and we wanted to learn more about them and how they lived. So one day we visited the group of small houses where most of the foreigners lived. We chose a house seemingly at random, gathered in a semicircle around the door, and knocked loudly. A woman opened the door and gasped, startled by the two veiled women and the little girl standing before her.

'We want a drink of water,' Grandmother grunted, but the woman didn't understand Arabic. Grandmother repeated the request, louder this time; still to no avail. Then Aunt Hameeda raised her cupped hand to her lips and tilted her head back.

A smile broadened on the European woman's face. She pointed her index finger in the air (as a sign for us to wait, I realized later), but the gesture meant nothing to us. When she disappeared from the door, leaving it slightly ajar, Grandmother and Aunt

Hameeda stepped into the house, pulling me with them. They wanted to see what a European's house looked like on the inside.

When the woman returned with a tray and three glasses of water, she discovered us in her living room gazing in wonder at the paintings and antiques on the walls, turning in circles to take everything in. The woman couldn't have been more accommodating – perhaps it wasn't the first such visit. Yemenis are extremely inquisitive by nature and do not shrink away from taking the initiative to satisfy their curiosity. The woman invited us to sit down while we drank our water. She listened, uncomprehending, to Grandmother Amina and Aunt Hameeda's chatter about the wonders to be found in the dwelling, then waved goodbye when we departed a few minutes later.

I also heard fascinating stories about foreigners from Azeeza Abu Lahum, whom I called 'Mother Azeeza' as a sign of respect. Azeeza, the daughter of the Nihm *shaykh* Abdullah Abu Lahum, was married to Muhsin al-Aini, the brother of my Aunt Hameeda's husband. Muhsin al-Aini became Yemen's Prime Minister in November 1967, a post he would occupy three more times at various intervals. Beginning in 1978, he served for two years as Yemen's ambassador to the United Nations, four years as ambassador to Germany, then crossed the Atlantic again, where he stayed as ambassador to the USA from 1984 until December 1997.

Azeeza, who accompanied her husband abroad, is a highly intelligent, strong-willed and courageous person, said to be one of the first women in Sanaa to drive a car. She took full advantage of her many years in America and Europe to study the people and the English language.

When Azeeza and Muhsin returned to Yemen for a holiday each year, Mother and Grandmother took me with them to visit. Azeeza loved to talk about America and I hung intently on every word. Many of the stories seemed outlandish to me, such as the description of how men and women sometimes danced together under flashing lights at night clubs.

On a few occasions, Azeeza brought a European friend with her to visit Aunt Hameeda and I heard them conversing in English. Awestruck, I wished more than anything that I might grow up to be like Azeeza, and she encouraged me to get a good education.

Just before turning 14, I decided I wanted to learn a foreign language, too. After a couple of years at the television station, I had moved from hosting children's programmes to anchoring the news, spending an increasing number of hours at the station each day. But I wanted desperately to learn another language.

One of my colleagues spoke English and he told me of language classes in Cambridge, England, offered by the British Embassy in Sanaa. Though I gave part of my salary to Mother and Grandmother, there was still enough left over each month for me to put aside for just such an occasion. I used these funds to pay for the tuition and prepared to leave for the one-month study programme the following summer.

As soon as school finished, I headed for England. During a two-day stopover in Cairo, I stayed with my friend from the Guides, Amat al-Aleem al-Suswa, then studying in Egypt. The second evening, I went to visit my classmate, Siham Makawi, who had already returned to Cairo for the summer break. Policemen and security guards patrolled outside the apartment building and on the Makawis' floor, provided by the Egyptian Government after the murder of Siham's brothers.

When Siham left the living room for a few moments, I planted myself in front of their aquarium. I had never seen anything like it before, with goldfish swimming back and forth. Growing up in Sanaa, far from the sea, I hardly knew what a fish looked like. A small stream used to wind through Sanaa, but it had dried up a few years before my birth, and today Yemen is devoid of perennial rivers.

England proved to be irresistibly exciting, in particular London. The lights, the buildings, the traffic, the strangely dressed people: it was another world for me, full of unimaginable novelties that even Azeeza and Nadia Zayn had not prepared me for.

I lodged with a cheery widow named Mrs Clark. The tiny grey-haired woman ran a private boarding-house not far from Cambridge University. I was the only one of her boarders to help her clear the table after the meals she served us, and she seemed to take a special liking for me as a result. She loved to take me around to her neighbours and show them my long hair. I couldn't understand what she said very well, but we got along nonetheless.

Cambridge was a beautiful city, and I loved its flower gardens and neat houses. Walking through the peaceful, well-kept parks on my way to classes reminded me of the heaven Grandmother Amina had described to me so often. And being from such a dry, dusty country, the clouds and rain in England didn't bother me in the least. I couldn't understand why everyone complained about the weather so much.

I didn't learn a great deal of English in England. Cambridge was delightful, but its history meant little to a young teenager, particularly one from a biblical land like Yemen. Only the modern aspects of the country interested me, and lively London proved far more attractive than a traditional university city. I attended few of my classes after the first week, instead taking the train into the capital almost every weekend. When I didn't feel like returning to Cambridge, a Yemeni woman I met in London let me stay with her. Her husband was a well-known Yemeni businessman who took her to London each summer on holiday.

I noticed many girls riding bicycles through the parks and on the streets in England, and it struck me that no stigma seemed to be attached to it. I had never ridden a bicycle before, though I had wanted one ever since a young girl in Sanaa had caused a scandal by riding around the town on one a few years before. Bicycles were considered to be for boys, and I never dreamed at the time that I might be lucky enough to have one myself some day.

Having mastered the use of escalators during my first week in England, I felt confident I could learn to ride a bike. I bought one and pushed it from the shop straight to Hyde Park where I felt most secure, surrounded by flowers and trees, ponds and birds, with no one to bother me. Just as I began to get the hang of it, a large dog arrived on the scene to give chase. I was resting on a hilltop when the playful canine came bounding towards me. Terrified, I pedalled away, picking up speed on the incline. Weaving and wobbling, halfway down the slope I lost control and ended up sprawled on the ground with a gaping hole in my trouser leg and a bloody knee. But I returned the following day, undeterred, and was soon riding all over the park. I could not have experienced any greater feeling of achievement.

I went back to Yemen at the end of the summer. My knowledge of English showed little evidence of the weeks in England, but the experience had transformed me into a new person, intent on seeing more of the world.

My father, Muhammad Murzah, had never recovered from the psychological problems he suffered in 1968. But for a receding hairline and a few more wrinkles, he had changed little during the years since his return from the battlefield that fateful day when I was not yet two years old.

After much urging from neighbours and friends, his father began petitioning government offices and ministries in Sanaa to pay for Father's treatment abroad. His efforts bore fruit, and Grandfather Hamud accompanied his son to Cairo sometime in the early 1980s.

Father's condition had improved remarkably when they returned to Sanaa a few weeks later. For the first time in over a decade, he could speak intelligibly and was conscious of what went on around him. He inquired immediately about Mother and me, but the Murzahs told him only that Mother had divorced him and remarried, growing old and withered over the intervening years.

He eventually learned that Mother had divorced her second husband, and Muhammad made it known that he wanted her to return to him. He pestered until his father finally acquiesced. Grandfather Hamud visited Mother's brother, Uncle Ali, to ask if

Mother would be willing to take Father back. Uncle Ali agreed to talk the matter over with his sister.

The Egyptian doctors had placed Father on a daily regimen of tranquillizers, and the progress he had made encouraged Mother. Uncle Ali informed Grandfather Hamud that his sister would accept to remarry Muhammad, but only on the condition that Hamud buy them a house to live in, separate from the Murzahs. After much stammering, he finally consented.

Grandfather Hamud returned a week or two later with the property deed for the house he claimed to have bought for his son and daughter-in-law. Uncle Ali checked and discovered the document to be a forgery. Hamud then grudgingly purchased a typical four-storey home on Aqeel Street near Bab al-Shaub, the main northern entrance to Old Sanaa. The house satisfied Mother. Though it lay around the corner from the open square where handicapped donkeys are stabled to live out their years in idle luxury, it was also close to the Suq al-Zumur vegetable market, convenient for shopping.

Mother once again married Father, who seemed as if he had snapped out of a long coma since returning from Cairo. He recognized Sanaa with the joy of an immigrant returning home after many years abroad, and he could roam anywhere through the convoluted maze of its old streets and know just where he was at any moment.

But Father had no recollection of anything that had occurred since the civil war. Though he remembered and spoke often of me, he experienced difficulty in comprehending just who I was when I came to sit with him. He couldn't believe that the daughter he remembered as a toddler had turned into a young woman. When he saw my younger sister, Nejla (born to Shaykh Hameed), he called her Khadija, since Nejla was only a year or two older than I had been the last time father had really known me. And Nejla bore a striking resemblance to me.

Father learned with distress of the abuse Grandfather Hamud had inflicted upon us since Father's illness. The house they now resided in on Aqeel Street represented the only wealth Grandfather

Hamud ever restored to the couple from the inheritance Muhammad's grandfather and mother, Khayriya, had so earnestly intended for him. Hamud and his second wife, Sadiya, now controlled everything else, and after so many years, they were not prepared to return any more.

Following weeks of painful reflection, Father finally decided he could do little to remedy the situation.

'I forgive my father,' he confided to Mother one day as tears welled up in his eyes. 'It is for God to dispense justice. Not me.' But his father's cruelty had a more profound impact on him than even Father wished to admit.

After a few months, Father grew careless in taking his medications, and steadily reverted to his former incoherent mental state. This time, Mother sold her jewellery in order to pay for her husband to return to Cairo for further treatment.

Once back home, Father still refused to take his medication regularly, and his condition deteriorated. He lamented that life seemed so meaningless: 'Why are we born at all if we're only going to die later?' he would ask rhetorically. As he sank deeper into his own world, further from his wife and children with each passing day, he spent his time calculating in his head and on his fingers, mumbling numbers that represented the inheritance he reckoned his father had deprived him of. After determining how much his mother's land in Sanhan would have fetched, adding various other valuables and subtracting the price of their current home, Father would peer blankly before him.

'Give it back, you devil!' he cried every few hours. 'Give me back my money!'

Father repeated this ritual day after day, year after year, sitting cross-legged on a cushion in a corner of his little room, illuminated by a bare light bulb. Mother fed and cleaned and watched over him diligently until he passed quietly away over a decade later, in 1995.

As Grandfather Hamud lay on his deathbed a year or two after Mother and Father remarried, he called Mother to his side.

'I hope you can forgive me,' Hamud whispered with pleading eyes, choked with emotion. Mother closed her eyes and nodded gravely.

'I have forgiven you,' she whispered back.

When Grandfather Hamud finally died a few days later, one of Sadiya's sons opened the carved wooden chest his father had always kept locked. Hamud never took the key from around his neck and everyone in the house had always been extremely curious to know exactly what he kept inside. His son found a will and other documents in the chest, which he refused to show my brother Hamud when he asked. Mother believes he did not want our side of the family to discover the extent of Grandfather Hamud's assets and ask for the inheritance due to my father.

My half-brother, Tariq, had been born to my mother and Shaykh Hameed just two weeks before Uncle Salih al-Salami died in the Jawf. Tariq had moved around with his parents, to Ibb and Dhamar, and then back to Sanaa with Mother after she divorced Hameed. As he grew older, he spent most of the time in his father's native village of al-Sharara in Jahran.

In December 1982, a violent earthquake rocked Jahran and the surrounding areas. Several thousand people lost their lives and hundreds of thousands saw their homes reduced to rubble. Mother feared for her son when word of the devastation reached Sanaa. She couldn't telephone, for al-Sharara has no electricity even today, so she decided to travel to the village to see if nine year-old Tariq was all right.

Mother took a minivan south from the capital, crossing the Yislah Pass to the Jahran plain an hour and a half away. The tremor had badly shaken Tariq's village. She found most of the 100 or so inhabitants sheltering in makeshift shacks of zinc slabs thrown up beside their homes, which threatened to collapse in the periodic aftershocks.

Mother rejoiced at finding her son unhurt, but the news was not all merry. Hameed al-Maamari had been involved in a long-standing contention with a neighbour over a plot of farmland beside the village. Yemenis often avoid officially registering land purchases to avoid paying property taxes and, as a result, sometimes several 'private' deeds to the same plot of land circulate simultaneously, causing serious disputes.

Nearly a month earlier, long before the earthquake, Hameed had gone to the man's house to discuss the problem. As the two conversed, Hameed let his temper get the better of him. He slapped his adversary on the cheek, one of the worst insults a tribesman can suffer, and stormed out of the house under the victim's startled gaze.

Later that afternoon, Hameed emerged onto the roof of his house, the highest in al-Sharara. As he signalled to his brother working in the garden below to come in for lunch, the man he had gravely offended a few hours earlier happened to notice Hameed on the rooftop. He plucked the loaded rifle from beside his front door, eased the stock to his shoulder, and fired through an open slit in the house at a range of 75 yards.

As the shot echoed through the valley, the sniper could hardly believe what he had done. Revenge was sweet, but the consequences, which he only now began to consider, could be much less appealing. He collected his wits and came up with a plan even before the ringing in his ears had subsided. Throwing on his sandals, the man sprinted out the door and headed for Hameed's house. Just before reaching it, he slowed his pace, took a deep breath and pounded sharply on the door.

'Oh, Hameed, Shaykh Hameeeeed!' he shouted.

Hameed's sister opened the door.

'Where's Hameed?' the man asked, trying his best to smile calmly. But the effort seemed conspicuously awkward. 'I want to invite him to lunch at my house, so we can discuss our problem.'

Even had no rifle been fired, the man's unusually amicable behaviour would have alerted Hameed's sister that something was up.

'Who fired that shot?' she asked, sweeping the village with her eyes for any clues.

While his aunt answered the door, Tariq ascended the interior ladder and surfaced through the open trapdoor to get his father. On the roof, the boy discovered Hameed lying on his stomach in a spreading pool of blood. He kneeled and shook him.

'He's dead!' Tariq shouted from the rooftop. 'Someone has killed Father!'

Shaykh Hameed's sister knew immediately what had happened.

'You did it!' she growled, pointing her finger at the man outside the door. 'You killed him!'

The murderer turned and fled.

A week later, the police summoned the al-Maamaris to the police station. They had found Hameed's killer hiding in Dhamar, 15 miles away. The man was exhausted and dishevelled, but the near certainty of death had swept the fear from his heart.

'What do you want done with him?' one of the soldiers asked Shaykh Hameed's brother, Ahmed.

Hameed's widow (he had remarried after my mother divorced him) positioned herself for a better look at the killer. She would not leave the house between sunset and sunrise for four months and ten days after her husband's death, the traditional mourning period. When completed, Hameed's younger brother would take her as his own wife.[1] She glared menacingly at the man, but his fate rested with Ahmed.

Hameed's brother might have accepted the *diya* from the killer's family and spared his life had he believed that would be the end of it. But the blatant manner in which he had killed Hameed meant that many in the al-Maamari family would never consider the payment of blood money sufficient compensation for the death. Some of Hameed's uncles, cousins and in a couple of years even Tariq, would be likely to have schemed to kill the man themselves, or a member of his close family if he chose

[1] It is suggested that this custom dates back to Semitic tribes in biblical times, who considered that no fertile woman should be left unwed and prevented from conceiving for any length of time.

to flee, and that would lead to further reprisals. The man's execution would constitute the least violent course in the long run.

'Kill him!' Ahmed barked.

The policemen dragged their doomed prisoner away and shot him later that day.

Since returning from England I had made up my mind not only to pursue my studies to university level, a radical enough proposition, but I intended to do so overseas, this time in America. My classmates laughed when they heard the idea. They said I was crazy: 'Sanaani girls don't go abroad by themselves to study!' I suspected the girls made fun behind my back, so thereafter I devised my plan in silence.

I applied for a scholarship with the United States Agency for International Development (AID), a section of the State Department. Through its offices in Sanaa, the organization offered scholarships for a handful of Yemenis to study at one of several universities in the United States. The tuition fees were too expensive for me on my own, and I waited impatiently for several weeks until the AID finally informed me that it had chosen me for one of the scholarships.

Mother, though sad and worried to see her daughter leave, could not have been prouder. She had herself never studied as a child. She had no access to a girls' school, even had her parents been inclined to allow her to study. Her own mother liked to say that 'girls who learn to read only end up writing love letters to their boyfriends'. But Mother realized later in life that Grandmother Amina had been mistaken.

Grandmother, too, came to see otherwise. Her sister, Hameeda, had begun taking classes in Sanaa for illiterate people who wanted to learn to read and write later in life. Mother accompanied her a couple of times, but had too much work at home to continue. When Grandmother Amina saw that my studies had not ruined me, and that they would even allow me to travel abroad, she decided to attend the classes.

Grandmother Amina was very excited and would walk to class with her grammar books balanced on her head. Considering herself to be more modern now that she studied, she asked her son, Uncle Ali, to buy her a long coat like the young girls in Sanaa wore.

The only opposition to my going abroad to study came from my Uncle Ali. He made his disapproval clear by complaining to Mother, but I was independent of his authority now and he could not stop me easily. At 16 years old, I left for Washington, DC, in the summer of 1983 to study English intensively at Georgetown University.

America disappointed me at first. I had seen many television shows on the country, about its great wealth, the luxurious lifestyle of its citizens and its unfathomable technological advances. I half expected to be whisked away from Dulles Airport to my hotel on an automated conveyor belt straight out of a Jetsons cartoon. Visions of sparkling streets of gold and buildings whose tops disappeared into the stratosphere filled my head. The expectations, of course, had been exaggerated, and America turned out to be not unlike what I had witnessed in England the previous year. But my new life nevertheless took some getting used to.

Apart from the brief weeks in England, I had known no real peace in my life. The shadow of war and domestic violence, my marriage and divorce, separation from Mother, and the feeling I somehow bore responsibility for it all hovered above me like a vulture over a feeble lamb.

But in America the burden of my past, of trying to keep it all hidden, miraculously lifted from my weary shoulders. No one in Washington knew who the al-Salamis or the Murzahs were, or the size of my house in Sanaa. Few Americans had even heard of Yemen. They often thought I was trying to say 'German' when they asked where I came from. For the first time in my life, I lived in the present, and stopped dwelling on a painful past that until then had pervaded my every thought.

My adviser at the AID office in Washington assigned me to study at the University of Michigan in the autumn. When my classes at Georgetown finished later that summer, I packed my suitcase and flew to Ann Arbor.

A large Yemeni community resides in Michigan, many of whom originate from one of two villages in the Ibb region. They made their way to the Detroit area in the 1960s and 1970s to work in the car factories there, and an army of relatives had joined them over the years.

I befriended a few of the Yemeni families in Ann Arbor, mostly students studying for their master's degree in education under a scholarship agreement between Sanaa University and the University of Michigan. They often lived in the same building, and in the residence where one of my girlfriends lived, a particularly devout Yemeni student used to wake up every morning around 5.00 a.m. for the sunrise prayer. He called loudly down the hallway for anyone else who wanted to join him. A flood of complaints, from both Yemenis and non-Yemenis, eventually forced him to pray alone.

When this same student glimpsed the American girls sunbathing on the University of Michigan campus for the first time, he paced slowly across the lawn, staring critically. '*Astaghfurallah! Astaghfurallah* – God forgive,' he pronounced, gawking in wonder at the bare bodies.

He eventually took the big step of accepting shorts as a legitimate clothing item for men (but never for women). He displayed his approval by turning up on campus one warm afternoon dressed in a pair of the knee-length boxer-like undershorts worn by Yemeni men under their *zena* gowns. The other Yemenis, and quite a few Americans, laughed hysterically at him.

Before classes began that fall, one of my Yemeni girlfriends needed to renew her passport at the Yemeni Consulate in Detroit, an hour's drive away. I agreed to accompany her, but later regretted it.

One of the Yemeni officials seemed an exceedingly friendly man, striking up a conversation when we entered his office. With our business complete, my friend and I rose to leave. After shaking hands, the official innocently asked for our telephone numbers, 'In case I need to get in touch with you,' he said.

The next evening, the official rang my dormitory room to invite me for dinner. I said I was too busy with my studies just then, but he insisted vehemently, making his romantic intentions clear. Angry and insulted, I told him not to call me again.

But the official felt equally offended by the rejection. Or perhaps he thought he must prepare his defence in case word got out of his solicitation. When he telephoned again the next day, I assumed he wanted to apologize for what between Yemenis constituted a serious insult. I was wrong.

'I've been informed that you've been smoking marijuana and drinking alcohol,' he stated coldly. 'You're giving Yemen a bad image.'

Before I could ask what he was talking about, he continued, 'I swear I'll have you sent back to Yemen for this.'

Stupefied that he thought he could scare me into giving in to him, I could hardly control my rage. I slammed the receiver down and the tears flowed for the first time since leaving Yemen. The official called back several times that night, but I didn't answer. I fell asleep praying that God would punish him. Revenge came only a week later when the man slipped in the bathroom, drunk, and broke his leg. It was he, and not me, that got shipped back to Yemen – for good.

Despite his departure, staying in Michigan through the winter did not appeal to me. My friends warned me of the snow and bitter cold, and I asked my AID adviser if I might study at a university in more temperate Washington, DC, instead. The adviser consented, and I returned to the capital late that summer to enrol at Mount Vernon College, a women's college in northwest Washington.

My three and a half years there could not have been more idyllic. The tiny college, with fewer than 200 students and a 24-acre rural campus, proved much more cosy than the overwhelming University of Michigan, with its student body of over 30,000. Like a curious infant, I soaked up what the college and the nation's capital had to offer, cramming my timetable with tennis classes, modern dance, aerobics and swimming, in addition to the more basic academic curriculum.

My English improved rapidly in America, but the first year of classes demanded my total concentration in order to follow the professors' lectures. I was surprised to learn that maths and science courses for first-year students started at levels Yemenis had to take in secondary school. I breezed through my algebra course, and many of my classmates came to me for tutoring.

College friends introduced me to life off campus. One Saturday night, a group of girls in my dormitory convinced me to come dancing with them at a night club. I loved it, but weekdays were reserved for studying, and first- and second-year students had to be on campus by 10.30 p.m. on weeknights, significantly curtailing the dancing excursions.

Mount Vernon College proved a perfect environment for me to adjust to life outside Yemen. The all-girls college enforced what most Americans would consider very stringent restrictions on a college student's social life, such as having to sign in all visitors to campus, and say goodnight to boyfriends by dark. But I still experienced more liberty than I had ever imagined possible, given the implicit social restrictions of life in Sanaa.

During my first few months in Washington, a college friend taught me to drive, and I quickly determined to get my own car. But not just any car would do. I browsed at the various car dealers around the town until finally finding what I wanted: a Fiat Spider convertible. The effects of consumer society had rubbed off quickly on me, or maybe it was that desire for independence engrained in every Yemeni bubbling to the surface again, symbolized in America by owning your own car.

The Fiat was expensive, but I had long since developed a knack for getting what I wanted. When I was 10 or 11, Mother decided we should apply for a telephone, a new and rare luxury in Yemen at the time. I went by myself to the phone company to request the installation of a line and a telephone in our house. When the company finally informed us several months later that the telephone was ready, Mother didn't have enough money to pay for it.

Rather than pass up the precious opportunity, I ran to my Aunt Hameeda's house to ask her husband, Ali al-Aini, if they wanted the phone instead. Though the insinuation was that it would belong to Hameeda and Ali, what I really intended was for the couple to use it only until Mother came up with the money to pay them for it. But I forgot to mention this in the excitement, and Ali gladly accepted the offer. He handed me the money, and I returned a few minutes later to give him the telephone.

Ali was then director of the electricity company and the brother of Muhsin al-Aini, who had been Yemen's Prime Minister up to the previous year. Ali unintentionally intimidated many people in the neighbourhood, especially the children, because of his family's prestige and influence; but not me. When I started work at the television station a few months later, one of the first things I did after getting paid was return to Ali al-Aini, cash in hand, to ask for 'my' telephone back.

The Fiat I set my heart on cost US$11,000. I had saved US$4,000 from my salary at the television station, but had no idea how to come up with the remainder. Then I talked to my banker at Riggs Bank in Washington, and he of course offered to loan me the money, provided I could find someone to guarantee the payments.

I thought long and hard. My college scholarship included a spending allowance that would just allow me to meet the monthly payments, but I still had to come up with someone to guarantee the loan.

Then an idea struck me. A couple of days later, a girlfriend and I visited the Yemeni Embassy in the Watergate Building in

Washington. I told the receptionist that we wanted to see the ambassador, and a few minutes later a secretary showed us in to his office.

Yahya al-Mutawakil was a slim, soft-spoken gentleman with short-cropped black hair and a thin moustache. He was a military man, the former aide-de-camp to Prime Minister al-Amri during the 70-day siege of Sanaa in 1968, though I knew nothing of that then. I had never met the ambassador, and neither of us suspected at the time that we would become such close friends. It would be largely through Yahya's encouragement and example over the coming years that I would continue to forge my own way in life, when at times the struggle seemed lost.

CHAPTER FOURTEEN

Unlikely rebel

The secluded town of 100 or so ancient stone houses where Yahya al-Mutawakil was born in the spring of 1942 is situated in some of Yemen's most rugged mountain terrain, 35 miles northwest of Sanaa as the crow flies. During both Ottoman occupations, Yemen's *Imams* frequently retired to the 8,000-foot summit on which Shahara village lies, using it as a base from which to organize the struggle against the invaders. Shahara is populated for the most part by *Sayid* families that have furnished their fair share of Yemen's rulers over the centuries. A harried *Imam* could expect a sympathetic welcome from Shahara's inhabitants.

Yahya was born into a prominent *Sayid* family. Like many *Sayids*, he traces his ancestry back to the Prophet Muhammad on an extensive family tree elegantly laid out on a poster-size scroll.

'The first *Imam* from my family was al-Qasim al-Mansur in the late 1500s,' Yahya explains proudly, with the air of an historian, when asked about his family. 'He and his sons expelled the Turks from Yemen and took the name *al-Mutawakil ala Allah*.'[1]

Yet being a *Sayid* provided Yahya with few privileges as a young boy – except the ability to daydream that he might some day follow in al-Qasim's footsteps to become *Imam*. And even that remote possibility entailed significant drawbacks, for governing Yemen has always been a complicated task fraught with danger.

---

[1] He who places his trust in God.

Yahya told Charles and me stories of his youth during his many trips to France. He was delighted someone took an interest in such banal details as his childhood, and Charles prodded him for more whenever an opportunity arose. My husband's curiosity makes many Yemenis suspicious, but not Yahya. Whether told at dinner or on a drive to visit a chateau outside Paris, Charles would return home and type the stories on his computer so that he wouldn't forget them.

'I lived on the upper floor of our family's two-storey stone house,' Yahya told us one day, 'which we shared with several uncles and their families. All of us were crowded tightly together, though we thought nothing of it at the time.

Most of Shahara's men worked in government administrative posts[2] in far-off districts of the country. Many of the tribesmen living around the village also left, heading for Sanaa to seek employment as personal guards of the *Imam*. So Shahara was nearly empty of working-age males, except on holidays when many returned to visit their families.

The main mosque in Shahara allowed a few students to continue their studies beyond the informal Koranic school. It offered more in-depth education, including Arabic grammar and religious doctrine, and completing the courses at the mosque qualified graduates for public service.

My father studied at the mosque, becoming a government *hakim* (judge) following his graduation. He was later responsible for collecting the *zakat*[3] in our area. My mother was also an al-Mutawakil, a distant cousin of my father. She died when I was only five, and soon afterwards the government transferred my father to the village of Mahabsha.

A 12-hour trek separated Shahara from Mahabsha, where Yahya and his father stayed for eight years. But Yahya returned

---

[2] The typical path laid down for *Sayids*.

[3] A $2\frac{1}{2}$ per cent annual income tax prescribed by the Koran.

frequently to his native village to visit his six brothers (he had no sisters) and his father's second wife, though he got on poorly with her.

He travelled freely through the countryside, unmolested by the ubiquitous conflicts between the tribes. Anyone committing an offence against a *Sayid* had to deal not only with the tribesmen under whose protection the *Sayid's* village fell, but also with the *Imam* if the victim had family employed in public administration.

Throughout his childhood and into his teens, Yahya ate little at meals but a thin gruel of beans and a piece of round, flat bread to scoop it up with. 'We ate meat once a week, on Fridays,' Yahya says, without the least hint of regret, 'and occasionally to celebrate the arrival of a guest, a marriage, or a religious holiday. I was 14 before I tasted a piece of fruit or any vegetables other than the green onions and long white radishes my mother and stepmother mixed in with the beans.'

Shahara, like the rest of Yemen, had no pumps for irrigation until the 1960s, and farming depended entirely on rain. Famine was not a rare occurrence, like the one that lay waste much of the country in the year of Yahya's birth. Refugees from the Tihama had lumbered into the highlands in search of food then, trailing an epidemic of typhus and lice-borne recurrent fever in their wake.

Yahya's father had his sons' lives mapped out for them while they were still infants. He intended each of them to marry at around 16, then move into their own homes nearby.

Like most *Sayids*, he had considerable respect for religious learning, but Shahara proved too unforgiving an environment to allow all of its inhabitants the luxury of an education. And while Yahya's father envisioned one or two of his seven sons studying to become government employees like himself, the others would inevitably grow up to farm the family's land around the village.

'But my brother, Ahmed, older by seven years, wanted desperately to leave Shahara and go to Sanaa to study,' Yahya explains. 'Father was not at all pleased, and only after long pestering did he finally give in. Ahmed wrote home regularly, describing his studies and the wonders of far-off Sanaa. Father noticed Ahmed's strange but elegant use of the classical Arabic language in his letters – the style found in the Koran, not the colloquial slang of the common people – and he swelled with admiration.'

Subtly at first, Ahmed planted the idea of Yahya joining him. Though his father had only recently chosen a wife for him in Shahara, Yahya soon set his heart on going to Sanaa, too. He wanted to learn more of the outside world he had heard sketches of on the radio at a merchant's house in Mahabsha when he was younger.

'A few friends and I used to mill around outside the merchant's home,' Yahya recalls. 'We could just make out the sound from the radio inside if we were quiet, because we didn't have the money to pay to go inside and listen like the grown-ups.'

'Our religion teacher at school called it "the little box that talked" and said it was bad, "a form of magic", and that we shouldn't listen to it. But of course that only encouraged us,' Yahya remembers with a devilish grin.

Yahya's father reluctantly discarded the hope that all of his sons would marry and settle down in the village, and he let Yahya go. He was 14 when he set out eagerly for Sanaa and a life that could never have been his had he remained in Shahara.

Yahya glimpsed his new home for the first time from atop his donkey as he crested the pass leading down to the plain a few miles north of the town. Though Imam Ahmed had moved the capital to Taiz eight years earlier, Sanaa was still a magical place.

'Inside some of the government buildings in the walled town,' Yahya recalls, 'I saw tiny balls of glass shining with a bright light, but without actually burning. It was only electric lighting fed by a generator, but I had never heard of such a thing then. In the alleys of Suq al-Milh I found fruit and vegetables, sweets, and so many other strange foods that I'd never seen. The market alone seemed to me bigger than all of Shahara.' Yahya paused for a moment and a broad smile broke over his face. 'I even ran away when I saw a boy riding a bicycle towards me. I had no idea what it was.'

Yahya enrolled in school and quickly settled into his studies. He loved the challenge and his competitive nature galvanized him to excel so that he consistently finished towards the top of his class. But two years after coming to Sanaa, Yahya received word from the village that his father had died following a bout of agonizing illness. Yahya and his brother returned to settle the family's affairs.

Once at home, Ahmed decided he had had enough of town life. He took a local girl for a wife and settled down near his old home. Yahya, however, soon returned to Sanaa. He rapidly made up the weeks he had missed while in Shahara and graduated from secondary school that same year, 1958, with the highest marks in his class. His father would have been proud.

Yahya debated what to do with his life after graduation. After considerable reflection, he finally decided on pursuing a career in the military, a radical choice for a *Sayid*. But unorthodox decisions soon became his forte.

Growing tension between Sanaa and the British in Aden resulted in small-scale skirmishing between the two during the late 1950s. The *Imam* purchased 30 military aircraft from Czechoslovakia to beef up the country's defences, then opened Yemen's first air force academy in Sanaa, bringing in an Egyptian General to train pilots at the school.

Abdullah al-Sallal, who in four years would become Yemen's first President, headed the Air Force Academy. He had worked his way up the ranks from a modest family background, serving Imam Yahya and Imam Ahmed for over 30 years.

Yahya applied to the academy and was accepted, but when al-Sallal noticed the name of al-Mutawakil on the list of that year's entrants, he questioned his staff: 'What's this *Sayid* doing in the academy?'

Service in the army was traditionally reserved for tribesmen, and the presence in the academy of an al-Mutawakil, a well-known *Sayid* family, was not an everyday occurrence.

'Take him off the list,' ordered an irritated al-Sallal. But the Egyptian General at the academy stood his ground, insisting that Yahya deserved entry thanks to his exam score. Al-Sallal gave in.

Yahya had no family in Sanaa to support him. He survived only on the meagre handouts distributed by the academy: five pieces of *kidam* – hard military bread – per day and two riyals each month.

'Every morning I sold two of my *kidam*,' Yahya says. 'I used the money to buy a cup of tea, something else I discovered for the first time in Sanaa. Normally the money from one piece of bread would have covered the cost of the tea, but I had developed a sweet tooth and couldn't drink my tea without a cube of sugar. It was imported and cost almost as much as the tea. My schoolmates called me *al-mayt*[4] because I was so emaciated from not eating all of my *kidam*.'

In 1959, Yahya and the other academy students nearly saw their military careers evaporate before they had even begun. On his return from medical treatment in Italy, the outraged Imam Ahmed suspected that Egypt had a hand in the tribal unrest engulfing Yemen. He deported the Egyptian General at the Air Force Academy and closed down the instituion.

'But al-Sallal believed the *Imam* would soon change his mind,' Yahya recalls. 'He knew that someone would eventually have to fly the country's expensive new aircraft. Though classes were suspended, along with our *kidam* rations and monthly stipends, al-Sallal told the students we could continue living in our dormitory rooms if we wanted, and he sold barrels of lubricating oil from the academy's stocks in order to feed us. Six months later,

[4] The dead one.

al-Sallal's hunch proved correct. The *Imam* reopened the school, but converted it into an airborne academy for parachute training, bringing in Russians to teach the courses this time.'

In March 1961, Yahya's class travelled to Hodayda to execute its maiden jump from the air. It happened that Imam Ahmed came to the port town at the same time, to have an X-ray taken with one of the country's two X-ray machines (X-rays fascinated the *Imam*, and he insisted on having one taken whenever he had the slightest ailment). While inside the hospital, a coup attempt left the *Imam* with a dozen bullet wounds. But, once again, he miraculously survived.

Ahmed suspected the Airborne Academy's Yemeni officers of implication in the plot. When an investigation eventually cleared them, the students resumed training and Yahya was the first one out of the aircraft in the Yemeni military's inaugural parachute drop.

On graduation, Yahya was promoted to second lieutenant and joined an artillery unit. It was here that he first came into contact with an underground reform movement called the Free Officers Organization. Inspired by Gamal Abdul Nasser and the overthrow of Egypt's King Faruk in 1952, the Free Officers in Yemen held clandestine meetings at which they plotted the downfall of the Imamate.

Planning progressed at a snail's pace over the years, until the *Imam* passed away in September 1962. The plotters soon noticed that Ahmed's successor, 35-year-old Muhammad al-Badr, neglected the armed forces during his first week in power. The military had displayed extreme loyalty towards his father, but officers felt much less comfortable with al-Badr at the helm, particularly given his efforts to play the tribes off against the army during Ahmed's absence in Italy in 1959. In those brief weeks of de facto rule, al-Badr had shown himself much less savvy at governing than either his father or grandfather. He would need all the help he could get, and committed a grave error in failing to meet with the military command right away to ensure their support.

The new *Imam*, like all his predecessors, had many enemies, none more formidable than the clique of Free Officers. With the death of Imam Ahmed, the Free Officers sensed a window of opportunity. But they would have to act quickly, before al-Badr consolidated his control.

In a few hours the plotters devised a plan, the opportunity for which had eluded them for several years. They divided their forces into five groups. One tank brigade (made up of three tanks) would initiate the coup with an attack on the palace. A second tank brigade would capture the Qasr al-Silah fort, with its stock of arms and ammunition. A unit of light armoured cars was assigned to seize control of Sanaa's radio station, while an artillery unit would surround and neutralize the military command headquarters. The fifth section, Yahya's artillery unit, was placed south of town with orders to bombard any pockets of resistance that emerged in Sanaa. All told, about 100 officers participated in the coup, aided by numerous tribal *shaykhs* whom the plotters informed shortly before launching the fateful operation.

On 25 September 1962, Yahya's 15-man unit moved into position with its three artillery pieces and a machine gun beside the al-Urdhi military barracks. Word spread among the ranks that the *Imam* would be overthrown the following day.

On the eve of the coup, 20-year old Yahya had convinced himself that the world was about to end. No one ever attacked the *Imam* and lived to tell about it. The cadavers of men who had tried littered centuries of Yemeni history. Yahya, along with probably every one of the men involved, harboured grave doubts about their undertaking.

With Judgement Day staring him in the face, Yahya's sweet tooth got the better of him. 'My best friend and I took the money left between us from that month's salary and headed for Suq al-Milh,' Yahya remembers nostalgically. 'We spent every last riyal on chocolate, stuffing it into the various pockets on our uniforms until we looked like we would explode. Then we waddled back to our post to prepare the equipment for the following day's mission. I lay down in a crater we had dug for one of the artillery pieces. It was wet and muddy from a recent rain shower, and the night air was freezing. But the chocolate in my pockets melted and felt warm.'

The *Imam*'s personal militia spotted the strange preparations being made by Yahya's and certain other units around Sanaa that night. But, frustrated with al-Badr's failure to consult them since coming to power, its commanders omitted to inform the *Imam* of the suspect movement.

With the launching of the tank assault on the palace the following day, some of al-Badr's guards nonetheless held their ground courageously. 'One managed to climb onto a rooftop and pour petrol onto the lead tank in the column heading towards the palace,' Yahya said of that historic day.

It burst into flames in a narrow lane, and stopped the other tanks from moving forward. Everybody began to panic with the road to the palace blocked, but one officer kept his head and radioed my unit for assistance. Adrenaline pumping, we threw everything we had at the palace. Within a few minutes we had gone through our entire stock of 45 shells.

But that was all they needed. Imam al-Badr fled in the mayhem.

Yahya was one of the few Yemenis of *Sayid* origin to rally to the revolution from the very beginning. He subsequently confronted an enormous amount of suspicion, despite the fact that his sacrifices on behalf of the revolution nearly cost him his life. He would even end up shelling his native Shahara on one occasion when Royalist forces occupied the town. Yet Yahya never wavered in his support for the Republic.

The revolutionaries called in Abdullah al-Sallal to serve as the Republic's first president. This former head of the Air Force Academy had not been intimately involved in planning the coup, but the revolutionaries believed his stature and reputation offered the greatest chance of generating broad support for the revolution. Meanwhile the *Imam* made his way north to rally loyal tribes and appeal to Saudi Arabia for financial support.

Three days after the coup, Yahya took command of a 120-man *block*. Equipped with three artillery pieces, three armoured cars, and three tanks, the unit made its way to the Shahara region to counter pro-Royalist tribesmen there. Yahya was the sole person in his *block* who knew how to operate the unit's artillery pieces.

One day in late 1962, Yahya led his men north across the sparsely populated plain of Udhr, in Hashid territory north of Shahara. Enemy troops lurking in the area greatly outnumbered Yahya's own, but he determined to prevent the Royalists from discerning his weakness and pressing home their advantage, which could have ended in disaster for the Republicans. He sent out two groups to flank the adversary, leaving his main force dangerously depleted as it advanced slowly up the centre. But the ploy worked and the Royalists withdrew in the face of what they believed to be a superior force.

The retreating enemy put up token resistance at hamlets and ridges, before pulling back to the next defensive position as the Republicans closed in. Yahya's force gained momentum, and opposition tapered off as they swept across the plain.

'By the time we reached the tiny village of Sukaybat,' Yahya remembered during one trip to Paris, 'we assumed that the Royalists had already abandoned the site, so I walked unsuspecting into the main street at the head of my men. The last thing I heard was the rattle of a machine gun from the window of a nearby house. At the same moment it felt like my left arm and thigh exploded.'

In the café where we sat on the Champs-Elysées, Yahya rolled up his sleeve to show Charles and me the scar. One of the rounds had severed the main nerve in his forearm before lodging in his chest.

After taking out the sniper, Yahya's men had their commander transported back to Sanaa. In critical condition, the doctors in the capital immediately shipped him by plane to Cairo for emergency surgery.

Yahya returned to Sanaa six months later, but the damage to his arm prevented him from returning to combat duty right away. In July 1963, President al-Sallal sent him along with the first group of Yemeni officers to study in the Soviet Union, at the Officers Infantry Academy.

Yahya lived in the school's barracks in Solnecnogorsk, 25 miles north of Moscow. He had weekends free, and usually took the train to Moscow to pass the time. The orderliness and efficiency of Russia compared to Yemen made a strong impression on him.

Yahya and his fellow students were subjected to extensive Soviet propaganda, not only from their instructors but also from some of the highly politicized foreign students at the Academy. Middle East politics interested the Arab students most, and they asked many questions about Soviet policy in the region. Officially, Moscow supported the Egyptian revolutionary, Gamal Abdul Nasser. Yet those fellow pupils schooled in ideology pointed out that Nasser's stress on Arab nationalism was incompatible with Marx's concept of a borderless world.

The Communists' harsh criticism of the Egyptian leader antagonized many of the Arab students. They considered Nasser a hero and most, like Yahya, refused to replace their modern-day idol with Karl Marx.

Yahya returned to Sanaa after graduating from the Infantry Academy in late 1965 to take a post as head of the army's military training. By then the war in Yemen had bogged down into a stalemate. Neither the Republican regime nor its Egyptian patrons made any effort to develop Yemen's regular army during the first few years of the war. Yemeni officers were sorely lacking and poorly trained, and the entire armed forces totalled less than 10,000 men in 1965. The Republicans depended to a great extent on tribal irregulars led by loyal *shaykhs* and, more importantly, on the 60,000 Egyptian troops dispatched to the country.

The Egyptian soldiers, however, who had trained in conventional warfare in the desert and on the Nile Valley plain, experienced great difficulty in adapting to conditions in the rugged Yemeni highlands. Their initial confidence in defeating the Royalists steadily eroded.

By mid-1965 a growing number of Republican political and military leaders, Yahya among them, felt that President al-Sallal had done all he could do. They wanted him to step aside and allow someone else to pursue a different strategy.

The Egyptians, too, had grown frustrated with al-Sallal's lack of success, both in prosecuting the war and in broadening popular support for his regime. Nasser summoned the Yemeni President for a lengthy visit to Cairo in September 1965. Al-Sallal's Prime Minister, General Hassan al-Amri, and the pre-Revolution reformist, Abdul Rahman al-Iryani, were given free reign over the country in his absence.

Desperate to turn the war to the Republic's advantage, al-Amri finally set about strengthening Yemen's regular army. But progress came slowly, and after a year Nasser lost patience with him, too. Al-Sallal prepared to return to Sanaa.

Many Republican officers, not least of all al-Amri, opposed al-Sallal's homecoming. The Prime Minister even declared that he would have the President arrested the moment he set foot in Yemen. Anticipating trouble, the Egyptians lined the road from the airport to central Sanaa with tanks as al-Sallal's plane landed on 12 August 1966. Egyptian troops escorted him to his home unhindered.

The Yemenis already begrudged the fact that every one of their officers had at his side an Egyptian 'advisor', a Siamese twin empowered to overturn the Yemenis' decisions if they failed to concur with Egyptian thinking. Al-Sallal's return accentuated the grievances of moderate Republicans against Egypt's strong-arm tactics. A clash loomed ominously over the horizon, but al-Sallal's opponents knew they could not defeat the Egyptians militarily, so al-Amri and his backers, including Yahya al-Mutawakil, removed to Taiz in protest.

'When Nasser contacted him by telephone,' Yahya remembered, 'al-Amri demanded a face-to-face interview with the Egyptian leader. Nasser sent two aircraft to Taiz to take him and the 50 or 60 ministers, military officers and government officials opposed to al-Sallal to Cairo. We believed Nasser had agreed to hear us out.'

But the Egyptian leader's true intentions proved altogether more insidious. The delegation included Prime Minister al-Amri; Yahya al-Mutawakil and his brother, Ahmed (then also a military officer); Shaykh Muhammad Abu Lahum (son of the Nihm *shaykh*, Abdullah Abu Lahum); his distant cousin, Dirham Abu Lahum; Ibrahim al-Hamdi (the future Yemeni President); Abdul Rahman al-Iryani (another future President); and dozens of other officials who would exercise considerable influence over Yemeni politics in the years to come.

'The Egyptians treated us with great respect – at first,' Yahya continued. 'The Prime Minister himself greeted us at the airport and assured us that the Egyptian Minister of Defence would come to hear our arguments. They took us to the Intercontinental Hotel, and a few days later gave us all money so that we could rent flats in Cairo, as though we were going to be there for a while.'

The importance the Egyptians appeared to place on their visit encouraged the Yemenis, particularly the fact that the Defence Minister himself would see them. They hoped to negotiate a de-escalation of Egypt's pre-eminent role in Yemeni affairs, while at the same time politely reiterating their support for the Republic and their appreciation of Egypt's past assistance.

One week elapsed before the Yemenis gathered in the Officers' Club in Cairo on 16 September 1966 for their long-awaited interview. Yahya coolly recalled what happened next:

Our optimism disappeared when the Egyptians informed us that the Defence Minister would not be available to meet with us after all. Instead, the Minister of Military Affairs would speak in his place, someone of much lower rank. Al-Amri and Abdul Rahman al-Iryani stood up and walked out of the club in protest.

The rest of us stayed to listen to what the Egyptians had to say. When the Minister of Military Affairs entered the room, right away he began patronizing us like a school teacher, lecturing us on the political and military situation in Yemen. We Yemenis are very proud people. It really irritated all of us.

When the minister rambled on and on, Ali al-Khawlani[5] raised his hand to say something. The minister tried to ignore him, but Ali kept waving his hand. Finally the Egyptian stopped his lecture and looked at him: 'You are here to listen, not to talk,' he said. At those words, every one of us stood up and filed out of the building.

We walked together to the house Abdul Rahman al-Iryani was renting, which wasn't very far away, to talk over our next move. But as we arrived at the house, we saw that Egyptian soldiers had surrounded it. Al-Iryani and al-Amri were prisoners, and we realized it wouldn't be long before they arrested us too.

Muhammad Abu Lahum recalls the unfolding of events as if it happened yesterday. 'We decided to split up and each take a chance on his own,' he says. 'Dirham Abu Lahum took Tariq[6] with him and headed for the city centre to lie low in a flat owned by Muhsin al-Aini.[7] I thought long and hard and finally came up with the idea of going to the Kuwaiti Embassy and requesting political asylum.'

I wanted Dirham and Tariq to do the same, so I went to Muhsin's flat to get them. When I arrived at the building, I noticed Egyptian police cars parked outside. I saw a

---

[5] The Yemeni Chief of Staff.

[6] Muhammad's teenage nephew.

[7] To whom the Abu Lahums are related by marriage.

telephone and rang the flat to see what was going on. Dirham answered the phone, his voice shaky and nervous, and I could hear several Egyptians talking loudly in the background.

'Who's with you?' I asked him.

Dirham hesitated. 'Just the guys,' he mumbled.

Then I heard one of the Egyptians' voice come closer and suddenly the telephone receiver slammed down and cut off.

I was so upset I didn't know what to do. I started towards the Kuwaiti Embassy, but stopped after a few steps. I couldn't ask for asylum with Dirham, and particularly young Tariq, under arrest, so I turned around and went back to Muhsin's flat. The Egyptians arrested me along with Dirham and Tariq.

After separating from the other members of the delegation, Yahya al-Mutawakil wandered around the streets of the Egyptian capital. 'I knew things were tense,' he remembers, 'but I had no idea that everyone had been arrested, so I decided to go to a film. I used to go to the cinema all the time when I was in Cairo recovering from my wounds more than three years before that. Nobody makes films like the Egyptians, and they took my mind off all the troubles back home for a couple of hours. Some Egyptian security agents had followed me to the cinema, but I decided they were only trying to harass me. As the closing credits came on the screen and the lights switched on after the film, the agents came in, took hold of me, and said I was under arrest.'

Nasser ordered a dozen of the Yemeni delegation's more distinguished members kept under house arrest. The remainder (with one or two exceptions) were hauled off to the military prison near northeast Cairo's Heliopolis neighbourhood, not far from today's international airport.

The Egyptians had in fact intended to make the arrests during the meeting at the Officers' Club earlier in the day. But many of the Yemenis showed up wearing pistols, and their hosts thought it pragmatic to detain them separately.

When his captors threw him in prison, Yahya found most of his despondent comrades already assigned to cells. Their treatment came as a shock to all, and they sat soberly trying to work out what the future held in store for them.

The jail was a foul, sinister place and the Yemenis received no special treatment. Each cell measured some seven feet by seven feet and had a small horizontal slit about five inches long and two inches wide located just over the door. Each prisoner took the bucket that served as his toilet, turned it upside down, placed his folded blanket on top, and stood for hours on end peering into the prison courtyard through the slit.

'Sometimes the guards played soccer matches in the prison courtyard,' Yahya laughed. 'One of the guards played really well and he liked the prisoners to watch him, so he would unlock our cell doors and let us have them open a crack, just enough to see the game. One of the Yemenis, Hassan Makki, got carried away with the excitement and stuck his head all the way out of the door for a better look. A guard came up to him and smacked his baton loudly against the door beside Hassan's head, scaring all of us, Hassan most of all.

'Put your head back in there,' the guard yelled.

'What do you mean, treating us like animals?' Makki said with the look of a hurt puppy. 'We're respectable people.'

The guard looked at him with raised eyebrows and smirked. 'If you were respectable,' he said, 'you wouldn't be in this place.'

The days turned to months and the Yemenis began to despair that they would ever see freedom. As the chill of winter set in, Yahya tried to remain active in order to keep warm. It had been very hot the day of their arrest and he was dressed only in thin cotton trousers and a short-sleeved shirt. For hours each night, he used his metal belt buckle to laboriously scrape away the mortar from the wall separating his cell from that of his close friend, Ali al-Muayad.

'After several weeks of digging,' Yahya says, 'I managed to dislodge one of the bricks. I removed it every night after the final guard check so I could tell Ali about the films I had seen, and Ali could recite poetry to me in return. In the daytime, I would seal the brick back in place with cooking oil. So many flies swarmed on the grease that they were like a coat of black paint over the brick, so the guards never noticed that the mortar had been removed.'

Prison in many ways resembled the war back home: endless days of boredom, punctuated by brief but intense moments of terror. Some of the Yemenis had suffered interrogation and beatings on their first day in jail, and the verbal abuse continued. But this paled in comparison to the punishment meted out to certain other inmates.

The Yemenis had their cells washed out every morning by jailed members of the Egyptian Communist Party or, on the other side of the political spectrum, the Muslim Brotherhood, a popular movement calling for Islamic government. Both underground groups vehemently opposed Egypt's ruler.

The prison guards reserved an unparalleled hatred for the Muslim Brothers in particular. The gruesome screams from their torture sessions echoed through the jail and rattled the prisoners badly, not least the other Muslim Brothers.

'One of them managed to break away from the guards escorting him back to his cell from one of the special torture rooms on the third floor of the prison,' Yahya told me once with a shiver. 'He threw himself over the railing before the guards could stop him. I watched from the slit in my cell as the prison director stood over the man in the courtyard and kicked him to make sure he was dead.'

As their release seemed increasingly remote, the detained Yemenis sensed that death lay near at hand. The rare bits of news they managed to obtain from the outside world did little to reassure them. A Yemeni man ended up in the prison several months after the delegation, and he updated everyone with the depressing news that Yemen's President had launched a bloody campaign back home to purge all opposition to his rule. As part of this effort, al-Sallal was demanding the extradition of the Yemeni delegation imprisoned in Cairo. He boasted publicly that he would execute them all on their arrival back home.

Sympathetic Yemenis frantically lobbied Arab leaders to dissuade Nasser from sending the Yemenis to certain death at home. Their efforts proved successful, but the prisoners in Cairo had no way of knowing it at the time. Every day they expected to be hauled from their cells and delivered into the waiting arms of al-Sallal.

Not all of the Yemenis could cope with the mental strain imposed by their precarious situation. 'One Yemeni pranced out of his cell to go to the toilet one morning wearing only his underwear,' Yahya says. 'He had wound the rest of his clothes around his head like an oversized turban, and with every step he took it looked as though the weight would make him topple over. We all felt sorry for him, but it gave us a good laugh.'

Others discovered different methods for dealing with the stress. The Yemenis were not supposed to receive anything from outside the prison – no mail or gifts – but one of them managed to have a package from his family delivered. A sack of raisins accompanied the letter inside, and the prisoner soaked them in a plastic yogurt cup filled with water for several weeks until they fermented. He took a sip of the home-made wine every day or two, savouring each drop.

In June 1967, nine months after the Yemenis' arrest, Egyptian troops suffered a severe military defeat at the hands of Israel. The Jewish state furthered its acquisition of Arab lands by seizing the Sinai Peninsula and Gaza from Egypt (as well as the West Bank from Jordan and the Palestinians, and the Golan Heights from Syria). Nasser solemnly and sincerely announced his resignation as President, but massive demonstrations by the Egyptian people demanded that he stay – and he complied.

The military debacle against Israel forced Nasser to focus his attention on issues closer to home than the remote mountains of southern Arabia. To get its own house in order Egypt needed Saudi financial aid, and funds would hardly be forthcoming while Cairo waged a proxy war against Saudi Arabia in the latter's own backyard. So Nasser let it be known that he planned to wind down Egypt's involvement in Yemen. The Republicans' interest, he warned al-Sallal, lay in coming to a settlement with the Royalists before all Egyptian troops left the country in four months' time.

Nasser finally released the Yemeni delegation from their Cairo prison cells on 10 October 1967. They remained in Egypt for a further 12 days to discuss the situation in Yemen, and this time the Egyptian officials treated them with considerably more respect than 13 months earlier.

'We flew from Cairo to Hodayda on 22 October,' Yahya remembers, 'just in time to watch the last Egyptian troops boarding their ships for home. When we stepped off the plane, someone in the welcoming committee turned up a radio so we could all listen to a speech Nasser was giving from Cairo. 'We persecuted the good people and supported the bad ones in Yemen,' Nasser conceded.'

Yahya and the other Yemenis laughed.

Al-Sallal bravely ventured to Hodayda to meet the returning Yemenis and attempt to reconcile with them. The Egyptian withdrawal rendered al-Sallal extremely vulnerable, both to the Royalists and to opponents within the Republican regime.

He told the delegation that he would leave for Baghdad and Moscow a few days later to seek military aid to bolster the Republic against the Royalist offensive that would inevitably follow the Egyptian departure. Somehow he still clung to the notion that his presidency might weather the storm of events unravelling swiftly before him. 'He even joked with us on the tarmac in Hodayda,' Yahya recalls. ' "I hope none of you are thinking of taking my job while I'm gone," he said.'

Al-Sallal left Abdul Rahman al-Iryani in charge of the country when he departed for Iraq in early November 1967. On 5 November, al-Iryani and Hassan al-Amri deposed the absent President.

After serving as al-Amri's aide-de-camp during the decisive 70-day siege of Sanaa, Yahya became Director of the Prime Minister's Office in 1968, then was promoted to Deputy Commander-in-Chief of the Armed Forces the following year at the age of 27.

One of his proudest moments came when he accompanied Muhsin al-Aini, Yemen's new Prime Minister and Foreign Minister, to Jedda in March 1970 to secretly negotiate a Saudi-brokered peace deal with the Royalists. Tense bargaining at the meeting eventually resulted in an agreement both sides could live with, though members of Imam al-Badr's immediate family were excluded from holding any positions in Yemen.

With the details hammered out, Yahya returned to Saudi Arabia two weeks later with a larger delegation, to sign the final peace agreement ending the eight-year old civil war once and for all.

Yahya remained active in government after the war. He became a member of Yemen's National Assembly in 1970 and Ambassador to Egypt in early 1971, where he would remain for over three years under very different circumstances from his earlier months in prison there.

The day before a group of officers deposed President Abdul Rahman al-Iryani in June 1974, the plotters recalled Yahya from Egypt. US President Richard Nixon was scheduled to arrive in Egypt on an official visit the very next day and one of al-Iryani's advisors found it highly suspicious that Yahya would return home on the eve of such an historic event in Egypt. But it was too late to do anything about it.

Yahya became a member of the all-powerful Command Council following the bloodless coup. This executive and legislative body soon named Ibrahim al-Hamdi as Yemen's new President, and Yahya became his Minister of Interior.

Besides studying together at the Air Force Academy in Sanaa, Yahya and al-Hamdi had shared a cell during the last four months of their detention in Cairo. The two had an even tighter bond, however, in that Yahya had saved al-Hamdi's life 12 years earlier.

Prior to the revolution, al-Hamdi's father was the *hakim* – government judge – in Dhamar. The family maintained close relations with Imam Ahmed, and when the revolution swept Imam al-Badr from power, al-Hamdi and his son, Ibrahim, landed in jail to await execution. Yahya, who knew Ibrahim from their academy days, intervened and had him and his father released. Al-Hamdi's narrow escape soured his view of the Republic, which he ironically came to govern 12 years later.

When Yahya resigned as Interior Minister, President al-Hamdi packed him off to exile in April 1976 as Ambassador to the United States. In the mid-1980s, Yahya went to Paris as ambassador, where he stayed less than a year before returning home and becoming Governor of Ibb province south of Sanaa.

Yahya's rise up the military and political ranks of the Yemeni Republic is nothing short of phenomenal. He had no strong tribe behind him to make him valuable to the government, or able to threaten it to get what he wanted. And his *Sayid* origins presented him with an overwhelming handicap in a movement that strove to eliminate the exalted status of that very sector of society. Yet Yahya persevered through daunting odds, and succeeded. He will forever remain an example for me.

Plate 1.1 Bayt al-Salami village in Heima, commanding the Sanaa–Hodayda road. It was built by the author's ancestors and is still inhabited by their descendents.
Photo credit: Charles Hoots

Plate 1.2 Khadija's oldest brother: Hamud Murzah.
Photo credit: al-Salami family collection

Plate 2.1 Khadija al-Salami –
approximately 9 years old.
Photo credit: al-Salami family
collection

Plate 2.2 Khadija al-Salami –
approximately 13 years old.
Photo credit: al-Salami family
collection

Plate 3.1 Amina al-Salami, Khadija's grandmother – 1990s.
Photo credit: al-Salami family collection

Plate 3.2 Grandmother Amina's house in Sanaa's Hurqan neighbourhood.
Photo credit: Charles Hoots

Plate 4.1 Khadija's father, Muhammad Murzah (right), with his brother-in-law, Ali al-Salami, in Cairo for medical treatment.
Photo credit: al-Salami family collection

Plate 4.2 Left to right: Amat al-Aleem Al-Suswa (Yemen's first female ambassador), Khadija al-Salami, and friend, Jameela Ali Rija – approximately 1978–79.
Photo credit: al-Salami family collection

Plate 5.1 Khadija meeting President Ali Abdullah Salih in Washington, DC, with Ambassador Muhsin al-Aini looking on – autumn 1989.
Photo credit: al-Salami family collection

Plate 5.2 Khadija in Washington, DC – 1983.
Photo credit: al-Salami family collection

Plate 6.1   Khadija working as a DJ at *Radio Orient* in Paris, France − 1986.
Photo credit: al-Salami family collection

Plate 6.2   Tariq
al-Maamari, the author's
half brother, in front of his
family's home in al-Sharara
village.
Photo credit: Charles Hoots

Plate 7.1 Yahya al-Mutawakil in Claude Monet's Garden in Giverny, France – late 1990s.
Photo credit: Khadija al-Salami

Plate 7.2 Yahya al-Mutawakil on far right, posing with Shaykh Abdullah al-Ahmar (with *jambiya* dagger) and friends.
Photo credit: al-Mutawakil family collection

صقر خانشد العمد البطل عبا الصادو ثاو ٢

Plate 8 Mujahid Abu Shawareb – 1970. Photo taken by unidentified female Lebanese journalist soon after the Battle of Saada. The journalist wrote *saqr hashid* – the falcon of Hashid – on the photograph and sent it to Mujahid.

Photo credit: Abu Shawareb family collection

Plate 9.1 Official visit to West Germany in 1970. Right to left: Mujahid Abu Shawareb, Yahya al-Mutawakil, Ahmed al-Matari, Abdullah al-Ahmar (principal *shaykh* of the Hashid tribes).
Photo credit: al-Mutawakil family collection

Plate 9.2 Left to right: Interior Minister Yahya al-Mutawakil, President Ibrahim al-Hamdi, Prime Minister Abdul Aziz Abdul Ghani, Chief of Staff Ahmed al-Ghashmi – 1975.
Photo credit: al-Mutawakil family collection

Plate 10.1   Mujahid Abu Shawareb (right) and Yahya al-Mutawakil at military parade in Sanaa, Yemen.
Photo credit: al-Mutawakil family collection

Plate 10.2   Khadija in her wedding dress, with Amat al-Aleem al-Suswa, Yemen's first female Minister (of Human Rights) with full ministerial powers – 1992.
Photo credit: Boushra al-Mutawakil

Plate 11.1 Khadija al-Salami in traditional wedding dress, on the roof of her mother's house in Sanaa – 1994.
Photo credit: Lyu Hanabusa

Plate 11.2 Khadija's husband – Charles Hoots – chewing *qat* at our wedding party. Hassan al-Lowzi seated on his left, Abdul Rahman al-Akwa seated on Hassan's left.
Photo credit: *26 September* Publications

الشيخ عبد الله صالح أبو لحوم

ميلاده سنة ١٣١٣ هجرية وتوفي سنة ١٣٧٤ هجرية

Plate 12   Abdullah Abu Lahum, father of Muhammad Abu Lahum, photographed in approximately 1945 on his way to meet the *Imam* near Sanaa.

Photo credit: Muhammad Abu Lahum family collection

Plate 13.1   Muhammad Abu Lahum (standing at centre with dark uniform and rifle strap over right shoulder) as tank commander during the 1960s. Future President Ahmed al-Ghashmi is standing (over Abu Lahum's right shoulder). Current President Ali Abdullah Salih is kneeling (to Abu Lahum's right, with tanker's cap on). Training exercises near Sanaa during civil war, late 1967 – early 1968.
Photo credit: Muhammad Abu Lahum family collection

Plate 13.2   Right to left: Rubish Kaalan (who killed the *Imam*'s bodyguard and fled to the desert), Salih Abu Lahum, his brother Muhammad Abu Lahum (who went to prison for Rubish's crime), and friend, Ali al-Shayba – 1972.
Photo credit: Muhammad Abu Lahum family collection

Plate 14.1 Muhammad Abu Lahum resolving problems with tribesmen and the army – 1970s.
Photo credit: Muhammad Abu Lahum family collection

Plate 14.2 The house on Sanaa's Aqeel Street that Grandfather Hamud purchased for the author's mother and father when they remarried.
Photo credit: Charles Hoots

Plate 15.1 Funeral procession for Yahya al-Mutawakil – January 2003.
Photo credit: al-Mutawakil family collection

Plate 15.2 Khadija and family. Left to right: Khadija, niece Hadeel (on Khadija's lap), Ali al-Mehwashi (Khadija's brother-in-law), Ghamdan and Ghadeer (Khadija's nephew and niece), Fatima al-Salami (Khadija's mother) and Hanan (Khadija's niece).
Photo credit: al-Salami family collection

Plate 16.1 Khadija from her balcony in Paris – approximately 2000.
Photo credit: al-Salami family collection

Plate 16.2 Khadija and Charles Hoots at Charles' parents' home in North
Carolina, USA – 2001.
Photo credit: Judith Hoots

CHAPTER FIFTEEN

France

Yahya al-Mutawakil greeted my girlfriend and me amiably in his office in Washington, DC's Watergate Building. We shook hands and sat down in the chairs facing the ambassador's desk. After introducing myself, I explained soberly that I wanted a car and needed the embassy to guarantee the payments in order to buy it.

'US$11,000!' Yahya blurted out when I handed him the credit agreement from the car dealership. 'That's a great deal of money for a student ... That's a great deal of money for an ambassador!'

Yahya, of course, had no intention of guaranteeing the financing – that's not what embassies are for. He would have to talk me out of it, for my own sake.

'Why don't you take some time to think about this?' he suggested. 'You don't want to rush into anything involving this much money.'

'I've already thought about it,' I said, prepared for his arguments. 'That's the car I want.'

After a half-hour discussion that led nowhere, Yahya knew that I would not be talked out of the car. He recognized his own stubbornness in me and, taking pity, he verified that the scholarship stipend would be sufficient for me to meet the payments. My friend and I left his office a few minutes later, letter in hand to guarantee the car financing.

The image some of my classmates had formed of me foundered the next afternoon when I drove onto the Mount Vernon College campus in a new sports car. One of my friends approached me later that day to ask if she could borrow some money.

'But I don't have that much money,' I protested, truthfully.

'Yeah, right. How'd you pay for that new car, then?'

The girl flew into a rage when I told her again that I couldn't loan her anything. 'Rich bitch!' she snarled as she walked away.

At the summer break between the second and third years, I felt the urge to discover more of America. I had become attached to the country in the couple of years I had spent there. It was my first real experience of meeting and getting to know people from different ethnic backgrounds, religions and countries I had never heard of before leaving Yemen. There seemed to be so many opportunities for so many people and I wanted to see more, so I set off to cross America alone in my car.

The intense green of the countryside struck me as I crossed the Appalachian Mountains and drove beyond. Then the remarkable similarities between Yemen and the desert southwest fascinated me as I raced across New Mexico and Arizona on Interstate 40.

I couldn't believe America had a place that looked just like Yemen, with its dusty buttes and red sand. Driving through it reminded me of the trips I used to take with my Aunt Hameeda and her husband outside Sanaa on Fridays. We never went more than about 30 miles from the capital, but we had to pass through at least four checkpoints, where soldiers would stop to look at identification papers. On my way across America, I marvelled at how long it would have taken if I had had to stop at checkpoints every five or 10 miles.

And in Yemen, when we went on long drives, I had to be careful not to drink much before the trip because there are no toilets along the roads. But that wasn't a problem on Interstate 40. The only thing I had to worry about was making sure I read the map correctly from time to time. I have never felt more independent as on that trip, as though my destiny was truly in my hands alone.

Los Angeles featured none of the similarities to Yemen that New Mexico and Arizona did. I lost my way as I drove into the city and could find no one who spoke enough English to direct me. In most of the neighbourhoods, the locals responded to my inquiries in Spanish, of which I knew nothing.

I was headed for the University of Southern California, which had accepted me to study cinematography during its summer session. I had decided to major in communications at Mount Vernon College and, while taking cinematography courses in California would complement my major, I also believed it would be a fun place to spend the summer break. I studied camera techniques, sound and editing, and completed the class by shooting two short films. I loved the experience, and resolved to pursue filmmaking further.

Taking summer classes allowed me to graduate from Mount Vernon College in only three and a half years, in early 1986. I returned to Yemen and a job at the television station, but things were not as I had hoped. I made a few suggestions to hopefully improve the station and submitted some proposals for new programmes. No one seemed the least bit interested, and I concluded that it would be difficult for me to use there what I had learned in my studies abroad.

On the personal side, life at home jolted me back to reality after four years of being on my own. My brother Hamud had by now taken on more of the role of family protector, and he did nothing but harass me from the day I returned, chaperoning me like a child, wanting to know where I was going whenever I left the house, criticizing if I came home late, insisting it was time for me to get married. When I resisted, he threatened to lock me in the house and to do whatever was necessary to make me behave as he thought I should. Our shouting matches lasted for hours.

It was as if my university diploma was nothing to Hamud, just wasted time, and now I should go back to a traditional role in society. I wanted no part of it, and with my job not exactly what I had hoped for, I decided to leave Yemen again within a month of returning home from America.

When I was around nine years old, I came across an Arabic translation of *Les Miserables* among the books piled high in the room of my stepfather, Shaykh Hameed. The jacket cover portraying a street scene in nineteenth-century Paris sparked my interest, and Hameed offered me the book to read. Taken in by the abandoned children depicted by Victor Hugo in the story, I immediately identified with them. I had dreamed of visiting France ever since, reinforced by the stories told to me by Nadia Zayn.

Now was my opportunity to finally see the city of *Les Miserables*, and I decided to go to France to study French. My brother Hamud knew nothing of my plans to leave again. He would have tried to stop me had he known, so I told only Mother and Grandmother. The day before I left, Grandmother Amina handed me her savings of 4,000 riyals (around US$1,000 at the time), which covered my plane ticket to France.

On arriving in Paris in the summer of 1986, I headed for the Sorbonne to enrol in a French language course. The US$2,000 I carried in my bag was to pay the tuition and provide me with enough to live on during my semester in Paris.

Entering an underground Metro station on my way to enrol, I bought a train ticket and passed through the turnstile, heading for the platform. While I fumbled absent-mindedly to put my change away, a man snatched the wallet from my hand, leaped over the turnstile, and disappeared up the stairs and into the street before I could even cry for help. The thief got away with my entire US$2,000 lifeline.

It never occurred to me to return to Yemen – not when I remembered my brother Hamud's behaviour. I would find some way to get the money to pay for school and support myself in France.

I had met Charlotte through a mutual friend soon after arriving in France. The tall, blond French woman in her thirties drifted from job to job whenever she felt the least bit bored. On learning of my predicament, Charlotte told me I could come live with her in the flat she rented on a quiet street in the fourteenth arrondissement. I graciously accepted.

A few weeks later, Charlotte came home from work one evening and told me about an Arabic language radio station in Paris called *Radio Orient*. My hunt for a job had shown few results up to then because my student visa didn't allow me to work. I called the station the next day and was delighted when the director offered me a position as an announcer on the basis of my television experience in Yemen.

I enjoyed my time at *Radio Orient*, though relations between the station manager and employees were often strained. He frequently launched into tirades and staff could never be certain they would be paid on time. Employees however were reluctant to file a complaint perhaps because, like me, they held no work papers in France and were paid off the books, so had little leverage. If anyone asked about late payments, the director insisted the station had no cash at the moment.

Fortunately he never directed his abuse towards me. Though usually long overdue, the pay more than sufficed to support my modest student lifestyle, in particular since I neither drank nor smoked. And I had great fun at the job, meeting and interviewing well-known Arab musical artists and disc-jockeying until the early hours of the morning.

From time to time, the elderly Egyptian singer Muhammad Abdul Wahab telephoned the station in the middle of the night from his home in Paris' luxurious Crillon Hotel. The man's melancholic bass voice had enthralled Arab listeners through much of the twentieth century. He couldn't sleep and just wanted someone to talk to, passing the time trying to describe my face using my voice as a guide and asking me to play some of his songs.

At 4.00 a.m. one morning I stepped out of the broadcasting room to collect some cassettes from the storage area. The doorstop gave way and the door slammed shut, locking me out of the broadcasting room. No one else worked in the studio at that hour, so I had to wake up the station manager at home to bring the keys and let me back in after more than half an hour of dead airtime.

Having studied at a conservative girl's college in America, I had led a sheltered existence before coming to Paris, which turned into a real eye-opener for me. At my work I saw another side of life. The petty rivalries at the radio station stunned me as employees intrigued incessantly to curry favour with the station manager, despite his mercurial disposition.

I was equally disgusted when a trusted Yemeni friend and his girlfriend took me to a party at the home of a wealthy Yemeni-Saudi businessman. As the evening wore on, cocaine and a few more exotic drugs made the rounds, and I soon figured out that most of the beautiful women present were prostitutes. The scene shocked me in that I knew that several of the Yemeni men sitting with the prostitutes had wives. While supposedly very conservative at home (insisting their wives cover up before going out, not work, etc.), they proved to be anything but conservative when out on the town in Paris. Their double standards infuriated me.

One of the Yemeni businessmen a few days later would tell a friend about the party: 'That Yemeni student, Khadija, was there. I couldn't believe it. It was really sad to see her at such a gathering.'

For his male friends and him it was all right. But for me, a girl, it was shameful, though I had had no idea what I was getting into before going.

The businessman at whose flat the party took place was very wealthy. During the party, the friend I went with mentioned to him that I was a student and worked at the radio station all night in order to pay for my studies. Later the man had the audacity to approach me with a proposition.

'Why do you slave all night to make ends meet?' he asked, his inhibitions dampened by alcohol. 'I'll pay for your studies and your food. I'll even rent you a nice flat to live in. All you have to do is be my girlfriend when I'm in Paris.'

I felt nauseated. The man could have offered no bigger insult, and I cursed him violently before storming out of the flat.

Paris, like any big city, features its temptations, and I paid special attention to avoid giving in to them. While many aspects of Yemen's conservative society angered me, at the same time I am grateful for certain of its values engrained in me as a child. As a result, much of what others considered tempting did not appeal to me at all, like drinking alcohol or taking drugs.

France opened my eyes in more positive ways too, awakening me to a way of life different from any I had known before. In Yemen I had undergone a daily struggle to lead my life as I wanted, and in America I had basked in the freedom from social pressures so prevalent at home. But in France I discovered a taste for life.

The City of Light and inspiration, Paris thrilled me every day with its food, architecture, fashion and gardens. I loved to stroll around the Latin Quarter, whose narrow alleyways reminded me so much of Old Sanaa where I grew up. Window-shopping along Boulevard St Germain, with its elegantly displayed shop windows, and the beauty of the bridges spanning the River Seine took my breath away. Sitting in the cafés in summer and watching the variety of passers-by is like attending an haute couture catwalk. I loved every minute of it.

With a job and some money coming in, now I could extend my stay in France. I moved from Charlotte's flat to a chic building near the Arc de Triomphe on Avenue Foch, one of Paris' more expensive strips of real estate. While the address was plush, the living quarters were not, and I occupied a tiny, 100-square foot maid's chamber.

After nearly a year at *Radio Orient* I decided the time had come to move on. When he heard the news, the station manager contacted the chargé d'affaires at the Yemeni Embassy, a mutual friend, to ask him to convince me to remain at the station (probably because I didn't give him a hard time about being paid so late). But the chargé d'affaires turned out to be the wrong person to call, for I had found a new job at the embassy.

I knew many of the handful of Yemenis living in Paris, most of them diplomats at the Yemeni Embassy. The diplomats' wives were often intensely jealous of me, a single girl in close contact with their husbands. They gossiped among themselves at private parties, warning each other to beware of Khadija, who would undoubtedly try to steal their husbands away from them. I pitied these women, who had nothing better to do than worry that their spouses might take another wife. Their behaviour discouraged me further from wanting to get married, fearful I might become like them.

A new ambassador, Salih al-Ashwal, arrived that year, and I got along well with him and his wife. I had studied with the al-Ashwals' daughters in Sanaa, and when I asked the ambassador for a job, he agreed.

The al-Ashwals treated me like a daughter during my year at the embassy in Paris. I enjoyed the work thoroughly, answering the telephone and clipping press articles of interest to the diplomats. It was, however, not something I relished doing for very long.

Just before leaving the job at *Radio Orient*, a journalist friend of mine from Yemen, Ahlam al-Mutawakil, came to Paris for a short visit. From a conservative family (distantly related to Yahya al-Mutawakil), Ahlam was a very religious girl. She never left home in Sanaa without a veil, and though she discarded the garment when abroad, she still covered her hair with a scarf in public.

Ahlam had become active in promoting women's issues. She called me at the radio one day to say that she and another Yemeni girl were going to meet Shaykh Mujahid Abu Shawareb. He was also passing through Paris at the time, and they wanted to thank him for the support he lent to women's causes, such as encouraging four women to run in recent local elections in Yemen. They hoped I would accompany them.

Shaykh Mujahid served at the time as Yemen's Vice-Prime Minister for Internal Affairs. Over a dozen wounds testify to the man's inimitable valour, while the crowd of tribesmen, beggars and other petitioners gathered perpetually outside his home in Sanaa bears witness to his excessive generosity. Both qualities have helped make him one of Yemen's most widely respected personalities.

Known for his frankness in both criticism and praise, Mujahid's candid nature seems unsuited to the manipulative games engaged in by so many political figures the world over. He has preferred the direct approach, steamrolling his ideas through with sheer determination, rather than subterfuge and shady diplomacy. A healthy dose of stubbornness and a highly competitive nature reinforce his unbounded energy. Though frequently hesitant in making a difficult decision, few can deny him when he finally decides just what he wants.

But I knew little about Shaykh Mujahid when Ahlam called that day, and had no particular interest in meeting him. Nor did I care much about women's issues. I resented certain aspects of Yemeni tradition, such as discouraging girls from pursuing an education or making men 'responsible' for their wives and sisters. But until then I had always viewed my own struggles over the years as a question of personal dignity and justice, rather than as a gender-based campaign for women's 'liberation'. Ahlam nevertheless pleaded with me to come along and I finally accepted.

Mujahid occupied a suite at the Hotel Raphaël in Avenue Kléber, one of the broad avenues radiating from the Arc de Triomphe. We found him deep in discussion with three Yemeni men when we entered the room, and he rose graciously to greet us.

I assumed a *shaykh* with Mujahid's reputation must be in his sixties or seventies, and was surprised to discover that he was only in his late-forties. His hairline had receded slightly, but the moustache and closely trimmed beard adorning his chin showed no signs of greying. Impetuous green eyes ricocheted around the room like a pinball player's. His movements were decisive and he still walked with a hint of the confident strut he had acquired in his youth. His perfectly tailored silk suit gleamed under the light of the chandelier, and he straightened his designer tie as he introduced his three visitors to the other men in the suite.

After Ahlam talked briefly with Mujahid and thanked him for his support, we left. I thought nothing else of the meeting, until a few weeks later when one of my Yemeni acquaintances in Paris called. He was also a friend of Mujahid and the men that had been in the hotel suite with him. He said that the *shaykh* and his entourage had returned to Paris and invited him for dinner that evening. He wondered if an Irish girlfriend of mine, whom the man had met once, and I wanted to come along.

In Yemen, such an invitation for a woman to dine with practical strangers would have been inappropriate. But I had grown accustomed to the ways of Europe and America, as had Mujahid and all but one or two of his companions. I had developed enough confidence to know that no one could force me into something I didn't want, so I accepted the invitation, in particular since the Yemeni man that called me was a friend and would come with us.

Midway through the meal, though, the man seated beside me touched my hand in a way that, though perhaps innocent for a Westerner, was grossly unacceptable for two unrelated Yemenis of the opposite sex, even in Paris. I withdrew my hand hastily and fumed with anger, yet uncharacteristically I held my tongue through dinner.

Mujahid told me months later that when Ahlam had called to make the appointment to see him at the hotel, one of the *shaykh*'s travelling companions had suspected that the girls simply wanted to 'have a good time', as the man put it. The man who made this comment was supposed to be educated and well travelled, but unfortunately his intellectual faculties had not evolved far enough to conceive of any other purpose for such a visit.

Back in my flat after dinner, my fury continued to simmer. I cried all night at the disrespect the man had shown me. I finally picked up the telephone and called Shaykh Mujahid to say that I was coming to the hotel the following day. Unaware of my intentions, the man with Mujahid must have believed this confirmed his preconceived notion of us girls, but he immediately realized his error when I marched into the suite late the next morning in a huff.

Mujahid raised an eyebrow in surprise at his visitor's brusque entrance. I peered with disgust at the three men lounging in the chairs strewn around the room.

'You may be rich,' I stammered, waving a finger threateningly at the man who had touched me at dinner. 'But don't think you can buy me with your wealth. I'm not what you think. I work hard to support myself. No one is going to control me with his money.'

Breathless, I marched out of the room without another word.

When a Yemeni man meets a woman outside of his immediate family circle, it is exceedingly rare for him to introduce the woman to his wife or daughters for fear they might be suspicious of her (and his) intentions. But the issue never surfaced between Mujahid and me, and the next time he visited Paris with his wife and children several months later, they called me to have lunch with them and go shopping. Since then they have made me feel like a part of the family, and Mujahid has come to represent an invaluable father-figure in my life (though he would prefer to say brother-figure).

CHAPTER SIXTEEN

The kingmakers

The earliest written record of the Abu Shawareb family dates back over 700 years. The family formerly went by the name of Zaher, until one of its patriarchs cultivated an enormous moustache and the people referred to him thereafter as Abu Shawareb – father of the moustache.

Mujahid Abu Shawareb, like his close friend Yahya al-Mutawakil, was born sometime around the beginning of the Second World War. His village of Warwar is part of the Kharif tribe[1] and comprises a fertile finger of land shooting off from the broad Dhi Bayn Valley 25 miles north of Sanaa. The remnants of ancient lava flows fill the crevices on the encompassing slopes, fanning out into the valley bottom and bathing the floor in a sea of ebony.

The home Mujahid grew up in sits alone in the centre of Warwar's richest soil. The small square house of rock and mud is dwarfed by a round stone tower three storeys high, where the women and children formerly sought refuge in times of trouble.

---

[1] Mujahid's Kharif tribe (*kharif* means the 'senile one') is one of the pillars of the broader Hashid tribes. It is divided into three sections, based on descent from the original Kharif patriarch who lived many centuries ago. One of the sections, the Kalbiyeen, is further divided into three subdivisions, called 'thirds' (*thuluth*). The other two sections, Bani Jubar (the sons of Jubar) and Sayad (the hunter), are each divided into five subdivisions, called 'fifths' (*khamis*). Every subdivision has its own *shaykh* but, in the spirit of tribal independence, there is no leader for Kharif as a whole.

The nearest village, a handful of buildings crawling like ivy up a cliff in the valley, lies a mile or so to the east.

Mujahid's father and grandfather acted as *shaykhs* of one of the five Bani Jubar divisions of Kharif. Mujahid followed in their footsteps, growing up to earn a reputation for unsurpassed bravery, no small accomplishment in a country whose people pride themselves on the trait. However, the courage he displayed later in life was first inspired not by his father or grandfather, but by his mother.

Mujahid remembers playing around his home in Warwar as a small child when a lion suddenly leaped over the courtyard wall and growled at Mujahid's mother, who was busy feeding the sheep there. 'As the lion came towards me,' Mujahid says, 'mother grabbed an axe and charged the lion without the slightest hint of fear. The lion snatched a lamb in its jaws and sprang back over the wall before she could reach him.'

But another memory from a few years later forged an even stronger impression on Mujahid of his mother's courage:

'I was a young boy – just nine or ten years old,' Mujahid told Charles and me during one of his story-telling sessions on a visit to Paris. 'My mother sent me off one afternoon to buy some things in the village of Dhi Bayn, an hour and a half's walk up the valley. The day was already well advanced, so I readied the donkey, grabbed my rifle and hurried as fast as I could up the narrow *wadi* bed towards the market, anxious to make it home before sundown.'

On the way back, I grew nervous as the sun set behind the mountains of Sufyan, catching me a half-hour short of home. A twisted [olive-like] *ilm* tree grew alone on the bank of the *wadi* bed, between two boulders. As I passed by it, the donkey, laden with groceries, suddenly refused to go forward. There must have been a rock in his way or something, but I didn't know it at the time because it was too dark. I yelled at him and pushed him but he refused to budge.

Then I heard a strange rustling sound from the leaves in the *ilm* tree. It grew louder and louder and I became petrified, realizing that it must be a *jini*. We always said that *jinis* take particular pleasure in harassing people carrying oil or butter, and it occurred to me that the donkey bore a tin of cooking oil on its back. 'So that's why the donkey stopped,' I thought. 'He's afraid of the *jini*.'

I fumbled with my rifle and raised it to my shoulder, shaking so much I had to hold my breath to keep steady. I fired several rounds into the tree, but the rustling continued. Then I remembered: 'Of course. Bullets can't harm a *jini*.'

I sprinted home without looking back, leaving the donkey with the groceries to fend for himself. Running through the door, breathless and empty-handed except for my rifle, I placed myself in the corner furthest from the door. 'A *jini*! A *jini* attacked us!' I yelled to mother.

Mujahid smiles as he remembers the scene.

Mother stood there with her hands on her hips and stared suspiciously at me.

'Where are the groceries, Mujahid?' she asked me.

'I left them with the donkey beside the *ilm* tree. But the *jini* must have already got them,' I told her, trying to sound as convincing as possible. 'There may even have been more than one.'

Mother burst into laughter, which angered me to no end. She wrapped a cloak over her shoulders and started for the door. I couldn't believe it.

'Where are you going?' I screamed.

'To get the groceries.'

'What about the *jini*?' I asked, but she was already out of the door. I had not the slightest doubt that my mother was the bravest person in the world when she came back with the donkey and groceries an hour later.

'The shots I fired must have scared them off,' I said.

At the age of five, Mujahid began to study at the school at the foot of the mountain across the *wadi* from Warwar. The building had but a single room and the students sat in rows on the floor, writing on individual wood-framed chalk boards. Two teachers sent by the government taught the boys mathematics and how to read the Koran. All ages studied together, and when a student learned everything the teachers had to teach, he left to make room for someone else. Mujahid 'graduated' at the age of 12, the same year tragedy struck his family.

Mujahid's father, Shaykh Yahya Hadi Abu Shawareb, spent much of his time mediating problems within the neighbouring Sufyan, a Bakil tribe located in the very heartland of Hashid territory. His reputation through much of the northern highlands, like that of other *shaykhs*, stemmed as much from his arbitration skills as from his bravery.

Yahya's mediation proved highly effective, so much so that the Sufyani *shaykhs* didn't look kindly upon this perceived usurpation of their duties. The last straw came when Yahya purchased a large plot of land within Sufyan's territory, along the border separating the two tribes.

Land sold to someone from another tribe does not become the territory of the new owner's tribe. The latter can farm it and live on it, but the land remains closely bound to the honour of the original tribe, which continues to be held accountable for any crime or offence that takes place there.

Yet certain of the Sufyani *shaykhs* resented the incursion by Mujahid's father, whose popularity seemed to rise daily at their own expense. A handful of these men one day fabricated a dispute between two Sufyanis and called in Yahya to resolve the problem. But his task seemed a bit too easy that day, though he couldn't put his finger on just why. The answer was not long in coming.

'The next afternoon mother began to worry,' remembers Mujahid. 'Father had said before leaving the previous morning that he was likely to be away only for the day, and we had heard nothing from him since. I went to find my uncle, my father's brother, in the tiny village where I went to school nearby. I asked him if he had seen my father.

'You mean he hasn't come back from Sufyan yet?' my uncle asked. I said no, and he thought for a few moments.

'Did you hear gunshots last night?' he asked me. I shook my head.

'I thought maybe it was a wedding,' he said. 'But I didn't hear anything about a wedding this week. We'd better go and take a look.'

My uncle gathered a dozen men from the village, and I went with them along the path between Kharif and Sufyan. We spread out on either side of the track, looking for any sign of my father. I was dying with anxiety, and moved well ahead of the others when I came to a low embankment of earth between two plots of land. When I climbed to the top and jumped down on the other side, I saw my father lying on his side against the embankment, his knees drawn up near his chest.

He looked so peaceful, and for a moment I thought he must be asleep. But as I got closer I noticed that he was shrunken and gaunt. Then I saw the dark blood-stained earth around his body and I knew he was dead.

I wanted more than anything to cry, to scream out, and it was all I could do to hold back the tears.

No one would have blamed him, but Mujahid feared his uncle and the other men would consider him a child, so he remained stoical. He was practically a man, and he had to act the part if he wanted to be treated like one, for a tribesman is constantly on stage, his every move scrutinized by his peers.

'My father and Imam Ahmed had a close friendship ever since fighting the Saudis together in Najran,' Mujahid continued, referring to the 1934 Saudi-Yemeni war. 'When the *Imam* learned that my father had been murdered, he dispatched 1,000 soldiers to Sufyan and arrested every one of their principal *shaykhs*.

They soon revealed that as my father was walking home after mediating that afternoon, 16 Sufyanis lay in ambush along the path back to Warwar. Only a couple would ordinarily have been more than enough, but they used 16 to make it all but impossible to determine whose bullet actually killed my father. That way it would be more difficult for Kharif to take revenge. The *Imam*'s soldiers rounded up the men involved in the ambush and threw them in jail.

But the Sufyanis' plan worked. The judge appointed by the *Imam* could not determine which of the men had fired the two bullets that had hit my father and killed him. I was furious when I went to see the judge.

'All of them were there!' I yelled at him. 'They're all responsible!'

But the judge said he could prove nothing, and nearly two years later he set the Sufyanis free. I was even more furious when I learned of their release, and decided to take matters into my own hands.

A few days later I tailed one of the Sufyani *shaykhs* into the Dhi Bayn *suq*. Violence inside a market area is a grave offence according to tribal custom, but my blood boiled so much that I didn't care.

The Sufyani *shaykh* had several guards, and I knew a frontal assault would be likely to fail. So I went inside an empty house beside the *suq* and sat down beside an open window to watch.

When the guards moved aside for a moment, giving me a clear shot, I pulled the trigger. The bullet hit the *shaykh* on the right side of the chest, knocking him to the ground. The shoppers cleared the alleyways in a panic, and the guards started shooting at the house I was in.

Some of the *Imam*'s soldiers in Dhi Bayn came running when they heard the shots. They arrested the Sufyanis and me and hauled us all off to prison in Sanaa. I remained there for seven months, until it became clear that the Sufyani *shaykh* I had shot would survive his wounds. Then I was released.

Mujahid speaks with no hint of bravado or pride in what he did. The society he grew up in considered it a duty to act as he had done, and there was little choice in the matter. Mujahid could have left the deed up to his uncle, or some other close relative, but it still had to be done. And shirking his responsibilities, no matter how unpleasant or risky, has never been Mujahid's style.

When the Army Inspector General led a revolt against Imam Ahmed in 1955, Mujahid was visiting the capital of Taiz to petition the *Imam* about something or other. The *Imam* continued to pay Mujahid the pension he had paid Mujahid's father after fighting in the 1934 war, but though Mujahid's father had been close to the *Imam*, Mujahid did not like him. When the short-lived revolt broke out, 15-year-old Mujahid took pot shots at the *Imam*'s palace alongside the army's artillery.

In 1959, Mujahid again became involved in unrest after Imam Ahmed left for medical treatment in Italy. The ailing *Imam*'s sudden return four months later shocked everyone. Mujahid, not yet 20 years old, was with the prominent Hashid *shaykh*, Hameed al-Ahmar, when a message arrived summoning Hameed and his father, Hussayn, to see the *Imam*.

Numerous military officers had pledged beforehand to rise up against Imam Ahmed should he ever return to Yemen, and Hameed quickly composed letters to them reminding them of their promise. Mujahid set off with the correspondence for the town of Khamir, 40 miles north of Sanaa, while Hameed escaped to the Jawf to avoid arrest.

When the officers read Hameed's letters, they reacted unanimously: Imam Ahmed was too strong. It would be suicidal to confront him just then. They refused to lift a finger.

When the *Imam*'s soldiers managed to arrest Hameed in the eastern desert, Mujahid fled to Warwar. He went into hiding on the tabletop mountain overlooking his home, but after two months the restless fugitive tired of his monotonous exile and turned himself in.

Imam Ahmed sent Hameed al-Ahmar and his father off to jail in Hajja, where they soon lost their heads. But Mujahid was young and did not yet represent a serious threat to the Imam. Ahmed sent him not to dreaded Hajja, but to Qasr al-Silah, the fortress whose slanted basalt base, merging into a vertical wall of red brick, looms ominously above Sanaa from the southeast. Mujahid remained within its impregnable walls for three and a half years.

The guards allowed the inmates out of their cells on Fridays to wander in the sun along the fortress's battlements, 40 feet above the town streets. The prison held other diversions, too, some of them quite beneficial. Numerous intellectuals and educated military officers languished in the citadel from the time of the failed attempt to overthrow Imam Ahmed in 1955. These highly organized men operated a makeshift school for the younger prisoners. Mujahid and the other teenagers studied mathematics, geography and history, taught from books printed in Egypt and smuggled into the prison by friends and relatives.

The prisoners' spirits rose to their highest point in months on 19 September 1962. News reached them that Imam Ahmed had died from a combination of old age and complications from previous wounds. The possibility that the new *Imam*, Muhammad al-Badr, would amnesty the prisoners heartened everyone.

But the very next day, news from back home dampened Mujahid's enthusiasm. A message delivered to the citadel announced that one of Mujahid's tribesmen had finally avenged his father's death at the hands of the Sufyanis. While not bad news in itself, the circumstances of the revenge nevertheless revolted Mujahid.

Muhammad Harash, another of Kharif's *shaykhs*, had virtually adopted Mujahid after his father died. The man had always been close to the Abu Shawarebs and Mujahid referred to him thereafter as 'father'. Harash had never been a particularly violent man. He rarely got caught up as an antagonist in any of the frequent land disputes that plague the area.

Not a few Kharifis dreamed of avenging Yahya Abu Shawareb's death, but they had feared the terrible wrath of Imam Ahmed. The disorder caused by continuing the vendetta would not have pleased the ruler, though he had loved Yahya as much as any of the Kharifis did.

Within hours of learning of the *Imam*'s death, Harash assembled a group of men and attacked the village of the Sufyani *shaykh* that Mujahid had wounded in the Dhi Bayn *suq* eight years earlier. The *shaykh* himself had died of natural causes a few years before, but Harash and his band shot the man's son and drove off the villagers' livestock. The Sufyanis defended themselves and each side suffered several casualties in the ensuing fight, but Kharif came away with the advantage and considered itself avenged of Yahya Abu Shawareb's death.

Though his family's honour had been restored, the news of the bloody raid on the village angered Mujahid.

'The Sufyanis killed only one of us,' he admonished Harash later. 'There was no cause to butcher a village.'

Mujahid's moderation, particularly at his young age, earned him great respect and helped ensure that he would follow in his father's footsteps as a prominent tribal leader. The role of *shaykh* is by no means passed down automatically from father to son in the northern highlands. Instead it must be earned through one's actions, and Mujahid more than merited the title of *shaykh* as he matured into a young man.

Four or five days after Imam Ahmed's death, the new *Imam* freed the numerous *shaykhs* imprisoned in Qasr al-Silah and summoned them to his palace. The men assembled before Muhammad al-Badr that day observed a very different *Imam* from the one they had grown accustomed to. His eyes twinkled gleefully and his smooth coffee-coloured skin shone when he smiled, disconcerting the tough, poker-faced tribesmen before him. He kept his moustache trim and combed, though the whiskers refused to grow below the creased corners of his mouth. Unlike his father and grandfather, al-Badr's beard sprouted only at the tip of his chin and a few tufts of hair along the ridge of his jaw.

Overshadowed and repulsed by his father's domineering character, al-Badr had developed into a kind, gentle man, qualities that would prove more of a hindrance than an advantage in his capacity as ruler of Yemen. The hardened tribal *shaykhs* could smell al-Badr's weakness and inexperience. They had already witnessed it during Imam Ahmed's absence in Rome three years earlier, and al-Badr had changed little since then. He hoped his goodwill would suffice to win over the support of the tribes and the people in general, but neither Yemen nor any other nation works like that.

'I'm sorry for the things that happened between you and my father,' al-Badr told the coarse *shaykhs* lined up before him. He hesitated, searching for the right words. 'It was wrong to have killed Hameed and Hussayn al-Ahmar, and it was wrong to have kept you all in prison for so long. I hope we can open a new page between us.'

Mujahid and the other *shaykhs* acknowledged his confession with a nod. Jaded and sapped of strength from years of inactivity, they nevertheless saw clearly that the tide had finally turned against the Imamate.

For several months prior to their release, the imprisoned *shaykhs* had been in clandestine contact with military officers in Sanaa, planning a coup against Imam Ahmed. After the interview with al-Badr, the *shaykhs* left the palace and contacted the conspirators. These Free Officers (to whose movement Yahya al-Mutawakil had attached himself) revealed their intention to move against the new *Imam* in a few short days. The excited *shaykhs* set off for their respective territories to gather their tribesmen to assist the impending revolution.

'I went straight back to Kharif,' Mujahid remembers of that exciting time, 'to set about raising an army among the tribes. But within a day or two, news arrived from Sanaa that sections of the military had attacked the palace and that Imam al-Badr had been killed. I gathered 500 men and started immediately for Sanaa.'

Halfway there a messenger met us to report that it seemed al-Badr had not died after all. He said the *Imam* had managed to flee the palace dressed as a woman and was making his way north to Saudi Arabia.

We turned northeast in order to find him and prevent him from rallying support to his cause. Marching from village to village, they told us in one place that al-Badr and his supporters had passed through only five hours earlier. We tracked him for two weeks, without success, and he finally made it into Saudi Arabia.

Following the revolution on 26 September 1962, the majority of the Hashid tribes sided with the newly proclaimed Republic. Their support stemmed to a large extent from the *Imam*'s decision to execute the two prominent al-Ahmar *shaykhs* in 1959, but other factors also weighed heavily in the decision.

In Mujahid's case, his imprisonment in Qasr al-Silah further embittered him towards the institution of the Imamate. But perhaps more importantly, the years of study and mingling with political opponents to the *Imam* during his detention in the fortress exposed him to new ideas, new ways of looking at the system of government in Yemen. The Egyptian literature smuggled into the jail, with its revolutionary overtones, opened Mujahid's mind onto a world beyond Warwar, beyond even the mountains of Yemen; just as the radio in the merchant's home in Mahabsha had enlightened Yahya al-Mutawakil. He came to believe that the Imamate had to be eliminated before the country could begin to move forward into the modern world.

'If only Imam Ahmed had been more open to the outside world, he would have been perfect for Yemen,' Mujahid declared many years after the revolution. 'He was strong, brave, educated, a poet, and he was the only one who could maintain security in the country. In his time, you could walk with a sack of gold from one end of Yemen to the other and no one would try to take it from you. Imam Ahmed saw everything. If only he had been more open to the modern world ...'

Only someone with Mujahid's unquestionable loyalty and dedication to the Republic could speak so candidly on such a sensitive topic.

The Republican leadership placed Mujahid in command of some 2,500 troops after the revolution. He led his men into countless battles, ending up seriously wounded a half dozen times.

One rifle round punctured a kidney before lodging in his lower abdomen. Though it left him in occasional agony, Mujahid declined to let doctors remove the lead when they told him the procedure might render him sterile. He was young and still had a family to sire.

'During the second year of the war,' Mujahid recalls, 'I was riding in an APC[2] near the town of Khamir with ten of my men. Suddenly we felt a violent shaking. It felt like something was pushing us – hard – and I was thrown between the driver's legs up front. I remember an explosion. The flash blinded me and I passed out.'

> When I woke up several hours later, I was lying in the back of a transport truck converted into an ambulance. My clothes had been burned off and my skin charred with smoke.
>
> 'What happened?' I asked the APC driver, who was lying beside me in pretty bad shape. 'Where is everybody?'
>
> 'They didn't make it,' he said gravely. 'A rocket tore the top off our APC. You and I were thrown to the floor, but they couldn't even find the heads of the others.'

[2] armoured personnel carrier.

Mujahid's mood could swing from one extreme to another within very short intervals, betraying a highly sensitive character underneath his indestructible façade. The war against the Royalists seemed a lost cause for the Republicans at numerous junctures during the struggle and Mujahid, more than most, rode an emotional roller coaster through it all.

One of the low points came when he witnessed the partial destruction of the house he grew up in at the hands of Royalist troops occupying the mountains overlooking Dhi Bayn Valley. But no matter how dejected his spirit, he concealed it as best he could from his subordinates.

During the fighting in Hajja province, Mujahid's martial skills and daring impressed Abdullah al-Ahmar. Shaykh Abdullah had filled the vacuum left by his beheaded brother and father (Hameed and Hussayn) to become the most powerful of Hashid's, indeed the entire country's, *shaykhs*. He honoured Mujahid by offering him his sister's hand in marriage.

Shaykh Abdullah is a slim man with piercing eyes, a long sharp nose, and striking intelligence. Boasting unrivalled leadership skills, he has mastered the art of steering even the most hopeless of situations to his desired conclusion. Mujahid, some 15 years younger than Shaykh Abdullah, respected the man immensely and was delighted to take his sister for a wife.

Many years later, long after the war, Shaykh Abdullah and Mujahid were strolling with several of their men near the town of Khamir, where Shaykh Abdullah lived much of the time.

'Shaykh Abdullah and I were talking,' Mujahid recalls, 'when a boy in his late teens walked up to us. No one even noticed him until he took a pistol from behind his *jambiya* scabbard, placed it to Shaykh Abdullah's stomach, and pulled the trigger. Shaykh Abdullah writhed his body like a belly dancer and slipped aside just as the gun fired. The bullet only grazed his skin.'

Our men levelled their rifles, but before anyone could shoot, Shaykh Abdullah grabbed the boy's thick shock of hair with one hand and threw him to the ground with the other, pinning him there with a knee on his shoulder blade. Shaykh Abdullah unsheathed his *jambiya* and held it up to strike. But instead of slicing the boy's throat, like most men would have done, he pointed the dagger at the rest of us standing around him.

'Anyone who harms this boy,' he growled, 'I will kill right here and now.'

We all jumped back in awe. Shaykh Abdullah had placed the boy under his own protection, and we knew he would die himself before he let anyone lay a hand on the boy now.

When I stepped towards the boy, Shaykh Abdullah pointed his dagger at me and I backed away. Then he took the pistol from the boy's hand and lifted him to his feet.

'Have I harmed you or someone in your family in any way?' he asked.

'No,' the boy stuttered.

'Then someone must have sent you to kill me. Who was it?'

The terrified boy blurted out the name of a *shaykh* from a tribe far away to the east. He said the man had offered him 1,500 riyals, about six month's salary at the time, to kill Shaykh Abdullah.

'The next time anyone comes to you and wants you to kill someone,' Shaykh Abdullah told the boy, 'you come to me. I'll double their offer. Understood?'

The boy nodded and Shaykh Abdullah sent him off with his tail between his legs, grateful to be alive.

Shaykh Abdullah's sister bore Mujahid three daughters and a son over the coming years. One of the girls arrived the day Mujahid and his men won a critical battle against the Royalists. The family named her Intisar – Victory – in celebration, but she died in infancy along with her three siblings.

Mujahid's wife grew distraught. She began to doubt whether she would ever bear her husband a healthy child, in particular a boy. After painful consideration, she made the ultimate sacrifice by suggesting that Mujahid take another wife in order to ensure an abundant posterity. He refused at first, but she pestered him until he finally gave in.

Within days of Mujahid's second wedding, his first wife became pregnant again. She gave birth to a sturdy son, Jibran, just two weeks before the second wife gave birth to a girl.

At the end of the civil war in 1970, President al-Iryani made Mujahid Governor and Military Commander of Hajja province, from where he commanded the 5,000-man Majd (Glory) Brigade.

In the early 1970s, a group of military officers, for the most part in their early 30s, began meeting informally at the home of Muhammad Abu Lahum in Sanaa. They included Mujahid Abu Shawareb; Colonel Ibrahim al-Hamdi; his brother, Abdullah al-Hamdi; Ahmed al-Ghashmi; Parachute Brigade Commander Abdullah Abdul Alem; Artillery Commander Ali Qenaf Zahra; Muhammad Abu Lahum; his brother, Ali Abu Lahum; and their distant cousin, Dirham Abu Lahum, then the Military Commander of Taiz province.

Conversation at the gatherings naturally revolved around politics. By 1974, several of them felt that al-Iryani lacked the necessary force and decisiveness to lead the country effectively. Fearing that other, less desirable, personalities might stage a coup if they did not themselves act soon, discussion at their weekly gatherings turned to conspiracy.

Part of the problem stemmed from the President's relationship with Abdullah al-Ahmar, Speaker of the Consultative Council, Yemen's legislative branch. The two men got along poorly and the animosity between them increased steadily in the early 1970s. The President viewed with misgivings the Hashid *shaykh*'s close ties to the Saudi Arabian Government, which al-Iryani continued to mistrust even after the end of Yemen's civil war.[3] The powerful Sinan Abu Lahum, Governor of Hodayda Province and Muhammad and Ali's older brother, tried reconciling the two men.

Sinan Abu Lahum is the prominent *shaykh* of the Nihm tribe in eastern Yemen and one of the more influential *shaykhs* of the broader Bakil tribes in general. He became Governor of Hodayda province in 1967, a position he would retain for nearly seven years. Sinan transformed the position into a personal fiefdom, deriving significant power from control of North Yemen's principal sea port.

Both Shaykh Sinan (whose name means 'teeth') and Shaykh Abdullah al-Ahmar have preferred for the most part to remain behind the scenes of Yemeni politics. They rarely participate directly in the sort of conspiring then brewing in Muhammad Abu Lahum's home. But they did keep abreast of the discussions and exercised considerable, usually decisive, influence over the decisions taken. They were the real king-makers in the country.

Sinan's attempt to resolve the crisis between Shaykh Abdullah and President al-Iryani failed. Sinan warned al-Iryani that his continued alienation from al-Ahmar would eventually force the President's key military officers, including the Abu Lahums and Mujahid, to choose between the two men. There was no need to bring up the fact that Muhammad Abu Lahum and Mujahid were both married to sisters of Shaykh Abdullah. Al-Iryani knew it all too well, yet the President refused a rapprochement with Shaykh Abdullah.

[3] After the revolution in Yemen, foreign governments began financing their favourite *shaykhs* in order to exercise influence over the government in Sanaa. After Egypt washed its hands of Yemen in the late 1960s, Iraq and in particular Saudi Arabia poured millions of dollars into the country. While much of the Saudi money went to the Yemeni government to cover budget deficits, prominent *shaykhs* also received enormous sums directly from Riyadh through the late 1990s.

A majority of the officers meeting in the Abu Lahum house felt that al-Iryani had to go. If he could not come to terms with Shaykh Abdullah, then the country would come to a standstill.

Opposition to the proposed coup surfaced from the two most unlikely sources. Ironically neither Muhammad Abu Lahum nor Mujahid had given up on al-Iryani just yet. They considered it shameful to depose such a venerated figure, whose intellectual brilliance and service in the cause of the revolution no one could challenge. That al-Iryani was of a very agreeable personality, and much older than any of the officers considering his ousting, only reinforced the two men's desire not to move against him.

The debate at the Abu Lahum home shuffled back and forth during the spring of 1974, until word of the underground councils inevitably leaked. Muhammad al-Kuhali, Vice Minister of Interior and al-Iryani's chief of security, knocked on the door one day as the officers gathered to chew *qat*.

'I looked out of the window to see al-Kuhali pacing nervously back and forth in front of the house,' Muhammad Abu Lahum says of that day, 'and I let him in. Al-Kuhali glared at everybody there, trembling – but no one knew if it was out of anger or fear.[4] "I know you're in here plotting," he said angrily. "Don't think you're going to get away with it." Then he stormed out of the house.'

Al-Kuhali's warning rang hollow, for he could do little but posture against the powerful men assembled at the Abu Lahum home that day, and they saw through his bluff. In the end, al-Kuhali's plan to intimidate backfired. Mujahid and Muhammad Abu Lahum, angered by the man's patronizing tone, reluctantly swung their support behind the coup.

The officers 'placed our hands one over the other on top of a Koran,' Mohammad Abu Lahum recalls. 'Each of us then pledged that we would never plot against, or otherwise make trouble for,

---

[4] They would later refer to al-Kuhali as the 'carpet lion', due to the harmless nature behind his fierce façade.

any of the others present there that day. Then we all agreed that whichever of us took over the presidency from al-Iryani, he would stay in power only long enough to organize elections for a civilian ruler.'

On 13 June 1974, after more than six and a half years in power, the group of officers ousted President Abdul Rahman al-Iryani in a bloodless coup. Following al-Iryani's departure into exile in Damascus, a 14-member Command Council convened to decide who would take over the country. In addition to the original conspirators, the Council also included Yahya al-Mutawakil (recalled from his ambassadorship in Cairo the day before the coup) and Muhsin al-Aini (brother-in-law of the Abu Lahums and Yemen's Ambassador to London ever since resigning as al-Iryani's Prime Minister). Al-Aini was the Command Council's only civilian member.

After more than two weeks of intense discussion, which continued to take place at Muhammad Abu Lahum's home in Sanaa, the Council could delay no longer. It would have to take a vote to determine who would be Yemen's new president.

Several of the members considered Abdullah al-Ahmar as the best choice. Shaykh Abdullah, as *shaykh al-mashaykh* of all the Hashid tribes in Yemen, was and is the most influential tribal *shaykh* in Yemen. The strong cohesion of Hashid's member tribes endows it with considerable leverage in relations with the central government (though both it and the Bakil[5] had been somewhat cowed under the strong hands of Imams Yahya and Ahmed).

Yet, though the presidency lay at Abdullah al-Ahmar's fingertips in 1974, he preferred to exercise his influence from the more discreet position of Speaker of Yemen's Consultative Council. He was clever enough to know that the head of a large and powerful tribe did not constitute the ideal choice for Yemen's ruler.

---

[5] The Bakil tribes, while more numerous than the Hashid, are today too politically and geographically fractious to even agree among themselves upon a single, paramount *shaykh* to represent them.

A *shaykh*'s prestige and power in the northern highlands depends to a large extent on his distribution of largesse to his constituents. This wealth may originate from the *shaykh*'s personal landholdings or funds cajoled from the Yemeni Government (and sometimes foreign governments) to provide roads, schools, and other services.[6]

Certain *shaykhs* might have the ability to make or break the central government (even while in many cases they depend on it as a source of wealth). But should one of them decide to take over the country's reigns himself, he would open himself to accusations of preferential treatment towards his own tribe and allies. The charge is not serious. In fact it is expected, within the tribal context. *Shaykhs* are constantly travelling to Sanaa to petition the President for funds to be spent in their respective territories. But were the *shaykh* directly controlling the public purse strings, the charges of bias would take on greater significance, while at the same time his own tribe would complain that they were not getting enough. His margin for manoeuvre as the nation's leader would be severely curtailed.

It did not take long to tally the Command Council's votes. 'Thirteen of the 14 members raised their hands to elect Mujahid Abu Shawareb to succeed al-Iryani as President,' Muhammad Abu Lahum says. 'Mujahid was the only Council member who did not vote.'

The confidence his comrades displayed in him flattered the 34-year-old Mujahid, but he felt strongly that skills in tribal and military affairs do not suffice to run a country. Furthermore, he felt that Yemen's Parliament should elect the country's new leader, not the Command Council, which is why Mujahid refused to raise his hand for the vote.

---

[6] Custom makes it shameful for a tribesman, in particular a *shaykh*, to be directly involved in a purely money-making activity such as trade. But they have few qualms with taking handouts from governments – in fact it is a sort of extension of the *shaykhs*' own relationship with their tribesmen, to whom they distribute money.

Mujahid hesitated to speak during the moments after his election and Ahmed al-Ghashmi, seated beside him, dug his elbow into Mujahid's ribs and whispered: 'Accept! Accept!' But Mujahid declined the presidency.

Al-Ghashmi approached Mujahid afterwards. 'Why in the world didn't you accept?' he asked.

'You must be stupid if you think running a country is something to be taken lightly,' Mujahid answered.

A new vote had to be held. Abdullah al-Ahmar and Sinan Abu Lahum, whose pervasive influence loomed over the Council even without their presence at the proceedings, favoured Ibrahim al-Hamdi, a former Deputy Prime Minister and the Deputy Commander in Chief of the Armed Forces at the time of the coup.

Yahya al-Mutawakil knew al-Hamdi better than anyone on the Command Council, since they had shared a cell for a time during their detention in Cairo and before that had studied together at the Air Force Academy. They became good friends at the academy, perhaps brought together by their highly competitive natures. But al-Hamdi's sensitive character clashed with the machismo of military school, where he frequently got into mischief and found it difficult to swallow the consequent punishment. Considering himself a scapegoat, he dropped out of the academy after six months.

Despite his friendship with al-Hamdi, Yahya opposed his candidature for the presidency. Only in his early thirties, al-Hamdi looked with a progressive-minded perspective on the many social and economic problems confronting Yemen. He considered it a priority to set the country on the road to development after nearly a decade of war.

These views in no way conflicted with Yahya's own appraisal of the situation. But Yahya believed that, despite outward appearances, al-Hamdi suffered from an acute inferiority complex that he attempted to conceal with inflated personal ambition – a dangerous combination, Yahya thought. He sensed that al-Hamdi would not remain content as a mere transitional ruler, as the

Command Council members had agreed upon prior to their coup. Once in the job, he would never relinquish it voluntarily.

Al-Hamdi, whose occasional drink of alcohol sometimes turned to excess, could also be extremely moody. While chewing *qat* with friends, he was known to rise from his seat in the middle of a conversation to insert an Umm Kulthum cassette in the stereo. No one listens to music while chewing *qat* (unless from a live musician). It is a social time when participants engage in lively chatter and, before television and cell phones, someone might read sections of a book aloud. But al-Hamdi didn't care. He returned to his cushion, shut his eyes, and laid his head back to take in every note of the great Egyptian singer's voice.

Yahya just had a bad feeling and he attempted to dissuade the Council and, more importantly, Shaykh Abdullah and Sinan, from choosing al-Hamdi as president. Yahya's opposition led some of the officers to suspect that he harboured his own designs on the post. But no one realized better than Yahya that, as a *Sayid*, his candidacy would be inappropriate so close to the end of the civil war that ousted the *Sayid Imams* from power.

Yahya, no less stubborn than Mujahid when convinced he is right, fought an uphill battle. The rest of the Command Council did not share his opinion. Like al-Iryani before him, al-Hamdi hailed from a family of *qadhis*. He was articulate and sophisticated in a worldly way that the others were not and, while appearing strong and decisive, he also came across as a jovial, kind-hearted man.

The majority of the Council felt that, after Mujahid, al-Hamdi met the most criteria for what a president should be. In the end, Shaykh Abdullah and Shaykh Sinan decided the debate. Twenty days after al-Iryani's ousting, al-Hamdi became the Republic of Yemen's third president.

Ibrahim al-Hamdi quickly showed himself to be a charismatic leader. He appealed not only to intellectuals and modernists but equally won the hearts of urban dwellers and rural regions in the southern and western highlands.

As a young girl, I remember the people in Sanaa cheering in the streets and waving photographs of al-Hamdi after one of his fiery speeches. They loved him not only for his enthusiasm, but also for his perceived modesty, which none expected but all admired in a president. This was most conspicuous in the old Volkswagen 'beetle' he drove alone around Sanaa, even after he became president.

Al-Hamdi produced an agenda introducing numerous changes to Yemen, aimed at building up the country's all but non-existent political and economic infrastructure. The future radiated with promise as roads were paved, electrification expanded, official corruption combated and business in general began to thrive.

The Command Council shrank to seven members by mutual consent following al-Hamdi's election. Those with active military commands, such as Muhammad and Ali Abu Lahum and the President's brother, agreed to resign as council members and return to their commands. The Parachute Brigade Commander, Abdul Alem, however, maintained his seat. As the Council's only representative of Yemen's southern areas, al-Hamdi considered it politically prudent to keep Abdul Alem on.

The President's next step entailed forming a government, and jockeying for position got underway early. The Abu Lahums persuaded al-Hamdi to name their brother-in-law, the intellectual Muhsin al-Aini, to another stint as Prime Minister. The President then conceded to combined pressure from the Abu Lahums and al-Aini to make Yahya al-Mutawakil the Interior Minister.

Yahya's hunch about his friend's colossal ambition soon proved right on the mark. Disregarding the oath of mutual support taken prior to the coup, al-Hamdi turned on those who had helped put him where he was: the prominent tribal *shaykhs* of Hashid and Bakil.

'Within six months of taking over,' Muhammad Abu Lahum remembers, 'al-Hamdi began calling odd meetings with Mujahid Abu Shawareb. He would pretend to take Mujahid into his confidence and requested his help in clipping the wings of the Abu Lahums by expelling them from their positions in the government. Then al-Hamdi would call one of us (the Abu Lahums) to say very secretively that he wanted to dismiss Mujahid from his posts and would we give him our blessing before he acted. I don't know what he was thinking. He knew Mujahid and I are very close friends, and it didn't take long for us to see what al-Hamdi was up to.'

In early 1975 the emboldened al-Hamdi ploughed fatefully ahead with his vision of the new Yemen. He began by dismissing Muhsin al-Aini from his simultaneous posts as Prime Minister and Foreign Minister in January. The move so upset Muhammad Abu Lahum that among confidants he proposed overthrowing al-Hamdi, but Muhsin al-Aini refused to allow it and Muhammad did not push the issue.

Then on the afternoon of 27 April Yahya al-Mutawakil learned from his office in the Interior Ministry that tanks had begun deploying mysteriously around the streets of the capital. He rushed off to find the President.

'What's going on?' Yahya asked when he finally located al-Hamdi.

'Everything is under control,' al-Hamdi assured him calmly. 'This evening I'm going to announce the dismissal of Dirham, Muhammad and Ali Abu Lahum from their military commands. The tanks are just a precaution.'

'I was shocked,' Yahya recalled later. 'But there was no use arguing. Al-Hamdi had made up his mind and the announcement came through on the radio a few hours later.'

Al-Hamdi's decision to dismiss al-Aini and the Abu Lahums was not taken alone. His relations with Saudi Arabia were very close when he took power and Riyadh, which did not like the pro-Iraqi Baathist sympathies of al-Aini or the Abu Lahums, encouraged, if not pressured, the Yemeni President to distance himself from them.

The following morning, an angry Abdullah al-Ahmar came to see the President. Shaykh Abdullah, who was hardly more

comfortable with the Abu Lahums' Baathist leanings than was
Riyadh, nevertheless stood by the family. He insisted that if al-
Hamdi wanted to purge the Abu Lahums then so too should he
relieve his own brother, Abdullah al-Hamdi, as commander of the
elite Amalaqa Brigade and Ali Qenaf Zahra, the President's faithful
ally, as head of the Seventh Armoured Brigade. Ever eager to avoid
a face-to-face confrontation, al-Hamdi consented. He promised to
announce Ali Qenaf and his brother's dismissal that very evening.

'But the declaration never came,' Yahya al-Mutawakil
remembered 25 years later, still with incredulity. 'I went the
next morning to ask al-Hamdi why he hadn't kept his promise to
Shaykh Abdullah.'

'Because I've made another decision, and I want your
support,' al-Hamdi answered.

I asked him what it was and he said, 'You're not going to
like it.'

'You mean you're not going to dismiss your brother and
Ali Qenaf?' I asked. Al-Hamdi shook his head.

'No. I'm not going to dismiss them.'

I was disgusted and started to leave. He stopped me.

'But I *am* going to dismiss Mujahid.'

I couldn't believe my ears. Mujahid was Deputy
Chairman of the Command Council and by now Deputy
Commander-in-Chief of the Armed Forces as well. More
importantly, he was Shaykh Abdullah's brother-in-law,
and the one people expected to succeed Abdullah as
Hashid's principle *shaykh*. I told al-Hamdi he couldn't make
Mujahid go away just by pronouncing a few words over the
airwaves, but he wouldn't listen.

Dumbfounded, Yahya left to warn Shaykh Abdullah to expect
the worst. The radio broadcast the momentous news of
Mujahid's dismissal later that day. Fearing for his life, Shaykh
Abdullah departed Sanaa for Khamir, where he denounced the
al-Hamdi government as 'illegitimate' and circled the wagons for
a showdown.

As the President locked horns with the tribal *shaykhs*, he simultaneously attempted to woo Yahya al-Mutawakil, hoping to play him off against Yahya's close friends, Mujahid and the Abu Lahums. Following Mujahid's dismissal, Yahya presented his letter of resignation as Interior Minister, but al-Hamdi refused to accept it. He pleaded with Yahya to stay and help him reconcile with the Hashid and Bakil *shaykhs*. When Yahya hesitated, al-Hamdi dangled the vice-presidency in front of him as an incentive. Yahya refused the offer, but considered helping his old friend nonetheless.

Yahya knew all about al-Hamdi's skill at deception. On one occasion, the President telephoned Abdullah al-Ahmar and literally wept to convince the *shaykh* of his sincerity on a particular issue. Deeply moved, Shaykh Abdullah called his brother-in-law, Muhammad Abu Lahum, to say that he wanted to see him immediately.

'You won't believe what happened,' Shaykh Abdullah told him when Muhammad arrived at his home a few minutes later. 'The President broke into tears on the phone with me this morning.'

Muhammad laughed. 'Is that the first time you've heard him do that? Don't let him fool you. He does it all the time.'

But though he doubted al-Hamdi's sincerity, Yahya believed it was worth giving reconciliation a try. He withdrew his resignation and the following day travelled with al-Hamdi to Khamir to meet with Shaykh Abdullah for the first time since their falling-out.

The President, complaisant and humble, welcomed the Hashid *shaykh* back to Sanaa as an adviser on government affairs.[7] But he rejected Shaykh Abdullah's insistence that the Abu Lahums be reinstated to their former government positions. The meeting ended in deadlock.

---

[7] Al-Hamdi had earlier suspended the Consultative Council, Shaykh Abdullah's power base.

Mujahid was away on an official visit to China when al-Hamdi announced his dismissal. To reach Beijing, he and his delegation had flown to Karachi, Pakistan, on the presidential aircraft. Moscow had supplied the plane with its Russian crew to al-Hamdi for his personal use. But with relations strained between the Soviet Union and China, authorities in Beijing refused permission for the Russian aircraft to enter its airspace. The Yemeni delegation had to take a China Airways flight for the last leg of the journey to the Chinese capital.

After the week-long visit, Mujahid's delegation returned to Karachi on China Airways. 'Al-Hamdi had promised to send his private aircraft back to Pakistan to fly us to Sanaa,' Mujahid recalls. 'But when I stepped off the plane in Karachi, I looked around and didn't see it anywhere. I found a telephone and called our ambassador in Pakistan.'

'Where's the president's plane?' I asked him.
'You mean you haven't heard?' he said nervously.
'Heard what?'

The news of the dismissals stunned Mujahid and, as the reality sank in, his disbelief shifted to anger. He couldn't let al-Hamdi walk over him and the Abu Lahums with impunity.

He and his delegation boarded a civilian flight to Cairo. Leaving his companions in Egypt, Mujahid continued on to Jedda alone. In Saudi Arabia, he requested permission from the Saudi Government to cross the border into Yemen by road. But al-Hamdi, foreseeing this possibility, had already requested that Riyadh prevent Mujahid from returning to Yemen by land.

Prince Sultan, the Saudi Defence Minister, advised Mujahid to fly to Sanaa and work out his problems with al-Hamdi face to face. Mujahid refused. The Yemeni President had already arrested many of his and Shaykh Abdullah's supporters, and he was likely to do the same to Mujahid if he turned up in the capital.

Mujahid is nothing if not strong-willed. He insisted so vehemently that the Saudis finally allowed him to return overland to Yemen. He made his way straight to his fief of Hajja, where his loyal Majd Brigade had been awaiting the arrival of its commander.

Mujahid had garnered considerable backing during his time as Governor of Hajja. As news of his return swept across the terraced valleys, many of the tribes gathered round the *shaykh* and pledged their support against al-Hamdi.

The President squirmed when he realized that the powerful ally he had transformed into an angry rival had returned, bent on turning the tables against him. Fearing an attack on the capital at any moment by the Majd Brigade, al-Hamdi convinced Yahya al-Mutawakil to open negotiations. Mujahid agreed to listen.

With Yahya acting as go-between, al-Hamdi offered his adversary his seat back in the Command Council. But Mujahid was adamant that al-Hamdi bring Shaykh Abdullah back into the fold before he would consider returning to the Command Council. The talks halted abruptly.

As Mujahid prepared for a showdown after the aborted negotiations, Yahya persuaded him to meet one last time with al-Hamdi, in Hodayda. A few days later the President came face to face with Mujahid, each surrounded by his entourage of several hundred soldiers armed to the teeth, two peacocks competing to impress and intimidate with a dazzling display of ornamentation in the bright Tihama sunshine. Yahya realized with alarm that a powder keg could ignite at any moment.

Al-Hamdi began the tense conversation.

'You have nothing to fear from me,' he claimed. But his knees quaked as the words came boldly from his mouth.

Mujahid gazed stoically at the pudgy, baby-faced man before him, indignant at the suggestion that he might be afraid of someone, anyone. The only person who had ever intimidated Mujahid was Imam Yahya, and Imam Ahmed to a lesser extent. But he had been only a boy then, and al-Hamdi was certainly not Imam Yahya.

'I want you to be the Governor of Hajja again,' the President continued, laying out his first and only bargaining chip. Mujahid had relinquished his post as Governor of Hajja province after the coup against al-Iryani.

But it was hardly a concession. After all, half the men lined up behind Mujahid came from Hajja. He already controlled the province; not al-Hamdi.

The talks went nowhere, and the Kharif *shaykh* prepared to return to Hajja. But before he left, Yahya managed to secure a pledge that he would not move against Sanaa for the time being.

'I'll wait and see how things develop,' Mujahid agreed.

The meeting's peaceful ending relieved and surprised both Yahya and al-Hamdi.

By July 1975, Yahya al-Mutawakil's continuing efforts at mediation had progressed little as al-Hamdi and the *shaykhs* refused any compromise. Yahya saw clearly now that the President had no intention of appeasing them. He had used the negotiations simply as a way to buy time.

In mid-July, Yahya submitted his resignation for a second time as Interior Minister and member of the Command Council. Al-Hamdi tried once again to convince him to stay, but this time Yahya had made up his mind.

In the southern and western highlands of Yemen (and to a lesser extent in Sanaa), society is organized more along the lines of village and regional ties than of tribe. Inhabitants in these places have complained for centuries that the plateau tribes north and east of Sanaa exercise an inordinate amount of sway over central government.

In only a few areas have the southern populations enjoyed the forceful backing of a tribe to pressure the government into giving them what they want. A few southerners have held some leverage with their large business interests, for southerners have historically tended to be more merchant-minded than the northern tribesmen[8]. Yet the great majority of southern high-landers are farmers with limited access to influential circles within the government. They have survived, in some cases thrived, largely because their land is considerably more productive than that of the northern plateau (and because large numbers have emigrated to Europe and America to find work, sending money back home).

Over the centuries, taxes collected from farmers in the fertile southern highlands represented a large portion of the Imamate's budget. But the arid climate of the northern plateau meant farms there rarely provided more than a subsistence yield. Little could be gained from taxing those areas, while much could be lost, in the form of rebellion.[9]

What the plateau could provide the *Imams*, however, was man-power, either to defend the *Imams* when threatened or to enforce their rule (including the collection of taxes in the country's more productive regions). And as the *Imams* occasionally presented them with gifts of land in the south to placate or reward them, northern *shaykhs* have come to make up many of the large landlords in the southern highlands today.

Ibrahim al-Hamdi claimed he wanted to correct the economic and political imbalance between the tribal and non-tribal regions of the country. 'Had that been the case,' Yahya al-Mutawakil explained years later, 'I might have shown more enthusiasm in supporting the President. But I soon realized that in breaking with the prominent Hashid and Bakil *shaykhs*, al-Hamdi simply

---

[8] This phenomenon is beginning to change, however as the sons of tribal *shaykhs* have become increasingly involved in business activities since the 1980s.

[9] Unlike on the northern plateau, a large proportion of farmers in the south and west are sharecroppers of land owned by absentee landlords. Though referred to as *shaykhs*, the role of these large landowners is very different from that of *shaykhs* further north. The latter derive their standing from distributing wealth to their tribesmen. The southern *shaykhs*, on the other hand, see themselves as recipients of wealth from the people working their land, who present them with anywhere from one-half to one-quarter of the annual harvest.

replaced them in his inner circle with smaller *shaykhs* or their supporters.'

Al-Hamdi attempted to emulate the former *Imams'* divide-and-rule tactics of playing big *shaykhs* off against smaller ones, for example by handing small *shaykhs* powerful government posts and allowing big *shaykhs* less influence in his decisions. Yahya, however, came to believe that the President's motivation for curtailing Yemen's powerful tribal leaders had less to do with improving the country and more to do with reinforcing the President's own hold on power.

Nine months after Yahya's resignation as Interior Minister, al-Hamdi sent him into exile as Yemen's Ambassador to the United States.

Sometime around late 1976, the President got wind of a coup plot masterminded by Ahmed al-Ghashmi, al-Hamdi's Chief of Staff and Mujahid's successor as Deputy Commander-in-Chief of the Armed Forces. Ever since al-Iryani's overthrow, al-Ghashmi proved to be even more ambitious than his close friend al-Hamdi. The Chief of Staff egged the President on in his power struggle with the tribes, intent on having him finish off the dirty work. Then al-Ghashmi planned to step in and take over himself.

But the scheme appeared to be thwarted when a confidant informed al-Hamdi of the plot. The President dispatched his Chief of Staff on a visit to Iraq during which al-Hamdi planned to announce his dismissal. Al-Ghashmi had second thoughts about what lay in store for him as he boarded his flight for Baghdad. He disembarked, forcing al-Hamdi to postpone his plan. It would be too risky to dismiss al-Ghashmi while he was in the country.

A few months later, another opportunity presented itself when al-Ghashmi once again felt confident enough to venture outside the country. He travelled to Paris, France, in early 1977 with the President's brother, Abdullah al-Hamdi, and Ali Abdullah Salih (Dirham Abu Lahum's replacement as Military Commander of Taiz province).

With al-Ghashmi in Europe, the President could finally get rid of his dangerous Chief of Staff. Al-Hamdi, in Hodayda at the time, sat down at his desk to review the prepared order dismissing al-Ghashmi. As he lifted his pen to sign the document, the telephone rang. It was the head of security in Sanaa checking in with al-Hamdi, as he did several times each day.

At the end of a brief conversation, during which the security chief informed him that all was well in the capital, al-Hamdi asked absent-mindedly: 'Where is [Abdullah] Abdul Alem?' referring to the Parachute Brigade Commander and Command Council member.

'He's chewing *qat*,' the man answered.

'Who with?' al-Hamdi wanted to know.

The security chief explained that the Prime Minister (Abdul Aziz Abdul Ghani) had invited Abdul Alem along with the Minister of Foreign Affairs and the Minister of Local Administration to chew *qat* that afternoon. When al-Hamdi hung up the phone, his thoughts raced out of control. The Prime Minister, Abdul Alem, and the other men chewing *qat* had one thing in common: they were all from Yemen's southern highlands.

The President stared blankly at the dismissal order on the desk before him, but his mind was elsewhere. The seemingly innocent *qat* chew in Sanaa worried him.

Yemenis love to scheme, coming up with intricate, complex plans aimed at influencing events to their liking. The plots often unravel following the authors' revelation to a third party, who unfailingly informs everyone even remotely connected. But they often move ahead nonetheless.

Al-Hamdi, whose family originates from a small village 30 miles northwest of Sanaa, was even more suspicious than most Yemenis. Muhammad Abu Lahum says al-Hamdi's favourite song was Umm Kulthum's 'Revolution of doubt', and doubt indeed plagued the President. When he considered the *qat* session in the capital, al-Hamdi's own scheming mind could conceive of only one possibility: his Prime Minister and the two ministers from the southern highlands were plotting against him to seize power for themselves.

Alarmed, al-Hamdi decided he might need al-Ghashmi's strong hand after all. He tore up the unsigned dismissal order.

From his informants among the President's entourage, al-Ghashmi nevertheless learned of his near demise while still in France. On the same day as the Chief of Staff arrived back in Sanaa, Muhammad Abu Lahum was driving past the Presidential offices when he saw al-Ghashmi drive out.

'I waved at him,' Muhammad remembers, 'but he didn't stop. He signalled for me to follow him, and we drove to his home and talked there.'

> 'Welcome back,' I said. 'If you'd returned any later you would have lost your job just like the rest of us,' I joked, referring to Mujahid, Shaykh Abdullah, Dirham (Abu Lahum) and my brothers and me.
>
> 'How do you know about that?' al-Ghashmi asked me, his moustache trembling with anger. The Military Commander of Hodayda province was a good friend of mine, and he had sent me a letter immediately when he learned that al-Hamdi intended to dismiss al-Ghashmi. But I didn't mention that to al-Ghashmi.
>
> 'By God, Muhammad,' al-Ghashmi said. 'You can step on my face if I don't grind al-Hamdi's head to a pulp.'

Within a few months al-Ghashmi had kept his promise to Muhammad Abu Lahum. The Chief of Staff had al-Hamdi shot on 11 October 1977 (with the two French women), then seized power for himself.

Ahmed Hussayn al-Ghashmi was in his mid-thirties when he became Yemen's fourth president. Muhammad Abu Lahum had known him since the civil war in the 1960s, when al-Ghashmi, along with his own successor as president, Ali Abdullah Salih, fought in a Republican tank unit commanded by Muhammad

Abu Lahum. Al-Ghashmi worked his way up to Lieutenant-Colonel in 1971, then took over the First Tank Regiment three years later before joining the Command Council after al-Iryani's overthrow.

The arrival of al-Ghashmi to power in the fall of 1977 filled everyone linked to Yemeni politics with dread, particularly after he reportedly had a handful of his fiercest political enemies executed. His extremely tenuous hold on the reigns of power probably explains his severity, as spontaneous demonstrations formed in the capital to protest the popular al-Hamdi's death, blaming al-Ghashmi for the murder.

The unpredictable al-Ghashmi telephoned Mujahid Abu Shawareb three days after the coup. 'Who's stupid now?' al-Ghashmi asked him, referring to their conversation when Mujahid had declined to become president following the Command Council vote in 1974.

'I may be the stupid one,' Mujahid conceded. 'But I don't envy you your position one bit.'

Al-Ghashmi then asked Mujahid to come to the President's private home in Dhala village, a few miles from Sanaa. 'He wouldn't tell me why,' Mujahid remembers, 'so I expected the worst.'

Al-Ghashmi's guards took my pistol before I went into the house, which of course didn't reassure me. They showed me into the waiting room, where lots of other high-ranking officials were already seated, waiting nervously to see al-Ghashmi.

Several minutes later the door at the back of the room burst open, nearly scaring several of the officials out of their chairs. Al-Ghashmi walked in with a very grim face.

'What do you want from me?' he asked when he saw me.

'Nothing,' I answered. 'You invited me here.'

'Surely you want a position in the government. What is it? Name it!'

'Nothing ... right now,' I told him. 'Let's see how things go for a while. Then I'll let you know.' I thought for a moment, then told him: 'The only thing I'm interested in right now is improving the infrastructure in Hajja. We need roads and bridges.'

When al-Ghashmi said he would see what he could do to help, I thanked him and left. While I was driving back to Hajja with my men, a car came up on us from behind at high speed. Waving us to the side of the road, I got out to see what the men in the car wanted. Al-Ghashmi had sent them to deliver a suitcase to me. I slowly unzipped it and found it filled with several million dollars worth of Saudi riyal notes.

'The President says you can start building your roads with this,' the man said, and drove away.

Al-Ghashmi was known for his generosity, liberally distributing the large sums of cash he received as subsidies from the Saudi Government. Mujahid was desperately short of funds to meet his soldiers' salaries in Hajja, so the suitcase relieved him of this concern for the time being. But it would take more than money to convince Mujahid, who distrusted al-Ghashmi as much, perhaps more, than he had al-Hamdi.

Al-Ghashmi predictably delayed offering Mujahid and the Abu Lahums official posts in the new government, but it mattered little. No one expected the new president to last very long, and he didn't. The bomb in the South Yemeni emissary's briefcase ended his rule after only eight and a half months.

By the time a second border war erupted between North and South Yemen in 1979, neither Mujahid nor the Abu Lahums had been reintegrated into the government of Ali Abdullah Salih, al-Ghashmi's successor. When fighting spread into the southern areas of North Yemen, Ali Abdullah Salih called on Mujahid to command North Yemeni troops in Ibb and the overrun border region of Qataba.

Mujahid accepted and his forces subsequently expelled the South Yemeni army across the border. The President named Mujahid Vice-Prime Minister for Internal Affairs after the war had ended, a post he retained for over a decade.

A top South Yemeni official lost a brother in the border war when Mujahid's forces overran 300 southern troops in heavy fighting in the mountains above Qataba town. On learning that his brother was among the dead, the official determined to take revenge and targeted Mujahid as responsible for his son's death.

A Socialist Party cadre in South Yemen at the time told Mujahid the story 15 years later over dinner at a restaurant in Paris. The dead man's brother had hired an assassin a few months after the war had ended to kill Mujahid. Mujahid was in Washington, DC, and supposed to travel to France, so the assassin (who was not a Yemeni) went to Paris to wait for him. But Mujahid changed his mind at the last minute and went to Geneva instead. The assassin aborted the operation.

Mujahid listened intently, but the story amused more than concerned him. Despite the initial failure, the South Yemeni official would not forsake his vendetta. In 1985, six years after the border war, Mujahid was inspecting his vineyard in Warwar when an elderly Sufyani man came to ask him for money 'to help pay some medical bills'. Mujahid handed him some money and as the man was leaving, he suddenly swung round, levelled the muzzle of his Kalashnikov, and let burst a hail of bullets in Mujahid's direction. The alert guards shot and killed the man before he could find his mark.

Within an hour thousands of tribesmen from the surrounding area had gathered in Warwar to find out what had happened. The Sufyani *shaykhs* were in no mood for compromise, and they insisted that the killing meant nothing less than war with Kharif. Mujahid summoned Sinan Abu Lahum (like the Sufyanis, a Bakili) from Sanaa to intervene before the situation veered out of control. But when the *shaykh* arrived on the scene, the Sufyanis remained intransigent.

'We don't want your help,' they announced to Sinan. 'We want revenge.'[10]

When Sinan threatened to withdraw and let them take their chances in a war with the surrounding Hashid tribes, the Sufyani *shaykhs* quickly sobered up. If Sinan, and probably much of the rest of Bakil, refused to help them, then their demand for revenge could end up getting them badly mauled.

The antagonists surrendered rifles and *jambiyas* to Sinan and a dozen *shaykhs* from Kharif and Sufyan sat cross-legged in a circle under a camel thorn tree. The Nihm *shaykh* listened intently to their arguments.

After several hours of heated discussion, Sinan finally came to a verdict. Kharif should pay Sufyan three times the normal *diya* of 300,000 riyals (US$75,000 at the time) in compensation for the dead man. Sufyan and Kharif both accepted the ruling.

Normally, in a dispute with another tribe, all of Kharif's sections would pitch in to raise the *diya* payment. The system reinforces the notion of mutual assistance and communal responsibility, and spreads the financial burden across the entire tribe. This was particularly beneficial in the days when no one, not even the *shaykhs*, had enough wealth to come up with the large *diya* payments by themselves. But things had changed now, with the introduction of bore wells and pumps to irrigate cash crops like grapes or *qat*. In an act of goodwill, and without soliciting contributions from any other Kharif clans, Mujahid went beyond the decision and paid Sufyan two million riyals plus a bulldozer to help with road maintenance in their territory.

Mujahid thought at the time that the old man's attempt to kill him had something to do with the land Mujahid owned in Sufyan territory, or with the feud simmering between Kharif and Sufyan since the murder of Mujahid's father. But Mujahid discovered a few years later that the South Yemeni official who had lost a

---

[10] The fact that the dead man had tried to kill Mujahid held little relevance. What matters in such cases is not the intention, but rather whose blood has actually spilled.

brother during the border war had contacted the Sufyani man and offered him money and a brand new truck in exchange for killing Mujahid.

A combination of luck and awareness has allowed Mujahid to survive so many close calls over the years, and it is just such a mixture that produces great leaders in Yemen. But the unlikely odds of living through a sufficient number of these ordeals to build up a personal following means such men are few and far between.

CHAPTER SEVENTEEN

Tying the knot — halfway

After a year working at the Yemeni Embassy in Paris, I decided it was time to move on. My heart was set on returning to America to study for a master's degree in film and video production, a subject that had interested me ever since my summer at the University of Southern California.

I doubted the US Agency for International Development would grant me another scholarship, at least not directly. But AID also offered financial assistance through various government agencies in Yemen, including the Ministry of Information, which officially employed me since I worked at the television station. The ministry submitted a list of scholarship candidates to the AID office in Sanaa each year for approval. With the ministry's backing, I might have a chance.

When Mujahid Abu Shawareb passed through Paris again, I asked if he would talk to Yemen's Information Minister, Hassan al-Lowzi, about submitting my name for another scholarship. Mujahid agreed, as did al-Lowzi, and the AID accepted my application. The organization assigned me to study at American University, a mile up the road from Mount Vernon College in northwest Washington, DC.

Two weeks before leaving for America, I telephoned my mother in Sanaa. She had been waiting anxiously for my call and became frantic when she heard my voice. I could make out little from her frenzied talk, except that my half-brother, Tariq, was in jail. I returned to Yemen on the first direct flight from Paris a few days later to find out what had happened.

Six months earlier, one of Tariq's relatives accidentally shot and killed the son of the man that had murdered Tariq's father on the rooftop over five years before. The relative immediately fled.

Suspecting the incident had something to do with Hameed al-Maamari's death, tribal *shaykhs* from the surrounding area intervened to prevent a feud. Employing a traditional and usually effective technique, they arrested a half-dozen men from Tariq's village, holding them in jail in the provincial capital of Dhamar until the killer turned himself in.

The *shaykhs* had intended to take Tariq's Uncle Ahmed, Shaykh Hameed's brother, but he anticipated the move and left home. Tariq, 14, was considered a man so they detained him instead.

Mother lost little sleep over Tariq at first. Usually a wanted man will turn himself in after a few days or weeks at most, when he learns that his family and tribesmen have been imprisoned for his offence. But in this case the killer headed south for the mountains of the al-Hada tribe, from whom he requested asylum. The al-Hada took him in, as required by the tribal code, and negotiations and threats from the government failed to convince them to hand the man over.

As the months passed, Mother grew increasingly anxious for Tariq. Her other son, Hamud, tried to help, but never with any results. Next she turned to her brother, Ali, who by now had transferred from the State Security's Criminal Division to a job in the Immigration and Passport Bureau.

For all his faults, I will always remember the professionalism with which Uncle Ali approached his work. Years later, more than one Yemeni businessman told me how they had offered Ali payment in order for him to speed up the paperwork necessary for foreigners invited by the businessmen to Yemen. Such bribes are standard procedure and many of the employees in Ali's department lived in nice houses and drove expensive cars obtained with the proceeds of these payouts. But Uncle Ali categorically refused to accept them, paying the mortgage on his modest home from his meagre salary alone.

Uncle Ali sought the assistance of his superiors and confidently vowed to mother that Tariq would soon be freed, but this route also proved ineffective. Desperate, Mother now placed her hopes in me. Promising nothing, I said I would go to Dhamar the following day to see what might be done. Uncle Ali happened to be visiting Mother that day and heard of my plan to visit Dhamar.

'So Khadija thinks she can succeed where I failed?' he commented to his sister, snickering. 'The only difference between her and a *nagah* (female camel) is that a *nagah* can't talk.'

Etiquette required me to call at the Ministry of Information while in Sanaa, to thank the minister for helping me get the scholarship in America and to say hello to colleagues from my television days. While hopping from office to office, I ran into the Deputy Minister of Information, Mutahar Taqi, in the corridor.

'What are you doing back in Sanaa?' he asked.

'I have some family business to take care of,' I explained.

'Anything I can help you with?' Mutahar offered.

'No, thank you. I just have to go to Dhamar.'

Mutahar reflected for a moment. 'Have you been there before?' he inquired.

'No,' I admitted.

'One of my assistants is from Dhamar. Come with me.' He led the way down the hallway to his office at the far end. Moving to his desk, he picked up the telephone and dialled.

'Salih,' he said into the receiver. 'I want you to take Khadija al-Salami to Dhamar tomorrow, first thing in the morning. Whatever she needs to do, you help her.'

I thanked Mutahar and returned early the next morning to the ministry. Salih, a friendly, humble man in his thirties, was waiting for me behind the wheel of one of the ministry's old Mercedes cars. I described to him my problem and he suggested we start by visiting the Governor's office in Dhamar.

Once there, a secretary ushered Salih and me in to see the Governor, Muhammad Abdullah al-Iryani, a distant cousin of former President Abdul Rahman al-Iryani. He worked in a spacious office, adjoined by a large sitting room furnished with couches and chairs for two dozen guests.

'I've been expecting you,' the kind-faced Governor said. The Deputy Minister of Information had telephoned earlier that morning to say I was coming.

I immediately felt the sincerity in the Governor's warmth, despite what might be expected from someone with his military background. After serving 13 months under house arrest in Cairo in 1966–67, at the same time as Yahya al-Mutawakil and the rest of the Yemeni delegation were imprisoned there, al-Iryani became Commander-in-Chief of the Armed Forces, essentially the number two man in the regime. Though he no longer headed Yemen's military (since the overthrow of Abdul Rahman al-Iryani), subsequent leaders continued to hold Muhammad al-Iryani in high esteem. I had met him before in Washington, where he had replaced Yahya al-Mutawakil as ambassador.

Gruff-looking tribal *shaykhs* who had come to see the Governor about some problem or other occupied all of the seats in the office. I was perhaps the first unveiled woman to enter the Governor's office, and my presence astounded the curious tribesmen.

'We were just finishing our discussion,' the Governor announced. 'Won't you come to my home for lunch? My wife would love to meet you,' he said politely.

'No, thank you,' I answered. 'I need to settle this matter of my brother.'

One of the *shaykhs* offered me his seat.

'And who is your brother?' the Governor asked.

'Tariq, the son of Hameed al-Maamari,' I replied. The *shaykhs* nodded their heads in unison, aware of the case.

'That was over the incident in al-Sharara village,' one of them reminded the Governor.

'You're in luck,' the Governor said, gazing around the room at his visitors. 'These are the men who can help you.'

One of the *shaykhs* from Jahran, wearing a pinstriped suit jacket over his white *zena* gown and *jambiya*, slid to the edge of his seat.

'Tariq and the other men from al-Sharara are not in prison to be punished,' he explained. 'It's not like in Sanaa. We tribesmen have our own way of doing things. They will all be freed as soon as the killer is caught.'

'It's been six months,' I protested.

'I know,' the *shaykh* said. 'And we're doing our best to come to an agreement with the al-Hada to get him back.'

'But Tariq is only a boy. He was in school. You have no right to deprive him of that.'

The *shaykhs* looked around the room at each other, unsure of how to proceed. Women, and a very young one in this case, weren't supposed to involve themselves in such matters.

'It's not right,' I continued. 'This is the way the *Imams* used to do things. The revolution was supposed to put an end to taking innocent people hostage.'

'But we can't free your brother and keep the others,' the Jahran *shaykh* argued. 'It wouldn't be wise. As soon as Tariq returned to his village, he'd be a target for the dead man's family. They're still demanding blood, you know.'

'Then he won't return to the village,' I said.

'And where will he go?'

'He can stay in Sanaa for a while,' I answered. 'With his mother.'

The *shaykh* reflected for a moment, then shook his head.

'No. Someone from Jahran will see him there, and news will get back that he's been set free. It'll be trouble.'

'Then I'll take him to America with me,' I declared. 'That should be far enough away.'

The men's faces turned blank at the unorthodox proposal. They looked to the Governor for help, but Muhammad al-Iryani sympathized with me.

'It sounds like a good idea to me,' the Governor said enthusiastically. 'I will order Tariq to be freed right now if you agree,' he added, looking at the Jahran *shaykh*.

My idea now had considerably more weight behind it. 'Are you agreed?' I said, turning back to the *shaykh*.

The farmer's callous hand fumbled with the string of prayer beads wrapped around his *jambiya*. He exchanged glances with the men around him, and one by one they nodded their heads slowly in consent.

The Governor instructed me to write down my request to release Tariq from jail – quickly, before anyone could change his mind. I handed it to the Governor, who signed it before passing it around to each of the *shaykhs*. Those who could write signed it. The others removed their personal ink stamps from their *zena* pockets and pressed them onto the document. Taking the letter, I thanked the Governor and the *shaykhs*.

Salih and I drove straight to the police headquarters to show the letter to the Director of Prisons, but he had gone home for lunch. When we knocked on the door of his house, the director's son told us he was not there either. Petitioners came every day soliciting help, and he had trained his children well in deflecting such house visits.

'But this is important,' I declared, aware that such matters could drag out for days, even months, if not carried through immediately. 'It's a letter from the Governor.'

The boy hesitated, intrigued by this unveiled girl who had come to see his father on such business. He disappeared into the house with the letter, then returned a few minutes later to hand the paper back to me. I unfolded it to find his father's signature on it.

Though lunchtime had come and gone, Salih didn't complain when I insisted we go directly to the jail, located just outside the town.[1] Tariq was flabbergasted when his sister arrived at the

---

[1] Incarceration in Yemen's villages is a less traumatizing, more personal experience than in the West. Inmates are frequently allowed to return home to take care of urgent family business, giving only their word of honour that they will return – and they do. It is not unheard of for a warden to leave the jail, keys and all, in the hands of one of the prisoners while he runs errands.

prison with a letter from the Governor ordering his release – and signed by one of his own Jahran *shaykhs*! He became even more excited on learning that he would have to accompany me to America as part of the bargain for his freedom. Tariq had never left Yemen before.

Yemen can be as maddeningly bureaucratic as any country when dealing with government administration. Yet there are unexpected situations when for some usually unknown reason all barriers are cast aside and everyone involved acts with the single-minded purpose of resolving a particular problem. This, fortunately, had proved to be one of those occasions.

Back home in Sanaa, Mother burst into tears of joy on seeing her son. I feared Tariq's imminent departure for America would upset her, but she loved the idea when I said Tariq would enrol in secondary school there. My older brother, Hamud, had left school at an early age, but now Mother could hope that at least one of her sons would get an education.

I applied to the US Embassy for Tariq's visa, which would take a couple of weeks to process. Meanwhile I had to be in Washington in less than a week to start classes. My brother stayed behind in Sanaa with the plane ticket I bought him, ready to follow when his visa arrived.

On arriving in America, I immediately set about looking for a place to stay. A girlfriend came with me to enquire about available flats at a building beside the American University campus. While we waited to speak to the office manager, a tall, blond boy in his late teens with a warm and ready smile came in, to which the office manager immediately turned his attention.

The manager's attitude angered me, but I pointed out to my friend how handsome the boy was who had come in. It was probably the first time I had openly complimented the looks of a member of the opposite sex, but I never expected to see the boy again.

The flat close to the university did not work out. I settled instead on one in Falls Church, Virginia, a 20-minute drive from the campus and where rent prices were lower. With a spacious bedroom and living room, my new home offered much more space than the tiny maid's quarters I had rented in Paris, and I was very happy.

Tariq arrived ten days later from Yemen, after a connection in Frankfurt, Germany. When his Lufthansa flight took off from Sanaa, Tariq turned to the Yemeni passenger sitting beside him.

'This plane is going to America, right?' he asked.

'No. We're going to Germany,' the man answered.

Tariq was horrified. But once in Frankfurt, he worked out that he had to board another plane for Washington.

City life didn't intimidate Tariq as it would have some of the people back home in Jahran. He had spent a lot of time in Sanaa, and grown accustomed to the hustle and bustle. But he knew people from his village who stopped to shake hands with the strangers lined up to buy tickets at Sanaa's cinema when they visited the capital. Tariq had to inform them that it wasn't necessary to greet everyone they passed in Sanaa.

My brother slept on a fold-out couch in the living room of my flat on the twenty-fifth floor, and I enrolled him in a local Fairfax, Virginia, secondary school a couple of days after his arrival. He knew no English, but that didn't matter. Many of the students spoke no more than a few words of it, and Tariq would end up learning more Spanish and Vietnamese than English at school.

In the afternoons, he would go with friends to the McDonald's next door to the flat. But he stopped going when a pretty Hispanic girl from class started working there. He didn't want to embarrass her by showing that he knew her family was so poor that she had to work. It would dishonour her, he believed.

I specialized in film and video production at American University (AU), where I frequently studied in the campus coffee shop. I was sitting one day with a friend named Paul when suddenly the tall, blond boy I had seen while flat-hunting a few weeks earlier bought a coffee and waved to Paul with indifference (feigned, he told me later). He came over to our table, as I had hoped he would.

His name was Charles Hoots, and he was tanned and in good shape from playing tennis three hours every day on the university tennis team. He was a junior at AU studying international studies, and he and Paul lived on the same dormitory floor. The two often tested each other on geography and Paul thought maybe he could stump Charles this time, but Charles was prepared.

'I want you to meet Khadija,' Paul said as Charles strolled nonchalantly up to the table. 'She's from Yemen.'

He emphasized the word 'Yemen' and stared into his friend's face with a sinister grin, taking in his reaction.

'Nice to meet you,' Charles said to me. 'Are you from North or South Yemen?'

'From the North,' I answered.

'Whereabouts? Sanaa? Taiz?' he continued.

Paul's grin dissolved as Charles had passed the test. After a short conversation, even I professed disbelief that Charles knew so much about my country. He didn't reveal his 'secret' until much later.

Before that meeting in the coffee shop, Charles had noticed me eating lunch every day in the campus's tavern restaurant, usually alone. Thinking I was Hispanic and hoping to practise the Spanish he had studied in Madrid the previous semester, he decided to talk to me. Twice he started over to my table, he said, but each time, just before reaching me, one of my friends arrived and sat down to talk. Charles walked right past without stopping.

By coincidence, around the same time, he met a Yemeni graduate student in the coffee shop. Charles had never met anyone from Yemen, which delighted the Yemeni, and he proceeded to tell Charles stories that seemed right out of *A Thousand and One Nights*: tales of the country's long civil war, of the unruly mountain tribes, of how the *Imam* used to drive his car into the countryside and villagers would ask what they could feed his odd beast while he rested. By the end of their conversation, a curiosity for this exotic land seized Charles and has yet to let go. He set off for the library to find out more, and that is how he knew about Yemen when we met a few days later, in the autumn of 1988.

Charles and I crossed paths frequently over the coming days, in the cafeteria and library. Knowing I had lived in France and liked films, he invited me to watch the classic French film *Hiroshima, Mon Amour* in the library's visual media department. It was my first date.

Charles and I spent an increasing amount of time together, usually studying and occasionally going out for meals. Charles had grown up in a small town outside Winston-Salem,[2] North Carolina, and had spent the last year and a half of secondary school at the Lawrenceville School, an English-style boarding school outside Princeton, New Jersey. He told me while we studied one day that one of his teachers at Lawrenceville travelled frequently to Afghanistan, where he had done his fieldwork in anthropology. In the evenings the teacher used to tell the students about life in Central Asia, stories that affected Charles so much that he couldn't wait to go there.

'I played on the tennis team at Lawrenceville,' Charles told me, 'and made extra money by stringing tennis rackets for a sports goods shop next to campus. With the money saved up, I bought a one-way plane ticket to Pakistan, the nearest I could come to Soviet-occupied Afghanistan at the time.'

I left for Kennedy Airport one Sunday morning in December 1985 with all of my possessions stuffed into three bags and dreams of returning a year or two later fluent in Pakistan's Urdu language and wiser in the ways of the world. But there was a hitch. Neither my school nor my parents were very happy, mainly because I hadn't told them I was going. I

[2] The second word in the name of his hometown derives from the same Semitic root as my name – 'Salem' and 'Salami' both refer to 'peace'.

wanted to go so badly that I decided not to tell them and risk them saying no. They only found out that Sunday afternoon when one of my classmates who knew what I was up to told the school headmaster.

The headmaster immediately phoned my parents and the police. The two officers sent to find me had no trouble picking me out at the Pakistan International Airlines check-in counter. They had all of my bags removed from the flight, escorted me to the police station in their car, and handed me a telephone to call my parents.

It wasn't an easy phone call, and it was one of the few times I remember hearing my mother cry. Half-wishing at this point that they would stop me, they told me that if I had made up my mind, I could go. 'You'll be 18 in a few months anyway,' my father said, 'and we wouldn't be able to stop you then.' So I was off to Pakistan.

At 17 years old, I couldn't help but be impressed. Everywhere I went people approached me and wanted to talk for hours about every subject imaginable, then argued among themselves over whose family I would stay with that night. The mother of one very poor family I stayed with even made me a beautiful cake on Christmas Day. I had to live on about US$2 a day, but it proved no problem.

In the town of Peshawar, not far from the border with Afghanistan, an elderly Afghan refugee and his son who owned a kebab shop invited me to visit their refugee camp, a two-hour bus ride north of the city. They insisted on paying the fare and served me an enormous lunch in the mud-brick refugee village they had built with several thousand other refugees – the majority of whom it seemed attended our lunch. I had to leave behind most of the gifts they gave me since I couldn't carry them all back to Peshawar. I'm not particularly sentimental, but their generosity really moved me.

A man I became friends with in Peshawar took me to his village a few miles west of the town to spend the weekend on one occasion. As we walked among the fields late in the evening, my friend pointed to the lights of some villages further away to the west, much brighter and more numerous than the few lights in the village where we were.

'Over there are the tribal areas,' he explained, 'where the Pakistani Government has only limited control. They have their own police force and do pretty much what they want. Ever since the Russians invaded Afghanistan, Communist spies have been coming across the border to offer the tribal leaders in those areas lots of money in return for their support. Some agree and some don't, but they almost all end up with lots of money or new trucks or a brand new generator that few villages outside the tribal areas can afford.'

Having absorbed much of the anti-Soviet rhetoric of the Reagan years, I was dumbfounded to learn that anyone might consider throwing in their lot with Communists of their own free will. My friend stayed up until nearly dawn answering my questions on how cold war politics played out in the villages of Pakistan's tribal areas. That was my first inkling that the world was not as simple as I had imagined.

After a couple of months in Pakistan I developed salmonella and various other intestinal disorders from my diet of train station food, losing nearly 30 pounds in weight. With a little financial help from my grandfather, I returned to America.

My teacher at Lawrenceville, the one who had got me interested in Afghanistan and whom many blamed for 'putting me up' to going there, always said that my parents were the heroes of this story, for realizing that letting me go was the best thing they could do. The older I become, the more I realize how right he was.

Charles' interest in the world impressed me and he asked lots of questions about Yemen and Islam, which I didn't mind answering in the least. While the stories of my homeland thrilled him, I refused to allow him to draw me into talking about my family or my own life in Yemen. He discovered that I had worked in television only when another Yemeni student came to our table in the coffee shop one day.

'Are you Khadija?' the student asked. 'Khadija al-Salami?' He recognized me from television back home.

The encounter embarrassed me and I had to tell Charles that I used to read the news in Yemen, which I feared might open a Pandora's box of further questions. Charles saw that I wanted to take things slowly and did not press, but as I realized his interest in me was genuine, I gradually began to open up.

As we grew closer, Charles became aware that I felt slightly uneasy around him, though he wasn't sure why at first. I finally explained to him one day that our seeing each other so often placed me in a delicate position. An unchaperoned Sanaani girl studying abroad was revolutionary enough. But spending a large portion of my time with a classmate who was obviously interested in me more than just as a study partner could only lend support to the assertion by some at home that a woman should not be sent off alone.

About a dozen Yemeni students attended AU. They ate, studied and spent time relaxing out in the same places Charles and I did, and any unusual behaviour on my part, or by any of the other Yemenis for that matter, would be known through the grapevine back home within a few days. Though our hearts drew closer together, outwardly Charles and I remained very reserved. We couldn't even hold hands.

That spring, with only a few weeks left until the end of term, I received a letter that nearly ended our relationship. Just before I met Charles, I had applied to transfer the following autumn to the University of Southern California's prestigious film school. The letter informed me that I had been accepted.

Seeing that this could mean my separation from Charles, I asked his opinion. 'I wouldn't want to stand in the way of your dream of attending USC,' he said.

I nodded gravely and changed the subject. I interpreted Charles' reaction to mean that he was not certain he wanted a serious relationship with me, though I had slowly come round to the idea that I did want one. Only the week before meeting him I had thought myself incapable of ever loving a man. But Charles was gentle and open to other cultures, not pushy and interested in only one thing with the girls, unlike so many others I had met. He never cursed and was very polite, always holding doors for me and letting me go first.

My feelings for him grew very strong, passionate even. I wanted more than anything to hold him, to be like the American girls, who were not so inhibited in their relations with boys. These emotions confused and frightened me, but at the same time I was happier than I ever remembered being in my life and I thanked God for the beautiful feeling he had given me. In Charles, for the first time, I found someone I might be able to spend my life with.

But his reaction to the possibility that I would go to California saddened and disappointed me. I disappeared from our usual haunts and didn't answer my telephone for a week. When I finally ran into Charles on campus, I acted very coldly. We strolled awkwardly along, talking little, until we finally stopped and looked into each other's eyes.

'I don't want you to go,' he said, pleading. A smile broke across my face. From then on there was no turning back.

Tariq did well in school, earning a B average at the end of his first term. He used to come with me to the AU campus to study in the evenings, and I introduced him to a Yemeni graduate student who had initially impressed me with his courage. He was blind and had come all the way to America to study in a foreign language. I hoped he would be a good example for Tariq, teaching him to appreciate what he had and encouraging him to do well in school.

The student befriended Tariq and I soon discovered that he was not the person I had believed at first. That he used Tariq to guide him around campus and describe the pretty girls they passed along the way could be excused. But he soon began influencing Tariq in more sinister ways, such as introducing him to alcohol. The most worrying for me, however, was the man's advice that Tariq need not listen to his sister.

'You're old enough to make your own decisions,' he told Tariq. An impressionable teenager, my brother began skipping school to spend the afternoons talking with his friend. The graduate student had succeeded in turning my brother away from his schoolwork and making my life much more difficult.

I gave Tariq a second term to straighten up, but as the winter's unusually deep snows melted with the approach of spring, he didn't change. I decided to send him home at the end of the school year, so that I would not spend all my time worrying about him and having my own marks suffer as a result.

In late May 1989, Tariq returned to Sanaa, where he put his English to use in a job at a popular tourist hotel. But after a year in the capital, and with the problems resolved in his village, he returned to Jahran to take a wife and farm his late father's land.

Tilling the earth in al-Sharara village, where no one could afford a tractor, turned out to be a more difficult task than he had bargained for. Massive emigration to Saudi Arabia and the Persian Gulf countries over the past decade and a half had resulted in an acute labour shortage in many rural areas of Yemen, including Jahran. Land sat unsown and untended for years on end. Fallow plots and unworked terraces that had taken generations to build disintegrated in a single rainy season, and locally grown sorghum and wheat cost more than imported grains. The few farmers that remained, many of them women, concentrated on cash crops like *qat*, that great redistributor of wealth from the cities to the rural areas. But *qat* grows poorly in al-Sharara's soil.

Tariq struggled to make ends meet. Like many tribesmen, he joined the army to augment his meagre income. After basic training, his superiors assigned him few duties, so he sold his rifle and returned home to farm, still receiving his army salary. Several years later when I saw him at Mother's house in Sanaa, he told me he regretted not having taken better advantage of the opportunity he had while in America.

As Charles and I entered our final year of university in the autumn of 1989, Yemen's President Ali Abdullah Salih travelled to Washington, DC, to meet President George Bush. It was Ali Abdullah Salih's first official visit to the United States since becoming President 11 years earlier, but the two men had met before. As Vice-President, Bush attended the opening of Yemen's first oil refinery near Marib in 1986. Exxon and Hunt Oil Company of Texas had made significant investments in the project.

One of my old colleagues at the television station accompanied the President's entourage to Washington in order to film the visit for Yemeni television. He asked me to assist him and his team and I agreed, happy to lend a hand.

It happened that one of my friends at AU had become involved with a small exiled Yemeni political movement opposed to Ali Abdullah Salih and based in the United States. The friend used to work at the television station in Sanaa and I had known him since I began working there at age 11. But I cared nothing about his, or anyone else's, political affiliations, nor had he ever brought the subject up with me.

On the day of the Yemeni President's meeting with Bush, a handful of Yemeni students involved with the opposition group in the USA demonstrated outside the White House, shouting protests and waving placards. Yemeni security officials wanted to know who had organized the demonstrations and as part of their investigation they asked one of the Yemeni television journalists, an old colleague of mine, what he knew. Frightened, he blurted out that I was a friend of the AU student who used to work at the television station in Sanaa. Everyone knew of his political affiliation and assumed he had participated in the demonstration. The security agents convinced the journalist to try to discover if I might be involved too.

The man telephoned my flat that night and, with little tact, inquired as to who financed my studies and how I paid my rent, insinuating that the Yemeni opposition group had me on its payroll. I became furious as I realized what he was up to and slammed the telephone receiver down.

The journalist's behaviour hurt me. He had seemed like a very nice person and so I had gladly helped him for the President's visit. I have long had a tendency to place my complete trust in people I like. If they show me later that the trust was misplaced, or maybe that it was just too idealistic, then the disappointment for me is intense.

The incident opened my eyes to how easy it is to point a finger at an innocent person and have the accusation stick, but I wasn't going to sit back and let it happen to me. Muhsin al-Aini, the Yemeni Ambassador in Washington, held a reception for the President at his home the next evening. I rarely attended such gatherings of the Yemeni community in Washington where, as a Yemeni girl alone in America, I found myself a popular focus of gossip. But that night was different. I was determined to tell the President what had happened to me.

The head security officer met me at the door as I entered and I paid him no heed. He tried to apologize, realizing that he had made an error, but he had angered me too much for me to make peace just then. I nevertheless cooled down enough that I decided not to broach the subject with the President, whom I met for the first time that night.

After giving a short discourse encouraging the many Yemeni students at the reception to work hard in their studies and return home to help their country move forward, an older Yemeni man in the crowd spoke up.

'The students can't develop Yemen all by themselves. The politicians must join in too,' the man said bitterly, a thinly veiled charge that the President wasn't doing enough.

I held my breath for the President's reaction, which I expected to be defensive and aggressive. But he maintained his cool, and responded quite diplomatically, which greatly impressed me. I had expected him to have his security people throw the man out. Yemenis were not used to expressing their disapproval of the government too openly at that time, and presidents were not used to hearing it. Critics were often seen as enemies of the state, and some had been imprisoned as such on the flimsiest of evidence. My ordeal with the President's security agents the day before only drove the point home for me.[3]

Charles never proposed to me. It was just understood that we would get married. But the logistics of a wedding proved anything but simple. The first step entailed Charles going to Yemen to meet my family and ask my older brother, Hamud, for my hand.

I could not be sure what the reaction at home would be. Numerous Yemeni men had taken foreign, even Western, wives, but Yemenis looked much more gravely upon handing their women over to foreigners. A few from Aden in South Yemen had taken foreign husbands when they went abroad to study, but such marriages are a wholly different matter in conservative Sanaa, where genealogy, and thus marrying one's daughter into a good family, is of capital importance. The future of one's descendents depends on it since they will be known by their father's name, and therefore carry with them much of his reputation.

Hamud had by now taken over responsibility for my mother and sisters from Uncle Ali. My brother knew I had a mind of my own, but he might still do his best to oppose my decision, in particular in choosing a husband. And Uncle Ali could be as unpredictable as a cornered snake. I feared he might try to stir up trouble alongside Hamud.

Charles and I both graduated from AU in the spring of 1990. As his first visit to Yemen loomed just a few short weeks ahead,

[3] Fortunately over the coming year or two Yemen experienced some radical changes that remain in place today (mainly as a result of unification between North and South Yemen). A multiparty-political system evolved almost overnight and opposition groups thereafter have held back little in their denouncements of controversial government policies regarding even the most sensitive of topics.

Charles realized that not only would he have to ask my older brother for my hand, but he would have to do it in Arabic, since neither Hamud nor anyone else in the family spoke English. He began studying the language feverishly, buying textbooks and listening to the Arabic radio station in Washington.

Charles suggested we be married in the United States before going to Yemen. That way we wouldn't have any problems with the US Government recognizing our Yemeni marriage. It also allowed his mother to throw a small wedding party with family friends in North Carolina. But we could tell none of our school friends, in particular the Yemenis, about the wedding in the USA. Some would inevitably interpret it as an insult to my family – marrying behind their back – which was certainly not the intention.

Charles' father, who ran the RJ Reynolds Tobacco Company's pension fund at the time, took Charles with him to a business conference in Santa Barbara, California, the summer before his first year at AU. On the return flight, a sprightly woman who turned out to be well into her nineties boarded the plane. She and her 60-year-old son sat between Charles and his father.

Charles was reading a book about Afghanistan and, when the woman noticed it, she proceeded to tell him about her visit to that country a decade or so before. Her name was Katherine Robinson Everett, and her determination and resistance to tradition, I would learn later, had earned her great respect and admiration. Mrs Everett, who graduated from the University of North Carolina School of Law in 1920 at the top of her class, became the first woman to argue a case before the North Carolina Supreme Court. In 1990 she was said to be the oldest practising attorney in the USA, at age 97.

Mrs Everett's achievements ran in the family. Her son, Robinson Everett, graduated from Harvard Law School in the top 1 per cent of his class at the age of 22, then taught at Duke Law School, where he was younger than any of his students.

Charles' father stayed in touch with the Everetts after their flight from California. When Robinson heard that Charles planned to marry in Washington, he asked if he might perform the ceremony in his capacity as Chief Judge of the United States Court of Military Appeals. We gladly accepted and set the wedding date for a fateful 2 August 1990.

What began as the happiest day of our lives slowly disintegrated into a nightmare. The *Washington Post* greeted us on the morning of 2 August with headlines proclaiming that Iraqi troops had invaded Kuwait.

I didn't initially grasp the importance this event would have on our future as I put on my dress and waited for Charles to pick me up for our wedding. The news upset us, but we put it out of our minds during the short ceremony.

Over the coming days the gravity of the situation became clearer. Washington staunchly insisted on an unconditional Iraqi retreat from Kuwait, while Saddam Hussein showed himself equally stubborn, refusing to consider a withdrawal and save his country from impending doom. The tension heightened as the USA began airlifting the first of nearly half a million US troops to the region, while United Nations, Russian and Arab mediation dragged on with little progress.

In addition to Hosni Mubarak of Egypt, King Hussein of Jordan and numerous other politicians from around the world, Mujahid Abu Shawareb travelled to Baghdad at the Yemeni President's request to convince Saddam Hussein to leave Kuwait. The two men knew each other well.

The Iraqi leader's vision of economic development and modernity for Iraq, as spelled out in the Baath Party manifesto, had inspired Mujahid many years earlier to play a prominent role in Yemen's own Baath Party. Mujahid had travelled often to Iraq during the 1980s. The country moved him intensely with its organization, its heavy industry, the participation of women in the workforce, and the high level of education, all of which evoked images of Western countries more than of other Arab countries.

Yemen and Iraq resembled each other in that their large populations rendered them dependent on aid from their sparsely populated, oil-rich neighbours in the Gulf. However, Saddam's folly in invading Kuwait greatly disturbed Mujahid, along with most of the leadership in Sanaa. Though he sympathized with the economic pressures that led the Iraqi leader down this desperate path, he knew it wasn't the right solution. Mujahid hoped more than anyone that Saddam would back down and avoid the fate looming over the horizon in the form of US and Allied military hardware.

Most Arab leaders publicly opposed Saddam and supported the US-led attack to expel his troops from Kuwait. Yet the overwhelming mass of the Arab people discerned hypocrisy in Washington's determination to employ force to ensure observance of the UN resolution calling for an Iraqi withdrawal. 'Why had the USA failed to support, and often used its influence to prevent, observance of other UN resolutions?' they asked. They referred in particular to numerous resolutions demanding an Israeli withdrawal from areas it has occupied in Lebanon, Syria and Jordan since the 1967 Arab-Israeli war, a highly sensitive issue with all Arabs.

While Yemen condemned Iraq's invasion of Kuwait, it was also one of the few governments to publicly express its reluctance towards the USA and Allied troop build-up in the region following the invasion. Sanaa insisted that every effort be made to find an Arab solution to the crisis before inviting foreigners in to solve the problem for them.

Sanaa's stance might have gone largely unnoticed if the presidency of the United Nations Security Council had not, by the luck of the draw, devolved to Yemen on 1 December 1990 in the middle of the crisis. Yemen's vote against the use of force to dislodge Iraq from Kuwait provoked the wrath of the USA and Saudi Arabia, whose king feared Iraq might next invade his own country and wanted Saddam out of Kuwait at any cost.

Riyadh immediately revoked the special status offered to Yemeni workers in the kingdom, which had exempted them from having to find a Saudi 'sponsor' in order to work in the country. Yemen soon found itself confronted with a wave of over 700,000 migrant workers returning home, while Washington simultaneously axed its annual US$20 million in development aid to Yemen.

Demonstrations erupted in many Arab countries against the preparations for war. In Sanaa, protestors peppered the US Embassy with rocks, but went home disheartened when the embassy's bullet-proof glass 'threw the stones right back at us', according to one participant. The authorities maintained control over the crowd, but it quickly became evident that this was not a propitious time for me to announce my planned marriage to an American in Yemen.

Obstacles to the wedding already appeared hazardous enough without offering potentially recalcitrant family members the added ammunition of a war in which Western countries were battling Arabs. Charles' visit to Yemen, and our 'second' wedding, would have to be postponed indefinitely. We had one leg over the precipice, but the rocks seemed to be crumbling beneath us.

CHAPTER EIGHTEEN

Mayhem

Charles and I flew from Washington to Paris on 1 October 1990. I stayed in France for two weeks before continuing on to Sanaa, for despite the postponed wedding plans, my AID scholarship required me to return to Yemen after graduation and work for the Ministry of Information.

In the meantime, Charles would look for a job of his own. He had visited France twice as a teenager and loved Paris as much as I did. We had talked about trying to live there after university, so while I worked out my time at the Information Ministry in Sanaa, Charles would look for work and a place to stay in the French capital.

It was an exciting yet emotionally difficult couple of weeks for us together in France. We had begun a new phase in our lives, but for the time being our paths led in separate directions due to causes beyond our control. We had no idea how much time would pass before we saw each other again. The day I left Paris was the saddest I had experienced in a long time.

A friend of mine sublet Charles her 300-square-foot flat in the thirteenth arrondissement, not far from Chinatown, and he started job-hunting the day after our arrival. With only enough money to last him about three months, he had no time to waste.

For weeks Charles walked to every newspaper, magazine, news agency and wire service he could find in and around

Paris, handing out résumés in the hope of becoming a journalist. He wore a hole in his shoes by December, when he found temporary work teaching English to French company executives. But finding a more solid job did not come easily. The Gulf crisis and uncertainties over world oil supplies had put the international economy on hold. No one was taking on employees in France, particularly someone without work papers, like Charles.

With time running out, despair began to set in. In mid-December 1990, Charles made a reservation for a return flight to the United States on 20 December. He would go home for the holidays and if no job turned up in the final days before he left Paris, he wouldn't come back. The money had run out.

But on 18 December a call came. It was the bureau chief at *Business Week* magazine in Paris, one of the dozens of publications Charles had visited over the preceding ten weeks. The magazine's editorial assistant had left and they needed a replacement. He could have the job if he wanted it.

The position paid just above France's minimum wage, about US$1,200 per month, but that didn't matter to Charles. It was his first job out of university and, more importantly, it meant he could come back after Christmas to Paris, where he wouldn't be so far from me.

Business Week generously agreed to apply for his French work papers while he worked. To succeed, the request would have to argue that the magazine needed an American-English speaker (as opposed to British-English), and that no such person could be found who was a citizen of a European Community country. It took a full year, but the papers finally came through.

Meanwhile, I started working at the television station in Sanaa. The country I returned to in October 1990 had changed substantially since my last visit the previous year. Just two and a half months before Iraq's invasion of Kuwait, North and South

Yemen finally fulfilled their cherished goal of unification, on 22 May 1990.[1]

In Sanaa, I tried to put my master's degree to good use, making documentary films on the country's history and culture for the Sanaa television station. While shooting a film on Aden and the ancient skyscrapers of the Hadhramawt Valley in eastern Yemen, I experienced the first in a series of unfortunate run-ins with Yemeni Socialist Party cadres.

The Aden television station director heard that I was in Aden and requested that my two-man crew and I meet with him after shooting one day. We found the station director in his office that afternoon, drinking tea and talking with several men seated around his desk. After introductions, the director tried to play to the crowd in his office.

'A woman can't carry a camera or direct a film,' he said condescendingly to his chuckling companions. 'Not one has ever made a decent film.'

The comment initially startled me. Then I began to boil and the words rolled off my tongue in a torrent.

'I thought you were supposed to be educated, you Socialists,' I fired at the director. 'You brag about what you've done for women in the South, and you make fun of the tribesmen in the mountains and call them backward. But it was a tribesman working at the television in Sanaa who sent me here to film, and he has never talked to me the way you just did. I much prefer them to you "progressives".'

---

[1] During the 1970s and 1980s, unity proved an unworkable dream. The antagonism and incompatibility of the Soviet-backed Marxist regime in Aden and the pro-Western, decentralized government in Sanaa precluded any merger, despite lots of rhetoric to the contrary. But with the imminent collapse of the Soviet Union in the late 1980s, Moscow informed South Yemen's rulers that they could no longer depend on Soviet financial aid to sustain the country. Leaders of the ruling Yemeni Socialist Party, the only legal party in the country, had little choice but to seek unification with North Yemen, or face economic ruin. The former police state opened its doors to the world for the first time in 21 years following the 1990 unification.

I stormed out of the office, leaving my baffled cameraman and sound man inside. That evening an envelope arrived at the hotel for me. A letter inside authorized me to take 'any television equipment you need', signed by the Aden station director. He had also included letters to the authorities in Hadhramawt, asking them to assist my crew and me in any way possible.

Word of the stormy encounter spread rapidly. When the Adeni director visited the Sanaa television station several months later, he spoke harshly to one of the employees there.

'Watch out, or we'll bring Khadija in here to straighten you out,' the employee berated him.

After nearly three months in Yemen, I managed to obtain a short holiday in early January 1991. I went to Paris where Charles and I had a joyful reunion, but our happiness ebbed away while we watched television late one night soon after my arrival. A news bulletin interrupted the normal programming to show live images of Baghdad, where anti-aircraft fire ignited the dark skies over the city in response to the first Allied air attacks on the Iraqi capital. We watched, distraught, for an hour or two until I finally cried myself to sleep. I understood what it was like to be in a city under siege.

My one-week stay in France turned into one month as flights to Sanaa were cancelled at the beginning of the war. When I finally returned to Yemen, I talked to my minister, Hassan al-Lowzi, and he graciously consented that I would be free to leave work after another three months.

The intervening weeks proved difficult. The air raids on Iraq climaxed in a ground war that expelled the Iraqi army from Kuwait, but at the cost of thousands of Iraqi lives. Despite the end of the war, the region promised to remain extremely turbulent for the foreseeable future.

I returned to Paris for good that spring. But with the situation in the Middle East still chaotic and anti-American sentiment rife, we could not yet reveal our plans to be married. We would have to wait for things to calm down.

Charles worked all day at the *Business Week* office just off of the Champs-Elysées. I soon grew bored and anxious for something to do, when a friend working at the United Nations Educational, Scientific and Cultural Organization (UNESCO) told me of a job opening at the organization's headquarters in Paris. The secretarial position didn't appeal to me, nor was I professionally qualified for it, but I took it anyway. It helped to pass the time until Charles' and my situation became more certain.

In the summer of 1992, with the Gulf War more than a year behind us, the political situation in the Middle East, or at least in Yemen, had stabilized somewhat. I decided we could finally take the leap.

With the scandal I imagined might be made over my marrying a foreigner, and in particular an American so soon after the Gulf War, I might easily have left Yemen altogether, stayed with Charles, and not worried about what people said about me back home. But that hardly seemed an option to my mind, so strongly did I feel that there was nothing wrong with what I was doing. I wanted people at home to understand that, and maybe even offer me their blessing.

I left for Sanaa in July to prepare for Charles' arrival. I told my mother and brother, Hamud, about Charles, and that he was coming to Yemen the following week. They fretted over what people in Sanaa would say, but I would have none of it.

'Why do I have to worry what anyone else thinks. He's my fiancé. I'm the one that has to live with him. What business is it of theirs?'

Mother agreed with me, though Hamud insisted on meeting Charles before offering his approval, which is as much as I could have hoped for from him. He also said he would pick Charles up at the airport.

My younger brother, Tariq, assured Hamud that he would have no trouble recognizing Charles. He described him as a blond *amalaq* – giant – and teased Mother that in order to talk to

Charles, she would have to climb to the second floor of the house and speak through the window.

After an all-night flight, Charles' plane landed in Sanaa at dawn. As he waited in the immigration line, a young Yemeni man pushed through, took his hand and ushered him to the front of the line without a word.

Hamud was a typical highland Yemeni: short and wiry, about five feet four inches tall, without an ounce of fat on his body. He had the long, thin al-Salami nose, and his almond-shaped black eyes seemed almost oriental. Whiskers sprouted in thin, isolated patches across his chin, and his slicked-back hair reminded Charles of James Dean. In his mid-twenties, he was extremely quick-witted and intelligent, though he had only a rudimentary education.

As a boy, Hamud loved taking apart electronic devices such as radios and re-assembling them. He did well in school, but our grandfather forced him to quit and find work after only a few years of study. Uncle Ali later managed to find Hamud a job in the Yemeni state security, where Ali worked too.

Hamud had a healthy sense of humour and loved to laugh. But he was also very religious and could blend in well with the stern-faced conservative Muslim activists that were becoming increasingly involved in radical politics in the late 1980s and early 1990s. Hamud's superiors in the security used him to infiltrate these groups and keep an eye on their activities.[2]

---

[2] Yemen has until recently proved to be relatively sterile ground for fundamentalism. Never having been colonized by European powers (with the exception of Aden) and remaining so long in isolation from the rest of the world, Yemenis do not feel their way of life challenged by the West the way that many other countries do. Yemenis have no doubts that their way of life is superior to that of anywhere else in the world, and they harbour few of the insecurities that have led others to seek solace in a more rigorous form of religion or politics.

However, conservative Muslim groups have made some inroads among the population. In the 1970s and 1980s, few educated Yemenis wanted to go out to rural villages to teach in schools. In order to fill the void, Yemen brought

Hamud also undertook less risky work. His resourcefulness made him good at his job, though blunders cropped up occasionally. During the mid-1980s, his boss assigned him to keep tabs on who went in and out of the Iraqi Embassy in Sanaa.

'Several days in a row, I would ride down the street on my motorcycle,' Hamud told me once, smiling. 'Each time I switched the motor off and coasted to a stop just across from the Iraqi Embassy, where I pretended I was having engine trouble. I would sit the rest of the day watching the entrance out of the corner of my eye, banging a wrench once in a while on the motorcycle frame.'

One day I was really tired and I fell asleep under the motorcycle. By the time I woke up, everybody in the embassy had long gone home for the day, and I felt pretty ridiculous. A few days later, my boss called me into his office. He showed me a photograph of me sleeping under the motorcycle. The Iraqi Embassy had sent it to him.

Nothing daunted the persevering Hamud. On another occasion, his mission involved following an Arab ambassador around Sanaa.

---

in Egyptian instructors to teach in isolated regions. The Egyptian government, struggling at the time with its own Islamic activists, used the opportunity to rid itself of some of the troublemakers by sending them to places like Yemen to teach. Of course their ideas spread with them. The more cosmopolitan Egyptians took the Yemeni villagers for ignorant savages and drilled their religious convictions into their students with all the more zeal.

Despite these Egyptian origins, Yemen's Islamic activists are commonly referred to as Wahabis, in reference to the strict Islamic code observed in Saudi Arabia and from which they take their more recent inspiration and financing. Many of these groups actively oppose the secular rule of Yemen today, and their attempts to expand their influence have made the Yemeni government wary.

Perhaps the most obvious evidence of the Wahabis' increasing popularity in Yemen is the return of many women to the veil in places where 10 to 15 years ago it was rarely encountered. This is particularly the case in rural areas. The recent arrival of greater wealth (from *qat* cultivation and the development of a market economy) and roads (allowing access to strangers) have worked hand in hand with the preaching of these religious groups.

'It was an especially chilly winter,' Hamud said, 'and I was still on my motorcycle. I had no doubt after a few days that the ambassador's driver had noticed what I was up to. So when the ambassador came out of a house after a long meeting one night, heading for his car, I walked up to him.

' "Excuse me," I said, shivering. "I know you've seen me following you. But I'm freezing. Do you mind if I ride with you?"

'The ambassador smiled, but refused.'

After Charles' arrival in Sanaa, Hamud took him to the hotel where Tariq had worked for a year after returning from America. Sanaa was no longer the tiny town Charles had read of in history books. It had completed its transformation into a vibrant, sprawling metropolis.

Since the end of the civil war in 1970, rural Yemenis had emigrated en masse to the capital. Its population of just over 50,000 in 1960 had exploded to over a million by the mid-1990s. The newcomers found employment in the booming construction industry, in restaurants and shops, hawking goods on street corners, or in the government's rapidly expanding public service sector. New buildings sprouted up daily around Old Sanaa, and the town's original mud wall deteriorated as the traditional tax on the *suq*'s butchers to maintain the wall faded away.

But thankfully Sanaa has not lost all the vestiges of its former self. The corridors winding through the vast Suq al-Milh market still convey visitors back to the Middle Ages. Families and neighbourhoods remain close-knit and Sanaanis still stare in wonder at the occasional foreign visitor. It is perhaps the only capital in the world where you can dial a wrong number and the person who answers asks who you are trying to reach, then gives you the correct number from memory.

Hamud left Charles in his hotel room, where he dozed until the call to prayer screeched from a loudspeaker across the street at sunset. Hamud returned soon after to take him to my sister Jameela's house. Near Grandmother Amina in Hurqan and not far from the hotel, her home is modern and spacious and the best place for Charles to meet the whole family.

Twenty-two year old Jameela, her husband, and their six children welcomed Charles with timid smiles. Tariq and my youngest sister, Afrah (born to Mother and Father soon after their remarriage), showed up later with Mother, followed by my sister, Nejla, and her husband and daughter.

Initially tense, the gathering soon lightened up. The children sat in front of Charles on the cushions lining the walls, giggling at his every move until they eventually mustered the courage to tell him jokes and dance for him to a Michael Jackson cassette. And Mother did everything she could to make him feel at home, showering him with tea, and biscuits she had baked.

Mother had not been sure what to expect of the foreigner coming to ask for her daughter's hand. The few Westerners she had seen in Sanaa in recent years tended to be hippie backpackers with long hair and tattered clothes. She assumed that all Westerners were of the same nature, so Charles' short hair and coat and tie caught her off guard.

The warm reception pleasantly surprised me. A handful of distant cousins refused to attend, but otherwise we couldn't have asked for more. The only snag, and it was minor, came from Uncle Ali.

The last to arrive, he sat silently across from Charles, staring suspiciously with tilted head and stroking his moustache as if trying to figure out this strange creature his niece had brought back from America. Uncle Ali had previously let it be known that he wanted nothing to do with the wedding, but he had effectively acquiesced by simply showing up to meet Charles. I finally forced him to speak.

'So, what do you think?' I asked.

The whole family grew silent, turning to Uncle Ali. He squinted and removed his turban to scratch his head.

'How do we know he's not a spy?' he finally replied eruditely. 'He should stay here for two or three months, so we can make sure.'

The laughter from the rest of the family embarrassed Ali.

'That's ridiculous,' Mother piped in. 'Even if he stayed here for a year, what would that prove?'

Uncle Ali, uneasy, finished his tea and slipped quietly out.

Charles talked to Hamud alone that evening about the marriage, explaining as best he could in very rudimentary Arabic that we both wanted to get married and that we wanted Hamud's blessing. Hamud said he would think it over, and by the following morning he had made up his mind. He had had a revelation during the sunrise prayer, he said, in which God instructed him to approve his sister's marriage.

Hamud took Charles alone to the Nahrayn (two rivers) Mosque later that morning. The low brick building, devoid of a minaret, perched over the western bank of the *sayla* canal. Al-Muayad, a prominent Yemeni religious scholar who led Yemeni pilgrims to Mecca each year for the *Haj*, served as the mosque's *imam*.

Hamud and Charles removed their shoes and carried them across the Oriental carpets to the *imam*'s office at the back of the mosque, hidden from the entrance by numerous pillars. Al-Muayad, probably in his eighties, sat on a thin mattress reading the Koran under a naked light bulb dangling from the ceiling. He picked himself up with surprising agility and greeted the two gaily with moist, inquisitive eyes.

After inquiring about his visitors' health, he gathered some papers from a pile of documents beside the door, fumbled a pen with his trembling, wrinkled hands, and began filling out the marriage contract between Hamud and Charles. Ideally, Charles' father would have represented him, but that was hardly practical in this case.

After writing a few lines, al-Muayad looked up from the paper into Charles' face. He studied him for a moment, and seemed only then to notice that he was not Yemeni. When Charles walked around the city, children spotted him above the crowd from 200 yards away and summoned their friends for a look at the 'giant' as he passed by. But al-Muayad didn't see very well, nor did he ever expect that a Sanaani girl would be marrying a foreigner, though he in no way showed any disapproval.

'Your sister is marrying this?' he asked Hamud, still looking Charles up and down. Hamud smiled and nodded.

'It's the first time I've been asked to marry one of Yemen's daughters to a foreigner,' the *imam* continued. 'But I guess there's no law against it.'

He snickered, glancing up from his paper to see if they appreciated his humour.

Hamud and Charles sat on the mattress beside al-Muayad as he filled out the marriage contract. Age had detracted not only from his sight, but also his hearing. He had great difficulty in writing out 'Charles' (which sounds strange to Arabic speakers even with perfect hearing). Hamud shouted the name first in his right ear, then in his left, until al-Muayad finally looked down and entered it on the document as best he could.

'Where was he born?' he asked next, always addressing Hamud.

'America,' Hamud replied loudly.

'But what province?'

'North Carolina,' Charles broke in, since Hamud didn't know.

'What?' the *imam* asked.

Hamud frowned in frustration. He reached over and politely but firmly lifted the pen from the *imam*'s hand. Pulling the paper and the book on which it rested over to him, he wrote 'North Carolina' on the appropriate line of the contract, then returned it to the *imam*.

'Thank you,' al-Muayad mumbled.

With the document complete, the three of them signed the bottom of the contract. Hamud then pulled a handful of almonds and raisins out of the chest pocket of his *zena*. He dropped them on the floor between them, in accordance with Sanaani tradition, to seal the bond between our families. Hamud gathered them up again as fast as he could, until he realized that Charles didn't understand and was only watching him.

'Grab them,' Hamud told him. 'In Sanaa it is said they will make your teeth strong and healthy the more you can pick up and eat.' Charles joined in.

After the mosque, Hamud brought Charles to see me at my Aunt Hameeda's house. Friends and relatives busied themselves making me up for the wedding party that evening. A woman used a tiny brush to paint my arms, hands and feet in flower patterns with a black liquid made from crushed vegetable oils. The liquid hardens when dry and fades after a couple of weeks.

I wore a full-length silk dress, its golden brilliance rivalling the bracelets on my arms. A string of threaded jasmine was placed over my coral necklace with a silver amulet at the end to ward off the evil eye. Basil leaves and other sweet-smelling herbs draped over both ears from the pointed crown on my head, made from the same material as my dress.

When Charles came in to see me, the woman painting my arms looked at him admiringly. It is not often that Sanaanis see six-feet-five-inch blond men.

'Does he have a father that wants another wife?' the woman asked me jokingly (she was already married).

Charles couldn't stay to see my completed outfit. A car waited outside to take him to another party, this one reserved for the men. Ali al-Shater (who had shown the South Yemeni envoy into President al-Ghashmi's office before the briefcase explosion) had heard about the wedding and insisted on throwing a party at his home. Unfortunately he had gone to Marib with the President and Mujahid Abu Shawareb earlier in the day, but he insisted the celebration go on without him.

Fifteen guests were already seated on cushions around the walls of al-Shater's living room, chewing *qat*, when Charles arrived. They stood up to greet him as he wound around the room shaking hands. Several of them complimented him on the *zena* and *jambiya* he wore. Hamud had had the *zena* specially tailored for the occasion, but it barely reached Charles' calves and looked comical to the Yemenis, though they were too polite to say anything and proud that at least he tried to dress like them.

Beside Charles sat Abdul Rahman al-Akwa. He had lived next door to me in the Hurqan neighbourhood many years before, and now occupied the post of Deputy Minister of Information. The al-Akwas are a family of *qadhis* from Sanhan, just south of Sanaa. Abdul Rahman moved to the capital when he was a boy in order to study. He stayed with an uncle who lived next door to Grandmother Amina and I knew him well. The uncle, a military man and former Governor of the Jawf, welcomed several other nephews and nieces into his home too. He and his wife, who was deaf from birth, cared for them as their own children.

Abdul Rahman found growing up in Sanaa difficult, with its deeply ingrained sense of sophistication compared to the uneducated tribesmen from the countryside. He had played and worked outdoors all day before moving to the capital, and the sun had burned his skin a dark coffee colour. The kids in the neighbourhood in Sanaa made fun of him, calling him *al-aswad* – the black one – and refused to let him play with them.

As a teenager, Abdul Rahman tried to make extra money after school by selling sweets from a cardboard shack he built on the street near his house. Before long, he had a thriving business fuelled by the neighbourhood children. He never gave any sweets away for free, and didn't even take any for himself, no matter how hungry he became. But he eventually allowed one exception to his rule.

One morning Abdul Rahman passed the well behind Grandmother Amina's house, where I went every day to fetch water. He glimpsed a girl there washing a bundle of carrots she had gathered from the nearby communal garden. She had lowered her veil while drawing the water and normally would have pulled it back over her nose and mouth at the approach of a man. But when she noticed Abdul Rahman, she conspicuously neglected to replace it, beaming a beautiful smile at him.

She was very pretty and Abdul Rahman immediately developed a crush. The girl passed by his sweet stall on her way home and handed him a carrot. He hadn't eaten all day and thought she must be not only the most beautiful, but also the most generous creature on earth. Abdul Rahman, too embarrassed to do it himself, gave me several sweets and asked me to take them as a gift to the girl, who lived nearby.

Next to Abdul Rahman at the wedding party sat Hassan al-Lowzi, Yemen's Minister of Information at the time. He had organized the party for Charles. A very sensitive and caring person, Hassan is a talented writer and close friend of Abdul Rahman and Ali al-Shater.

In October 1977, Ahmed al-Ghashmi summoned Hassan and Ali together into his office to inform them of President al-Hamdi's death. Hassan had cherished the President, and news of his death devastated him. He choked up with grief in front of the stoic al-Ghashmi.

'But ... who could have done such a thing?' Hassan asked al-Ghashmi, uncomprehending.

Beads of sweat formed on Ali al-Shater's forehead. He knew instinctively that al-Ghashmi, as Chief of Staff, was most likely behind the murder.

'Do you know who did it?' Hassan repeated.

Al-Ghashmi's face flushed red with anger. Ali mustered all his force to keep from landing a sharp kick to Hassan's shin to keep him quiet.

While they chewed *qat* at the party, two well-known Sanaani musicians took turns playing the lute. At the Hour of Solomon (the hour or so before sunset), when the effects of chewing *qat* for several hours renders everyone calm and reflective, each of the 20 or so guests composed his own verse that was combined into a wedding song. The musicians improvised the tune while the others sang, and when all was perfected someone recorded the song on a cassette and handed it to Charles. It is our favourite wedding gift.

Mujahid Abu Shawareb and Yahya al-Mutawakil also expressed their delight that I had finally decided to marry. Mujahid invited us to his home in Sanaa, where the two dozen guards and retainers who keep watch over his walled home welcomed us when we drove in to the courtyard.

We saw Mujahid in the garden that separates the houses of his two wives, listening intently to the grievances of two dozen men who had come from all over Yemen to seek his assistance. Such people turn up every day before sunrise, seeking Mujahid's help on any number of issues: his intervention to resolve a dispute, his money for a family emergency, his signature authorizing a promotion in the military or perhaps a raise. Many visitors from the former South Yemen wanted to have land returned to them that the Marxists confiscated – a very thorny issue.

The silk *zena* and expensive *jambiya* Mujahid wore in Yemen highlighted his forceful personality better than the Brioni suits he wears in Europe. I had witnessed Mujahid's warm, sociable side in Europe and America, but in Yemen he was all business. He so intimidated many of the men petitioning his aid that they could hardly look him in the eye.

Mujahid, who greatly impressed Charles, soon excused himself and joined us inside. He had a sheep slaughtered and prepared for lunch in honour of our wedding.

Any worries I had about the reaction to my marrying a foreigner dissolved with the blessings offered by my family, Mujahid and Yahya. I felt the lifting of an immense burden from my shoulders, accumulated over 20 years of people trying to dictate who I could and could not be. My life was finally nobody's but my own.

CHAPTER NINETEEN

Spiral to war

Charles and I returned to France a few days after the wedding. During a visit to Paris in 1993, Deputy Minister of Information Abdul Rahman al-Akwa suggested that I might be useful working at the Yemeni Embassy in Paris on behalf of the Ministry of Information. I had recently left my job at the UNESCO and found the thought of working at the embassy appealing, in particular doing something related to what I had studied at university.

The Yemeni Government had begun to cut back spending and new appointments were handed out sparingly, particularly abroad. But with a master's degree and fluent French, I felt I could justify a position at the embassy, and I had backing from some crucial people.

In addition to Abdul Rahman al-Akwa's support, Mujahid encouraged the President to agree. And Amat al-Aleem al-Suswa, the former Guide,[1] supported my cause. Amat entered President Ali Abdullah Salih's office a few days after the request for my embassy posting had reached his desk. Vice-President Ali Salim al-Baydh, the former head of South Yemen, was in the office too. He overheard Amat when she expressed her hope that the President would approve the request.

'When will you learn that politics is a man's world, not a woman's?' al-Baydh taunted Amat.

---

[1] Who went on to become Yemen's Ambassador to the Netherlands in 2000 and Minister of Human Rights in 2003.

Exasperated, Amat pointed out to al-Baydh the example of Shaykh Mujahid, who had talked to the President not only about me but two other women who hoped to obtain appointments in Yemeni embassies abroad. Mujahid thought having women represent the country abroad was a good idea.

Al-Baydh snickered and insinuated that there must be 'something going on' between Mujahid and the three women for him to be taking such an interest in our cases. Amat's skin crawled at this comment from a man who claimed to have done so much for women under his rule in the former South Yemen.

I remembered the television station director in Aden when I heard the story later. The Vice-President's attitude disgusted me and reinforced my image of the Socialist leaders in my country as hypocrites.

President Ali Abdullah Salih ended up signing the authorization for me and the other two women, to work as diplomats abroad. I became press attachée at the Yemeni Embassy in Paris's sixteenth arrondissement, a five-minute walk from the Champs-Elysées.

But I began my new job in late 1993 under the shadow of a rapidly deteriorating political situation back home. The leaders of North and South Yemen had rushed through the 1990 unification of their two countries several months ahead of schedule in an effort to head off mounting pressure against it. Certain religious elements in North Yemen, such as Shaykh Abdullah al-Ahmar's conservative Islah Party, opposed any deals with the Marxist 'atheists,' as they saw them. And Saudi Arabia, a major financier of the Islah, feared a unified Yemen with some 16 million inhabitants dominating vast stretches of the Red Sea, the Indian Ocean and the strategic Bab al-Mandeb strait. It could pose a formidable counterbalance to Saudi's traditional leadership role in the Arabian Peninsula.

As unification approached, Riyadh strove with renewed vigour to divide the leadership in Sanaa. Saudi officials contacted Shaykh Mujahid several times when he travelled to Europe. They suggested that he take power in Yemen, with the understanding that Riyadh would support him if he did so.

But Mujahid had come to place unification on a pedestal above all else. He would do nothing that might give either side an excuse to back out. Furthermore, he knew his would-be backers would eventually see him in the same suspicious light as they viewed the current president if he were to take power. Mujahid, like President Ali Abdullah Salih, valued his independence too much to allow anyone to pull his strings.

Much remained to be done to ensure the success of the unification, even after its official declaration in May 1990. Until precise quotas could be established, civil servants from the former South Yemen simply came to Sanaa and set up shop alongside the former North Yemen's own bureaucracy. Each ministry found itself with two ministers, one from the North and one from the South, two deputy ministers, etc., on down the line to the lowest levels of administration.

But the real problems surfaced at the top of the hierarchy. South Yemen contained a population of around two million people, compared to the North's nearly 14 million. Added to this imbalance was the disastrous state of the South's economy.[2] These inequalities dictated that Ali Abdullah Salih, rather than Ali Salim al-Baydh, would preside over a unified Yemen.

But misunderstandings over just how much say Ali Salim al-Baydh would have in the country's affairs as vice-president inevitably cropped up within weeks of the euphoria generated by unity. As the wrangling grew in intensity, each side prepared for a decisive showdown.

The risks of civil war proved all the greater in that the armies of the former North and South had yet to be merged. Some 15,000 southern troops had been transferred to the north while 8,000 northerners moved to garrisons in the south in an initial step

---

[2] Some US$6 billion in foreign debt and the evaporation of financial aid from Moscow.

towards full integration. As a result, units under separate commands literally faced off within a few yards of each other at some bases.

Mujahid mustered all his mediation skills in trying to reconcile the President and Vice-President. He shuttled between Sanaa and Aden, where al-Baydh frequently retreated when he wanted to demonstrate his displeasure with Ali Abdullah Salih. But he could do little to bring them together.

After several months of virtually non-stop arbitration, Mujahid came to Paris for a break in early January 1994. He had just been named Vice-Prime Minister, but he knew that any post in the government would remain hollow until the differences between the President and Vice-President were settled.

Though exhausted, he continued to spend the greater part of his time on the telephone until the early hours of the morning, trying to convince the two antagonists to compromise on one issue or another. Both men respected Mujahid and listened to what he had to say, but Mujahid felt the country slipping steadily towards war.

'What should I do?' he asked in exasperation one afternoon while Charles and I watched the news with him in his flat. 'I don't feel like being involved in this squabbling any more.'

'Mediate, but don't take sides,' I suggested. 'Maybe neither of them will give in. But the unification is too important to let it go so easily.'

By early 1994, the Yemeni Embassy in Paris had split down the middle. Half the diplomats, including the ambassador, were Socialist Party cadres sympathetic to Ali Salim al-Baydh. The other half, including the chargé d'affaires (the number two man at the embassy), was from the former North Yemen, or otherwise southerners who opposed the Socialists. These backed President Ali Abdullah Salih.

The two sides retired to their respective corners, each going about its business with as little interaction as possible. But the tension mounted in step with the deteriorating situation back home.

After only three days in Paris, Mujahid flew to Aden where he and Sinan Abu Lahum attempted to convince al-Baydh to return to Sanaa after a lengthy absence. A few days later, they helped narrowly avert the outbreak of full-scale war when aircraft from the former South Yemeni Air Force bombed northern army positions.

As both sides readied for confrontation, Mujahid and Sinan cajoled the President and Vice-President into meeting each other the following day for the first time in several months. Tempers eased and the talks resulted in the creation of a three-man 'Grievances Committee', aimed at putting an end once and for all to the dissension.

The two adversaries would each choose one member of the committee, while Mujahid would name the third. But when Ali Abdullah Salih and al-Baydh both nominated hard-line representatives to the committee, Mujahid saw that it wouldn't work.

'I will decide who is on the committee,' he declared. 'It will be Jarullah Omar, the key to the Socialist Party; Abdul Karim al-Iryani, the key to the General Peoples' Congress;[3] and Abdul Wahab al-Anisi, the key to the Islah Party.'

'And you, Mujahid. You will be the master key,' someone in the crowd quipped in admiration. Everyone laughed.

Optimism ran high a few days later, on 21 February, when Ali Abdullah Salih and al-Baydh travelled to Amman, Jordan, to sign a definitive accord. Both sides stated their satisfaction with the agreement, but its implementation left much to be desired.

Mujahid returned to Paris for a much needed rest following the signing of the Amman accord. He also wanted to consult with

---

[3] The President's party.

his close friend, Muhammad Abu Lahum, who lived much of the year in a flat in the same building as Mujahid in Paris.

Muhammad had been a top military officer in Yemen during and after the civil war in the 1960s and, like Mujahid, Governor of Hajja province from 1979 to 1981. But in late 1981 he grew frustrated with politics. He resigned his governorship and purchased a flat in Paris, where he then spent the majority of his time.

Though Muhammad had given up his government duties, he could not so easily relinquish his tribal responsibilities. He returned home two or three months out of every year to mediate disputes, of which the hubristic Nihm are never short. And while in Paris, he maintained close contact with various *shaykhs* and politicians back home, keeping his finger on the pulse of events.

The Bakil tribes, of which Nihm comprises a key component, had their own reasons for being dissatisfied with the government in Sanaa in the early 1990s. The strain between the two had grown steadily since the overthrow of the *Imam* in 1962. During the ensuing civil war, the Bakil furnished the bulk of the Royalist forces, though by no means all Bakilis joined the Royalists (the Abu Lahums, for example, were staunch Republicans). And the fact that politics in Sanaa tends to be dominated by Hashidis does not sit well with the Bakil. Though some of their *shaykhs* have occupied important posts over the years, many Bakilis believe that, as a rule, their more capable tribesmen have been blocked from government positions in which they might yield effective power in the country.

The Bakil generally took an ambiguous stance during the crisis between Ali Abdullah Salih and Ali Salim al-Baydh following unification. This was partly because, as usual, they failed to come up with a coherent policy on which all of their disparate tribes could agree. But it was also at least partially a calculated move. It provided them with a means of displaying to the government their disgruntlement over what they perceived as their imposed isolation from decision-making over the years.

Yet despite their public neutrality, the Bakil had no illusions that their situation was likely to become infinitely worse if the Socialist hardliners under al-Baydh took power in a unified Yemen. Party leaders spoke out frequently against the independence of the northern tribes, and would undoubtedly do their best to reign them in once in the driver's seat.

Bakil support could prove crucial if war broke out, and supporters of both the President and Vice-President engaged in considerable behind-the-scenes manoeuvring to ensure their loyalty. Bakil's loosely allied tribes do not enjoy the cohesiveness that lends the more compact Hashid a near unanimous voice in most matters. There is no such thing as 'winning over' all of Bakil, for some of the Bakil tribes will inevitably oppose the majority no matter what the issue. But the jockeying for position went ahead in early 1994 with all sides dangling carrots and brandishing sticks in front of the Bakil in a timeless game that rarely left anyone content but the Bakil, who are experts at playing off outside interests.

Mujahid had come to Paris to sound out Muhammad Abu Lahum on the views of the various Bakil *shaykhs*, whom he frequently contacted by telephone. If anyone could claim to speak for a majority of the Bakil at that time, it was the Abu Lahum brothers: Sinan, Ali and Muhammad.[4]

I had moved with Charles in 1992 to an apartment building a quarter of a mile from Muhammad's building, overlooking the miniature Statue of Liberty on the Seine, half a mile from the Eiffel Tower. I didn't know Muhammad well before that, though I knew his sister Azeeza (who used to thrill me with stories of her time in America with her husband, Muhsin al-Aini – whose brother married my Great-Aunt Hameeda).

Muhammad treated Charles and me like family when we got to know him better, and he invited us to his home for lunch regularly. We profited not only from the excellent Yemeni food, but also from the endless stories that, like many Yemenis, Muhammad has a knack for telling.

---

[4] Sinan lived in Sanaa, while Ali served at the time as Yemen's Ambassador to Jordan in Amman.

CHAPTER TWENTY

Like father like sons

The Abu Lahum family has served as *shaykhs* of the Nihm tribe for so many generations, even they have lost count. The Nihm are one of Yemen's largest tribes in terms of area. Their territory stretches from the base of the Khawlan escarpment in the southwest to the confines of the Khala desert northeast of Marib.[1] Rainfall is scarce in the land and Nihmis are for the most part livestock breeders inhabiting a handful of permanent settlements of stone houses. Emasculated farms provide just enough sorghum to feed the sparse population in a good year, but an onslaught of locusts or failed rains mean famine, of which the Nihm have seen their share.

Long ago the Abu Lahums acquired farmland on the Tihama coast, between Zabid and Mokha. In the early 1800s, inhabitants of the Tihama began harassing government representatives in the region. Assuming the Abu Lahums to be behind this challenge to his authority, Yemen's *Imam* seized two Abu Lahum brothers and beheaded them.

---

[1] Four principal tribal sections make up the Nihm. Their names could have inspired street gangs in American cities: Iyal Sayad (the sons of Sayad, the Hunter), Iyal Mansur (the Victorious), Iyal Hanashat (the Snakes), and Iyal al-Ghufayr (Forgiveness). The Abu Lahums (whose name means 'father of the meat') belong to the al-Ghufayr, the easternmost of northern Yemen's settled inhabitants, referred to collectively as the *Bayt al-Hajar* – those who dwell in houses of stone. Further east, in the desert, roam the nomadic *Bayt al-Shair* – those who dwell in houses of hair (i.e. wool tents).

Muhammad Abu Lahum tells how 'the sister of the executed men, Muhsina Abu Lahum, addressed letters to all the Bakil tribes around Sanaa, reminding them that their honour demanded retribution for the death of her brothers, fellow Bakilis. In a rare display of unity, they rallied to her cause and rose in revolt. Fearing that Sanaa would be sacked, the Imam offered Muhsina several large tracts of land in the rich valleys around Jibla[2] as *diya* for her brothers' deaths.'

Muhsina returned several years later to the Abu Lahum's native land of Milh, a bone-dry *wadi* bed cutting through the white mountains of Nihm in eastern Yemen. A single acacia unfurls its green canopy above the *wadi*, the only tree for miles around. The rest of the land is a geological dumping ground, seemingly devoid of any organic matter. Millennia of erosion have carved the surrounding slopes into a series of gigantic steps leading up to the flattened summits above the *wadi*. Small parcels in the hollows, ploughed up and cleared of stones, are sown with corn and sorghum each year, often to be ploughed under a month or two later as a failure.

Muhsina erected a house in the Abu Lahum's village of al-Shariya, at a bend above the Wadi Milh, a few hundred yards downstream from the acacia tree. It towered six storeys high, built of mud-smeared stone. Sturdy timbers, their tips poking through the outer walls, held up the floors. Animals spent nights on the packed dirt of the spacious ground floor, with its ten-foot ceiling. A large sitting room occupied most of the second floor, for use in entertaining guests. Grain storage chambers with bins sunken into the floor, and rooms featuring raised clay platforms for beds were situated on the upper storeys, along with a bathing room. The kitchen and a hand-turned millstone made up the last level.

Tiny window openings, some filled with a polished translucent rock, kept the interior of the house cool through the cloudless afternoons. A clay wall surrounded the fortress-home, and several

[2] 120 miles south of Sanaa.

pits, an arm's length in diameter and 15-feet deep, held more grain within this outer courtyard.

All of Nihm looked forward to the occasional parties thrown by the Abu Lahums, a tradition that continued into modern times. 'Guests showed up wearing exotic costumes of animal skin mantles,' says Muhammad Abu Lahum, 'and the heads of cows or camels for masks. People walked sometimes the whole day to arrive at sundown for the beginning of the festivities. Guests sat on the ground and stretched their bare feet out in front of them, waiting for villagers to come and massage their legs with butter. When they felt refreshed, they got up and sang and danced all night, before returning home the next day.'

Several decades after Muhsina's death, the *Imam* passed through Milh while fleeing from the advancing Turkish army. When the Abu Lahums granted him refuge, the Turks attacked al-Shariya in retaliation. As if in divine tribute to her own steadfastness, Muhsina's home remained one of the few buildings still intact after the smoke cleared. It still stands today, handed down to Sinan Abu Lahum by his father, Abdullah.

Abdullah was an honest and proud man, uncompromising in his principles, as rigorous and sturdy as the environment he lived in. He insisted on frugality within his own family, setting the example by neither smoking cigarettes nor chewing *qat*.

However, towards guests Abdullah's generosity went unsurpassed. *Nihm* means 'greedy' in Arabic, but Abdullah would gladly have handed over any of his possessions to the most humble passer-by – and he expected to be treated in like manner by others. He usually was.

With a reputation for inordinate bravery over several generations, the Abu Lahums have earned the hereditary title of *naqeeb*. The name is used only in regions east of Sanaa, bestowed upon families that exercise considerable and long-standing influence over regional affairs.

Abdullah habitually dressed in a colourless wrap-around skirt under a baggy white *zena* gown and indigo-dyed cloak. He tied the cloak's enormous sleeves behind his neck, to keep them from drooping to the ground when he straightened his arms. A tightly wound turban crowned his head, which he never failed to hold high, his stern face clouded in grave contemplation. Dark blue or red vegetable dye coloured the turban, and when he sweated, the dye streamed down his face and neck in what passed for the fashion of the time.

Throughout eastern Yemen and beyond, people held Abdullah in the highest esteem. Laying down his wooden walking stick sufficed as a guarantee for his tribe's behaviour, where other men would have been required to hand over a dozen rifles.

He abhorred anything smacking of injustice. 'When the *Imam* allowed Yemen's Jews to emigrate to Israel in 1948,' his son Muhammad remembers, 'my father made sure that all of the houses in the Jews' mud village a mile northwest of al-Shariya were purchased at fair prices from the departing owners.'

Though a family of *shaykhs*, the Abu Lahum's desolate homeland enforced a strict equality of poverty between the lowliest and the noblest of tribesmen. Only a few servants distinguished the one from the other. Abdullah's four sons, for example, received a new *zena* each year during the Festival of the Sacrifice. They wore it every day, until presented with a new one at the following year's festival.[3]

Abdullah owned half a dozen slaves, not uncommon in Yemen during the first half of the twentieth century. Of African ancestry, slaves lived and worked with their own wives and children in the service of a tribal family, usually of *shaykhs*. Some had served the same masters for generations. Abdullah's slaves lodged in a small one-storey mud house just outside the courtyard entrance to his home (the one Muhsina built).

---

[3] The Festival of Sacrifice celebrates Abraham's willingness to sacrifice his son to God. Muslims believe it was Ismail, rather than Isaac, whom Abraham intended to offer. According to Arab genealogy, Isaac's descendents became the Jews, while his half-brother, Ismail, fathered the Arabs.

On the advice of his sons, Abdullah freed his slaves in the 1940s. But the families elected to remain with the Abu Lahums after their emancipation, continuing their lives just as before. They could not have been more loyal to Abdullah had they been his own children. Though not members of the tribe, and therefore non-combatants according to custom, the men nevertheless volunteered to fight in defence of the family when necessary.

A year or two before Imam Yahya's death, a land dispute in Milh turned nasty, pitting the Abu Lahums against the neighbouring Shinayfi clan, also of Nihm. During a normally uneventful skirmish, when foes flex their muscles through a flurry of random, usually harmless, potshots, a Shinayfi bullet took the life of one of Abdullah's former slaves. The Shinayfi offered the *diya* due for the killing of a slave, which, as for Jews or other protected classes, can reach 11 times that demanded for a tribesman.

'But my father loved his servant,' Muhammad recalls. 'His mother had bought him for more than half a *qudah* of wheat[4] when my father was still a child, and the slave helped raise him. Father was adamant: no *diya*, only revenge.'

Abdullah al-Wazeer, Imam Yahya's representative in Sanaa, got wind of the dispute and called my father and the Shinayfis to Sanaa. He told my father that the feud must end, that insisting on blood for the dead man would only make matters worse. 'Besides, no one demands revenge for the death of a slave,' al-Wazeer said.

Father and Abdullah al-Wazeer were friends, but my father was furious.

'You call him a slave,' he told al-Wazeer. 'But I say he was a free man. He deserves a life for a life!'

The original dispute involved ownership of a plot of land and the *Imam*'s deputy worked with the Nihmis over the next couple of days to find a solution to that problem first.

---

[4] One *qudah* of wheat equals about 70 pounds.

When al-Wazeer finally announced his decision, my father protested.

'It is unjust,' he said. 'I will not accept it.'

'Do not be stubborn, Abdullah,' al-Wazeer told him. He was not pleased to have his judgment questioned. 'I must enforce this decision. Otherwise my pen will break.'

Al-Wazeer was a religious scholar and the pen symbolizes a learned man's honour. He considered a refusal to accept his ruling as a personal affront, but my father would not give in.

'And if your decision is enforced, then my *jambiya* will break,' my father answered, and he unfastened his belt and raised the scabbard up with the *jambiya* still in it.[5] Al-Wazeer and the mass of tribesmen looking on held their breath, fearful that my father would break the sheath across his knee, a virtual declaration of war.

Imam Yahya had greatly improved the security situation in the country during the decades since the Turkish withdrawal. He treated agitators, bandits and unruly *shaykhs* harshly. The *Imam* would not take such defiance of his deputy lightly, even from so close a personal friend as my father.

To everyone's relief, my father replaced the *jambiya* around his waist, and tempers cooled. Al-Wazeer eventually forged a resolution to the disputes and my father dropped his demand for revenge on behalf of his former slave. The blood spilt between the Shinayfi and the Abu Lahums was forgotten as quickly as a child forgets a scolding from a parent.

Abdullah Abu Lahum demanded the highest standards not only of himself, but of his four sons as well. The youngest, Muhammad, used to herd the family's sheep and goats out to pasture in the

[5] Like the pen for a scholar, the *jambiya* has come to symbolize a tribesman's honour. It is commonly offered as a guarantee to someone to whom a promise has been made. And to unsheathe a *jambiya* in anger, even if no blood is drawn, constitutes a grave offence for which custom prescribes a heavy fine.

mornings as a young boy. His shepherding duties interested him little, and he constantly sought entertaining diversions from the task.

But one day Muhammad's father happened to watch from near the village as his son drove the herd down Wadi Milh. Abdullah could just make the boy out in the distance, throwing rocks at the boulder under which one of his nieces had given birth while out with the flock a few years before (she had returned home in the evening with firewood balanced on her head and a newborn baby in her arms). Absorbed in his imaginary world of single-handedly holding off an army with his stones, Muhammad failed to notice one of the lambs wandering around the mountain side.

Abdullah raised his rifle to his shoulder and took careful aim. His son heard the crack at the same moment as a stone exploded in a cloud of dust within inches of his feet, the bullet ricocheting off harmlessly. Hopping from one foot to the other, he swivelled round and round, trying to make out where the shot had come from. Only then did he see the straying lamb, and his father heading slowly back towards the village in the distance. Abdullah never mentioned the incident to his son, but Muhammad needed no explanation. He never took his eyes off the flock again.

When Muhammad Abu Lahum was five or six years old, he served as one of the numerous hostages taken by Imam Yahya from the sons of the country's tribal *shaykhs*. Imprisoned in Sanaa's Qasr al-Silah fortress, Muhammad and the other hostages received four riyals each month as 'pay'. The guards allowed Muhammad to visit relatives in Sanaa on Thursdays and Fridays. On the other days, he learned to read and write from one of the older prisoners.

When the *Imam* freed Muhammad after a year in the citadel, he went to Ibb to live with his mother for a few months before returning to Milh. The Abu Lahums formerly owned vast landholdings in the southern highlands, from Sumara in the north to Warath village 25 miles to the south.

An old stone fortress marks the summit above the breath-taking Samara Pass, with its cluster of stone houses. On all sides but the north, the mountains drop off thousands of feet from Samara village, in narrow terraces kept green by nearly four feet of rain annually.

The western slope of the pass, beyond where it disappears behind a crag in the ravine far below, formerly belonged to the Abu Lahums. It was the land handed over to Muhsina by the *Imam* in the early nineteenth century, in compensation for her brothers' deaths. But a few generations later, one of the Abu Lahums sold the land to pay off a *diya*.

As a young boy Muhammad sometimes accompanied his father from Milh to Sanaa or al-Rawdha village, a half-hour northeast of Sanaa where Imam Yahya had a palace, to discuss affairs with the ruler. On one occasion, the group of a dozen or so men began the 12-hour journey late, and sunset caught them short of their destination.

'We arrived in the dark at al-Malika village, an hour from al-Rawdha,' Muhammad remembers. 'It began to rain so we decided to stop there for the night. Father went to the village mosque to pray the evening prayer, where he found the village men assembled for the same purpose. He knew the people of al-Malika well and of course he expected someone to welcome us and find us somewhere to spend the night. But after the prayer the villagers returned to their homes without offering an invitation.'

We decided to sleep in the mosque. Our horses had to keep dry, so we led them into the mosque with us for the night. In the morning, when people started showing up for the sunrise prayer, they made a big scene when they saw the horses inside and the mess they had made during the night. They hurled insults at us and virtually chased us away. Father dismissed their behaviour as typical of townsfolk, and thought no more of it as we continued on to al-Rawdha.

But later that day, while my father was discussing affairs with Imam Yahya, a group of villagers from al-Malika requested an audience with the *Imam*. They were shown in and declared that they had come to lodge a complaint regarding the previous night's irregularities in their mosque. Then they proceeded to lay out their demand for reparations to be paid by our group.

After my father calmly explained his side of the story, Imam Yahya turned to the men from al-Malika.

'And what did you serve the Nihmis for dinner?' he asked them.

'Why, nothing, my Lord,' the leader among them spoke up. 'It was very late.'

The *Imam* nodded gravely.

'And what did you offer them in the morning, to break the night's fast?' Yahya asked.

'Nothing, Oh Commander of the Faithful. We were so upset to find the horses in our mosque that ...'

'So you offered neither food nor drink nor a warm bed to your guests?' the *Imam* interrupted. 'Is al-Malika made up of nothing but stingy merchants? Surely there remain some tribesmen among you, men who recall the obligation of hospitality to a guest?'

The notables started to fidget as the *Imam*'s anger became clear.

'If you cannot act as tribesmen, then I will act as one for you,' the *Imam* continued. 'I will *not* fine the Nihmis for the charges you lay against them.'

'But ...' one of the notables protested.

'No!' Yahya growled above him. 'I will fine *you*, the village of al-Malika, four riyals for the price of the breakfast you failed to provide your guests!'

The notables handed my father the money and returned to al-Malika without another word.

Muhammad was still a teenager when his father passed away, but he had ripened into manhood long before. For years Muhammad had been going to Sanaa alone to discuss issues with the *Imam*'s deputy on behalf of his father.

Departing on the 35-mile trek at sunrise, he would reach the capital on foot just at sunset, whether summer or winter, for the length of day varies but little so close to the equator. From Milh, the track to Sanaa snakes west through a canyon, before rising steadily to the 7,500-foot Bin Ghaylan Pass. The route descends sharply on the other side, towards the rolling hills of Wadi Baran, the only part of Nihm consistently blessed with more than an occasional raindrop each year. The sorghum and barley grow healthier here than in Milh. The vivid green crops stand in marked contrast to Jebel Hareem Mountain further west – a bald, massive slab of granite poking hundreds of feet out of its sandy base. Its smooth rounded peak is known to locals as 'the penis of Nihm'.

The track hugs the northern base of an undulating mountain range the rest of the way to Sanaa, the sharp ridge providing occasional shade for travellers. But Muhammad, impatient, usually cut straight across the plain to gain time. Enormous slabs of flattened granite cover areas of ground half the size of a football field, patterned with limestone and black basalt in between. Muhammad might have leaped from one stone to another all the way from Milh to Sanaa without ever touching the soil.

If he got a late start, he would lie up for the night under a boulder, or inside a cave hollowed into a cliff face, where the ancients had placed their dead. If he glimpsed the warm glow of a cooking fire, Muhammad would make for the Bedouins' tent and share in a fortuitous meal. Meat and a gooey pile of ground sorghum mixed with water, buttermilk and clarified butter were the standard fare; better than sleeping on an empty stomach. And he would learn the news of the desert, for the Bedouin know everything that goes on around them. Every chance passer-by is invited for a meal, not only to forestall an attack (desert custom strictly forbids violence between people who have recently shared bread together), but also to catch up on the goings-on of the desert.

As Muhammad grew older, his hosts frequently insisted on slaughtering a lamb or goat in his honour, despite his protests.

Some had precious few livestock to spare, and he began avoiding the nomad camps altogether so as not to put them out.

But if threatening weather or bitter cold eventually led Muhammad to a tent for the night, he would push aside the best pieces of meat and a healthy portion of sorghum gruel, knowing that the womenfolk and children would eat what the men did not. The better the meat left behind, the more ginger and cardamom the women would grind into the strong after-dinner coffee, roasted over a brazier of glowing charcoals. Before departing the camp in the morning, he received a bowl of clarified butter with which to anoint his long hair against the dry air and intense sun. Then he would set off without a word, for thanks are rarely rendered verbally in this land where generosity is the norm rather than the exception.

Muhammad heard a noisy commotion as he passed a village while walking back to Milh from Sanaa one day. 'Some item had been stolen from one of the villagers' houses,' Muhammad remembers with a wide grin. 'And the owner was determined to find out who had done it. He was so irate that the headman finally dispatched a messenger to a nearby village to fetch a frail, elderly sage, known for his ability to discover the guilty party in any crime.'

Once at the village, the sage told everybody to form a line outside. While they filed into order, I noticed the man give the jute sack he carried with him the slightest tug with his wrist. When he did, whatever was inside thrashed back and forth and the man had to struggle to hold the sack closed.

The villagers were watching and wondering what on earth could be inside. Then the sage held up the sack for them to see clearly and told them that he had brought a *jini* along with him. Everybody gasped.

'Be still, you devil!' he yelled at the *jini* as it jerked violently inside. 'I know you know who the thief is. But you must be patient.'

By now the villagers were nearly in a panic, and I thought some would run away, but the sage knew just how far he could push them. He walked slowly along the line of villagers, looking each one in the eye.

'Yes, he knows who among you is guilty,' he repeated. 'But I will give the thief a chance to confess. If he refuses, then I'll let the *jini* show us.'

'Will he hurt us?' a boy asked, nearly crying.

'Oh, he will punish the culprit as he sees fit. I have no say in that,' the old man told him.

The villagers looked nervously around, each one urging the next to do something. Finally a voice, crackly with fear, rose above the murmur.

'I did it,' a man said, trembling as he stepped forward. 'But please. Do not loose your *jini* upon me. I meant no harm.'

The other villagers let out a sigh of relief, except the thief's victim, who demanded that the sage free the *jini* to punish the thief. But the old man refused.

I followed the sage home. A mile or two from the village, I watched him bend over and empty his sack of a three-foot agami lizard, the blue kind. It scrambled under a rock, and the old sage grinned and continued on his way.

It was in a similar manner that Muhammad got his family into a tight spot when he was around 18 years old. Haj Salih, a middle-aged man living in Milh, did not have all of his wits about him. He couldn't read, but that didn't prevent him from lugging around an enormous book wherever he went.

I ran into him one day in our village. 'Haj Salih,' I said. 'Everyone knows you can't read. Why do you insist on carrying that book around with you?'

He smiled at me as though he'd been waiting a long time for someone to ask him that question.

'This book ...' he said, holding it up for me to look at, though there was nothing on the cover. 'When someone comes to me with a sick cow or sheep, it tells me exactly what illness they have, and the best way to treat it.'

I wasn't overly impressed. I'd become sceptical about a lot of things since I saw that old sage with a lizard for a *jini*. A few days later I met one of our neighbours on his way to see Haj Salih, and I asked what he wanted with him.

'One of my cows is sick,' he said.

'Is she shivering?' I asked, trying to sound as if I knew what I was talking about.

'Yes.'

'And is the hair standing up on her hide, like so?' I said, pointing my index finger in the air.

'Why, yes, yes! How did you know?' he said.

Of course I didn't tell him, but I had heard of several other cows in the village suffering from the same symptoms. I told the man to mix certain herbs together and feed them to his cow, a remedy I had heard someone mention once before. He was very excited and rushed home to try it.

It apparently worked, because a few days later ten men showed up at our home early in the morning.

'We heard that you are even better than Haj Salih at treating cattle,' one of them said. 'We need your help.'

I thought it was all rather funny at first, but then a half dozen big *shaykhs* from villages much further away began arriving to ask me to help with their own herds. Of course we had to slaughter a sheep in honour of each of the guests; *ras li al-ras* – a head for a head[6] – as we say, and insist they stay the night. And some of them ended up staying several nights, which meant slaughtering more sheep for every meal.

'Finally my older brothers decided to send me into exile in order to salvage what was left of our flock of sheep,' Muhammad laughs. 'They sent me to Sanaa "to take care of some family business",

[6] ie. a sheep slaughtered for each guest.

they told anyone new who turned up. When I returned a few weeks later, everyone seemed to have forgotten my veterinary skills. Haj Salih, who had been very angry with me for taking away his livelihood, was back in business.'

Muhammad Abu Lahum's destiny would lead him to jail for a second time before his twentieth birthday. In the mid-1950s, Rubish Kaalan, one of the seemingly endless number of sons sired by the infamous Jidaan raider, Mabkhut Kaalan, was passing down a secluded *wadi* bed at the foot of the Khawlan escarpment one day when he came upon a lone traveller.

The traveller donned the plain brown *jambiya* sheath typical of the Bakil (unlike the Hashidis' scabbard, plaited with light green twine), but Rubish had never seen the man before. He appeared ignorant of the ways of the eastern regions, for he had no escort, and committed the grave error of sporting two magnificent pistols at his waist that evoked the envy of everyone he met, not least of all Rubish. The Jidaani fox could not resist the temptation. He lifted the coveted pistols, but at the price of the owner's life, who had resisted.

When a detachment of the *Imam*'s troops marched through the area in search of the missing man, Rubish learned with horror that his victim, a Bani Matar tribesman from west of Sanaa, served in the *Imam*'s personal bodyguard. News spread rapidly that Rubish had been seen with the dead man's pistols, and the Jidaani fled northeast to take his chances in the empty wastes of the Khala wilderness.

Had the killer not been identified, the Nihm, in whose territory the crime had taken place, would have convened a gathering of 44 prominent members of the tribe to swear an oath that no Nihmi had committed the crime. They would then have collected funds from the various Nihm clans to pay off the *diya* to the murdered man's family. The victim's tribe would not be justified in seeking revenge among the Nihm, since Nihm denied under oath the implication of any of its tribesmen. But in this case the killer was known. And it was not only with the victim's tribe that he would have to deal, but also with the *Imam*.

Rubish Kaalan is fearless, demanding and reserved with strangers to the point of paranoia. The Bedouin sense of justice is engrained deeply within him: he takes what he desires and is strong enough to seize. Abdullah Abu Lahum once said, 'If a Bedouin becomes your friend, he eats you. If he becomes your enemy, he kills you.'

Rubish realized he had committed a grave error in killing the guard. An enraged Imam Ahmed ordered the taking of hostages not only from the Jidaan (which comprises a sub-division of the Abu Lahums' own al-Ghufayr clan), but from all of the Bakil tribes, until Rubish turned himself in.

Soldiers led Muhammad Abu Lahum off to the al-Nafa fortress above Hajja town. Though still a teenager, he turned out to be one of the older hostages in the prison. He found some of the inmates, mainly from the turbulent Jawf and Barat tribes in the northeast, chained to their cell walls as punishment for some crime committed by their tribesmen long before the Rubish incident. But the younger boys always remained free to move around.

'The Bedouin hostages, used to the open spaces of the desert, seemed unable to adapt to prison life,' Muhammad remembers with sadness. 'I watched several of them die from the stress of being confined after only a month or two in the fortress, though they showed no signs of physical ailments. I felt sorry for them. They reminded me of some of the Bedouins that used to visit our house. They tend to be much taller than Yemenis from the mountains, and they always seemed to strike their heads on the doorframe of our house whenever they came to visit.'[7]

---

[7] Rubish's son cut short a two-week visit to Paris in the mid-1990s to return to Yemen. 'I miss the open spaces of the Jawf,' he told Charles and me as we strolled up the Champs-Elysées on a beautiful summer evening, the sun setting beneath the Arc de Triomphe before us. 'There are too many buildings and trees here. I've got to get back to the desert.'

Through intermediaries, Rubish negotiated a settlement several months later in which the *Imam* agreed to spare his life. But despite the settlement, Muhammad Abu Lahum remained in prison for two years to guarantee Nihm's good behaviour.

Imam Ahmed, unlike his father, never trusted the Abu Lahums. Abdullah Abu Lahum had loved Imam Yahya and would have done anything for him, but he did not have the same affection for Ahmed. The two had fought together against the Zaraniq in the Tihama in 1928. Abdullah, courageous and confident, bowed down to no one, treating the Crown Prince as an equal. The future *Imam*, however, expected those around him to cede the centre stage to him and Abdullah's proud demeanour offended him. The two never got along after the Zaraniq campaign.

When Ali Nasser al-Qurdai (renowned for losing his nose in a run-in with a lion) assassinated Imam Yahya in 1948, Abdullah Abu Lahum was furious. But his loathing for Crown Prince Ahmed led him and most of Nihm to throw their weight behind the conspirators. The bid failed, however, and Ahmed was none too happy with the Abu Lahums.

On his return from Italy in 1959, a year or two after the Rubish affair, Imam Ahmed learned that Muhammad Abu Lahum's eldest brother, Sinan, had acted as one of the ringleaders in the plot to overthrow him. He summoned Sinan and the other mutinous *shaykhs* to Sukhna, a village near Hodayda where his ship had landed from Italy. But Sinan suspected he might well lose his head if he obeyed the order.

When Sinan failed to arrive, the *Imam* called Muhammad Abu Lahum, some 15 years Sinan's junior, to answer for his brother. Muhammad feared the *Imam* would kill him in Sinan's stead, though Muhammad had had nothing to do with the conspiracy. So he and a companion, Jarullah al-Qurdai (the result of a union between Imam Yahya's killer and a slave woman), determined to make their way to Sukhna together and do away with the *Imam* before he did away with them.

'When we arrived,' Muhammad remembers, 'the guards refused to let al-Qurdai enter the *Imam*'s chambers with me. So I would have to carry out the plan alone. But the guards suspected that something was up. They couldn't take my *jambiya* away from me without insulting me, so one of the guards wound a long strip of wool around the *jambiya*'s hilt. It would have taken me several seconds to unwind the cloth and free the dagger, giving the bodyguards time to stop me before I could do any harm.'

I trembled as I realized my plan was now useless. I entered the *Imam*'s chambers and saw Ahmed's bulging eyes and harsh scowl. I wondered whether I could have acted even had the turban not been wrapped around my *jambiya*.

'Where is Sinan?' the *Imam* said. I tried to keep from shaking.

'Oh, Sinan? But he's a small, unimportant *shaykh*,' I stuttered. 'He had nothing to do with this. Why do you want him?'

The *Imam* looked up from his desk at me for the first time, and I thought he would explode. 'Bring Sinan!' he yelled.

I don't know how I did it, but I told the Imam that he must first guarantee Sinan's safety. He nodded.

'I want it in writing,' I told him.

So the *Imam* called in Muhammad Ahmed al-Basha,[8] his deputy in Hodayda, to write a letter of safe passage

---

[8] Al-Basha came from a well-known family of *Sayids* in Taiz province. Formerly called al-Mutawakil, one of Ahmed's ancestors travelled to Istanbul with two other Yemenis as part of a delegation to meet the Sultan in the nineteenth century. On their departure from the Ottoman capital, the Sultan enquired of the three Yemenis what they desired to take home with them. While his companions asked for silver and expensive carpets, al-Mutawakil asked only to be given the official title of Pasha (pronounced 'Basha' in Yemen, since the Arabic language has no 'p' sound). His companions mocked him, until their ship foundered in a storm, taking the silver and carpets with it to the bottom of the Red Sea. The two men lost everything. But al-Mutawakil still had his title, and he changed his family name to al-Basha on returning home.

for Sinan. Al-Basha wrote out the safe-conduct letter and handed it to me.

'Bring Sinan in the Dakota,' the *Imam* said, referring to his personal plane. 'I'll send it to Sanaa. I want no delays.' The *Imam* then placed 50 riyals in my hand and sent me on my way. Al-Qurdai and I flew back to Sanaa in the Dakota. It was the first time I had been in a plane.

Back in Sanaa I ran into Hussayn al-Ahmar.[9] 'Have you heard any news from Sinan?' I asked him.

'He went to Bayhan,' Hussayn said. 'Hameed sent a letter with Mujahid Abu Shawareb asking the military to revolt, but they refused. Hameed was arrested and flown in the Dakota to see the *Imam* a couple of days ago. Then they arrested Mujahid, too. Sinan knew he was next, so he spread the word that he had been killed, and headed for Bayhan.'

'Come with me to Bayhan to talk to him,' I said.

'I can't,' Hussayn answered. 'I've got to settle things here first.'

'What will you do?' I asked.

'Crown Prince al-Badr has invited me for lunch this afternoon.'

'You mustn't go,' I told him. 'He will surely arrest you and send you to Sukhna with Hameed.'

'Al-Badr has given me his word that no harm shall come to me,' Hussayn said.

'But al-Badr fears his father,' I said. 'He will do what the *Imam* tells him to do.'

'I'll have to take my chances,' Hussayn said, and he left.

Al-Badr did not arrest Hussayn, but he did end up convincing him to go to Sukhna of his own accord. Sinan was right to stay away, for the *Imam* had Hussayn and Hameed beheaded soon afterwards.

---

[9] The principal Hashid *shaykh* and father of Shaykhs Abdullah and Hameed.

Sinan's feigned death did not hold water and the *Imam* soon learned of his exile in Bayhan, and later to Aden. Adept at playing off the tribes, the ruler ordered 1,000 tribesmen from the al-Hada area south of Dhamar to proceed to Milh and destroy Sinan's home. When they arrived several days later, Salih was the only one of Sinan's three brothers still in the village.

'The al-Hada announced they had come to dynamite Sinan's home,' Muhammad Abu Lahum explained, 'the same one Muhsina Abu Lahum had built a century and a half before. But Salih could be very convincing, and he spread some money discreetly among the al-Hada leaders to persuade them to change their minds.'

'Sinan doesn't live here,' he told them, pointing to the big house. 'Of course, he stays here from time to time, but this house is part of the family inheritance. Only a small portion belongs to Sinan. The rest is divided between our brothers and sisters and cousins. For some of them it is all they have.'

The al-Hada were unsure of what to do. They would have to destroy something, if only to appease Imam Ahmed, but at the same time they had no interest in sparking a problem with the Nihm.

Salih saw them hesitate, so he pointed to a small two-storey clay house 100 yards further down the *wadi*.

'That's where Sinan stays when he's here,' Salih told them.

It was an old run-down building that no one had set foot in for years, but the al-Hada played along. They blew it up and returned home, mission accomplished as far as they were concerned.

Muhammad Abu Lahum did not have to experience many more unpleasant encounters with Imam Ahmed like the one in Sukhna. The ruler's health declined steadily, and three years after returning from Italy, he died.

Like many young tribesmen, when Muhammad was a teenager he wanted to join the army. Imam Ahmed, ever distrustful of the Abu Lahums, refused the boy entry into the military, offering him a desk job in the Ministry of Labour instead. But Muhammad needed no one to teach him how to use a rifle. He eagerly joined the revolutionaries in overthrowing the new *Imam*, Muhammad al-Badr, just a week after Imam Ahmed's death.

During the ensuing civil war, the Abu Lahums never wavered in their backing for the Republic (unlike many of the other Bakil tribes). Muhammad's brother, Ali, led the assault on the radio station in Sanaa on the morning of the revolution. He suffered 13 bullet wounds and had to be flown to Cairo for surgery, one of the revolution's first casualties.

Muhammad Abu Lahum became a second lieutenant under the fledgling Republican government. Growing up in a family of *shaykhs* proved better training in leadership skills than any military college.

In November 1962, barely a month after the *Imam*'s demise, Muhammad's unit of mixed Egyptian and Yemeni troops entered the Khawlan mountains south of the capital to engage Royalist tribesmen at Bayt al-Khardal village. His cousin, Dirham Abu Lahum, and future prime minister Hassan al-Amri accompanied the unit.

A bullet struck Muhammad in the mouth during the fighting, and his men evacuated him to a Sanaa hospital. After the battle, Muhammad's unit withdrew from Khawlan to camp among the deep gorges of a *wadi* system in Bani Hushaysh territory east of the capital. Almost immediately they came under attack from Royalist tribesmen in the area. The fighting was fierce and Egyptian soldiers soon showed up at Muhammad's hospital bed to take him back to his men. 'They need you,' they told Muhammad, who could hardly speak because of his wound, and had to mix his bread in with a glass of water in order to swallow it.

Muhammad joined the battle once back with his unit. 'I climbed up the rocky scarp overlooking the *wadi*, from where I could get a good view of everything,' Muhammad remembers.

'Our camp had turned into a battlefield and thick smoke blanketed the *wadi* bed.'

Suddenly a bullet whizzed past my head from close range. I looked up and saw a teenage boy on the opposite wall of the *wadi*, not 80 feet away. I remember his turban spread out to nearly twice the size of his head, and his *jambiya* seemed enormous compared to the boy's small size. He was so scrawny; I wondered how he could even lift his rifle. But then he sent a second bullet right past my cheek.

I raised my rifle and took aim. I could see the terror in the boy's eyes as he fumbled to reload, but I knew he would shoot me if I didn't shoot him first. I fired, and the boy looked at me as he fell forward onto the rocks holding his chest.

I stared at the body and suddenly became overwhelmed with sadness, despite the fighting all around. I wondered who the boy's father was, whether I knew him, how his family would feel when they learned of the boy's death. But all of the sudden the boy sprung up and darted out of sight over the crest of the hill. I laughed for the first time since getting shot in the mouth, though it still hurt.

Blood filled the dry *wadi* bed below Muhammad, and the dead soon appeared to be more numerous than the living. Somehow the Republican camp managed to prevent a rout by their foe. When the Royalist tribesmen finally retreated up the valley soon after sunset, Muhammad and the other survivors collapsed on the ground in exhaustion.

'In the morning,' Muhammad says, 'dozens of Egyptians and Yemenis lay dead or wounded among the boulders in the ravine. I found half a dozen bullet holes in my shirt and trousers, but I was fine.'

Anwar al-Sadat, Speaker of the Egyptian Parliament and that country's future president, was visiting Yemen when the battle in Bani Hushaysh broke out. Yemen's President Abdullah al-Sallal thought a visit to the area with al-Sadat might boost the soldiers' morale.

'Before we could bury the dead,' Muhammad Abu Lahum says, 'a convoy of military vehicles arrived on the road from Sanaa. They stopped and we saw al-Sallal and al-Sadat get out of one of the jeeps. At the same time, a sniper on the cliff wall further down the *wadi* started taking potshots at our unit. Some of our men were shooting back at him, but he pranced around like a mountain goat from rock to rock, twirling around between shots like he was dancing. It was as if something was protecting him. No one could hit him. It spooked us all, and the men finally stopped shooting at him.

I walked over to the convoy, in my tattered, dusty clothes, saluted al-Sallal and al-Sadat, and took them up to the scarp above the wadi to get a look at the battlefield. Al-Sadat gasped when he saw the Egyptian corpses lined up on the ground waiting to be buried. He stopped and just stared blankly at them.

'My God, my God,' I could hear him whisper. Then he buried his face in his hands and wept while his escorts looked around and pretended not to notice.

I could see that al-Sallal was quite angry. He led me away from the others. 'Why did you have to show us this?' he demanded. He was worried that the Egyptian casualties might push al-Sadat to encourage President Nasser to withdraw Egyptian troops from Yemen.

'What's wrong with you?' al-Sallal continued. 'What were you thinking?'

I just turned and walked away.

The visit to the battlefield apparently had an enduring impact on the future Egyptian president. When Muhammad Abu Lahum attended Gamal Abdul Nasser's funeral in 1970, al-Sadat recognized him among the Yemeni delegation as it passed to offer its condolences. Al-Sadat gripped Muhammad's hand long and hard. He held up the line as he stared into Muhammad's eyes, recollecting their meeting eight years earlier in the Bani Hushaysh *wadi*. The two men nearly broke into tears.

Muhammad Abu Lahum left Yemen in January 1964 to study at a military college in Baghdad. He returned home a year later to teach tank warfare at the military school in Sanaa, before moving back to the fighting front as second-in-command of an armoured unit (under an Egyptian officer).

Muhammad expected that the end of the Imamate would also mean an end to his days in jail, but he was wrong. He travelled to Cairo in 1966 with the delegation opposed to President al-Sallal, spending 13 months in prison.[10]

Back in Yemen, Muhammad took command of his old tank unit from the departed Egyptians and helped repel Royalist tribesmen during the 70-day siege in December 1967.[11]

The collapse of the Royalist attack raised hopes that the Republic might survive after all without the backing of Egyptian soldiers. But the new-found optimism turned into a curse as the diverse Republican factions lost sight of the Royalist enemy, concentrating instead on securing their own pre-eminence within the Republican ranks.

A group of left-wing officers from the southern highlands had proved instrumental in defending the capital during the 70-day siege. Many Yemenis from the southern highlands had emigrated during the Imamate to British-occupied Aden and beyond to study and work. Offered few opportunities to participate in government service under the *Imams*, this burgeoning educated class saw the 1962 revolution as their chance to correct the imbalance. Many returned from abroad to help defend the Republic.

But their vision of post-war Yemen diverged sometimes radically from that of other Yemenis. Some southern officers grew frustrated

[10] See Chapter 14, 'Unlikely rebel'.

[11] See Chapter 2, 'Earliest memories'.

when the Royalist threat began to subside following the 70-day siege. They expected to be rewarded for their crucial role in Sanaa's defence with military promotions and important government postings. But the leadership, dominated by men from the northern highlands, proceeded too slowly for their liking and one group decided to force the issue.

The most disciplined, and left-wing, segment of these disgruntled officers hailed from the Hujariya region, along the border with South Yemen. Though this area has produced several of North Yemen's big merchant families, it has also harboured a strong Socialist sentiment.[12]

The Egyptian military command spotted the tight organization of these men from Hujariya and took them under its wing during the civil war. They offered them special training and rapid advancement, particularly within the state security apparatus. These elite officers tended to consider the northern tribesmen running the show in Sanaa as uncouth yokels and they longed for the day they could run the country themselves.

A month after the lifting of the 70-day siege, a large shipment of Soviet-supplied tanks and other war *matériel* arrived by ship in the port of Hodayda. Sinan Abu Lahum, Hodayda's Governor, sent his soldiers to collect the arms, but the Hujariya officers had the same idea. When Sinan's troops, including his brother Muhammad, blocked access to the quay, the Hujariya contingent returned to the city centre and incited the people to revolt against the Governor. Some of Hodayda's inhabitants joined in, and it looked for a few crucial hours as though Sinan could lose control of the city. But the revolt soon petered out.

Not yet defeated, the Hujariya officers readied themselves for a final showdown. When a handful of their supporters were dismissed from important military posts five months later, they kindled an insurrection among the units under their command. On 22–23 August 1968, the mutinous soldiers gathered inside

[12] The former South Yemeni President, Abdul Fatah Ismail (widely believed to have killed President al-Ghashmi with the briefcase bomb), came from Hujariya.

the al-Urdhi military garrison across the street from Bab al-Yemen and prepared to storm Sanaa.

Mujahid Abu Shawareb assumed responsibility for repulsing the attack. He placed his troops, mostly tribal irregulars, on the battlements astride the city wall for a quarter of a mile, from Bab al-Yemen west to the *sayla* bed. Muhammad Abu Lahum joined in, bringing his unit to the city from its base in the northern suburb of al-Rawdha.

But the mutineers, strong and highly motivated, threatened to overrun the defenders. Holed up in the two-storey stone garrison of al-Urdhi, like cats ready to pounce, they awaited the order to charge the rampart 50 yards across the street. Heavy machine guns and RPG rockets suddenly ripped apart the stones of al-Urdhi and the mud of Sanaa's south wall as the combatants engaged in battle. A parachute brigade loyal to the Hujariya officers occupied the fort atop Jebel Nuqum Mountain. It pounded Mujahid's positions far below as the Hashid *shaykh* roamed back and forth across the narrow passageway on the town wall, encouraging his men, helping out where needed.

For a moment the firing from al-Urdhi seemed to taper off. Suddenly the mutineers burst forth from their redoubt and rushed the wall. The defenders beat them back, but they quickly regrouped for another attempt. One of the waves of attackers managed to climb the fire escape of a two-storey motel recently built outside Bab al-Yemen's gate. As they swarmed over the wall, Mujahid sprinted from near the *sayla* to help plug the hole.

When he stopped along a battlement a few hours later to survey the enemy's positions, a bullet struck Mujahid over his right eye, sending him crashing to the clay floor. The sight of the puddle of blood forming under his head tetanized the men crouching beside him. News of their commander's demise raced up and down the wall, and the defenders began to lose heart.

A sigh of relief released the unbearable strain when Mujahid regained consciousness and sat up. The bullet had struck his skull at an angle, ricocheting off but leaving a nasty concussion.

A doctor bandaged his head, helped him to his feet, and began to lead him away.

'What are you doing?' Mujahid exclaimed.

'I'm taking you to rest.'

'I can't rest,' Mujahid insisted. 'My men need me. If we don't win this battle, it's all over for us.'

Shouts of joy rose from the men when Mujahid returned to the wall to continue the fight. The mutineers had taken advantage of the confusion by breaking into the town again, this time through a breach near the *sayla* in the west. When Mujahid and his men repulsed them again, the tide of battle turned definitively in their favour.

'It took us three days to put down the revolt,' Muhammad Abu Lahum recalls. 'We might have done it sooner had Royalist tribesmen in the mountains not heard the fighting and decided to take advantage. They moved on Sanaa from the northeast, and as they marched beneath Jebel Nuqum, the parachute brigade spotted them from the fortress on top and radioed the news to the Hujariya officers.

Their commander used his field telephone to ring Abdullah al-Ahmar, who was in constant touch with Mujahid during the fighting. He warned Shaykh Abdullah that the Royalists were coming. Both sides turned their guns from one another, abandoned their positions and raced together to cut off the approaching Royalists. They drove the tribesmen back into the mountains, then returned to Sanaa to resume fighting each other.

When the mutineers realized they couldn't penetrate the capital, sections of their line began to surrender. The insurrection soon fell apart and their officers fled with a handful of their supporters to South Yemen.

Some 300 civilians inside Sanaa perished in the fighting. The defenders suffered 70 dead, while the mutineers lost many more.

The Hujariya-led mutineers remained active following their defeat. Both North and South Yemen sponsored guerrilla groups to sow turmoil on the other's territory. In an effort to end the urban bombing campaign in North Yemen, the Sanaa Government held public executions of captured saboteurs, one of which my six-year-old classmates and I witnessed in the square in front of our school. Many of those beheaded included the remnants of the Hujariya-led insurrectionists.

With the simmering guerrilla campaigns, tensions between Sanaa and Aden climaxed when South Yemeni troops fought North Yemeni irregulars in a week-long border war in late September 1972. Just days before the full-scale fighting broke out, Muhammad Abu Lahum's brother, Salih, took it upon himself to bring the two sides together in a bid to avert war.

Salih Abu Lahum, some six years older than Muhammad, always advocated bringing foes together to discuss their differences before resorting to bloodshed. Though he had little formal education, Salih's eloquent speech often swayed the most hard-headed of antagonists. His calm eyes and full beard, greying in thin vertical lines on either side of his chin, disarmed as much as his conciliatory words did. Though he abhorred violence, no one ever called Salih a coward. When peace efforts failed and war seemed the only path, Salih was at the front of the fighting.

Salih gained a reputation for his generosity, too. 'Once he bought an expensive *jambiya*,' Muhammad recalls with affection. 'It had a very rare stone embedded in the tip of the hilt, said to drain the poison from a snake bite when rubbed on the puncture. People came from miles around to borrow the dagger for someone or other that had been bitten by a snake, and Salih never refused a request. Within three months the stone had worn away and the *jambiya* had become worthless.'

It was to the region of Damt, 10 miles south of Radaa, that Salih set out in late summer 1972 to try to avert the war brewing between North and South Yemen. Certain tribes around Damt harboured forces of the defeated Hujariya officers. Salih went twice to the area for discussions, but in the end even he proved unable to halt the tide of war.

Following a shaky ceasefire, the undaunted Salih gathered 18 *shaykhs* and returned to Damt in November 1972 for a third attempt at forging a permanent solution. But political events beyond his control were about to overwhelm him.

At that very moment, North Yemeni President Abdul Rahman al-Iryani, Salih's brother Sinan Abu Lahum, his brother-in-law Muhsin al-Aini, and Yahya al-Mutawakil were in Tripoli, Libya, for talks with South Yemeni leaders. The ambitious discussions aimed not just at improving relations between North and South Yemen, but at bringing about full political unification between the two neighbours. Though Sanaa and Aden had come no closer to settling their differences than before their war, pressure from Arab states pushed the Yemeni leaders to at least pretend to be moving towards a merger.

Libyan leader Muammar al-Qadhafi, a great proponent of Arab unity, proved most adamant that the two Yemens become one. His generous financial assistance to Sanaa, and Socialist sympathies with Aden, earned him influence with both camps. He insisted they come to Tripoli for talks.

Like primary-school students, al-Qadhafi sat President al-Iryani and South Yemen's leader, Salim Rubaya Ali, in chairs and used chalk and a blackboard to draw a map of the two Yemens and explain the mutual benefits of their unification. But when the negotiations made little headway, the frustrated Libyan leader took the Yemenis for a ride in his four-wheel drive vehicle. Speeding recklessly across the desert outside Tripoli, al-Qadhafi lectured the two men, swearing he wouldn't allow them to leave Libya until they signed a unification agreement. He studied the two Yemenis for a reaction as he raced over the dunes, taking his eyes off the track for several seconds at a time.

The two passengers were mortified as the Libyan narrowly missed a large rock that could have sent the speeding vehicle into a fatal roll. Glancing at each other, they blurted out in unison their intention to sign a unity accord, if only the Libyan leader would slow down and take them back to Tripoli before he killed them all.

With the announcement of the tentative merger, the guerrilla leaders in Damt grew worried. They feared that improved relations between North and South would spell the end of their financial and military aid from Aden.

The arrival of Salih Abu Lahum and the 18 *shaykhs* presented an ideal opportunity to disrupt the growing entente. As the truck carrying Salih and his companions crept over rough ground towards the extinct volcano towering above Damt, guerrillas emerged from the brush along the road and opened fire. Salih and every one of the *shaykhs* with him died in the hail of bullets.

I was six when Salih died. I was playing at Aunt Hameeda's house where Azeeza, Salih's sister, happened to be visiting that day. When news arrived of the deadly ambush in Damt, she and the other women erupted into a horrible wailing, clawing their faces in grief. My Aunt Hameeda cried so hard she fainted and they had to bring a doctor. I had never met Salih, but would never forget the sorrow caused by his death.

Nearly 14 years later, when the fighting erupted between the various Socialist Party factions in Aden in January 1986, all of the men who had participated in the order to kill Salih Abu Lahum died in the carnage; except one, named al-Audi.

Muhammad Abu Lahum's desire to avenge his brother never subsided through the years, though the killers were beyond his reach in South Yemen. A year or two after the 1990 unification, Muhammad was with President Ali Abdullah Salih one day when al-Audi's name came up.

'Where is that al-Audi these days?' Muhammad asked with an air of feigned indifference. 'I haven't heard anything about him for years now.'

The President thought for a moment, until the motive behind Muhammad's interest in the man dawned on him.

'Oh, him. He's studying in Moscow,' the President finally answered.

But Muhammad didn't believe it.

'Studying?' he said. 'But he's over 50 years old.'

'It was a long time ago,' the President told him. 'Let it go.'
But Muhammad can't.

As President Ibrahim al-Hamdi schemed to dilute the political
influence of the prominent tribal *shaykhs* in the mid-1970s, some
of al-Hamdi's confidants persuaded him that the Abu Lahums
presented a dangerous threat to his plans. Muhammad Abu
Lahum had recently touched a sore spot by commenting to al-
Hamdi that he appeared to be in no hurry to hold elections for a
civilian president.

'You should choose between your post as Commander-in-Chief
of the Armed Forces and President,' Muhammad told him. 'One or
the other, as we all agreed before the coup.'

'I want both,' al-Hamdi retorted.

The President had little doubt that the Abu Lahums would be
dangerous once he implemented his plan to sever the family from
its power base in the military. They would become like cornered
lions and much of Bakil would rally behind them. Al-Hamdi
abhorred violence, but many of those closest to him, including
Ahmed al-Ghashmi, tried to persuade the President it would be
more prudent to eliminate the Abu Lahums than to disgrace them.

Al-Hamdi invited Muhammad, Ali and Dirham Abu Lahum to
the Presidential Office for lunch one afternoon in early 1975.
'After the meal,' Muhammad remembers, 'the President wanted
to take all of us to chew *qat* at al-Ghashmi's house in Dhala.[13] He
was pushy, but Ali Abu Lahum insisted he had things to do, so
only Dirham and I went.'

> We had been chewing *qat* for an hour or so when Ali Qenaf
> Zahra, one of the President's confidants, entered the room.
>
> 'Everything is prepared, sir. We're ready now,' Zahra told
> the President.
>
> Zahra was very nervous, and it was obvious to Dirham
> and me that he wasn't referring to coffee. But al-Hamdi

[13] A village a quarter of an hour's drive northwest of Sanaa.

waved his hand to dismiss him and we didn't think anything
of it. Then, about a quarter of an hour later, Zahra came in
again.

'We're ready, sir,' he said, even more nervous this time.

Whatever he was talking about, Dirham and I were clearly
not meant to know what it was. I was a little annoyed and
stood up from the cushions on the floor where we were seated.

'If you're ready, then we're ready!' I said, looking angrily
at Zahra.

'Go!' the President shouted at Zahra. 'And don't disturb
us again.' Zahra nodded and hurried out of the room.

I suspected nothing at the time. I was just irritated. But
years later one of al-Hamdi's former bodyguards told me
that Zahra had in fact been waiting for the President's
signal to burst into the room and shoot Dirham and me. He
said that when I had stood up and said, 'If you're ready, then
we're ready', it confused them and al-Hamdi decided not to
go through with it.

Muhammad was shocked to discover years later that al-Ghashmi
had encouraged the plan to assassinate him. The two men had
forged a close friendship over the years.

During the al-Iryani presidency, al-Ghashmi served in
Muhammad Abu Lahum's tank brigade, where Muhammad
promoted him through the ranks to be his number two man. He
taught al-Ghashmi, with his Charlie Chaplin-moustache popular
among officers at the time, how to sign his name and how to tie a
necktie on the rare occasions when he needed one.

Soon after the end of the civil war, al-Ghashmi developed a
chronic headache. He petitioned his commander for money in
order to seek treatment, and Muhammad helped him. But the
doctors in Yemen could do nothing for him. When the pain grew
more intense, Muhammad sent his friend to Asmara, across the
Red Sea in Eritrea, where doctors discovered a brain tumour.
They operated to remove it, and al-Ghashmi remained several
months in Asmara to recover.

The future president, Ali Abdullah Salih, along with another of al-Ghashmi's friends in the tank brigade, alternated month-long visits to keep their comrade company. Muhammad Abu Lahum visited on several occasions too, and al-Ghashmi always remained grateful for their care during that period.

On the afternoon of 27 April 1975, Muhammad Abu Lahum was chewing *qat* at his house in Sanaa with his brother-in-law, Abdullah al-Ahmar. Muhammad then commanded the Sixth Armoured Brigade, one of the most powerful military units in the country. While they chewed, one of Muhammad's men turned up in a huff, from the garrison in al-Rawdha. Sections of the army had begun deploying around the city, the man said. And no one seemed to know why.

Muhammad called al-Hamdi's office, but the President was out. Then he recalled running into Ahmed al-Ghashmi that same morning.

'I'm at a fork in the road,' the Chief of Staff had told him cryptically. 'And I don't know which way to go.'

Muhammad didn't understand what al-Ghashmi had meant. But he was about to find out.

The sun had nearly set by the time Muhammad drove back to his garrison. Within minutes of his arrival, he and his men tuned in to al-Hamdi on the radio, announcing the dismissal of Muhammad as Sixth Brigade Commander, his brother, Ali Abu Lahum, as Commander of the Special Forces, and their cousin, Dirham, as Military Commander of Taiz Province.

To attack the Abu Lahums head on was to play with fire. The divergent personalities of the brothers and their distant cousin complemented and reinforced each other in politics and tribal affairs. Salih (until his death), while the peace-maker, was also known for his quick temper. His frank words held great sway over much of the country, and could not be taken lightly. Ali is the born politician, the diplomat of the family, adept at tough negotiations and making big decisions, while Muhammad, calm and collected, exudes sober self-control – the 'good cop'. Sinan, clever and determined, excels at convincing nearly anyone to follow him. And those who hesitate can often be swayed by the threat of Sinan's Bakil tribesmen hovering in the background. Dirham, their distant cousin, keeps everyone guessing with his unpredictability.

It is rare for a son of a great *shaykh* to surpass, or even equal, his father in ability. Such men are as rare as the watering places of the eastern desert. Yet Abdullah Abu Lahum produced not one, but four such sons. And they were not to be taken lightly.

The announcement of the Abu Lahums' dismissal stunned Muhammad and he considered what to do next. He still enjoyed the Sixth Brigade's unswerving loyalty. Without any prompting, his men had sprinted to their tanks and dispersed from the vulnerability of their base before al-Hamdi had even finished his radio address that evening. Muhammad could use them to crush al-Hamdi like an insect if he chose.

The President, however, did enjoy one advantage: his charismatic personality, which filled many Yemenis with hope for a promising future. Soon after taking power, al-Hamdi announced his determination to fight endemic corruption in the country – no easy task.[14] An integral part of al-Hamdi's anti-corruption agenda included sharply diminishing the power of Yemen's big tribal *shaykhs*.

Sanaanis who had lost their ties to the countryside, inhabitants of the detribalized southern and western regions of the country,

---

[14] Bribes have long been a necessary part of getting things done in Yemen. The salaries of civil servants are so low that they are expected to, indeed they must, resort to accepting payment for services rendered in order to feed their families. The salary of a Yemeni government minister is equivalent to US$550 per month in 2003. That would suffice were it just the minister and his immediate family that lived on it. But a minister's high position means he is constantly solicited by an array of relatives and even unrelated inhabitants of his native village for much-needed financial support. He would be highly negligent in his social duties were he to refuse them. Of course just where to draw the line between an acceptable supplement to one's official salary and unabashed personal enrichment is not always easy, and abuse of the system had become common and visible by the time of al-Hamdi.

and even portions of the tribal population greeted al-Hamdi's campaign with enthusiasm, believing that influential *shaykhs* had merely stepped in to replace the *Imam* in a system that had changed little despite the revolution. Wealth was squeezed out of their hardworking hands and poured into the tribal areas, whose inhabitants did little but make trouble and demand more money from the government, they complained.

Al-Hamdi's popularity in Sanaa and the southern regions attained heights unknown before in modern Yemen. But popular support would have little role to play during the short time it would take for Muhammad Abu Lahum and his tanks to devour the President.

Then news arrived that al-Ghashmi, loyal to the President, had deployed his own tanks around Sanaa to counter any resistance from the Abu Lahums. Muhammad then understood the 'fork in the road' to which al-Ghashmi had referred that morning.

If he moved against al-Hamdi, Muhammad just might plunge the country into civil war. He had little doubt he would come out victorious in the end, yet the prospect of more fighting repulsed him and he hesitated. The phone rang through the night, friends and fellow officers begging Muhammad to exercise restraint. He conceded and stood down his troops.

The President knew he was treading on dangerous ground in locking horns with the *shaykhs*. But the source of al-Hamdi's downfall two and a half years later would emerge from another quarter altogether.

Salih Hedayan, the Saudi Arabian military attaché in Sanaa, exercised considerable influence in Yemen, particularly for a foreigner. Representing the interests of his patron, a prominent Saudi prince, Hedayan met regularly with the Yemeni leader, offering advice and ensuring that the President took his boss's interests to heart.

But al-Hamdi's sacking of Mujahid Abu Shawareb the day after the Abu Lahums alienated Shaykh Abdullah al-Ahmar, a staunch ally of Saudi Arabia in Yemen. Al-Hamdi further antagonized his neighbour to the north by reducing Hedayan's access to the President, significantly curtailing the Saudi military attaché's ability to pull the strings in Sanaa. Enough was enough, and Hedayan joined hands with al-Hamdi's ambitious Chief of Staff, Ahmed al-Ghashmi, to remedy the situation.

After eliminating al-Hamdi, the former Chief of Staff seized power and liquidated several of his political enemies. Like al-Hamdi, he quickly forgot the pledge made by the clique of officers meeting at Muhammad Abu Lahum's house prior to launching the 1974 coup, in which each man promised never to make trouble for the others. Ali Qenaf Zahra was one of the first to die in al-Ghashmi's purge, and Parachute Brigade Commander Abdullah Abdul Alem soon fled the country in fear of his life.

On 22 June 1978, Muhammad Abu Lahum informed the President that he was taking his family for several months of vacation in Cairo and London. Al-Ghashmi had been in power over eight months, but he had yet to broach the subject of bringing the Abu Lahums or Mujahid Abu Shawareb back into the government. Muhammad's departure implied a subtle protest to this state of affairs.

His generosity never failing, al-Ghashmi handed his old friend a bundle of cash, a couple of expensive watches, and called the Director of Yemenia Airlines to reserve seats for the Abu Lahums on the flight to Egypt that evening.

'But the plane is already overbooked,' the director protested.

'You get them on that plane or I'll break your head,' al-Ghashmi growled and hung up. He turned to Muhammad.

'Come back in a month,' he said. 'I'll have a good position ready for you then.'

Muhammad placed little faith in the promise. His intuition proved correct, for two days later al-Ghashmi was dead.

When the second war with South Yemen broke out in February 1979, al-Ghashmi's successor, Ali Abdullah Salih, asked Muhammad to command troops in the Marib region. He accepted, and after the brief conflict he returned to Hajja, this time not as a prisoner but as Governor of the province.

By 1994, when Mujahid Abu Shawareb came to see him to feel out the Bakil's stance on the political crisis threatening to engulf Yemen in civil war, Muhammad had been in semi-retirement in Paris for several years.

CHAPTER TWENTY-ONE

Showdown

Less than a week after President Ali Abdullah Salih and Vice-President Ali Salim al-Baydh signed the Amman accord on 21 February 1994, the situation in Yemen turned explosive. Skirmishing between the northern and southern armies broke out at several bases around the country. The powder keg of full-scale war seemed ready once again to ignite.

Mujahid Abu Shawareb was still in Paris meeting with Muhammad Abu Lahum when he heard the news. The Amman agreement had failed and the disheartened Mujahid believed that only one thing could head off further bloodshed now. At 1.00 a.m. on the morning after the skirmishes, he talked to Ali Abdullah Salih on the telephone from his Paris flat.

'You should both resign,' Mujahid asserted. 'You and al-Baydh cannot overcome your differences. You should just step down and give more moderate heads a try at running the country.'

'All right,' the President consented. 'You may be right. I will tender my resignation immediately, if al-Baydh agrees to do the same.'

Encouraged, Mujahid left the next day in a bid to secure al-Baydh's resignation in Aden, where the Vice-President had returned after the signing of the Amman agreement, instead of going to Sanaa. But Mujahid ended up shuttling ceaselessly between Aden and Sanaa for the next few days, unable to make any headway.

On 3 March, Mujahid and Sinan Abu Lahum issued a joint declaration to the press. They warned that the current situation in Yemen was leading the country down a path to war, that they had done everything within their power to avert such a catastrophe, and that henceforth they relinquished any responsibility for future events.

Mujahid returned to Paris the next day. Charles and I visited him in his flat, where we found him drained and crestfallen.

'I'm tired. So tired,' he groaned. 'Maybe I'll emigrate to Canada, buy a farm and forget about politics.' His spirits improved slightly at the thought.

He disconnected the telephone in his flat, then proceeded to torture himself over the coming three days over what to do. As much as he would have liked to separate himself from his country's woes, Mujahid is a man of action. He could never sit idly back and watch events unfold from afar.

For the next two months he predictably forgot his promise to wash his hands of the situation in Yemen. He plugged his telephone in again and talked with Yemenis until the early hours of the morning: proposing, bargaining, cajoling and negotiating.

In late April, Mujahid flew to the United States for surgery to correct a deviated septum. He cut his convalescence there short when Yemen began to spiral out of control. Several dozen northern and southern tanks, faced off against one another in Amran, had opened fire from point-blank range. Mujahid returned to Paris, where the one-hour time difference with Yemen made contact more practical than from the USA.

On 4 May 1994, the inevitable could wait no longer. Heavy fighting broke out between the northern and southern armies at a joint army barracks in Dhamar province. The battle spread like a cholera epidemic to half a dozen military bases around the country. The southern air force swooped in to attack the north's two power stations, plunging Sanaa and other towns into darkness for the coming weeks.

I called home that night. Distraught, Mother informed me that my brother Tariq had returned to duty with the Republican

Guards a few months before, when political tensions began to mount. He was stationed at the base in Dhamar, where the fighting had started that day. We would receive no word of Tariq for the next two months.

The following morning, each side announced that victory was imminent. The foreign press and Middle East analysts echoed the sentiment, predicting that the war would end within a week at most. Mujahid is the only one I know who believed otherwise.

'This will not be a quick war,' he forecast gloomily. 'Nobody's going to help Ali Abdullah Salih after Yemen's stance during the Gulf War. And al-Baydh's forces are too weak to take advantage of it.'

On the second day of the fighting, the Socialist leadership in Aden upped the ante by firing half a dozen Soviet-made Scud missiles on Sanaa. One landed between Mujahid's house and one of the President's private residences 600 yards away.

Outraged, Mujahid called Salim Salih Muhammad, a member of the Presidential Council, former Deputy Secretary-General of South Yemen's Socialist Party, and a confidant of Ali Salim al-Baydh. Though in London at the time, Salim Salih maintained close contact with the Socialist leadership in Aden by telephone.

'This is outrageous,' Mujahid stammered, choked with emotion. 'Your Scuds have absolutely no military value. You know as well as I do that the President is safely underground. Your missiles are killing only innocent people.'

Mujahid's mood swung like a pendulum. Updates on Yemen from friends came through in a constant stream and we all stayed glued to the Arabic satellite television channels in his flat. He drifted from severe bouts with depression following reports of heavy casualties, to exhilaration at the slightest indication that the war might soon end.

On day five of the war, Mujahid received a call at his Paris flat from a man I will call Ali, a close advisor to Saudi Arabia's King Fahd.

'You must go back to Yemen,' Ali urged. 'If this war bogs down, you'll be the only man acceptable to Yemenis to lead the country.'

'There's nothing I'd like more than to return,' Mujahid admitted. 'But it has to be under the right circumstances. I can't go back to Yemen and just proclaim myself President without having consulted anyone first,' he pointed out. 'That's crazy.'

I listened to the conversation through the phone's second earpiece (attached to many French telephones at the time). I tapped Mujahid on the shoulder and he cupped the mouthpiece with his free hand.

'If he wants you to go back, tell him to get Shaykh Abdullah's accord,' I whispered, referring to Mujahid's brother-in-law, Abdullah al-Ahmar. This would reveal whether the Saudis were really serious, for Riyadh was close to al-Ahmar and would have to secure the Hashid *shaykh*'s agreement before encouraging Mujahid to return to Yemen.

When Mujahid repeated the demand to Ali, the Saudi hesitated. He had obviously not broached the idea with al-Ahmar, who all along advocated crushing the Socialists completely. Al-Ahmar would not be pleased if Mujahid arrived on the scene to halt the war before al-Baydh and the hard-line Socialists had been thoroughly defeated.

Noncommittal, Ali ended the conversation. An aid to King Hussayn of Jordan called later that evening to say the king would send a private aircraft to convey Mujahid to Yemen if he wished to return. Mujahid said he would let them know, but he had no intention of taking up the offer.

The tension at the Yemeni Embassy in Paris approached boiling point once the fighting started back home. Following the first week's exaggerated claims of a speedy victory from both Sanaa and Aden, the wisdom in Mujahid's assessment of a drawn-out conflict became evident. With telephone lines shut down for security reasons throughout Yemen, the embassy staff in Paris stayed glued to radios for any news.

I had long hours to reflect on what it might mean for me if the Socialists managed to gain control of the entire country. It could be years before I would be allowed to return to Yemen or see my family again, and many of the people dear to me could be killed or forced into exile too. I tried not to think of how little it would take for such a scenario to come to pass: a change in sides by this or that tribe, some key support from a neighbouring country, or a poorly considered decision here or there.

The fighting, of course, weighed heavily on my mind, though it was over 3,000 miles away. Even the gay streets of Paris seemed sad and scary to me, and as I drove to and from work listening to the news of the war on the radio, I felt as though tanks were rumbling all around me and missiles could explode at any moment. I realized for the first time how deeply the trauma of warfare had affected me when I was a child.

I busied myself fielding telephone calls from French journalists wanting to know what was going on in Yemen. Others prepared to travel there to cover the war. I filled them in as best I could and supplied them with telephone numbers of officials in Sanaa whom they could interview. But the other embassy staff and I knew little about the actual progress of the fighting.

When an official at the Ministry of Information in Sanaa managed to ring me on a special line, I asked why he was not supplying me with any information so that I could keep journalists informed.

'But we've been sending you loads of press releases,' he told me.

I hadn't seen a single one. The fax machine was located inside the ambassador's office and it turned out that some of the Socialist sympathizers at the embassy were intercepting the faxes before I could get them.

For its banking needs, the Yemeni Embassy used a small institution located in a Paris suburb. Many of the embassy staff did their personal banking there, too. When Jazm Abdul Khaliq, chargé d'affaires and the second man at the embassy, went to the bank to handle some personal business one afternoon during the war, a bank manager came out to see him.

'Someone from your embassy called this morning,' the man explained. 'He said he was coming to withdraw all of the funds in the embassy account.' It was a pro-Socialist diplomat.

'What did you tell him?' Jazm asked.

'We said we would need at least two days to have such a large amount of cash on hand. With the problems in Yemen, I didn't know exactly how to handle his request.'

The chargé d'affaires thanked the manager and immediately called Sanaa. The following day, the President recalled the ambassador to Sanaa, along with several other pro-Socialist ambassadors in various countries. All refused to return.

The outbreak of war had caught neither side with its trousers down in Yemen. In addition to stockpiling weapons in Sanaa, the Socialist Party leadership had distributed hefty sums of cash to certain Bakil tribes to induce them to march on the capital in their support in the event of a full-scale conflict. The President and his supporters worked with equal diligence to ensure the support of various tribes.

All of Yemen held its breath for the Bakil tribes to make their intentions known. Rumour had it that some considered backing the Socialists. In April, just days before the war began, the Bakil had joined together in a rare display of unity. Following a perceived insult by a government official directed at the Abu Lahum family, hundreds of Bakil tribesmen closed the main road running north from Sanaa to Amran for several days. But in the end many of the Bakil hesitated to join the fray when war broke out.

Mujahid, Charles and I had dinner in Muhammad Abu Lahum's flat on the tenth day of the fighting, 13 May. When I talked about my work with the journalists interested in Yemen, Mujahid kidded me about my loyalty to the President. But I detected a hint of irritation in his voice. Being somewhat sensitive on the issue, I didn't appreciate the humour and took the comment as a personal affront.

'It's easy to sit there and criticize. But what are you doing to end the war?' I lashed out, rather unjustly. 'You and the other *shaykhs* will be the first to be killed if al-Baydh and the Socialists take over, just like they did in South Yemen before.'

Muhammad and Mujahid nodded in agreement.

'I'll never go back if the Socialists win,' I added. 'Even if they let me.'

My support for the President more than anything else reflected the loathing I felt for al-Baydh and the system he stood for. The Socialists, highly effective at public relations, portrayed the war in Yemen as a battle pitting primitive tribal forces, incarnated in President Ali Abdullah Salih, against a progressive underdog, Vice-President al-Baydh. The image they described was of Socialists, having overcome tribal allegiances, now struggling in the cause of women's rights, personal freedom and economic development for the country.

Up to then I had had little but regrettable experiences with Socialists I came into contact with since the unification,[1] and I did not buy their claims. I had already seen what al-Baydh thought of women from his comments to Amat al-Aleem al-Suswa about politics being 'a man's world'. And the Socialists' favourite criticism, that the northern tribesmen are 'divisive and backward', also rang hollow for me. I recalled the internecine violence between Socialist leaders in Aden in January 1986, when up to 10,000 people lost their lives. The bloodbath started following a shoot-out at a meeting of top officials in the South Yemeni capital. The antagonists immediately coalesced around tribal and regional groupings that 17 years of Marxist rule had 'officially' eliminated.

With the war in 1994, I noticed that many journalists for leading French newspapers and magazines echoed the Yemeni Socialists'

---

[1] After the war, I would meet several Socialist Party figures that I liked and respected.

line in their press articles. They seemed genuinely sincere in their desire for the country's well-being but, as is so often the case, they focused on issues important to Westerners yet of little concern to Yemenis. Many foreign journalists would take up the destruction of a beer factory in Aden by the conservative Islah Party as a rallying call in support of the Socialists. And correspondents covering the war from the former South Yemeni capital pleasantly discovered that the veil is much less common there than in Sanaa.

'Those poor women in the north', one female journalist lamented to me after returning from Yemen. 'How oppressive it must be to have to cover yourself from head to toe. Certainly *you* don't dress like that when you're there, do you?

'I personally don't want to veil,' I explained. 'So I don't. But many women want to wear it. It's a tradition they feel comfortable with; not something to be liberated from. The Yemeni women who come to Europe are just as shocked at how the women dress here. It would never enter their minds to go out in a short skirt and sleeveless shirt, for example. There are so many other issues to be addressed in Yemen that would "liberate" women infinitely more than telling them to stop wearing their veils.'[2]

---

[2] The veil is believed to have been introduced into Arabia before Islam by the Christian Byzantines in what is today Turkey, where females of upper class families concealed their faces in public as a sign of prestige. In much of the Muslim world, including Yemen, the veil has traditionally served the same purpose: a status symbol for women wealthy enough not to have to work outside the home. The common folk, labouring daily in the fields, found the veil cumbersome and rarely wore it. While the Prophet Muhammad's wives veiled themselves in public, it is not universally accepted that Islam requires all Muslim women to do so. A Yemeni girl today begins wearing a veil in her early teens because society, and often her mother and father, encourage it. In time, however, she wears it because she doesn't feel comfortable without it.

Women in Yemen enjoy a sort of protected social status. They are in many instances discouraged from mixing with men outside the immediate family or from working outside the home. Some women, often those that have travelled abroad, dislike such restrictions, but the vast majority do not complain of any

I explained to the journalist my feeling that education is the key to improving the status of women in Yemen, or in any other country for that matter. Education better prepares a woman to defend herself against ideas others wish to impose on her, to confront them with strong arguments and constructive dialogue. It makes her aware of the choices open to her, allowing her to take her destiny into her own hands. The struggle for secondary issues, such as the veil for women not particularly fond of wearing it but who feel pressured to do so, can only come later.

When I finished, the journalist returned to the subject of the veil and sighed again in pity. She seemed incapable of understanding that other cultures might see the world differently from her.

Mujahid's cold demeanour the following day betrayed the hurt provoked by my verbal attack during dinner at Muhammad Abu Lahum's flat the previous night. He announced he was leaving for Geneva to meet a representative of Saudi Arabia's King Fahd. 'I'm going to see what I can do to end the war,' he said, referring sarcastically to my comment at dinner.

Mujahid called the next day from Geneva.

'Maybe you're right,' he told me. 'Maybe I should go back to Yemen and try to mediate again. I'll call the President and see if he's still open to the idea.'

I thought for a moment.

'Tell him that if he thinks they can win the war in the next two or three days, like they keep saying, then there's no need for you to get involved. But if they can't win quickly, then you'll go back.'

'lack of freedom' or 'oppression' any more than a Yemeni *Sayid* might complain of discrimination because he is traditionally not supposed to serve in the military.

Most Yemeni women take pride in, even demand, the nearly sacred status society offers them, and they can sometimes prove the most diligent in upholding custom. My Grandmother Amina used to yell at me when I watched the street from the window of our home in expectation of her return in the evenings: 'Why do you have to show your face for the world to see?' she would yell at me when she entered. 'It's shameful.'

When Mujahid called Sanaa, the President told Mujahid that the war was progressing well. 'We're picking up momentum, and will be in Aden soon. There's no need for you to come now,' he said.

Mujahid returned to Paris, delighted the war seemed to be nearing an end.

Over the years, Mujahid had his differences with the President over just how to run the country. But he nevertheless held Ali Abdullah Salih in the highest esteem as a person.

'He's probably the bravest man I know,' Mujahid told me, on learning that the President had gone to the front to observe the fighting on the second day of the war against the Socialists.

Ali Abdullah Salih had done the same thing with Mujahid 15 years before, during the 1979 border war against left-wing guerrillas backed by South Yemeni forces. As Mujahid and the President had approached the front, they met their own tanks fleeing north from the approaching enemy. The major town of al-Baydha had fallen and the North's troops were being routed.

'The commanding officer stopped and got down from his tank to tell us that the situation was lost,' Mujahid says. 'But Ali Abdullah wouldn't accept defeat.'

'Get in your tanks, turn around, and take back al-Baydha,' the President yelled.

'The officer argued with him, but the President screamed him down. The man got back in his tank and turned it around – but only halfway. Pointed straight at the President and me standing a few yards away, the tank suddenly came towards us. I moved for cover, but Ali Abdullah ran forward with a rifle in his hand, enraged, and began smashing the front of the tank with the butt. I couldn't believe it. As the tank shifted into a higher gear, someone pulled the President out of its path – just in time. He would have been crushed in another instant.

Ali Abdullah Salih[3] was born in 1945 and grew up in a small village in Sanhan territory south of Sanaa. His father died when Ali and his two brothers, Muhammad and Salih, were still young boys, and their widowed mother soon married a close relative of her late husband. She gave birth to two more boys and named them Ali and Muhammad too, just like their half-brothers.

Ali Abdullah Salih worked his way steadily up the military hierarchy, his break coming when President al-Hamdi named him Military Governor of Taiz after Dirham Abu Lahum's dismissal in 1975. He became Deputy Commander-in-Chief of the Armed Forces and a member of the four-man Presidential Council following President al-Ghashmi's death in June 1978. Within a month, the youthful Ali Abdullah had taken over as the new President of Yemen.

The position had few takers at the time. With two presidents assassinated in eight months, the prospects for maintaining the reigns of power for any length of time appeared minimal. Furthermore, Yemen's economic, political and social problems were overwhelming. Few people wanted the responsibility of having to deal with them.

It would not be smooth sailing for the inexperienced Ali Abdullah Salih. A protracted counter-guerrilla campaign, a brief border war with South Yemen, and several assassination attempts in the first years of his rule offered little hope for stability in the country. But the President slowly consolidated his position. Twenty-five years later, he is Yemen's longest-running ruler since Imam Yahya.

Mujahid's gamble in refusing to take sides in the conflict between President Ali Abdullah Salih and Vice-President al-Baydh in 1994 paid off initially. His neutrality made him perhaps the sole Yemeni acceptable to both Sanaa and Aden as an arbitrator.

---

[3] Like many Yemenis in the countryside, he uses no family name, identifying himself only as Ali, the son of Abdullah, the son of Salih.

With the civil war entering its third week and Ali Abdullah's troops nearing Aden, Mujahid received urgent telephone calls from Palestine Liberation Organization Chairman Yasser Arafat and a Saudi royal advisor on 19 May. They both urged him to try to bring Ali Abdullah and al-Baydh together and end the fighting.

I considered it a bad idea. 'If they're really about to capture Aden,' I said, 'there's no point in stopping now. Nothing will be settled, and al-Baydh will regroup and wait for a better day to fight again. The situation will be right back where it started.'

Though he agreed with the assessment, Mujahid, true to form, refused to sit back and wait. For the next three days he juggled phone calls with officials close to Ali Abdullah and al-Baydh, trying to determine the mood.

Alongside the President were Interior Minister Yahya al-Mutawakil[4] and a confidant of Ali Nasser Muhammad, the former South Yemeni leader ousted by al-Baydh in the deadly fighting in 1986 and now allied with President Ali Abdullah. Contact with al-Baydh came through Yemen's Socialist Prime Minister Heidar Abu Bakr al-Attas and al-Baydh's close advisers: Salim Salih Muhammad in London and Muhammad Selman, who remained in Aden with al-Baydh and al-Attas.

But the timing was not ripe for a ceasefire. Troops loyal to the President had indeed pushed further south, to within 20 miles of Aden. If they could capture the former South Yemeni capital, the war would be over. And further east, with the help of local tribes resentful of the Socialists' land reform programmes in the 1970s,

---

[4] Yahya al-Mutawakil had moved to Paris as ambassador to France soon after he gave me the financing guarantee for my sports car in Washington. By now he had returned to Yemen and, following the April 1993 legislative elections, became Interior Minister for the second time.

This cabinet post may well be the most difficult in Yemen, all the more so in that Yahya strove to do a good job and enforce many of the laws that others had found expedient to ignore. The early 1990s was a hectic period as the government struggled with the complexities of unification. Internal security tended to be neglected in order to deal with more immediate problems.

Ali Abdullah Salih's forces had succeeded in driving through Shabwa province almost to the Indian Ocean. This cut the Vice-President off from potentially critical support in his home province of Hadhramawt.

Ali Abdullah felt he had the upper hand now and insisted on an unconditional ceasefire, but al-Baydh had one last card up his sleeve. He would consider a ceasefire, he declared, but only after the President's troops withdrew to the pre-unification border between North and South Yemen.

Al-Baydh had by then given up hope of taking control over all of Yemen. His goal now focused on using international diplomacy to dissolve the unification. That would leave him to rule over the former South Yemen, a return to the pre-1990 status quo.

Having secured assurances from neighbouring Gulf countries of diplomatic and financial support, al-Baydh publicly proclaimed an end to Yemeni unification and the creation of the Yemen Democratic Republic within the borders of the former South Yemen. If he could just hold out a little longer, al-Baydh and his allies in the Gulf could work through diplomatic channels to gain international recognition for the secession at the United Nations.

Al-Baydh's gamble finally forced Mujahid (and many other political figures up to then opposed to the war) to take sides. He publicly condemned the Separatists and their self-proclaimed Yemen Democratic Republic, for unification was too dear to Mujahid to be sacrificed to the whims of a few men. Ye he still strove to bring the two sides closer together, hoping most importantly to convince al-Baydh to renounce his secessionist intentions. But the Socialist leader continued to demand a withdrawal of troops to pre-unification borders.

'No,' the President insisted. 'We will accept nothing less than an unconditional ceasefire.'

'Unconditional ceasefire?' Muhammad Selman, al-Baydh's adviser, bragged when Mujahid relayed the message by telephone to Aden. 'You must be kidding. Our troops are standing over piles of their dead soldiers at al-Anad,' a key military base north of Aden.

The news shook Mujahid and for once he was at a loss for words.

'Tell Ali (Abdullah Salih) and Yahya (al-Mutawakil) they must withdraw to the border,' Selman repeated.

Listening on the second earpiece, I cupped the mouthpiece of Mujahid's receiver. 'He's bluffing,' I said.

Mujahid regained his composure. 'I haven't been able to reach them today,' he told Selman, winking mischievously at me. 'They're not returning my calls. I think they're angry about the Scud you fired on Sanaa last night.'

Mujahid hung up and called the Presidential Office. Yahya answered.

'I think the Separatists are having trouble around al-Anad,' he told Yahya. 'Is anything going on there?'

'Our troops arrived at the base yesterday,' Yahya pointed out. 'We haven't attacked it yet. The Separatists seem pretty well dug in, but you think they're weak there?'

'It's just a hunch,' Mujahid admitted.

The next morning government troops launched an offensive against al-Anad. When the defenders withdrew late in the afternoon, falling back towards Aden, Muhammad Selman called Mujahid from Aden to complain about the siege.

'But Yahya told me they didn't attack,' Mujahid answered with rare duplicity. 'He said they were just defending their positions, that it was *you* who attacked.'

'It's not true! It's not true!' Selman screamed into the phone. 'He's lying. Don't listen to him. *They* attacked *us!*'

Mujahid realized with those words that the Separatists had grown desperate. He pressed home the advantage and by the end of the conversation Selman and the Socialists in Aden had agreed to an unconditional ceasefire.

The next day, Mujahid told President Ali Abdullah Salih and the Separatists that the truce would be followed by negotiations between six delegates, three chosen by Ali Abdullah and three by al-Baydh. But the talks quickly became ensnared when the President insisted before anything else that the Socialists renounce the secession. When Mujahid stated that he agreed with this demand, the Separatists grew angry.

'I feel like you've tricked us,' Selman told Mujahid on the telephone.

The accusation disturbed Mujahid. He had made clear all along that the essential aim of his mediating was to preserve the unification, Yemen's proud contribution to the cause of Arab unity. That al-Baydh continued to pursue his secessionist goal angered Mujahid.

The ceasefire fell apart before it even began, and fighting resumed the next day.

With the pro-Separatist ambassador dismissed and the chargé d'affaires, Jazm Abdul Khaliq, now in charge of the embassy, the other pro-Separatist diplomats in Paris turned bitter. Several stayed late one evening at the embassy to discuss the situation over glasses of vodka. Several hours later, the inebriated employees ripped the framed photographs of President Ali Abdullah Salih from the walls and danced joyfully over the shattered glass.

'We won't consider ourselves men until Khadija is dead,' an embassy employee heard someone announce one evening, and the others toasted his declaration. 'Then we'll dance over *her* body.'

The pro-Separatist diplomats focused their wrath on me for a reason. While the other staff had for the most part kept to themselves since the outbreak of the war, as press attaché, I had by necessity become even more active. And I did not back down from confrontation with the pro-Socialist diplomats. I angrily confronted them on such issues as the disappearing faxes and the fact that they were sending out their own pro-Separatist press releases to their journalist contacts on the embassy fax.

Jazm, now the acting ambassador, threatened to expel the Socialist diplomats if they continued to promote the secession. One of the Socialists made it known through a mutual friend that they had a car loaded with weapons and explosives parked nearby. They would use it to attack the embassy if they were prevented from entering.

The threat only angered Jazm, who is not easily intimidated. After requesting round-the-clock police guard for the embassy from the French Foreign Ministry, he told the Socialists not to come to work any more.

I received a telephone call at home a couple of evenings later. 'We're going to get even with you,' the man on the other end whispered. 'You'll see.'

Despite the poor attempt to disguise his voice, I recognized it as belonging to one of my former colleagues. The threat outraged Mujahid when I told him about it the next day.

'If they so much as touch Khadija,' he reassured my husband, 'I'll cut off all their heads, put them in a sack and send them to her mother!'

I have no doubt he meant it.

The day after the ceasefire talks broke down, an exasperated Mujahid asked Yahya al-Mutawakil in Sanaa: 'Why don't you hit them harder, and get it over with?'

'We've hit them with everything we've got,' Yahya answered. 'We can't advance any further.'

But the Socialist leadership nevertheless saw their world closing around them. Muhammad Selman called Mujahid from Aden two days later. The Socialist leaders were considering the use of chemical weapons if the President's troops continued their advance on Aden, he said.

Mujahid nearly choked. He never imagined that al-Baydh would resort to such extremes.

'They're not crazy,' I said, trying to calm Mujahid after he hung up the phone. 'They're about to lose the war and they're going to use chemical weapons? I don't think so. They're not that stupid. They know they would all hang if they did.'

Ali Abdullah Salih's troops continued to tighten their stranglehold on Aden over the coming weeks, but the Socialists never mentioned chemical weapons again.

The war was now seven weeks old, when few but Mujahid had believed it would endure beyond seven days. But time was running out for the Separatists.

Al-Baydh's only hope lay in his allies in the Gulf countries. If they could force through an internationally brokered ceasefire and a withdrawal of Ali Abdullah Salih's troops to the former border between North and South Yemen, he might be saved. But the chances of such a scenario playing out faded as the tide of war shifted squarely in the President's favour.

With Ali Abdullah in a position to deal the final blow to his enemy, the need for Mujahid as mediator disappeared. I suggested again that maybe it was time he return to Yemen. 'Otherwise, when it's all over, people will say you were with the Separatists,' I argued.

Mujahid dismissed the advice, irritated. With the war winding down, he felt going back now smacked of hypocrisy, no matter how much he abhorred the Socialists' and their attempt to destroy the unification.

'No,' he answered. 'I told them they were heading for war, and I did everything I could to prevent it. I'm not going back now and pretend I supported it.'

'But you don't have to go home in defeat,' I argued. 'You acted in good faith with everyone. You did your best.'

On 7 July 1994, troops loyal to President Ali Abdullah Salih entered Aden and several other key towns held by the Socialists. Al-Baydh and other top Separatist officials managed to flee across the border to Oman, whose ruler offered them asylum but forbid them any involvement in politics. Some continued on to Saudi Arabia, unwilling to abide by the Omanis' condition.

Relieved that the war had ended, Mujahid decided against returning to Yemen for a few months. His pride wouldn't allow him to go home immediately and face the inevitable interrogations from the people: 'Where have you been? Why weren't you here to help out during the war?' no matter how unfair such questions were.

Despite its tragic nature for the country, on a personal level the war boosted my confidence – in Yemenis and in myself. While I certainly played no part in the decisions that had been made, the fact that someone like Mujahid would listen to and consider my opinion on such an important topic meant a lot to me. Not only did it make me feel that I had something to contribute, but I was pleased that a prominent *shaykh* with supposedly conservative ideas did not hesitate to listen to a woman on issues that typically are reserved for men. Such seemingly small things filled me with hope for the future.

Epilogue

I called Mother a few days after the end of the war to learn that everyone in the family was safe. My brother Tariq had survived not only the battle in Dhamar in the first days of the conflict, but also the bloody struggle for al-Anad base and the mopping up operations around Aden at the end.

A degree of normalcy returned to my life at the embassy in the following weeks.[1] I continued my job as press attaché, and was recently promoted to Director of the Communications Centre at the embassy. Through this work I assist journalists and film directors who want to visit Yemen, facilitating their trips. In addition, I make news reports for Yemeni television and continue to organize cultural exhibitions throughout France to allow French people to discover a small part of my country through photographs, films, traditional clothes, handicrafts and jewellery.

Though I enjoy this work very much, I occasionally use my holiday time to make documentary films on Yemen for French and Yemeni television stations. I have discovered and filmed remote areas of Yemen that I never knew existed before: from the mountainous abode of the Flower Men in the northwest – where the men spend their days applying make-up and searching for sweet-smelling flowers to wrap around their heads – to the 70-mile long island of Soqotra in the Indian Ocean, many of whose

[1] The pro-Socialist staff, including the ambassador, all returned to Yemen under an amnesty guarantee for politicians, diplomats and soldiers that had worked on behalf of the secession. Those from the embassy in Paris all found jobs again within the Ministry of Foreign Affairs in Sanaa, while a new group of diplomats arrived in France to take their place. The former ambassador in Paris received another ambassadorship to an Arab country within a few months of the end of the war.

inhabitants are nomads and fishermen who live in mountain caves, and which was until recently closed off to the rest of the world for several months each year during the rainy season. I have come to appreciate my country and its people in a way that would have been impossible had I never left it.

Everywhere I go, Yemenis are always surprised to learn that I too am a Yemeni, and that I don't always travel with a family member to protect and watch over me (as most women do). But from the moment I look them in the eye and speak to them as an equal, they treat me with the utmost respect, and soon appoint themselves as my protector while I am among them.

Sometimes my husband, Charles, accompanies me to shoot films. His passion for nature, history and anthropology makes Yemen the perfect holiday for him. The great joy he finds in my homeland and his appreciation and respect for it have opened my own eyes to the beauty of its land and people.

When the Yemenis we meet in our travels around the country learn that I am married to a Westerner, their eyes glow with wonder. In the beginning, I had imagined that my marrying Charles would make for one of the most difficult battles of my life. But the reception Yemenis consistently offer Charles and me could not be warmer and more sincere. Like my friends and family in Sanaa, the rural Yemenis we have met while shooting films accept Charles almost instantly as one of their own, and their natural curiosity soon comes to the surface in an avalanche of questions about Europe and America and what life is like there.

Within these Yemenis, toughened by a lifetime of hard labour, so firmly attached to their independence, I can see clearly the remnants of an ancient civilization intimately tied to their spirit. It fills me with awe and pride to call their land and culture my own.

My father died suddenly about a year after the 1994 war ended. Mother had cared for him attentively in the small room from which he had hardly moved for the past 15 years.

My older brother, Hamud, passed away a year after Father. The excruciating stomach pain he suffered led Mother to believe the chemicals sprayed by farmers on the *qat* crops played a role in his death. He chewed the leaves up to 12 hours every day.

Hamud left five young children and a pregnant wife living with my mother. Soon after Hamud's death, his widow decided she wanted to move into her own place with the children. Mother agreed to sell the house and pay her daughter-in-law Hamud's share as inheritance.

A few days before the sale was complete, Abdullah Murzah, Father's half-brother, stepped in to counsel Hamud's widow and children.

Abdullah told his nieces and nephews that if Mother didn't give them their share of Hamud's money from the sale of the house, he would find them a good lawyer to make sure they received it. Abdullah's sudden concern for justice flabbergasted even my immune Mother, who would never have dreamed of cheating her grandchildren out of their inheritance.

Grandmother Amina died on New Year's Day 2001, one month after my husband and I last talked to her about stories in this book.

Yahya al-Mutawakil became the Deputy Secretary General in charge of Political Affairs in the ruling General People's Congress, one of the top positions in that party. With legislative elections scheduled for April 2003, Yahya busied himself campaigning on behalf of the party's candidates. I telephoned him at his home in January 2003 and asked him to send me some information on the upcoming elections. He was leaving the next day for Aden and said he would ring me when he returned the following week.

A few days later, Mujahid spent a night in France on his way back to Yemen from the United States. The morning of his departure from Paris, our telephone rang at 7.00 a.m. Neither

Charles nor I got up to answer the phone, and the caller left a message on our answering machine. When Charles got up a little later, I heard him playing the message over and over. I thought it was strange, and I got up to see what it was. I heard Mujahid's voice saying the name 'Yahya', followed by 'God have mercy on his soul.'

I could hardly catch my breath when I realized that something had happened to Yahya. Mujahid was still at Charles de Gaulle Airport waiting for his flight and I immediately rang him on his mobile phone, praying that I had misunderstood him. A friend of Mujahid's answered the telephone and said Mujahid was too upset to talk to anyone. But when he heard me sobbing he passed the phone to Mujahid anyway.

'Are you sure? Are you sure it's true?' I pleaded with Mujahid.

I could hardly hear him as he told me that Yahya was riding with seven other men in his Lexus SUV near Aden early that morning on their way to a campaign event. A truck forced their car off the road, sending it into a high speed roll. Yahya and three of the other passengers died.

'It can't be,' I said. 'Yahya must be one of the survivors.' But Mujahid kept saying 'God have mercy on him', and I knew there was no doubt.

I was in my second month of pregnancy, and the news struck me like a dozen knives piercing my stomach. I lost the baby a few days later.

I remembered how a few years earlier I had broken the news to Yahya of my first pregnancy. He couldn't have been more excited and happy.

'This is going to be my first grandchild,' he said. His enthusiasm touched me deeply and I was very sad, as much for him as for Charles and me, when I eventually lost that baby too.

My reaction to Yahya's death surprised even me. When my father and older brother died within a year of each other, I was sad but did not dwell on their deaths. Yahya's disappearance, however, shook my whole outlook on life and made me question whether it has any purpose. He had been a father to me and, as is so often the case, I took him for granted when he was alive.

He had always been there for me when I needed him. He encouraged me when others felt I was doing the wrong thing. He had replaced the mountains I looked to for strength as a girl on my rides with Aunt Hameeda and Uncle Ali outside Sanaa. And how many times he embarrassed me with his non-stop praise of me to others.

One quality Yahya and I shared was our extreme stubbornness. But though he would rarely directly admit defeat, he had other ways of acknowledging that he was wrong. I remember when Yahya's daughter, Boushra, asked him to buy her a car. He refused, telling her she should save money from her work to buy one. I argued with Yahya, reminding him that he had bought his son, Muhammad, a car, and that to refuse his daughter one would be unfair.

'I want her to be like you,' Yahya defended himself. 'Strong and independent.'

'But I didn't have a father like you,' I said. 'I was forced to depend on myself.'

Yahya would not give in, but two weeks later he called me to say that he was buying Boushra a car.

I couldn't imagine that morning in January 2003 that I would no longer see Yahya, never talk to him, argue with him or make him proud again. The only consolation has been the memory of his optimistic outlook on life, an optimism that I did not share before I met him.

Yahya's second son, Ahmed, a quiet and extremely considerate boy, graduated from Georgetown University in Washington, DC, with an A average at the age of 20. He completed his master's degree two years later, and his father couldn't have been prouder of him.

Nearly three months to the day before Yahya's death, Ahmed returned to Sanaa from Japan where he was taking training courses for his job in the Yemeni Ministry of Planning. On one of his first nights back home, a plumber came to the house to fix a clogged pipe. Ahmed went into the small room where the plumber was working and found the man had passed out from the fumes of a chemical he was using. Ahmed tried to drag him out, but he too passed out. Their bodies were found the next morning.

Yahya was in Taiz when he heard the news. I was very worried about Yahya's state of mind and called him from Paris to see how he was. When I finally got through to him, his calm manner impressed me. He even asked about my recent trip to the United States with a delegation from Yemeni television and radio.

Yahya had been passing through Paris earlier that month when the Director General of Yemeni television and radio called to ask me to go with him and his group to the USA. Washington had just announced that arriving visitors from certain countries, including Yemen, would be fingerprinted and photographed at the airport as part of the post-9/11 security tightening.

'I wouldn't go if I were you,' Yahya advised me then. 'I know how proud you are. You would be too humiliated if they fingerprint you and take your picture just because you're an Arab.' He knew me well.

When I phoned him after his son's death, I told Yahya that Immigration had not given us a hard time when we arrived in the USA. But, to cheer him up, I told him about the customs official who had asked our group if we were carrying any fruit or vegetables. The Director General of the television and radio, never one to miss an opportunity to joke, answered: 'We've come to visit your television stations, not to open a restaurant.'

Yahya laughed at the story and it made me so happy to cheer him up just a little at such a difficult time. His serenity in the face of such a tragedy inspired me and made me see that life is a journey full of good and bad surprises that we must come to grips with. The memory of his positive outlook delivered me through the tragedy of his own death and helped ensure that I would no longer take for granted others that are dear to me.

Had it not been for meeting the likes of Yahya al-Mutawakil, Mujahid Abu Shawareb and Muhammad Abu Lahum and seeing what kind of men they are, I might have remained forever disappointed in my country. Through them I have seen that the future of Yemen is not so bleak, that even men and women who have grown up in a traditional society, with as many social pressures as I had been subject to (but without the advantage of a thorough education, as I had) could evolve to see their wives and daughters as something more than a symbol of the family honour – to see their country as more than just a source of wealth, to be milked as much as possible for personal gain.

Yemenis are moving increasingly towards this outlook, and in recent years I have come to meet many other men and women with a similar philosophy. Needless to say, the changes delight me.

When my husband's 83-year-old grandfather came to Yemen with us in 2000, he was so excited to see children riding their donkeys to school in some of the villages we visited.

'I used to ride my donkey to school too when I was a kid,' he said nostalgically.

I realized that in many ways Yemen today is not all that different from America and Europe 70 years ago. The thought fills me with hope for my country – not necessarily that we become exactly like America or Europe, but that Yemenis can perhaps obtain a higher quality of life than what most know today.

While I carry many painful memories of my childhood, I have come to see some of the positive aspects of these hardships. The trauma hardened me to the ubiquitous social pressures in Yemen and made me work harder to overcome them. Had I lived a more typical childhood, I would never have had the incentive to work at such an early age, or to study abroad, and marrying a foreigner would have been all but out of the question.

I would by no means recommend such an upbringing to others, for I suppose I was lucky not to have been irreparably scarred by the ordeal. With the encouragement of my husband, I have recently begun to seek an explanation for what I see as the injustices of my early life, kept carefully hidden away for the past two and a half decades. I hope that by sharing my experiences it might prompt others not to give in to cruelty and ignorance, not to remain passive, but to strive even harder to overcome. Vengeance, as well as justice, are complete when the pain inflicted is finally conquered.

Many of the very family members who opposed my education, my working at the television station and my travelling abroad today profess to be proud of what I have accomplished. They marvel that I have been able to provide for my grandmother, mother, sisters and even brothers, while my uncles, grandfather and other relatives could, or would, not. Now they even encourage their own daughters to continue studying through secondary school and beyond. And they no longer berate and threaten Mother about me when they visit.

Overcoming the barriers put in place by tradition and contributing, even to a tiny extent, to the notion that a person can be both different and accepted at the same time are what I believe I will look back on one day as most worthwhile in my life.

Chronology

1000 BC – AD 500	Incense trade leads to rise of powerful South Arabian kingdoms.
AD 525	Abyssinians (Ethiopians) conquer Yemen.
575	Persians expel Abyssinians and rule Yemen.
628	Yemen's ruler converts to Islam.
897	Yahya al-Rassi arrives in Saada, becomes Yemen's first Zaydi *Imam*.
1538	Ottomans occupy Yemen's coastal plain.
1636	Ottoman troops leave Yemen.
1839	British occupy Aden.
1849	Second Ottoman occupation of Yemen begins on coastal plain.
1869	The Suez Canal opens.
1871	The Mukarama revolt against the *Imam* in Haraz Mountains.
1872	Ottoman troops capture Sanaa.
1904	Yahya becomes *Imam* of Yemen.
1911	Accord between Ottomans and Imam Yahya brings peace in Yemen.
1915	Asiris invade Yemen.
1919	Ottoman troops withdraw from Yemen after defeat in the First World War.
1927–29	Imam Yahya puts down Zaraniq rebellion.
1931	Campaign to bring eastern desert tribes under the *Imam*'s rule.
1934	War between Yemen and Saudi Arabia.
1948	Imam Yahya is assassinated. His son, Ahmed, suppresses plot and becomes *Imam*.
1955	Imam Ahmed puts down an army mutiny.

1958	Yemen unifies with Egypt and Syria. Ahmed leaves for medical treatment in Italy, leaving Muhammad al-Badr in charge. Unrest erupts and Ahmed returns, quelling tribal rebellion.
1961	Yemen breaks its union with Egypt.
1962	Imam Ahmed dies. Yemeni officers overthrow his son, Muhammad al-Badr. Civil war erupts. Egyptians send troops to help Republicans, while Saudi Arabia aids Royalists.
1967	Egyptian troops leave Yemen.
1967	Al-Sallal is ousted as President, replaced by Abdul Rahman al-Iryani. Royalists launch unsuccessful 70-day siege. British evacuate Aden. NLF takes over.
1970	Peace treaty ends civil war.
1972	Border war erupts between North and South Yemen.
1974	Al-Iryani is overthrown by military officers. Al-Hamdi becomes President.
1977	Al-Hamdi is assassinated. Ahmed al-Ghashmi becomes President.
1978	Al-Ghashmi dies in briefcase explosion. Ali Abdullah Salih becomes President.
1979	Border war between North and South Yemen.
1986	Fighting in South Yemen brings Ali Salim al-Baydh to power.
1990	Unification of North and South Yemen.
1994	War of Secession leads to Socialist Party's defeat.

Glossary

Al-	Arabic article 'the'
Ashraf	(sing. *sharif*) descendents of the Prophet Muhammad
Bab	door or gate
Bani	children of
Bayt	house, extended family
Block	military unit made up of approximately 100 men
Diya	money paid in compensation for a death
Doshan	town crier
Evil Eye	what in the West would be called 'a jinx'
Hajama	female folk doctor
Hamam	bathouse
Hijra	a protected area, such as a town, where violence is strictly forbidden.
Imam	leader of the Zaydi Shiite community.
imam	head of local mosque
Jambiya	curved dagger
Jebel	mountain
Jini	a mischievous, sometimes evil spirit
Kafir	unbeliever
Khol	a pigment extracted from antimony
Mudafin	a shaft dug in the ground for storing grains
Qadhi	judge – now a hereditary title
Qat	shrub whose small leaves are chewed by Yemenis
Qishr	coffee husks
Ramadhan	Muslim month of fasting between sunrise and sunset
Sayid	descendent of the Prophet Muhammad

Sayla	drainage canal
Sharaf	honour
Shaykh	tribal leader
Shaykh al-mashaykh	'*shaykh* of *shaykhs*' – leader of all the *shaykhs* in a tribe.
Suq	marketplace
Thar	revenge for a killing
Ulama	religious scholars
Wadi	valley
Zaydi	form of Shiite Islam prevalent in Yemen's northern highlands
Zena	long gown worn by men

Bibliography of principal sources

Admiralty (UK), *Western Arabia and the Red Sea*, London: Naval Intelligence Division, 1946.

Al-Rashid, Ibrahim, *Yemen Under the Rule of Imam Ahmad*, Chapel Hill: Documentary Publications, 1985.

Al-Akwa, Ismail Ali, and Muhammad Ahmad al-Hijri Al-Yemani, *Majmua Buldan al-Yemen wa Qabailha*, 2 vols., Sanaa: Ministry of Information and Culture, 1984.

Bethmann, Erich W., *Yemen on the Threshold*, Washington, DC: American Friends of the Middle East, 1960.

Burrowes, Robert D., *The Yemen Arab Republic: The Politics of Development, 1962–1986*, Boulder, Colorado: Westview Press, 1987.

Bury, G. Wyman (Abdullah Mansûr), *The Land of Uz*, London: Macmillan, 1911.

Bury, G. Wyman, *Arabia Infelix, or the Turks in Yemen*, London: Macmillan, 1915.

Chelhod, Joseph, *et al.*, *L'Arabie du Sud: Histoire et Civilisation*, 3 vols, Paris: Maisonneuve & Larose, 1984–1985.

Daum, Werner (ed.), *Yemen: 3000 Years of Art and Civilisation in Arabia Felix*, Innsbruck: Pinguin, 1988.

Douglas, J. Leigh, *The Free Yemeni Movement 1935–1962*, Beirut: American University of Beirut, 1989.

Dresch, Paul, *Tribes, Government, and History in Yemen*, Oxford: Oxford University Press, 1989.

Ingrams, Harold, *The Yemen: Imams, Rulers and Revolutions*, London: John Murray, 1963.

Leger, David, *Shifting Sands: The British in South Arabia*, Peninsular Publishing, 1983.

Maréchaux, Pascal and Maria and Dominique Champault, *La Route de l'Encens*, Paris: Imprimerie nationale Editions, 1996.

Pridham, B.R. (ed.), *Contemporary Yemen: Politics and Historical Background*, New York: St Martin's Press, 1984.

Robin, Christian (ed.), *L'Arabie antique de Karib'îl à Mahomet*, Aix-en-Provence, France: Edisud, 1992.

Schmidt, Dana Adams, *Yemen: The Unknown War*, New York: Holt, Rinehart & Winston, 1968.

Scott, Hugh, *In the High Yemen*, London: John Murray, 1942.

Stookey, Robert W., *Yemen: The Politics of the Yemen Arab Republic*, Boulder, Colorado: Westview Press, 1978.

Tutwiler, Richard and Sheila Carapico, *Yemeni Agriculture and Economic Change*, San'a: American Institute for Yemeni Studies, 1981.

Wenner, Manfred W., *Modern Yemen 1918–1966*, Baltimore: Johns Hopkins Press, 1967.

Wenner, Manfred W., *The Yemen Arab Republic: Development and Change in an Ancient Land*, Boulder, Colorado: Westview Press, 1991.

Whitaker, Brian, http://www.al-bab.com/yemen/

Zabarah, Mohammed Ahmad, *Yemen: Traditionalism vs. Modernity*, New York: Praeger, 1982.

Index